SEARCH
A Handbook for Adoptees and Birthparents, 3rd Edition

Jayne Askin

ORYX PRESS
1998

The rare Arabian Oryx is believed to have inspired the myth of the unicorn. This desert antelope became virtually extinct in the early 1960s. At that time, several groups of international conservationists arranged to have nine animals sent to the Phoenix Zoo to be the nucleus of a captive breeding herd. Today, the Oryx population is over 1,000, and over 500 have been returned to the Middle East.

First edition copyright © 1982 by Jayne Askin
Second and Third edition copyright © 1992, 1998 by The Oryx Press
4041 North Central at Indian School Road
Phoenix, Arizona 85012-3397

Published simultaneously in Canada

Printed and bound in the United States of America

∞ The paper used in this publication meets the minimum requirements of American National Standard for Information Science—Permanence of Paper for Printed Library Materials, ANSI Z39.48, 1984.

Library of Congress Cataloging-in-Publication Data
Askin, Jayne.
   Search: a handbook for adoptees and birthparents / by Jayne
Askin.—3rd ed.
      p.   cm.
   Includes bibliographical references and index.
   ISBN 1-57356-115-0 (alk. paper)
   1. Adoptees—United States—Identification.   2. Birthparents—
United States—Identification.   I. Title.
HV881.A8   1998
362.82'98—dc21   98-22656
                                                            CIP

To my sister
January 31, 1937 - December 5, 1994

The family of
Joy Patrick Reinhardt
would like you to
join us in a
celebration of her life.

CONTENTS

SAMPLE LETTERS
AND FORMS

Sample No.

PREFACE

Search: A Handbook for Adoptees and Birthparents is a reference book for all those searching, considering a search, or wishing to know more about the plight of adoptees or birthparents. While directed to the searcher, this book also offers the nonsearcher or the person considering a search insight into the problems and choices that the searcher faces and needs to consider. Although helpful with genealogical research, *Search* is not a genealogy handbook; for help and assistance in tracing your family tree, you should also consult your local librarian or a professional genealogical researcher.

Adoptees and birthparents often reach a time in their lives when sealed records and secrecy conflict with a medical, genetic, genealogical, or personal need-to-know. Many years will have passed since the adoption took place and more current information may be needed. While those opposing adoption search like to talk of the abundance of information taken from birthparents at the time of relinquishment, the reality is that 20 years later the data will be incomplete: medical problems that show up after the relinquishment, new genetic findings, incomplete or inaccurate information given at the time of relinquishment.

Search provides listings and information that cover a wide range of topics and issues relating to adoption search. Among these are deciding to search, getting moral support and handling resistance from family and friends, the costs of searching, search and support groups, searchers/researchers, search consultants, intermediaries, dealing with adoption agencies and the courts, reunion registries, finding and using various types of records, using computer resources to search, and ending your search. In addition, readers will find a searcher's checklist, sample letters and forms, print and nonprint reference sources, a reading list of adoption-related books, and a state-by-state listing of addresses and applicable state laws.

This third edition of *Search* is completely updated. Over 500 search and support groups and search consultants were contacted to learn of their current status of activity and to ensure all information presented was correct. A letter, fax, or e-mail went to each state asking for current addresses and information on the state adoption agency, court of jurisdiction, reunion registry, age of majority, and laws governing opening records and inheritance. All references to birth, death, marriage, and divorce records were verified. An updated list of archives/record holdings and departments of motor vehicles was compiled.

Many hours were spent in the Arizona State Law Library reviewing legal suits relating to adoption search that have been filed since the first edition was published in 1982. Medical journals were read and several genetic counselors were contacted to obtain current medical information. Much other information came from the public library and the Family History Center located nearby. A particularly fruitful correspondence was carried on with Dr. Thomas J. Bouchard of the Minnesota Twins Study.

This edition includes a new chapter titled "Searching on the Computer" (Chapter 9). It provides information on how to start a computer search, keywords needed to find the information sought, and useful Web sites the searcher may wish to use. Correspondence with searchers on the Internet provided me with information about this valuable resource.

Search offers anyone who has decided to try to find a birthparent or relinquished child the information needed to conduct the search effectively and to maximize the chances of success.

ACKNOWLEDGMENTS

I wish to thank the Phoenix Central Library, the Scottsdale Main Library, and the Scottsdale Mustang Branch reference librarians for their advice, support, and many hours of help. I also wish to thank the state adoption counselors, the Arizona State Law Library, the Latter-day Saints Family History Center, and the Minnesota Twins Study for the information each provided. Without their help, I could not have compiled the individual state laws and learned of the kinds of projects, plans, and future policies being considered. A special thanks to Curry Wolfe and her Adoption Reconnection Directory which provided information that enabled me to locate many resources. Without the help of Denny Glad and Jalena Bowling at the Tennessee Right to Know I could not have presented the lawsuit in progress and its enormous impact on "open records." When I was lost and needed direction, I turned to Karen Tinkham and Alice Syman, my Arizona neighbors and adoption advocates.

I wish to acknowledge the search and support groups listed and thank them for their responses to requests for verification of their names, addresses, and current status. To all those searchers and those offering search help through the Internet, thank you for introducing me to the new world of computer searching.

As always, I wish to thank my husband, Bob Askin. Through the many months of this project there never was a time I didn't receive your help and support.

To Josephine, who ended where I began.

INTRODUCTION

"Where did I come from?" "Who am I?" "Whom do I look like?" "Does my relinquished child look like me?" "Do my birthparents ever think about me?" "What medical problems might I have inherited?" "Why was I relinquished?" "Do I have any full siblings?"

If you're an adoptee, you don't need an explanation of how much these questions haunt you throughout your life. If you're not, imagine for a moment that you've never known the answers to questions like these. Hard, isn't it? Whenever you've thought about things like this, you had someone to ask; your questions were answered. As a child, you may not always have been given complete answers to your questions, but by the time you were a teenager you had a sense of your own and your family's history. You consider it yours by birthright. An adoptee has no birthright in this respect—at least the adoption laws don't recognize one.

As a birthparent you're put in a somewhat different situation, but the result is the same. You relinquished your child—often because you had no choice—and the adoption law is so structured that you never again receive word of that child. Somewhere your child comes into a new home, matures, and grows to adulthood. You know this, but never get the opportunity to reassure yourself that your child is all right. For a relinquishing birthparent, the emotions other parents can freely express are held hostage for a lifetime.

Is there any other way? After all, there are still the child's best interests to consider. Somehow a stable, secure environment has to be provided for the child. Can adoptive parents do that when birthparents are in the picture vying with adoptive parents for the affections of the child? Wouldn't that cause the child conflict and insecurity? Under the circumstances, it seems logical that the relinquishing parent should step out of the picture.

That's the argument continually raised against efforts on the part of adoptees and birthparents to reconnect. But there's one thing this argument ignores by citing the best interests of the child: There's no child involved per se. As an adoptee searcher you aren't a child anymore. You're an adult who feels entitled to know your own background. And as a searching birthparent you're seeking contact with your child who is now an adult. This grown child is—or should be—as free to say yes or no to having any relationship with you as with any other adult.

Those in the adoption movement who are working and fighting for an opening of opportunities to establish a new connection between birthparent and son or daughter are doing so on behalf of adults on both sides. They are not working for some imagined right to interrupt the rearing of children. They claim no such right. What they do ask is why adults continue to be regarded as children, as though they were incompetent to decide whether or not to establish a relationship with another adult to whom they are genetically connected.

You may note that I haven't spoken of adoptees "finding their families." I've consciously held back from doing so. Adoptees have been raised as sons or daughters by adoptive parents who provide them with a family and a home where they are loved. The adoptive parents have cherished and cared for the child they've adopted and have earned the right to be called Mother and Father. Those of you who are adult adoptees recognize this better than anyone else. What many people do not understand is that adoptees aren't searching for new families. Adoptees already have one, thank you. What an adoptee doesn't have is a complete sense of connectedness with the past. There's a blank wall drawn across it. As an adoptee, you may feel cut off from a piece of yourself by that wall. Now that you're an adult, you feel you should be allowed to look beyond that wall, to make the connection that will tell you where you came from and what set you on the road to where you are. Many of you have in fact won the support of your families in this effort—of your real families, those who provided you with a home and who continue to love you.

For similar reasons I shy away from the term "natural parents"; it seems to make adoptive parents somehow unnatural parents. The adoptive relationship isn't that, however. Adoptive parents are playing a natural role. They are in a most fundamental sense natural parents. Where others may commonly think in terms of natural versus adoptive parents, those in the adoption movement who promote the right to search prefer to speak of both birthparents and adoptive parents as natural parents.

For many of you who are birthparents, the irony is that so often you are judged unnatural parents. Part of society habitually thinks in terms of careless, uncaring playboys and loose women. But it's not like that as a rule. Many of you relinquish children you would rather keep and love, watching them grow into adulthood. Personal misfortune, economic pressures, or family pressures pushed you to do something you would rather not have done. And like the natural parents you are, you hope one day to see your child grown, to know whether you might have grandchildren, to learn what your child has made of him or herself. You are not trying to take the child away from those who have loved and provided a home for him or her.

Thus, throughout this text I will use the term birthparent to represent the genetic parent of a child. A brochure published by Concerned United Birthparents called *The Birthparent's Perspective* offers the best explanation of this term.

> We find the terms "biological" and "bio-parent" descriptive of a me-chanical incubator or unfeeling human baby machine. We are neither; our continued love and concern for our birthchildren is akin to any parents' for their children. Although we do not object to the term "natural parent," we find many adoptive parents rightly resent the implication that they are "unnatural" parents, for they may parent quite naturally, indeed. Therefore, we choose the term "birthparent," one word, analogous to terms like "grandparent," "grandmother," or "grandfather." We remain the child's progenitor and thus find the term "birthparent" both accurate and sensitive to our place in the child's existence.

This book is written to present choices and alternatives available to adoptees and birthparents who wish to search (and to adoptive families and others who support and participate in—or simply wish to understand—the search activities of a son, daughter, or friend).

If you are contemplating a search, the first and most important question you will need to answer is "Should I search?" The fact that you are reading this book is an indication that you have considered—are still considering—this question. Even so, I cannot tell you that to search is or ought to be a foregone conclusion. I can only present it as a choice available to you. And I can tell you how to go about your search.

If you decide to undertake a search, you hope to find a loving, honest, healthy person (or persons) who has thought of you over the years, who will reach out to you and answer the many questions you have. You hope to locate a birthparent, a relinquished child, a brother or half-sister, who is like you, who may even look like you or think like you. But are you being totally realistic and honest with yourself?

Can you face what you may find? A birthparent who denies your relation-ship. A birthfather who never knew of your birth. A grown child whose interests and lifestyle are radically different from your own, who may harbor resentment and bitterness at your "abandonment" of him or her. A birthmother who can't tell you which man of many is your birthfather. A birthfamily with an "undesirable" background. An account of conception and birth under other than socially acceptable circumstances. Are you ready to risk rejection, this time with no possible flight into fantasy or rationalization to ease the pain?

Read through this book, and when you are finished, reread this Introduction. If you decide "No, I'm not ready to search," consider reading this book to have been well worth the conclusion reached. If you decide to search, know that all along the way there are new friends to help you and groups dedicated to opening your records. Most important, whether or not you locate a specific person—and chances are better than ever that you will—you will discover important things about yourself and who you are.

You'll probably come out somewhere between the worst and the best possibilities at the conclusion of your search. Whatever the reception you meet with in the process of search, there will have been questions of long standing answered, new contacts made. And there is the possibility of a new relationship that can grow to fill an old void.

We see that although the desire to search has always been there, buried and seemingly lost except for the occasional thought, daydream, or outburst, the actual commitment to search is a special stage in itself. It is arrived at over a period of time, as the self gradually evolves from one level of consciousness to another, striving for authenticity and self-autonomy.

Betty Jean Lifton, *Lost and Found*

CHAPTER 1

Deciding to Search

As an adoptee or birthparent who initiates a search for those from whom you have been separated through relinquishment and adoption you instinctively feel you have a right to information. It seems only natural that you be allowed the opportunity to reestablish the kinship connection broken years earlier. And yet when you begin to search, you immediately come up against a system of administering relinquishment/adoption records that insists you have no such right. Frequently you face outright hostility from agencies holding records, administrations that feel you have no right to the information you're seeking.

Searchers are hard put to understand this opposition to what they consider their right to know. They generally hold onto their deep conviction that they *do* have rights, regardless of present administrative attitudes. As the search movement grows, searchers are becoming increasingly outspoken and articulate in defense of the rights they claim. In addition, they are learning to turn to their advantage the rights that *are* accorded them as citizens, in particular the right of access to public records.

WHAT *ARE* MY RIGHTS?

Under the American system of government, citizens (either as individuals or organized into groups pursuing defined interests) can raise a challenge to any federal, state, or local statute or administrative policy affecting them that appears inconsistent with the guarantees contained in the Constitution of the

United States. Such challenges can be pursued through the federal court system. Since relinquishment and adoption procedures are governed by state laws, citizens can challenge any state or local law or administrative policy that appears inconsistent with guarantees contained in the applicable state constitution. State courts can also be asked to give their opinion on whether a state law is in violation of the United States Constitution. The court's ruling, however, has effect only within the state's borders, whereas a federal court ruling can have a broader application.

Searchers do not contest society's need to balance conflicting rights. However, it does seem unprecedented to those seeking to change the laws that efforts simply to establish contact with another individual—and that individual the closest of blood kin—should be seen as a violation of another's right to privacy.

Several legal challenges have been made to address these fundamental rights. In the case of *Petitioner–Appellant v. The People of the State of Illinois*, the petitioner's attorney argued as follows:

> The fact that we are dealing here with a fundamental right is illustrated by the questions we all have about ourselves. What are the physical characteristics to which my children may be genetically prone? What is my ancestral nationality or religious persuasion? What sufferings and endurances are in my roots? What achievements or feats can I point to with ancestral pride? Can anyone seriously deny that one's identity is an inalienable and fundamental right? Thus, the right to know one's individually created identity must be considered a fundamental right. For those persons that are adopted, however, the only way that this fundamental right can be meaningful is to include within it one's liberty to know the identity of his genetic parents. In my opinion, this inclusion is demanded within the quintessential meaning of the fundamental right to know one's individually created identity . . . . [1]

Adult adoptees and birthparents continue to feel that being denied the right to know who their birthparents are and what has become of their relinquished children violates basic human rights that the United States Constitution guarantees. They ask how having such knowledge, in itself, can amount to any violation of another's guaranteed rights.

The state of Tennessee is the first state to pass legislation re-opening original birth certificates and some other adoption records to the adoptee upon request.[2] Challenge after challenge has been made and rejected as this law passes through the various courts. As of this writing, the following provisions were in place in Tennessee:

> *Provisions Pertaining to Pre-1951 Adoption Records:* These records were opened in July 1995 and allow all adult adoptees to obtain ALL records pertaining to their birth, relinquishment, and adoption. Direct descen-

dants of the adoptee (birthparents, birthsiblings, adoptive parents, adoptive siblings) may obtain records with proof of their relationship by either adoption or birth to an adopted person. Persons obtaining these records under the provisions are under no restrictions and may proceed as they wish in using the information they receive to locate and make contact with the persons whose identities are revealed.

Provisions Pertaining to Records of Adoptions after March 1951: Under these provisions, adult adoptees may obtain all records pertaining to their birth, relinquishment, and adoption. However, before such records may be released to them, they are required to sign an affidavit, by which they are legally bound, stating that if any person whose identity is revealed in the records has filed, or elects to file, a contact-veto, they may not make contact with such persons, or make use of any information in the records to cause harm to anyone named therein. The existence or placement of a contact-veto does not prevent the release of records to the requesting adoptee. However, should there be a contact-veto, and should the adoptee violate that contact-veto, he or she becomes subject to both criminal and civil penalties. If the person being sought agrees to contact, or does not file a contact-veto within 90 days of being notified of a request for records, or is found to be deceased, or simply cannot be located, the requesting adoptee is under no further restrictions and may proceed as he or she wishes in using the information.

Also under these provisions, birthparents and birthsiblings may request information or search services with respect to the adult adopted person to whom they are related. The adoptee is not required to file a contact-veto. However, unless he or she files express written consent, no information may be released to the requesting party.

For the latest information on this Tennessee law and the fees involved to open records, contact one of the groups listed in Appendix I under Tennessee, the Tennessee Department of Human Services, or query one of the Web sites in Chapter 9, "Searching on the Computer."

One interesting note regarding the Tennessee case is the following, taken from The American Adoption Congress newsletter, *DECREE:*

The *amici* [friends of the court] and their attorneys submitted affidavits to the court (a) explaining why the adoptees needed access to their records and why their birthparents and adoptive parents needed and wanted them to have access, (b) reporting that search programs in Tennessee and around the country had found that at least nineteen out of twenty birthparents wanted to be contacted by the children they had surrendered for adoption, (c) containing testimony of social workers that open records promoted adoptions and (d) reporting statistics from England and from New South Wales, Australia, showing that opening adoption records in those countries had neither decreased adoptions nor increased abortions and had probably done the reverse.[3]

I would be remiss if I did not include information on a federal suit that took place in 1993. The Musser Foundation worked to reunite adoptees with birthparents through search. The foundation charged search fees that were within an acceptable range and its results were laudable. Due to the large number of those seeking a reunion, Sandy Musser, founder and president of the foundation, did not do all the searches herself, rather she "farmed" them out to independent "investigators" or "searchers" who did the actual searching. The independent investigator/searcher agreed on a reduced fee rate to do the search and the balance went to the Musser Foundation to cover overhead expenses. The client was charged a flat fee by the Musser Foundation which in turn paid the investigator/searcher.

During a busy time, Sandy gave some search cases to a long-time associate named Barbara. Barbara began searching and collecting information on the case in question.

> Having previously obtained the name of the person for whom she was searching, Barbara needed only a current address. It was more efficient for Barbara to make one simple phone call to Social Security for the current address information than to search many other public records for the same information. By trying to obtain a current address from Social Security, Barbara violated the U.S. Code. The evidence was indisputable that Barbara had obtained information illegally from Social Security.[4]

The problem arose when it was discovered that Barbara, the investigator/searcher, had illegally impersonated a federal employee to obtain information from Social Security. The federal government claimed Sandy Musser knew how the information was obtained by Barbara and was therefore also guilty. To make matters more confusing, Barbara testified against Sandy in exchange for immunity. Barbara was never charged with the crime even though she was the one impersonating the federal employee. The case went to federal court where Sandy was found guilty and ordered to spend four months in a federal prison.

While I cannot guarantee adoptees and birthparents protection from future lawsuits, I do believe it would be most difficult to prosecute a person for seeking information or records on him or herself. It seems highly unlikely that someone would be pronounced guilty for obtaining updated medical information not provided by the agency, for seeking knowledge of full siblings, or for asserting the right to know his or her heritage. Obtaining records on oneself is not a crime; how you obtain the records can be.

STATE LAW

Adoption laws are enacted and administered by the states, although a few states give this role to the counties. Each state differs from the others in some respect. There is no uniformity. Practice varies from relatively open records to difficult-to-search records.

In most states, the law generally defines which records are available. In almost every state, a birthparent has a right to all documents issued before actual relinquishment. As a birthparent, you are entitled to your child's original birth certificate, but not the amended certificate bearing the adoptive parents' names. As an adoptee, you are usually entitled to all records issued after the relinquishment. You may receive an amended birth certificate but not the original. Upon finalization of an adoption, the original birth certificate is sealed and cannot be opened without a court order. In some states, the adoption agency and hospital records are also sealed. The purpose of sealing records is to "protect" the identity of the relinquishing birthparent, the adoptee, and the adoptive family.

In undertaking research for the reference section in the back of this book on state laws regarding open records, I became aware of how unclear the situation often is, despite the generally followed policies described above. And I'm not the only one who has discovered the potential for confusion and frustration in state adoption practices. The following statement is from the *National Conference of Commissioners on Uniform State Laws*:

> At present, the legal process of adoption is complicated not only by the different kinds of children who are adopted and the different kinds of people who seek to adopt, but also by an extraordinarily confusing system of state, federal, and international laws and regulations.[5]

Identifying Information

The general practice for states nationwide is to withhold information considered to be identifying in nature. "Identifying information" is whatever the authorities have decided might make it possible for you to pinpoint the name and address of your relinquished child or of your birthparent. Only "nonidentifying information" may be released. Here is how a Task Force on Confidentiality in the Adoption Program Report to the California State Department of Health defined nonidentifying information:

> Nonidentifying information is to be considered any information other than that which would lead to the identification of a member of a biological family. Information such as personal, social, and medical history is normally considered nonidentifying. Examples of identifying information are names, address, and other details, such as the specific job title of a biological parent.[6]

There is no national standard on identifying information. Depending on the state involved, interpretation may be more or less restrictive than in California. In some states, the name of the hospital where the child was born or the name of the attorney who handled the court proceedings will be considered identifying. Other states will fairly routinely release an adoptee's first name if this has subsequently been changed.

One's race has usually been considered nonidentifying information, but in the following case this did not prove true. Betty Chase was raised as a foster child. Her first foster parents were white and she was considered white. At an early age her skin color raised questions and after a time she was placed in black foster homes and raised as a black. She then culturally identified herself as black and married a man of that race.

On February 10, 1978, when Ms. Chase was 33 years old, county authorities responded to questions from Ms. Chase and added that her race was white: "Our records indicate that all your immediate forebears [sic] were white with the exception of your maternal grandmother's mother who, it is reported, was an American Indian (no tribal identification)."[7] After a lengthy battle with county authorities and a difficult search, Ms. Chase finally located her birthmother. She discovered her birthmother was black and her heritage was black, Native American, and white.

In any state there will be something of a gray area between what is considered clearly identifying and what is not. State authorities and agencies licensed by the state, in drawing the identifying/nonidentifying distinction, implicitly acknowledge that you have a right to any nonidentifying information you request. You can be pretty sure that asking outright for a name and address will run you up against the brick wall established by the law. However, at times you may ask for information that you do not feel is clearly identifying and still run into the same brick wall. You're in that gray area where sometimes records administrators lean one way, sometimes the other.

In this situation, challenge the person who refuses to give you what you feel is nonidentifying information. But do so in a tactful manner. Belligerently asserting your rights to a social worker or civil servant rarely wins you cooperation. Sometimes, if you respond to a refusal to provide a point of information with a question—"Is that identifying?" or "How is that identifying?"—the person facing you may reconsider and give you more details than if you just quietly accept his or her interpretation of the law. Persistence in pursuit of your rights to information can pay off. Familiarize yourself with the state adoption laws that apply to you. It is here that you will discover the distinctions between identifying and nonidentifying information. You will have a better sense of when to persevere and when to back off. I've included a summary of state laws in the state-by-state reference lists that make up the final portion of this book. However, since these laws are under review in a number of states, also check further for recent amendments or additions that may affect your rights.

Your library probably has a copy of your state constitution and an index to state laws. If not, ask for a photocopy of the pertinent material through interlibrary loan (see Chapter 4, "Reference Resources") or refer to a nearby law library. You can also ask for help from a search and support group that closely follows changes in state adoption laws or view one of the Web sites dealing with state adoption laws listed in Chapter 9, "Searching on the Computer."

When searching, you will be gathering information from a much wider range of sources than just those having custody of your adoption/relinquishment records. In directing inquiries to those sources, the question of identifying versus nonidentifying information rarely comes up as such. You will simply be depending on the general right of free access to public documents and publicly held records. In some cases, the law or administrative code that applies may require that you state a particular relationship to a person you wish information on—considerations of privacy occasionally come into the picture. But many records can be reviewed more freely.

Even when searching through records to which you theoretically have a right of access, it is best to avoid mentioning adoption search as the reason for desiring information. Some records are open only to those indicating a reason deemed acceptable, and what constitutes "acceptable" is sometimes so vaguely specified that whether or not you obtain access is left up to a determination made by the civil servant you're dealing with. Giving "adoption search" as a response to a question on why a certain record is desired too often leads to a decision not to release information. If you cite "genealogy search" as a reason for requesting records, you will get a different reaction, even though the objective is much the same. You can also cite a need related to inheritance and estate settlement or a medical need-to-know. The thing to remember is that when you put your request in the context of adoption search, you may in effect find yourself denied "identifying" information in a situation where the records administrator normally does not distinguish between identifying and nonidentifying information.

The following was stated in a response to an article on the "Sealed Record Controversy in Michigan" in a recent issue of the *University of Detroit Law Review*:

> ... the court refused to conclude that there had been a showing of good cause. The court failed to specify what would constitute good cause in Michigan, but stated that compelling medical reasons, and occasionally psychological reasons, had been sufficient to fulfill the requirement.[8]

State Inheritance Laws

In considering the question of what rights you have under state law in the context of inheritance and disposition of your estate, James R. Carter made the following observation in the *Tulane Law Review*:

> In some states, the decree of adoption, while almost totally severing the relationship between the natural parents and the adoptee, does not divest the adoptee of the right to inherit from his natural parents. In fact, when an adoption statute is silent on the question of whether an adoptee can inherit from his natural parents, some courts have allowed adoptees to inherit under the laws of descent and distribution. If these same states deny an adoptee the right to see his adoption records to ascertain whether he had inherited property from his biological parents, it may be argued that the adoptee is being deprived of property without due process of law.[9]

How can adoptees know whether or not they have an inheritance if they do not know the name of the person leaving an estate? How can birthparents leave an inheritance to children whose names they do not know?

For clarification purposes, an inheritance does not necessarily mean money. A birthparent may leave to a relinquished child the original birth certificate or the story of the relinquishment. An adoptee may use inheritance laws to help open records with no hope or intention of receiving cash benefits.

Depending on what the law is in your state relative to adoptee inheritance rights, you may be able to cite the right of inheritance as a reason to open adoption/relinquishment records to you. That is not to say you will automatically be given the information you want. To the extent there is conflict between adoption laws and those covering inheritance, adoption records administrators may well choose to follow the code that is most directly addressed to their area of responsibility. But in seeking out other records, it can be helpful to present your interest as based on inheritance considerations.

In the state-by-state reference lists in the back of this book, I've indicated states' replies to my question on adoptee inheritance rights. Again, double-check for any updating in the laws. (Adoptees of Native American [Indian] heritage should be aware of certain rights of inheritance they have under federal law. See Chapter 4, "Reference Resources," for details.)

Uniform Adoption Acts

Several attempts have been made to present the states with a "model" which, if accepted, would make adoption laws uniform across the nation. These model laws are only recommendations, and states are not required to adopt them as law. Until your state legislature (or the legislature in your state of search) adopts a model as law, you cannot cite it to support your claim to information. The following are various attempts at writing such a comprehensive model law.

- The National Conference of Commissioners on Uniform State Laws (NCCUSL) drafted *A Uniform Adoption Act* in 1953 and continued revisions through 1994 when it was approved on February 15, 1995. A complete copy may be found at the following Internet address: <www.alt.net/~waltj/shea/uaa.html>.
- *The Model State Adoption Act* was proposed by the United States Department of Health and Human Services early in 1980.
- *A Model State Adoption Act* was prepared by the American Bar Association (ABA) during the 1980s. The model act was never approved by the ABA.
- The Child Welfare League of America (CWLA) released their revised *Standards for Adoption Service* in 1988.

States are not required to adopt any recommendations and each state still reflects its legislature's attitudes toward adoption. To learn of your state's use of a model law, contact your state adoption agency. Adoption groups are another source of information on model laws. STop the Act Coalition (STAC) is a series of groups working in over half the states to stop the enactment of "model laws" in their states. (See Chapter 10, "Search Resources and Services," to learn more details.)

THE ADULT QUALIFICATION

A considerable amount of the opposition to open records comes from those who see open records as a threat to the stability of the adoptive family. They fear open records may enable a birthparent to locate an adopted child and move to take that child from the adoptive parents. Much of the negative comment refers to "the child" even when his or her age is well beyond the age of majority.

But those who follow this line of thinking overlook the right that adoption groups and searchers traditionally claim is the right of adults to make free contact with other adults. The question of "best interests of the child," which is used as partial justification for sealed records, is irrelevant because neither of the involved parties is a child.

As long as "the child" is a child, adoptees and birthparents have overwhelmingly supported the need to consider the best interests of the child in the matter of sealed records. Those who want open records recognize as well as anyone the potential for disruption of the family environment and for resultant psychological damage to the child when a situation is created that leads to a contest for affections. But the "best interest" of the child is not found in sealing the records and thus preventing updated medical information.

Each state, in establishing its own age of majority for adoptees, must look closely at the rights of both adoptee and birthparent. While there are some birthparents who believe they should be allowed to search for their relin-quished children, even if these children are under the age of majority, this book deals with adults searching for adults. It ought to be easy to establish an adult qualification in state adoption laws so that the rights of adults are not compromised as the result of concern about the best interests of the child.

When it comes to the other justification for sealed records—protection against invasion of privacy—those contacted as the result of a search already have the same legal protection provided every citizen. Present law actually imposes a restrictive privacy on birthparents and adoptees that many find burdensome. As the growing record of reunions shows, many of those con-tacted in supposed violation of their right of privacy are genuinely pleased at the opportunity presented to establish some link with the family member who located them. In some cases, those whose right of privacy was supposedly being protected had themselves made efforts to locate the individual who was searching for them. What kind of protection is it that thwarts efforts by adults who are the closest of blood kin to make contact with each other?

FEDERAL LAW

Federal legislation does not grant birthparents or adoptees any specific rights to records withheld from them under state law. The states have full authority to establish policy in this area, although always subject to the limitations set out in the United States Constitution.

However, federal legislation does grant searchers the right to certain information kept on the individuals at the federal level. Your rights here are established principally by the Freedom of Information Act (5 U.S.C. 552) and the Privacy Act of 1974 (U.S.C. 552a).

The Freedom of Information Act requires the federal government to release to individuals upon request material that pertains to them and is contained in executive agency or department files. The agency is required to respond to an appeal within 20 working days after receiving the request. The agency must also specify any fee for document search and duplication.

Agencies may withhold information only in specified categories, such as trade secrets and other confidential business information, classified material, and, according to Sarah P. Collins, "information which, if disclosed, would constitute a clearly unwarranted invasion of privacy."[10] The Freedom of Information Act allows the individual to request the appropriate federal district court to order an agency to produce records that the agency is withholding without apparent good cause.

The Privacy Act is primarily aimed at restricting the federal government in its collection, use, and disclosure of information on individuals. However, it also allows individuals access to information the government holds on them, and so supplements the Freedom of Information Act in that respect. The provisions on access appear to be somewhat broader in the Privacy Act than they are in the Freedom of Information Act, so you may do well to cite your rights under both laws when writing to an agency for information it holds on you.

Examples of agencies that may hold useful information on file are the Passport Agency of the United States Department of State and the Immigration and Naturalization Service of the United States Department of Justice. The latter will be important for American citizens or permanent residents who are foreign-born, as records of entry into the United States may contain information that an adoption agency does not have or will not release. One adoptee I met discovered her original birth certificate through filing for information from the Passport Agency under terms of the Privacy Act.

For more specific details on exercising your rights under these two federal laws, check your library for books or articles explaining their workings. The *Freedom of Information Guide* from the Know Your Government Series is an excellent information source. Computer users can contact <www.spj.org/foia/index.htm> for the complete text of the Freedom of Information Act and <www.foia.com/PRIVSTAT.html> for the Privacy Act.

Native Americans

Native Americans are in a unique position when it comes to adoption rights. They are the only group of citizens whose rights of inheritance are governed by federal law, and these rights cannot be changed in any way through adoption.

Native Americans must be able to prove a tribal affiliation to qualify for inheritance rights that attach to membership in a particular tribe. If you are a Native American by birth, either wholly or in part, contact the Department of Interior, Bureau of Indian Affairs, Office of Public Affairs, 1849 C Street NW, Washington, DC 20240-0001, (202) 208-3711, fax (202) 501-1516, for information on how you can claim whatever inheritance rights you may have through your tribal affiliation.

Somewhere in that process you may also uncover leads to your birthparents. As a birthparent with a Native American background, you can press adoption/social service agencies to make it possible for your child to claim his or her federally protected birthright. Chapter 4, "Reference Resources" offers many places to contact and books to read, while Chapter 9, "Searching on the Computer" lists multiple Internet sites to view.

NEED-TO-KNOW

> How many times in your life have you Clicked into place? Like opening
> a safe, it's searching and finding the right combination to Future Fit
> into a new life. Mastering control, becoming clear. Too many people
> spend their whole lives feeling slightly off-kilter, slightly out-of-step
> with their expectations. Something doesn't work—a job, a place, the
> totality of what you're doing.[11]

You do not rely only on rights established by law to justify your search
efforts. A compelling need-to-know is the usual reason for someone to undertake this difficult, often frustrating search process. Searchers rarely pursue
their goals simply out of some idealistic sense of right. They are working to
resolve an intensely personal life-adjustment difficulty. Since laws—and consequently the rights established under these laws—are presumably based upon
perception of social needs, a review of searchers' rights cannot be complete
without a look at searchers' needs.

Psychological Need-to-Know

Self-identity and establishment of a sense of connectedness are uppermost in
searchers' minds. The remark below, from one of the individuals connected
with the ALMA lawsuit in New York, reflects how deeply painful the lack of
this knowledge can be:

> We are not separate or different from those born with a heritage they
> have always had knowledge of . . . and the freedom to investigate
> further if they so choose. Being denied information concerning myself
> that is not denied a nonadoptee is degrading and cruel . . .what an
> invasion of humanity! . . . [to] close up a human life as a vault
> somewhere and say, You may not know about yourself—you have not
> the right even to ask . . . . Your anxieties are neurotic, your curiosity
> unnatural . . . . [12]

Fortunately, awareness of the psychological need-to-know is occasionally
seen in remarks from the bench in cases involving adoption rights. Judge
Wade S. Weatherford, Jr., of the Seventh Judicial Circuit of South Carolina,
presiding over a case concerning the opening of adoption records, put the issue
of the relationship between needs and rights into particularly sharp focus when
he stated:

> The law must be consonant with life. It cannot and should not ignore
> broad historical currents of history. Mankind is possessed of no greater
> urge than to try to understand the age-old question: "Who am I?"
> "Why am I?" Even now the sands and ashes of continents are being
> sifted to find where we made our first step as man. Religions of

mankind often include ancestor worship in one way or another. For many the future is blind without a sight of the past. Those emotions and anxieties that generate our thirst to know the past are not superficial and whimsical. They are real and they are "good cause" under the law of man and God.[13]

It's unfortunate that up to now so few administrators, legislators, and judges have thought to look at the psychological need-to-know as a valid reason for opening records. But many adoptees have written movingly on this subject. Read their accounts. You'll find the titles of some of these books in Chapter 10, "Search Resources and Services."

Birthparents suffer a different psychological burden, although one that is equally painful. To begin with, whatever inherent parental love they possess is totally thwarted by the present blanket censorship of records. Circumstances of relinquishment and adoption necessarily require a birthparent to step back, however painful that often is. Why in later years may relinquishing parents not know their child's adult identity, not be assured that their child is well, and not reach out and touch that someone they gave life to?

What mother who has ever held and looked with love at her own newborn child cannot imagine the years of anguish another such mother has suffered because circumstances forced her to relinquish that child? What loving father cannot imagine the painful helplessness a man experiences at having to give up his child? Yes, reality dictates that the choice of relinquishment has to be made, that it has necessary consequences of separation. But what reality dictates that a relinquishing parent ought never have the opportunity of personal assurance that his or her child is all right, never experience pride in the child's accomplishments, never share with the child any of the life experience that is naturally a part of the child's heritage? What makes the emptiness suffered by these birthparents during years of separation so desirable that they must suffer it forever? Why must they carry a life sentence without hope of parole or pardon?

Although a relinquishing birthparent is often thought of as a cold, uncaring individual, the truth is more often something else. In the words of one birthmother, "I didn't take the easy way out. I didn't lack mother love—I just lacked everything else."[14]

Birthparents frequently have to deal with an enormous sense of guilt about relinquishing their child. And this is so even when they have been as much victims of circumstances beyond their control as has the child itself. Despite this, the present system of administering relinquishment/adoption records demonstrates little compassion. What it does instead is to reinforce the guilt, to treat the birthparents as if they were lifelong enemies of the child. What is the social advantage here, especially when the child has matured to adulthood? It may be that the child has no desire to establish or maintain any relationship with his or her birthparents. However, in that event, he or she as an adult can wield the same power that is exercised in deciding not to pursue any relationship—the power to say no. But current law deprives the child of an opportunity to speak for him or herself. The law dictates the answer for everyone, despite massive evidence that many would, in exercising their own adult right of free choice, answer differently.

It is primarily in these contexts that the psychological need-to-know has been expressed up to now. However, recent research findings suggest another psychological need that may be cited in the future—a psychological need to understand genetically influenced behavior patterns.

Minnesota Twins Study

The Minnesota Twins Study began on March 11, 1979, when a pair of twins, separated, adopted, and reared apart, arrived at Dr. Thomas J. Bouchard's office at the University of Minnesota. Since that time, Dr. Bouchard has published a number of papers and amassed volumes of information that have only just begun to present facts to the world on genetic influences as they relate to personality and other traits. Twins reared apart, says Dr. Bouchard, "provide the simplest and most powerful method for disentangling the influence of environmental and genetic factors on human characteristics."[15] In the Minnesota Twins Study, Dr. Bouchard has sought to enlarge the study's base of participants (currently over 70 pairs of identical twins and over 50 pairs of nonidentical twins) to address the issue of the degree to which personality traits are acquired (nurture) and inherited (nature). Many personality traits previously thought to be learned traits are being studied by Dr. Bouchard with the help of adult identical and nonidentical twins who were separated and adopted by different families.

Today's searchers, or those considering a search, should take note of the following statements found in three different reports from the Minnesota Twins Study:

> It is well known to naturalists and to animal breeders that there are wide and heritable differences in behavior within other species, but there is a curious reluctance among some scientists . . . to acknowledge the contribution of genetic variation to psychological differences within the human species. Our findings support and extend those from many family, twin, and adoptive studies, . . . a broad consilience of findings leading to the following generalization: For almost every behavioral trait so far investigated, from reaction time to religiosity, an important fraction of the variation among people turns out to be associated with genetic variation. This fact need no longer be subject to debate . . . rather, it is time instead to consider its implications.[16]

> Our findings lend additional support to the small body of literature (Martin et al., 1986) suggesting that social attitudes are in part genetically influenced. . . . It will no longer be possible to interpret parent-child correlations, sibling correlations, or other familial correlations as merely reflecting the impact of common family environments. . . . Social scientists will have to discard the apriori assumption that individual differences in religious and other social attitudes are solely influenced by environmental factors.[17]

> Three converging lines of evidence . . . all lead to the conclusion that parent-child relations and common family rearing environments have effects of minor magnitude, if they have any reliable effect at all, on adult personality. These finds are entirely consistent with many other lines of evidence generated by behavioral geneticists (Plomin & Daniels, 1987) as well as other critics of the conventional wisdom . . . .[18]

Magazines and newspapers report stories of unexpected "coincidences" surrounding reunions of those separated by adoption. These "coincidences" are only now beginning to be understood as more than happenstance. They are now looked at by geneticists as having a genetic basis.

It seems increasingly important that this aspect of psychological need be considered. Contact between adoptees and birthparents will afford the adult adoptee the opportunity for a better understanding of behavior patterns which may be genetically influenced. In light of these findings, depriving the adoptee of knowledge of his or her genetic heritage could be seen to deprive him or her of an important dimension of self-knowledge.

If you are searching and are a twin separated and adopted, Chapter 10, "Search Resources and Services," has more information on how to contact the Minnesota Study of Twins Reared Apart.

Medical Need-to-Know

The medical need-to-know cannot be separated from genetics. Neither can genetics be separated from the adoptee. Anyone first visiting a doctor or a dentist is asked to fill out a medical information sheet detailing diseases they have had, medicine they are allergic to, and a history of family illnesses. This becomes complicated for an adoptee who is denied access to information on family genetic tendencies and illnesses.

Genetic research is making new discoveries every day. These genetically based connections are only starting to be accepted by the general public as stories and reports appear more frequently in newspapers and magazines. The importance of this issue is made clear by the following quote from *Family Diseases: Are You at Risk?*

It is believed that genetic factors may be involved in 25 percent of diseases. Frightening as this figure is, many genetic disorders once thought to be incurable can now be controlled or treated successfully if they are diagnosed *early*. Family health histories can provide descendants with an invaluable tool, alerting them to watch for early warning signs of such illnesses as breast cancer, diabetes, and glaucoma.[19]

Birthparents are not always able to update medical information for the relinquished child and many more are simply not aware that they may be able to place a doctor's report or a letter in their relinquished child's file. What happens when a birthparent prepares a letter providing updated medical information and then sends it to the agency? Probably nothing, unless the adoptee contacts the agency in which case the information may be passed along.

Geneticists may have a solution for adoptees' lack of current, updated medical information. Since it is impossible to predict what information will be needed five, ten, or twenty years from now, it has been suggested that a sample of the birthparents' blood be obtained and included with other adoption material. The ability to look at the birthparents' DNA structure could provide medical information on the adoptee. This suggestion is an attempt by geneticists to reconcile the issue of sealed records with the adoptee's medical need-to-know.

Among the long list of ailments that have been found to include some genetic factors are Alzheimer's disease, allergies, arthritis, asthma, several forms of cancer, cardiovascular (heart) diseases, diabetes, multiple sclerosis, sickle-cell anemia, and certain visual disorders. More than 3,000 genetic diseases have been identified, and many other conditions thought not to be genetic do tend to occur more frequently in some families than others.

State adoption laws usually do take some notice of medical need-to-know, but they are not always clear to what degree you have a right to know. Can you at any time claim a right to whatever medical information is kept in your files? Or can you only claim that right in a situation of compelling need, such as when you are ill and doctors require a more complete medical background? Preventive medicine allows individuals to manage or watch for possible conditions before symptoms appear. It may entail changing eating habits or stress levels, seeing your doctor more frequently, and watching for potential illnesses. But how can you use preventive medicine if you don't know, are hindered from knowing, what to be on guard for?

Several years ago I spoke with an adoptee who had located her birthmother. It was only through conversation with her birthmother that she discovered a history of breast cancer in her family. She related this to her doctor, who confirmed that this knowledge would make early detection of any breast cancer she might develop more likely.

Those adoptees with a medical need-to-know are continually faced with obstacles that prevent the unsealing of their records. In an affidavit prepared for a pending trial, Melanie Sandoval spoke of her medical and psychological need-to-know:

> As an adult adoptee, deaf since birth and divorced mother of two children . . . I have overcome many obstacles to life. Perhaps the most difficult obstacle could not be overcome but instead was circumvented —statutory secrecy as to who I am, whether my deafness, and my children's early hearing problems, is congenital, whether I was given up for adoption *because* I am deaf or because my birth parents could have been deaf.[20]

From the later 1940s to 1971, more than two million pregnant women used the drug Diethylstilbestrol (DES) to prevent miscarriage. The federal Food and Drug Administration banned DES when an apparent link was established between its use by pregnant women and development of cancer in children they carried during that pregnancy. In October 1978, the United States Surgeon General issued a physician advisory to every medical doctor and osteopath, warning of the hazards associated with the use of this synthetic estrogen. While the advisory warns of danger primarily to the female child, DES is suspected of having potential for damage to male offspring as well. An abstract providing DES information can be found on the Internet at The Cancer Web, <infoventures.com/cancer/canlit/des0995.html>.

In certain parts of the country—New York City, for example—public awareness campaigns have urged mothers who have used DES to contact local health authorities or their doctor for information and advice on recognizing and dealing with possible health problems associated with DES. Young adult women are also the target of this sort of campaign. But what of the adoptees whose birthmothers are unknown to them? How can they determine if they are under risk if their birthmothers' medical records, as contained in the adoption file, are incomplete? And they probably are.

Incomplete medical information is a common problem for adoptees. Omissions in adoption records are often as important as what is included. And that's not necessarily the fault of the birthparents. The present system does not encourage them to maintain an up-to-date medical history in the records held by the adoption agency. Older adoption records are especially scanty on medical information. In previous decades, the genetic factor was not considered as important as it is seen to be now for predicting potential health problems. Adoptees have no source to turn to for answers to questions that may be vital to them. The birthparent who has important information cannot easily pass it on, may not realize it matters that it be passed on. The health risks that adoptees face would be much more apparent and the parental responsibilities that many birthparents feel could be carried out more naturally and fully, if the opportunity for contact were allowed.

The right to updated medical information is addressed as follows in North Carolina's General Statutes (Section 48–25 d.):

> While the statute assists the adoptee in gaining some medical informa-
> tion, it does not always solve the adoptee's problem; too often the
> records themselves are incomplete. When the adoption takes place,
> the natural parents may fail to divulge all of the relevant medical
> history concerning the child and the child's natural family. Moreover,
> the medical history of the natural parents changes over time; and even
> if the natural parents disclose all ailments affecting the family at the
> time of adoption, new illnesses may arise long after the records have
> been sealed. Incomplete records therefore result.[21]

There has always been a concentration on the birthmother's genetic information. Today, however, there is evidence suggesting that the birthfather's
contribution is more important than previously thought. *Time* magazine recently published an article titled "The Sins of the Fathers" which noted that
"The list of substances suspected of harming children through their fathers is
growing steadily."[22]

RECENT TRENDS

For years, adoptees and birthparents have faced the realities of searching for
black market babies or foundlings (see Chapter 5, "Beginning to Search:
Primary Sources of Data"). Today, some searchers are looking at records
concerning those conceived by donor insemination or "surrogate" mothers
(see Chapter 5). Future searchers will need to be aware of laws regarding in
vitro fertilization (IVF), egg donation, and other forms of third-party repro-
duction. A metamorphosis is taking place as we approach the twenty-first
century, a transformation that will surely impact future searchers just as black
market adoptions, foundlings, "surrogate" mothers, and donor inseminations
affect searchers today.

I do not by any means wish to give the impression that there is no progress
being made in recognition of adoptee/birthparent rights, that there is no
consideration of their needs. There is a growing awareness of these, both
among the public and among government decision makers.

Psychology Today recently published an article titled "Turning Two Identities into One." This article ended with the following statement: "The law calls
adoption complete when the judge signs the papers; in reality, it has barely
begun."[23] As encouraging as this awareness is, searchers still find themselves
faced with a system of records administration that discriminates against them
as they begin their search.

State reunion registries are growing, but most still require consent forms from the adoptee as well as the birthparent(s). The age of majority for an adoptee is simply the age he or she may try to access records, not when the records are available. States are starting to recognize medical need-to-know, but most put this need after the birthmother's right to privacy.

Adoptees, birthparents, and adoptive parents are taking a hard look at the adoption policies followed in the past. One policy that continues to plague the searcher is the state's obsession with secrecy. This policy is founded on the belief that sealed records offer protection to the birthmother and the adoptive families and that secrecy and protection are preferred by all those involved to maintain a normal life. Yet, comments from those actually involved show just the opposite. Susan Darke, both an adoptee and a birthmother, states the following:

> All my life I have been told, "If you find her [the birthmother] it will ruin her life; it will ruin your parents' lives, you'll hurt them so badly." And when I talked about knowing the child I had given up, I was told the same thing. At some point I stopped and said, "Now wait a minute, what is it about knowing me that's going to ruin people's lives?[24]

Karen Golden, an adoptive mother, reveals her feelings about secrecy in adoption. "I really believe that openness makes for a healthier child. . . . After all, we strive for openness and honesty in the rest of our lives; why should adoption be the exception?"[25] This simple sentence could easily be overlooked in an article, yet its sincerity sums up what searchers are saying. Their need-to-know stems from this lack of honesty as well as from state laws barring openness in adoption.

BALANCING RIGHTS

In closing this chapter, I would like to point out to you the importance of balancing rights. Because when all is said and done, your rights and needs exist in a social setting that includes other people with rights and needs of their own.

As a searcher, you have to be aware of the potential for conflict between your right to know and another's right to privacy. You must set standards that guide you appropriately. With these standards firmly established in your mind, you will be aware when pursuit of your right to know infringes on another's genuine right to privacy. Remember that the way you pursue a line of inquiry—the people you contact, for example—can often prove more an invasion of another's privacy than the actual line of inquiry itself. Setting standards here will guard you against irresponsible action that might be taken in moments of excitement, when under pressure, or at times when you don't quite know what to say.

There are no groups, professionals, or other individuals who can weigh your needs better than you can, so setting guidelines on respect for privacy must be a result of your own decisions. A pressing medical need for information, for example, can weigh differently than a need to establish a connection with a past. There are groups that say anything goes—your rights supersede all others. Present society has a tendency to state that your rights have no precedent over anyone else's, and, in practice, to put them at times in the back seat relative to others.

You will probably find yourself somewhere between these two positions as you draw up your rules of self-conduct. Much time and thought should go into this, because time and again your guidelines will be tested as you come into contact with new people and encounter difficult situations. By setting and following standards you feel to be appropriate and by defending your rights when necessary with a clear conscience on how they balance against rights claimed on behalf of others, you will be able to maintain your own sense of pride and dignity more certainly.

NOTES

1. From an article by Ruth B. Ward, "...by any civilized standard," *The Humanist*, September/October 1995, p. 32.
2. The Plaintiffs are Promise Doe, Jane Roe, Kimberly C. and Russ C., and Small World Ministries, Inc. vs. Donald Sundquist, Governor of the State of Tennessee, Charles W. Burson, Attorney General of the State of Tennessee, and Linda Rudolph, Commissioner of the Department of Human Services for the State of Tennessee.
3. From the American Adoption Congress newsletter, *DECREE*, vol. 14, no 1, Spring 1997, p. 3.
4. A reprint of an article by Jon Ryan, President of National Organization of Birthfathers & Adoption Reform as printed in *To Prison with Love* by Sandy Musser, p. 226.
5. A fuller discussion of the generally confusing body of state laws regarding open records can be found in Revised Draft of NCCUSL Proposed Uniform Adoption Act (Chicago: National Conference of Commissioners on Uniform State Laws), February 1995 Draft, Prefatory Note, p. 3.
6. The definition of nonidentifying information comes from Mary Sullivan, "Task Force on Confidentiality in the Adoption Program—A Report to the California State Department of Health," Sacramento, CA, 1977, p. 24.
7. The case of Betty Chase was chronicled in "Under 'Race' She Puts a '?'," *Los Angeles Times*, July 9, 1978, Metro Section, p. 1.
8. *University of Detroit Law Review*, vol. 62, 1984-85, p. 307.
9. The complete text of James R. Carter's comments on the question of adoptee inheritance can be found in "Confidentiality of Adoption Records: An Examination," *Tulane Law Review*, 1977-78, vol. 52.

10. Sarah P. Collins' interpretation of the Freedom of Information Act and the Right of Privacy Act are from *Citizens' Control over Records Held by Third Parties* (Washington, DC: Congressional Research Service, Library of Congress Report No. 78-255), p. CRS-22.

11. Taken from *Clicking* by Faith Popcorn and Lys Marigold, New York: HarperCollins, 1996, p. 3.

12. The psychological harm felt by adoptees who lack a complete family medical and psychological history can be seen in the affidavits of Anita McCarthy and John Franklin Filippone, filed in support of the ALMA lawsuit in New York before the U.S. District Court for the Southern District of New York on May 23, 1977, and reported in the *ALMA Searchlight*, Autumn 1977, p. 14.

13. The comments of Judge Wade S. Weatherford, Jr., on the relationship between needs and rights when considering opening adoption records can be found in "Report of the Governor's Commission to Study the Adoption Laws," issued by the State of Maryland and presented to the governor and legislature in 1980.

14. Concerning the stereotyping of relinquishing birthparents, see Edna Ewald, "Homecoming," *Good Housekeeping*, March 1981, p. 118.

15. *Science* Magazine, "Sources of Human Psychological Differences: The Minnesota Study of Twins Reared Apart," vol. 250, p. 227.

16. Ibid., p. 227.

17. "Genetic and Environmental Influences on Religious Interests, Attitudes, and Values: A Study of Twins Reared Apart and Together," *Psychological Science*, vol. 1, no. 2, March 1990, p. 141.

18. "Genetic and Rearing Environmental Influences on Adult Personality: An Analysis of Adopted Twins Reared Apart," *Journal of Personality*, vol. 58, p. 289.

19. From *Family Diseases: Are You at Risk?* by Myra Vanderpool Gormley, Baltimore: Genealogical Publishing, 1989, p. 7.

20. Affidavit and Brief of Melanie Sandoval, Amicus Curiae #7, United States District Court, District of Connecticut, Lori Carangelo, Thomas Schafrick v. William O'Neill, Governor, State of Connecticut.

21. "The Adoptee's Right of Access to Sealed Adoption Records in North Carolina," *Wake Forest Law Review*, vol. 16, August 1980, p. 581.

22. Andrew Purvis, "The Sins of the Fathers," *Time*, November 26, 1990, p. 90.

23. Kenneth Kaye, "Turning Two Identities Into One," *Psychology Today*, November 1988, p. 46.

24. Brian Kologe, "The Gifts of Secret Storks: Adoptive Children Come of Age," *Essex Life*, Summer 1984, p. 52.

25. David Ruben, "Option," *Parenting*, November 1989, p. 96.

CHAPTER 2

Getting Moral Support

A lthough it may be possible for an individual to undertake a search without having to deal with the highs and lows others face, I have yet to meet such an individual. You will need support from someone right from the start.

WHY WILL I NEED MORAL SUPPORT?

Two factors work together to lead even the initially casual searcher to seek out moral support. The first is the impact of directly facing the emotional stress that an adoption or relinquishment search produces. The second is coming up against the lack of consideration for the needs of searchers displayed by lawmakers and those who control records containing essential information. Let's look briefly at what is involved for adoptees and birthparents in either case.

The Adoptee

Although society as a whole may not seem to attach a stigma to an adoption situation, the fact is that you may be one of the many adoptees who carry a sense of stigma or emotional scarring with you. And that is often the case whether or not your adoptive parents have been matter-of-fact with you about your adoption.

As an adoptee searching for your birthparents you may be seen as a neurotic individual not content with your family. Some few adoptees may fit that image, but for the most part adoptee searchers are average citizens who function capably and responsibly in society. They are not set apart by reason of poor adjustment to the realities of day-to-day living. They are not a group of eccentrics with a radically different view on social issues from those held by the general public. The typical adoptee searcher is just a John (or Jane) Doe, a Mr. (or Ms.) Middle America. You are probably like almost everyone else, a person with emotional needs and curiosity and wonderment at where you came from. The difference that exists is not an outgrowth of the experience of unusual psychological needs. It is primarily an outgrowth of the very different circumstances surrounding your origin and the adjustments to a situation that was beyond your control. You do not know the answers to questions naturally raised by everyone. Because most people so routinely obtain these answers, they rarely consider how very important such answers are for the development of a complete sense of self-identity. For you, the absence of answers about where your roots lie results in a feeling of "unconnectedness" that the average person never has to face. This can at times create serious emotional conflicts, but such conflicts should be seen as a natural consequence of the circumstances that have deprived you of a socially conventional sense of rootedness, not as an indication of innate abnormality.

In initiating a search you are, on the whole, no more or less neurotic than the adoptee who does not choose to search. However, in initiating a search, you are ultimately confronting conflicting feelings that may be misunderstood by those around you. This kind of confrontation, I maintain, is typical of an individual with a positive drive to self-fulfillment and is not a form of neurotic behavior. However, for you, the searcher, it is almost always an unsettling process, requiring adjustments that cannot be anticipated and that may prove hard to make. Many times, adoptees try to explain that their search is for themselves—who they are—not for a birthparent. But to fill in the missing facts—to learn how you began, the factors that make you what you are—you must seek the person who has those answers. You might very well prefer to get those answers from your adoptive parents but realize this choice is not possible. You must stress, again and again, what you hope to do, what your needs are, and what choices are available to you. Any moral support serves to keep you anchored and focused in your day-to-day life, which must go on. It provides you an outlet for sharing or expressing emotions that otherwise could overwhelm you.

The Birthparent

As a birthparent who has relinquished a child, you are likely to be faced with a stereotyped judgment of your past actions. Society is apt to think in terms of a cold, uncaring, irresponsible woman or man who abandoned a helpless child, then went on to further escapades in life without second thoughts. All too often birthparents themselves carry the burden of a self-image that contains an element of this judgment, even though the circumstances of relinquishment were usually too complex to warrant this simplistic view.

At a Concerned United Birthparents (CUB) meeting, a young woman, very nervous and distressed, asked to be excused from identifying herself. After a while she entered into the conversation. No one pressed her to speak and the moderator stated she was welcome to remain silent or say anything she wished; no one was there to make judgments.

This young woman had never been able to tell her story before and could not hold back her tears in telling it now. She had relinquished a child when she was 15. Her parents had pressured her into the relinquishment because it was "best for the child"; she herself would soon forget all about it. That had been six or seven years ago. Since then she'd married and now had a two-year-old child from the marriage. But the pain she'd suffered in relinquishing her first child had not dissipated. She had come to the group, not in hopes of searching, since the relinquished child was still small, but to help her come to terms with a decision she now feared was wrong. She spoke of much anger and resentment towards her parents; since the birth of her second child, she had hardly had any relationship with them at all. She could not forgive their attitude and the pressures that led to relinquishment of their first grandchild.

It is rare that the decision to relinquish a child is made for the sake of convenience. Usually there are considerable pressures and complicating factors at work. But because it was your decision—an extraordinarily difficult and unpleasant one in most instances—you need to recognize that you're susceptible to feelings of guilt about whether it was a correct choice.

When you embark on a search, you are inevitably confronting feelings that are deeply disturbing. These may be near the surface or deeply buried. In either event, having the open support of someone close to you, or at least sharing a common understanding with another birthparent who experiences the same "need-to-know" or reawakened sense of responsibility for a child, will make your own search less racked by guilt, anxiety, or any feeling of being "out of sync" with the world around you. Support will help keep you centered in the here and now, and will make it easier to reject any negative judgment you may feel saddled with, either by others or by yourself. It will enable you more readily to see yourself in a new—and probably more accurate—light, as a mature person who now wishes to deal differently with a problem than he or she did at a younger age.

Chances are, as an adoptee or a birthparent conducting a search, you will encounter a variety of frustrations as you work to achieve the goal you've set for yourself. Some of the frustrations will be minor; others will be more substantial, the kind of blockages that virtually anyone would find hard to tolerate, let alone accept.

Take the example of Katrina Maxtone-Graham, an adoptee searcher who fought for many months against the Children's Aid Society in New York in an effort to obtain a full record of her adoption history. The Society repeatedly rebuffed her attempts to learn of her birthmother's identity. The social workers she encountered were obstructive on almost every front. She comments as follows on the conclusion of one visit to the Society's offices:

> We were about to leave when Mrs. Meinhauser [the social worker] made a final pronouncement: "Your mother has made a new life for herself. The episode is forgotten . . . . It is all over with for your mother. It's over, and done with, and finished." Sometime afterwards . . . I realized that, were my mother to walk into Mrs. Meinhauser's office tomorrow, she would be told, "Your daughter . . . has made a new life, and it's forgotten, Mrs. X. It's all over and done with for your daughter, it's over with and finished."[1]

The attitude of this social worker is, unfortunately, not uncommon. And it takes no great imagination to see what a devastating effect this can have on an adoptee or birthparent who is only trying to gain a sense of connectedness that others take for granted. As a searcher, you'll expose yourself to this frustration and humiliation, perhaps often. You may see yourself remaining steadfast throughout all such experiences, but you'll find the sympathetic support of someone who accepts your motivation and right to know to be an invaluable aid in keeping things in proportion. It's difficult for most people without support to maintain morale and purpose when up against a cold, bureaucratic system that denies them an element of their identity, either in manner of treatment or as a result thereof.

Note also that the frustrations can mount beyond anything you may have braced yourself for. In Katrina Maxtone-Graham's case, for example, she eventually discovered that the policy of noncooperation on the part of the Children's Aid Society was carried out despite a notation in her file by her birthmother that read: "I want it understood that if Judy [Katrina's birth name] is ever in need and the . . . [agency] knows of it, they will be sure to call on me for help."[2] Clearly, Katrina's birthmother was not all that opposed to the possibility of reestablished contact with Katrina; the agency nevertheless pursued its policy of blocking any contact. Perhaps your search will not be met with such obstructiveness, but it may be. In any event, you'll find the expression of moral support encouraging and reassuring during the experience of similar or other frustrations. Keep in mind that as you face these experiences, you're also likely to be dealing with personal anxieties and doubts related to the decision to search. You handicap yourself from the outset if you deprive yourself of any possible source of support.

THE STAGES OF A SEARCH

You may assume that once a decision to search has been made, you will plunge right into the process with an aloof, assured, businesslike manner, able to face and deal with all the conflicts and frustrations as they come up and to finish the search in the same emotional frame of mind you began it. The reality is that most searchers pass through a series of stages in their quest. The impact of conflicts and frustrations varies in each stage, but moral support is important through all of them. This is so for the broad reasons already given, but also because you yourself at times will become confused and bewildered by changes in the intensity of your own reactions to what is happening in each stage. That is to say, in addition to dealing with resurfacing or already present emotional conflicts, you might also be thrown off balance by shifts in your own perspective from one stage to the next.

Let's briefly look at what typically happens to the searcher's own reactions during the search process.

Separation

In this first stage, the searcher is commonly somewhat removed from the emotions of searching. You often express the reason for starting the search in very neutral terms: you are undertaking it to make your life more interesting, or out of simple curiosity, or from a medical need-to-know. You begin by concentrating attention on the mechanics of search, feeling no need to make a strong commitment to it. Often you respond to queries about what you are doing somewhat defensively, maintaining that the outcome is not so important to you, that if you get bored with it you can easily give it up.

This first stage does not last very long for most. And those whose support or interest is enlisted at this point may find themselves puzzled when you become progressively more involved and passionate about this quest, notwithstanding early assurances that it is only a matter of limited significance. "But I thought it didn't mean all that much to you—you said it didn't" is a common expression of puzzlement from family members or friends.

It is this awakening of deeper feelings and needs that proves so confusing for many a searcher. In the first stage, you are often convinced that this process you've begun is genuinely in response to an incidental kind of curiosity. You may realize the intensity of your desire to know, but it hasn't become an essential part of your life. However, before long the intensity builds and you are swept along into the further stages of search without quite knowing what is happening or why your initially controlled reactions seem to have snowballed.

This reaction also complicates the gaining of support. How do you ask for understanding if you yourself don't understand what your real aims are? This understanding is often beyond the comprehension of the person who has offered to help. That person often can fully help and understand your needs only after you have sorted through your own thoughts. And yet you are likely to feel a need for support before this process is complete.

Because of this pattern, it is best to avoid stating a categorical reason for your endeavor when you first begin your search. Sure, you can probably think of a reason that others will accept without too much challenge or question. Medical need-to-know will usually serve as an acceptable reason; heredity is now a known factor of concern in relation to susceptibility to common serious health problems. As you pass from the first stage through those that follow, there will probably be a growing awareness of other, more complex motivations that can be difficult to express. What becomes apparent now as you more intently pursue your search is that you are uncovering the hidden reasons pushing you to search. That is not to say that previous reasons were not valid; they were simply incomplete.

People respond to reasons that make sense to them. Don't necessarily hesitate to indicate the reasons for your search. Just avoid making them definitive. Be alert to the fact that they will probably undergo some kind of change; tell those from whom you seek support that such reasons as you can provide—whether logical or emotional—may gradually take on a different character. Impress upon them that it's not possible for you to know exactly what you will be seeking, although you wish you did. Possibly your needs have been pushed so far back into the recesses of your mind for so long that you are able to open up to them only a little at a time. Possibly there are deep hurts that cannot be faced all at once. What you hope for in having someone's support is to be able to share feelings that well up in response to each aspect of the experience as it develops. If you can express yourself in this fashion when first going into your search, others will be more prepared for the varying emotional conflicts you are likely to experience as you go through the subsequent stages of search.

When turning to someone who hasn't shared the adoptive or birthparent experience, it's best not to insist on a complete understanding of what you are going through. After all, how can those who haven't shared the experience understand it? Try rather to bring them to some awareness of how important this process is to you. Though they can never fully understand what it all means to you, you can make clear its link to your sense of who you are.

Indignation

The second stage of search is marked by an intensification of feelings. The neutral attitude typical of the first stage is dropped. These feelings commonly surface as indignation or rage at the frustrations encountered in attempting to gather information, rather than as anxieties, fears, or doubts connected to the personal significance of the search activity. The sentiment most expressed at this point is "How dare anyone violate my right to information that is kept on ME!"

Although the initial experience of indignation is genuine enough, don't focus on your indignation to such a degree that it prevents you from thinking about the deeper feelings that have also been awakened. This rage may cover feelings of rejection, insecurity, and guilt that have started to surface, or may sharpen them in instances where the searcher was already somewhat aware of these feelings.

At this point, having someone to turn to for moral support becomes very important. You are probably confused. With support from others, you will have more courage to face the mishmash of emotions you now find rising within you; you will feel less vulnerable and alone in dealing with both the growing turmoil within and the frustrations imposed on you from without. In your search for that connectedness that has heretofore eluded you or that you have previously sacrificed, having moral support helps maintain a proper balance in your day-to-day life.

By now you may begin to understand that there are deeply felt needs which prompted you to begin your search. If in enlisting the support of a family member or friend you stressed an attitude or reason that is now undergoing some change, realize that some confusion or uncertainty may attach to their reactions now. Enlist their patience in accepting your consideration of deeper, more personal motivations; be as patient as possible in allowing your support- ers time and room to come to a new perception of your involvement in this pursuit as well as of your frustrations.

Obsession

There comes the time in your pursuit of information when you become more and more involved in your search—nothing or no one can deter you. All your efforts and free time are directed toward correcting a gross miscarriage of justice against you, against anyone in your position. It may become a common event for you to confront friends, relatives, and even strangers you encounter with your burning determination to set things right. You are apt to be quick to judge others for their failure to see the issues as you see them. And yet you very well may not be facing the problem realistically.

During this stage the hurts and resentments that have usually begun to surface by now begin having a more sustained and disturbing impact. Think about what is happening. Is your crusading zeal possibly designed, in part, to keep those hurts and resentments from overwhelming you? And, if they have not already been considered, are there anxieties now about what you will actually discover? Do you ever think: "What if I find something terrible?" "What if the person sought doesn't understand my need-to-know?" "What if the child I relinquished doesn't understand my reasons?" Does your obsessive drive to locate that baby or birthparent to some extent grow out of a frantic desire to have such disturbing fantasies laid to rest?

It may be that coming to the decision to search was so difficult that now having to face obstacles that block the progress of your search causes anger and resentment. This anger and resentment toward those that withhold information and impede your progress is understandable, but your severe reactions to those hindering your progress may be influenced by doubts as to the decision itself.

During this stage you need moral support more than ever, but the obsessive nature of your pursuit often makes it difficult for your supporters to continue their help. The constant focus on getting to the identity of your birthparent or relinquished child can create tension with someone who now at times may wish you'd forget the whole thing or, at least, that you'd keep it "in perspective." You have to accept that at times it will be difficult for your supporters to respond to your needs for sympathy and involvement as completely as you'd like. Perhaps you'll find that you do have a friend or relative who at every turn will be right there in the trenches with you, fighting for total vindication of your rights. But recognize the likelihood of uncertainty or weariness intruding at times. Remember that this war you're fighting is at times strange to one who doesn't share the experience of adoption or relinquishment.

Suppression

Following a period of obsessive determination to achieve the search goal—and perhaps also to change the system as it relates to adoption or relinquishment records—you may find yourself withdrawing from the fray. The reasons vary. It may be as a result of the cumulative effect of frustrations encountered, of disruption of previously established routines, of anxieties that develop, and so on. It may simply be that you feel the need for a rest. Or the halt may be called at a point where a critical piece of information has actually been uncovered.

Whatever the prompting factor, it's important to understand that this reaction represents another stage for most searchers. It's not necessarily the end. You have put your search aside. It may be that you seldom even think about it anymore; your conscious desire to go on with it seems to have evaporated. You may feel this way for a few days, a week, a month, or forever. A few individuals stop their search permanently, but you are more likely to find that you eventually move on to the fifth stage.

From the vantage point of your supporters, your behavior may again prove a puzzlement. There may be surprise and shock that you're apparently giving up on a quest that has been so critically important to you. Or there may be relief that you've stopped, with the potential for a reaction of shock or confusion at whatever time you decide to resume searching. Whichever the case, for a moment you may once again find yourself seemingly out of step with those supporters who have been traveling the search road with you. As before, give your supporters a chance to make their adjustment to what is, in effect, your adjustment to your experience. You can't realistically expect that this adjustment will be completely synchronized with yours.

Acceptance

This stage comes when you accept *whatever* it is that you've discovered. This can mean you accept that you do want to continue your search, or that you're not ready to carry it through to the conclusion you'd originally hoped for, or that you now have and want to take the opportunity to try to develop a new relationship not previously possible for you.

Now you must deal with the qualms you probably have. Preparation for a reunion is very difficult; you don't know what you will find. Will the birthparent be receptive? Will the relinquished child (who may be conflicted about role models or a sense of loyalty to the adoptive parents) wish to talk to you? Will you find an undesirable birthparent or child? Will the medical histories you find bring new concerns into your life?

Realizing that you're willing to accept whatever the results of your search might be does not lessen your need for moral supporters. As your search comes to an end, and especially if the possibility of a reunion exists, you may find yourself more dependent than ever on your supporters. As much as all searchers hope this isn't the case, no searcher can overlook the possibility of rejection. If you've decided to seek a reunion you run the risk of attempting to establish a relationship, the intensity of which may run the gamut from love to hate. Whether a relationship develops or not, the entire situation is a trying one for you and your supporters.

One adoptee I know carefully tracked down her birthmother. It was a long and tedious process, but finally a current name and address were found and the phone call for initial contact was made. A very cheery, bright woman answered. She was astonished, sympathetic, and willing to help in any way, but stated it was impossible that she was the birthmother. After much conversation both agreed the facts had somehow been distorted and that possibly a college friend must be the birthmother. The woman promised to help, to relate all the facts she could remember.

The adoptee hung up the telephone devastated. She had searched so long and hard, coming up with the wrong name meant starting all over. During the next few days she retraced all her steps in an effort to discover where she'd made her mistake. Her frustration mounted at her inability to figure it out. Then, after several days, a phone call came through from the woman she had thought was her birthmother. She stated that she was in fact the birthmother, that she had realized this might eventually happen and so had mentally prepared herself for it. However, she'd never told her husband or children about the birth and she'd denied being the mother to have time to tell her family the truth. After several days of sorting out facts and feelings, she was now calling back to say she was the birthmother and that her family fully supported her getting to know her relinquished child.

This story has a happy ending, but you can imagine the value of moral support to the adoptee through those few days of seeming defeat. Her attitude of acceptance still could not prepare her for the shock of initial denial.

Even if you do not find the person sought, you will emerge from the search with a heightened self-awareness that can be channeled in a positive direction. A search should bring a sense of pride and dignity when you review the difficult tightrope that had to be walked, weighing your need-to-know against another's right to privacy.

No two people experience the stages of search in the same way. Each deals with unique circumstances and contends with very personal hopes and fears. Virtually all who search will find that the pattern of their search to some degree mirrors the general pattern, although often this is clearer in retrospect than during the process itself.

THE FEAR OF FAILURE OR REJECTION

Many an adoptee or birthparent has been stimulated to search as a result of the publicity others have received when their search has ended happily. Pleasant reunion stories appear in newspapers and magazines every week, giving the impression that all is well when the search ends. And the idea of their own happy reunion stirs them to decide whether to proceed or not: "If the possibility of a happy reunion exists for another, why not for me?"

Even so, I doubt that any searcher really feels secure just in knowing that others have found a "happy ending." There are haunting uncertainties that grow as the search progresses. Of course, the way you express these doubts to yourself influences exactly how disturbing they will be; some individuals will be able to handle them more readily than others. No one, however, will escape a brush with them. And when that comes, having your supporters standing by is invaluable.

Although there is always a chance you won't locate the person you're seeking, you should know that the odds are good that you will. Search techniques are more refined than ever; the network of search and support groups is constantly growing; at least some improvement is occurring in the general attitude toward searching; and we live in a records-oriented society, so a wide range of potential leads can be pursued.

In the process of search, you are also confronting deep-seated feelings about a fact of your past that has greatly influenced who you are today. This is perhaps more apparent with adoptees than with birthparents, but my conversations with birthparents reveal a similar significance to them of their search. In carrying the search through, you are to a considerable extent reviewing feelings about yourself. It's noticeable, for example, that many of those who enter into a search do so at an important time in their lives: after marriage, after the birth of a child, after passage of a significant age milestone (achieving legal age, turning 40 or 50), or after a death in the family. Such events prompt many to reflect on who they are, on what their life has thus far been, and where they feel a need for change. For adoptees, it means a consideration of the circumstances surrounding adoption and their impact; for birthparents, those surrounding relinquishment.

You may initially feel a compulsion to justify the rationale for your search, but this ultimately becomes less a consideration than the experienced need to justify actions taken through the search. It is your responsibility to set appropriate guidelines for yourself. Be cautious, as these guidelines will be tested again and again in moments of excitement, when under pressure, or at times when you suddenly don't know quite what to say. In searching for someone else, you pursue a course that makes it possible to discover something more of yourself. And that, to my mind, is not failure, whether you locate a birthparent/relinquished child or not.

As for the fear of possible rejection, the key, I believe, lies in accepting whatever it is you will find. In addition, be alert to this: The initial contact you eventually make will be a surprising, emotional event to the other person. This person cannot have anticipated your call or self-introduction, even if perhaps he or she has considered the possibility of it "some day." It will probably take more than a moment just for the realization to sink in that suddenly here is an opportunity for establishing a new relationship. It may take days or weeks to adjust to that fact and then to act on it. Don't be too quick to assume you've been totally rejected. Many searchers do find that acceptance ultimately awaits them. Those few who are rejected naturally experience pain and disappointment, but recognizing and accepting the risk of rejection generally serves to fortify them substantially. And at least they have raised the veil of secrecy that has been drawn across an important part of their lives; the uncertainty of not knowing has been resolved. That resolution provides a very positive feeling for many. Adoptees continually state that not knowing is worse than anything they might find. Consider these remarks of one adoptee:

> One of the things that has bothered me most about the partial information that my adoptive parents gave me about my natural mother was the fact that she had been institutionalized, without letting me know in what sort of institution. Was it a mental institution? Was it a prison? Without knowing these things, I will constantly feel anxious and in doubt. I would not mind knowing what sort of institution it was, but being in doubt produces lifelong anxiety.[3]

Facing the possibility of rejection is never easy, but we inevitably face that possibility in all areas of our lives. What are the resources you've fallen back on in earlier years? Certainly among them will be the moral support of people who care for you or who see in you a reflection of their own experience. As you pursue your search, during which you will wrestle with unsettling emotions and doubts, avail yourself of the moral support that is within your reach. It will make you more able to withstand whatever disappointments may lie ahead. In the face of possible rejection, it will be a vivid illustration of acceptance and caring.

WHERE WILL I GET MY MORAL SUPPORT?

You need not feel hopelessly alone in your undertaking, but finding support is not as simple as just identifying the possible sources and then availing yourself of them. You will be reaching for support from people with their own emotional needs and priorities. These have to be considered and dealt with.

Spouse

If you are married, the logical first source to turn to for support is your husband or wife. This is the person with whom you've entered into a life partnership. It seems only natural to be sharing your feelings about whether or not to pursue a search and about what you experience during your search with your marriage partner.

Ideally, your spouse will be strongly supportive. Not only will he or she take a positive interest in what you are doing and how that affects you, he or she will assist you in your search. You'll not only have the benefit of moral support, you'll find you have the full resources of two minds in tackling this problem you've decided to face. Together, you'll work out whatever emotional conflicts now exist or may arise in connection with your search. And at the conclusion, you'll have both the desired knowledge relative to your birthparent(s) or relinquished birthchild and a strengthened relationship with your spouse.

Well, it can work out that way for you, but you may find the dream of immediate, unstinting support from your spouse just that, a dream. Your spouse may find the significance of the search to you hard to understand. Why do you need a more secure sense of self-identity? What makes it necessary now to come to grips with feelings of guilt or responsibility that have troubled you for years? It's all water under the bridge, isn't it? Again, it's that inability of someone who doesn't share your experience wholly to understand what motivates you.

In addition, you may find that your spouse views your search as a threat to your relationship, that he or she resents the time and energy expended in an activity that seems to have no immediate relevance to life at home and that can complicate life at home. Suddenly, you're preoccupied with a problem and related issues that have their focus outside the marital relationship; you may seem to be putting your marriage and your responsibilities to family in second place to a pursuit that is rooted in fantasy.

Or it may be that your spouse hesitates or refuses to support you out of a sense of protectiveness. He or she may feel that you will only be opening yourself up to further hurts that will leave you emotionally shaken and scarred and so your spouse may attempt to dissuade you from undertaking or persisting in your search.

Or your spouse may react with indifference; it just doesn't seem all that important to him or her. If you want to do it, go ahead; just don't ask for his or her involvement.

As a birthparent, you may find another barrier to cooperation from your spouse: an unwillingness to accept your previous sexual relationship. Men typically find it harder to accept this than women, as multiple sexual relationships have traditionally been viewed as more tolerable in men than women. A birthparent-wife may find it more difficult to admit to a previous child—and thereby to a previous sexual relationship—than a birthparent-husband.

It's impossible to give one single piece of advice that will cover all such situations. If you want to initiate a search for a relinquished child your spouse knows nothing about, you will need to consider your marriage situation carefully. How do you think your spouse will react? Do you carry with you a constant anxiety that he or she will find out anyway? Would whatever risk might be taken in telling your spouse be compensated for by relief from that continual fear? Is there a mutually respected and trusted third party—a family member, friend, or member of the clergy—who might be able to help you resolve your fears of rejection by your spouse?

Occasionally, the birthparent will have shared the existence of a previous child with the marriage partner, but the fact will remain a secret from other family members and friends. In that circumstance, if you intend to undertake a search, you should realize that one result may be eventual wider knowledge of the existence of your child and of your relinquishment. Discuss this with your spouse. How many people will be told? Who will they be? How will the two of you resolve any discomfort that may arise in the face of shock or disapproval on the part of family members, in particular of in-laws, friends, coworkers, and neighbors?

If you are experiencing difficulty enlisting the support of your spouse, it may be because you have failed to share with your spouse your feelings about your adoption or relinquishment. If your spouse is confused by your needs or can't comprehend the reason for your search, perhaps you haven't given him or her sufficient opportunity to look at the issue from your point of view. If you are considering or have decided to undertake a search, plan time for discussing and sharing your feelings with your spouse. Think about what you are going to say, about what your spouse's reactions are likely to be. Keep in mind that how you present the problem can influence how your spouse reacts to it. An announcement made in passing while dinner is being prepared might be taken less seriously than one shared during a period of quiet time that allows scope for a thoughtful discussion of issues and feelings from both perspectives. With more information about your needs, with a clearer awareness of inner fears and hopes you may not previously have admitted, your spouse will more readily recognize the importance for you of a determination to search. Understanding may still not be immediately forthcoming, but support may be there, nevertheless.

In coming to a decision to search, it may be that you are reading books on the subject. Let your spouse read them too. Point out selected passages that reflect your feelings. Making him or her aware that others have feelings like your own can aid in winning acceptance for yours. If you are in, or plan, contact with a search or support group, ask your husband or wife to accompany you to a meeting. This again provides an opportunity for him or her to see that your experience is not just some neurosis of yours that is best resisted.

You may find that, despite your most reasoned efforts, your spouse remains unwilling to be supportive. Should this be the case, recognize that just as you will experience changing feelings, so may your spouse. You may find that once you've attended several workshops, written letters, received answers, or uncovered new leads, your spouse may become interested and express a desire to help. As this happens, remember that your spouse will have some questions of his or her own. Be patient and open in your response to them. Curb the temptation to answer with a remark like "I thought you didn't want to help" or to revive some other quarrel about a previous lack of interest.

Occasionally, you might find the support offered by a spouse (or other family member or friend) a problem. That person may go beyond the bounds of providing encouragement or assistance and seek to impose his or her views on the proper way to conduct your search. Should that happen, you will need to block diplomatically what amounts to an interference with the goals you have established. In a matter as personal as this, to follow priorities set by another contributes to feelings of conflict and uncertainty. Tell your spouse (or other supporter) that you appreciate the intent to help. Encourage suggestions on how an area of search might be approached; acknowledge that you value his or her readiness to listen to your expression of feelings. But be firm. Emphasize that you wish to avoid unwanted tension between the two of you, but that you must follow your own sense of priorities. Obviously, you have to deal with this problem in light of the relationship you have with your spouse.

Suppose that your spouse refuses to be supportive—what then? For one thing, it means a probable reevaluation on your part of whether you want to go ahead with your search anyway. The lack of support expressed in the form of general indifference may not give rise to any great conflict. If, however, your spouse declares absolute opposition to your proposed activity, you must reflect on what that means to you. You may go on to conduct your search in secret— you might receive correspondence via general delivery, a post office box, or via a sympathetic friend; you may arrange calls so as to avoid any chance of interception or being overheard by your spouse. But this creates an obvious situation of tension; the fear of discovery is constant. And should your spouse actually come to a realization that you've decided to disregard his or her opposition and to search in secret, there's great likelihood of marital conflict. You have to decide what course to take and whether it's worth it to you.

The one point of advice I will repeat here is that you keep the door as open as possible to a later change of heart on the part of your spouse if at first he or she refuses or fails to be supportive. The issue has an impact of its own on the marriage partner, arousing fears and uncertainties that may take some time to deal with. If in your disappointment and hurt at your spouse's first reactions you can keep this in mind, it will prove easier later to accept a change of heart as genuine. You're less likely to get locked into your resentment that this person who is supposedly most in tune with you has not immediately realized the significance to you of what you are undertaking. (I advise the same openness when other family members or friends similarly fail to declare support at the outset of the search.)

Family

The issues here vary for adoptees and birthparents. As an adoptee you have been transplanted into a family environment other than that into which you were born. In your search for your roots, you will often find yourself dealing with the question of loyalty to your adoptive family. Your adoptive parents may interpret the decision to search as a rejection of them, as a statement of dissatisfaction with the job they did in raising you. And there are also some adoptive parents who feel that the adoption itself is a secret that should remain hidden. If your adoptive parents feel this way, naturally this can place you under considerable strain.

At an early age you may have become aware that every child fears he or she is adopted and needs reassurance from the family that it is not so. But for you no such assurance could be given. It may be that the fact you were adopted and the loving reasons for the adoption are spoken of freely, but the fears and unspoken questions are never broached. It's as if you were born the day your parents walked into the room and "made their selection."

Your adoptive parents may be unsettled by your decision to search. Their feelings are in large part a reflection of a general attitude that adoption properly closes the door on a child's past history forever and provides a substitute family tree that is complete in every respect.

Many adoptive parents have introduced their children to the world of adoption through a book published in 1939, *The Chosen Baby* by Valentia Wasson (HarperCollins Children's Books, 3rd Edition). Although it has been updated in its illustrations, cover, and print style, the story remains the same. It begins, "Once upon a time there lived a man and woman named James and Martha Brown." It ends, "James and Martha and Peter and Mary Brown are a very happy family." Your expression to your adoptive family of a decision to search may be interpreted by them as an indication on your part that you are not happy or satisfied with them as a family. They may have swallowed the fairy tale that adoption, once accomplished, quite rightly wipes out a child's past, that any subsequent concern about your birthparents is perverse on your part or means that they have failed.

Suppose James, Martha, and Mary Brown were very athletic—tall and thin, agile and quick. While Mary was always playing ball or jumping rope, you would find Peter in his room drawing; he was always small and clumsy and he never enjoyed sports like the other members of his family. Now Peter and Mary have grown up and Peter still loves to draw and has chosen to make his living in a related field. He is very talented and wonders how he became so. Peter chooses to search and discover if his talent came from his birthparents. Peter's search is not a negative reflection upon his adoptive parents nor indicative of any unhappiness on his part. He is searching to reconcile his feelings of being different from the other members of his family. Now let's further suppose that, through it all, James and Martha and Peter and Mary Brown are a very happy family.

Suppose Mary Brown married John Smith. They decided to have a child and when Mary first believed she was pregnant she went to see their doctor. He confirmed her pregnancy and began asking medical questions concerning her and her parents. Since she was adopted, only her medical information was taken. Mary started searching to gain updated medical information for her and her unborn child. Now let's further suppose that, through it all, James and Martha and Peter and Mary Brown (Ms. Smith) are a very happy family.

In trying to win support from your adoptive parents, it is very possible that you will have to deal with their insecurities. Naturally, your first line of explanation will be that you are not looking for a new mother or father to replace them; locating your birthparents will not change the relationship established with them. It may help to cite a medical need-to-know. As already noted, this seems to be the least threatening reason for searching and also one of the most important. Indeed, it is a perfectly legitimate motive, but it may not be the only legitimate motive. And you want your parents to be supportive as you explore those motives which lie deeper. If, through your childhood and adolescence, you've been able to share feelings of insecurity and doubt with your adoptive parents, impress upon them that you hope they will be as open to your sharing the feelings you have now. Make them aware that this can afford you and them an opportunity to accentuate a relationship of closeness and mutual support. How could this kind of sharing be a threat?

Obtaining the support of your adoptive parents is important because they are your most available link to the past. Their recollections of the circumstances surrounding your adoption can provide valuable clues or leads for you to pursue as you seek out your birthparents. They may actually already have a crucial piece of information. One adoptee I know discovered his parents had a copy of a baptismal certificate that indicated his birth name.

Make an effort to broaden your parents' perspectives on your needs. Be explicit that your needs are an outgrowth of the fact of adoption, not a result of any shortcomings in their performance as parents. Ask them to read about the experience of others so that this fact will become more apparent to them. Ask them also to attend a search and support group meeting with you.

To avoid distressing your adoptive parents, you may choose to avoid discussing questions about your origin with them. You may feel that only upon your adoptive parents' death will you feel free of a conflict of loyalties in regard to searching out your birthparents. But then one of the most valuable sources of useful search information is beyond reach. In the words of one adoptee in this situation, "For my entire life I had been unable to approach my adoptive mother about my past and her death made me realize that my past was now dead, too."[4]

It may be that you find your adoptive parents absolutely unable to comprehend what your aims are in pursuing a search. The only thing they seem able to focus on is the threat of rejection or what they see as an implicit accusation that they have failed you as parents. In that event, it's probably better to pursue your need-to-know independently of them. Remember, this is your search and your need. While you would like support from people you love, you don't need to share this with persons who then translate your need into their hurt and fantasized failures.

Lest the focus in these paragraphs seem directed disproportionately to the possibility of a lack of support from adoptive parents, let me relate a personal encounter that illustrates a more positive reaction from an adoptive parent.

While attending a conference for searchers, I ran into an attractive woman one morning at breakfast. I asked whether she was attending the conference as an adoptee or birthparent. Neither, came the reply. She was an adoptive parent with three adopted children, ranging in age from 12 to 16. She had been reading lately about adoptees searching and felt it possible that one or all of her children might experience this need some day. She was aware of a certain inner pain in contemplating this possibility, but she recognized that her children would not actually be seeking a new set of parents and that the search would not affect feelings toward her. Even though her first reactions included fear, she discovered that facing the situation was not as difficult as she'd expected. She'd met many searching adoptees and heard what they had to say. She'd spoken with birthparents and realized that there was no real threat in the kind of relationship they hoped to establish with their relinquished children. As in helping a child through any difficult time, she wanted to be ready with meaningful support when the search question came up. I'm not sure many loving adoptive parents are similarly prepared to extend moral support once their children express a need to gain a connection to their birth origin.

As a birthparent searching for a relinquished child, you will be generally less dependent on your parents as a link with the past. You have your own memory of the events surrounding relinquishment. You were, after all, a principal in the decision and its subsequent implementation.

However, to the extent that family relationships are important to you, having the active moral support of family members is equally important. This can mean having to face any lingering sense of shame that may be harbored by your parents or other family members, which will influence their readiness to consider your needs openly. If they have not faced their feelings, if the subject of your child is one that by some silent agreement is never brought up for discussion, they are apt to resist your first efforts at bringing it up now. Their concern for what the neighbors might think, or what they still view as a shameful blight on the family name, may prevent them from being supportive. The possibility of enlisting their support depends in large part on the avenues of communication that remain open between you. If you now have a comfortable relationship with your parents, chances are excellent that you will in time be able to share aspects of your search with them. Allow latitude for a period of adjustment if at first they appear unable to understand your needs in pursuing your search.

Children

Often the decision to search out the missing connection with the past comes when you have a family of your own that includes one or more children. What do you tell them?

Two important factors influencing your decision will be your child's age and relative maturity. If your children are 3, 6, and 9, telling them will be much different than if they are 20, 25, and 30. What is your relationship with your children? Have they asked you questions about their family tree that would provide an opportunity to introduce them to the fact of your adoption?

Children react in different ways, according to their age and temperament. A friend of mine is searching. Her two teenage children find it very exciting and actively participate to the extent they can. Her 10-year-old, even though she is in the room when related conversations take place, gives no evidence of interest and does not participate.

As a birthparent you will find the question of what to tell your children more difficult. Your relinquished child is a sibling to the children who are part of your present family. Do they know of this other sibling? How do you feel they would react? Would their attitude toward you change? You will also have to consider their attitudes toward sex. Among young people there is often something of a double standard. They accept sexual openness and experimentation among their peers; they often find it difficult to accept that their parents may have indulged in that same openness and experimentation.

What about telling a small child about a brother or sister who was relinquished? In this case, confronting the child with an event beyond his or her capability to grasp would be irresponsible. It will not provide you meaningful support; it can generate unnecessary confusion or anxiety in the child. As a concerned, aware parent, you should know best when to tell your child and how to present the information most naturally. Adoption and adoption search are easily understood and accepted by children. Relinquishment is not as naturally introduced or as easily explained. With young children it is often advisable not to raise the subject until they need to know what is happening, possibly at the time of a find.

Whether to tell the children and how and what to tell them should probably be discussed first with your spouse, as with other issues that affect the family as a whole. It will be more difficult to come to agreement on telling the children when your spouse is not supportive. If you are pursuing your search despite your marriage partner's opposition and he or she is aware of that, it may be possible for you to compromise somewhat along these lines. You will agree not to confront the children immediately about the fact of your search and the reasons behind it, but at such time as their interest becomes apparent or it seems unavoidable that they will be touched by an aspect of the search—as when a reunion is imminent—you and your spouse will tell them together in a nonjudgmental, matter-of-fact manner. Obviously, the agreement you find yourself able to reach depends on the relationship you have with your spouse. If you feel obliged to search in secret, then it's evident you won't feel free to share your experience with the children in the home. Of course, the children's ages are a factor, too. If you have adult children—or perhaps even teenage children—you may not feel it imperative to "clear" what you tell them with your spouse first. Still, in most cases, I'd advise you to let your wife or husband know that you've shared this information with your children.

While I have discovered no instances of children failing to be supportive of a parent's search once they are told of it, that doesn't mean it hasn't happened. Parents who are concerned that their children will not be supportive may not tell them. I have encountered many instances of parents whose children are enthusiastically supportive of and participate in their search. I have met birthparents who spoke of difficulties bringing the subject up, but who found once the subject was out in the open that it was discussed freely in the home. (Most had not told younger children until the search reached a point where a find seemed near.) Birthparents with teenage or near-teen children noted that it wasn't a particularly comfortable way to approach sex education, but once the subject was broached, sex education was a natural byproduct. In each case, winning the support of the children had an unmistakable positive effect on the morale of the searcher.

Friends

When trying to explain my need to search, so often the friend listening would respond with the wrong question or conjecture. For instance, while I would be talking on a level of need-to-know, the friend would answer on a level of "What if the birthparents are rich and famous?"

Some people are able to grasp much of the significance of what you are doing quickly. Others can't. It is very painful for a searcher to find that a close friend is unable to lend support, can't understand, and may even disapprove, while another quickly recognizes needs within you and offers full support. Sometimes there's no alternative but to listen to a friend express an opinion that runs completely counter to your experience and feelings. In such a case, acknowledge that you've heard what was said and then proceed on to another subject.

You can keep friends who don't seem to understand updated in a brief or casual manner. Possibly, once they see the importance of this endeavor to you, they will express more interest. They will become open to a deeper sharing of feelings, to being educated in what search is all about. Some may even prove unable even to see your search as anything more than a subject that makes for interesting cocktail conversation. You will quickly get a feel for when and with whom you can truly share this very personal experience. Although it's likely that you will find yourself surprised and disappointed at the reaction of one or more close friends, chances are excellent that among your friends will be one or two who stand prepared to lend you support and aid, even if they at times find it hard to understand completely why you are so focused on what they see as a past event.

Other Adoptees/Birthparents

In 1978, the *Washington Post* estimated that there were some five million adoptees in the United States, approximately two million of whom were actively searching.[5] The newspaper did not provide an estimate of the number of birthparents searching, but one reunion registry reported that applications from birthparents now arrive in about the same proportion as from adoptees.

It is impossible to give an accurate number of those actively searching in 1998. Of the estimated two million active searchers mentioned above, there are no published figures on how many people completed their search; nor is there any estimate on the number of those unable or unwilling to reach their final goal. What can be calculated are the figures provided by states and search groups.

In 1997, reunion registries reported that they received more than 1,000 new enrollments each month. State reunion registries have as long as a six-month waiting list due to the large number of searchers. Search and support groups across the country tell of 20, 60, even 200 calls a week asking for search information or help.

The advent of the Internet has brought a new world of resources to the adoptee and birthparent searching. Computer Web sites report thousands of visitors to their pages. This new type of searcher may not join a search and support group, or even a registry, but quietly seeks a birthparent or relinquished child, going uncounted as one of the hunters for their past. All this would seem to indicate that the number of searchers has grown considerably since 1978.

To my knowledge, the number of searchers has not been tallied and the results of their searches not compiled. If these figures were available, the general public would be shocked to see the number of adoptees and birthparents making their quiet, private announcement to the world. Further, I believe that this announcement would be: "It's my right and a need I do not have to justify."

Look around you. Possibly you are a friend of or acquainted with someone else who is adopted or who is a birthparent with a relinquished child (although the latter may not as readily declare him or herself). All adoptees are at least curious about their origin. And I suspect that all birthparents have occasion to wonder about what may have become of their relinquished child. If you know you share either experience with someone else, it is usually easy to introduce the subject of search. That's not to say you'll encounter immediate, automatic support. Some adoptees/birthparents will not respond or may not be inclined to be particularly supportive. I assume that to mean they are not ready to consider a search for themselves. They may still be afraid of seeming conflicts in loyalty, or fear facing the unknown. They may feel they have an image to live up to which doesn't allow for search, or perhaps prefer to live with their fantasies. They may be so defensive that they feel constrained to dissuade you from undertaking your search. Then again, despite their fears or uncertainties, they may watch you pursue your search with a pointed curiosity that betrays an inner longing on their part to resolve the same unanswered questions. Every adoptee should have some concerns about genetic tendencies and updated medical information, and birthparents surely must realize their child's need for this critical information.

Reaching out for support in this context does not require that adoptees match up with other adoptees only or that birthparents line up only with other birthparents. Adoptees and birthparents can provide each other genuine support that can at times be even more meaningful than that offered by someone engaged in the same search. Adoptees may see in this acquaintance birthparent an encouraging example of concern and caring that they hope to find in their own birthparent; birthparents may similarly see in this searching adoptee an example of a relinquished child who sincerely longs for some contact with the parents who gave him or her up for adoption. The aim of the search/reunion is the same for both; the process of search is very similar; the fears that each encounters will be much the same. Motives may differ—for example, a need to gain a sense of connection with one's birth roots versus a need to resolve past guilt or failing with a new openness to responsibility. But these motives are largely complementary; there's no conflict between them. And the many similarities that exist make possible a broad sharing of experience and perhaps even a pooling of certain resources.

Approach your adopted friends; establish contact with a birthparent who has relinquished a child. You may be surprised at the reaction, even if up to now the other person has never dared consider the possibility of searching. You may find a person like yourself, feeling a need but unsure how to proceed. Using a "buddy system," you may both find you now have the necessary courage to undertake a search, something you hesitated or feared doing on your own.

Search and Support Groups

I have referred and will refer repeatedly to search and support groups. There are a variety of them. Some groups will work for adoptees and birthparents alike, other groups for only one or the other. Some groups concentrate on aiding actual searchers while others focus on efforts to influence legislation. Most do both. All have their origin in the uniting of people determined to promote the rights of adoptees or birthparents seeking information relative to their birthparents or relinquished children. They provide individual searchers with a network of support and resources far beyond that of anyone searching alone. They are established in every state in the Union; there are even a few links to similar organizations outside the United States.

Because search and support groups are composed overwhelmingly of people who have in the past responded or are now responding to the same need-to-know that pushes you, they constitute a source of genuine understanding. Yours may be a case where they are the only source of understanding you feel comfortable relying on. I attended a group meeting at which a divorcee with no other children than her relinquished child told of her relief at finding the group. "I thought I was all alone, no one to help me. I couldn't believe the first meeting I attended, the friends I made." And I've witnessed similar reactions over and over again. It is so heartening to find that others have gone through the same experience you are going through, have faced the same fears, have worked out similar problems.

Search and support groups are usually activist groups seeking to change attitudes and laws relating to adoption, relinquishment, and the right to know. They work actively for reform, but they do not enlist searchers as banner-waving members to be mobilized on behalf of the cause. The interaction with searchers is on an individual, sharing level. Their aim is to provide you support, not to recruit you into a movement. Your participation is welcomed; it is not demanded. Your privacy is respected fully and you are not pressured into support group policies or programs. Naturally, you will be invited to contribute so as to enable the group's support activities to continue. But the extent to which you participate in any group activities is up to you. You are almost always welcome to observe a meeting if you are unsure whether you are ready to reach out for the support the group can provide.

Search and support groups do not seek to take the place of any individual support you might otherwise reach out to; their purpose is to make additional support available, not to substitute for other available support. At one birthparent group I attended, I heard an embittered birthmother lash out against those who had disappointed her with their failure to be supportive. Her husband didn't understand; her best friend thought she was crazy; her parents were resentful that she was bringing up an old issue. Her only support came from the group. She went on to report that recently she'd spoken angry words to her friend and hung up the telephone without saying good-bye. The group suggested that maybe she had not given her family and friend the appropriate input and chance to support her. She felt so grateful to be with people who did not think her strange, neurotic, or crazy that she was willing to consider what the members of the group said. Their focus was on how to assist her in establishing the supportive links she so yearned for with those who were otherwise close to her.

Some groups make it possible for two searchers to join together in a mutually supportive buddy system. They are able to put people into contact who do not know each other but are in a position to help each other. Suppose you live in New York, while I live in California. You need records searched in Los Angeles; I need them searched in New York City. Through a contact arranged by the group, we are put in touch with each other. I then search for you while you search for me.

Another variation in approach works like this: Through the group, you spend time searching in New York on behalf of someone else while another person searches for you in Los Angeles. In this case, you are donating hours in return for hours spent on your search. The group coordinates. In a group I've been associated with, one adoptee was searching for her birthfather. She'd learned he lived in a small town in the Midwest, but she could only get telephone directory information, which was insufficient. She mentioned this at a meeting. After the meeting a woman approached her and said she had helped a birthparent with her search; this birthparent lived in the area mentioned. She gave her the birthparent's address and told her to write and request help in finding out the information locally. The birthparent was more than happy to help; she felt she was starting to repay a debt.

A third, and growing variation is volunteer help on the Internet. One such group, is Volunteer Searchers Network (VSN). This is a group of volunteers who will offer search help to those searching online, charging only for expenses, and offering a wide variety of search help (further information on VSN can be found in Chapter 9, "Searching on the Computer"). As the Internet continues to grow, more groups like VSN will offer Web sites and services for the searcher.

For more on the work that search and support groups do and how you can avail yourself of their help, see Chapter 7, "Search and Support Groups, Researchers/Searchers, Consultants, Intermediaries, and the Courts."

Professional Counseling

Some adoptees and birthparents develop feelings that are so conflicting and emotions that are so unsettling they must seek the aid of a psychiatrist, psychologist, or other professional counselor. It is never easy trying to live with guilt or needs we don't understand, and counseling or some form of therapy may prove beneficial.

I am not qualified to tell you when you need professional help, but I do urge you to keep in mind that it is available. One *thing* I do sincerely believe: The experience of a need-to-know is not of *itself* an indication that professional help is necessary. And yet you may find that friends, social workers, record keepers, and others around you may continually suggest this type of support. It may be that events that led to your decision to search (mid-life crisis, divorce, death) may be the reasons that cause turmoil in your life. The search itself may not be a contributing factor, but others may focus on this as the cause of your turmoil.

The idea that you are abnormal in wishing to know about your origins or your relinquished child is alien to me. You may, however, find yourself confused about an issue related either to your adoption or relinquishment. It can happen that the emotions stirred up during a search threaten to overwhelm you despite moral support you have, or because support has not been forthcoming from people you have counted on. In those cases, you will do well to recognize that professional help is available. But to seek counseling before you are aware of why you are seeking it, or before a problem threatens to become unmanageable, can be costly and nonproductive. Only you can know just when this kind of help becomes desirable or essential. If that moment comes, don't be afraid or ashamed to reach out for help.

If you do feel a need to consult a professional, consider carefully where you will go. Many adoptees and birthparents have discovered that the counseling they've received has not been directed toward their needs. When choosing your counselor or therapist, look for one who has some familiarity with needs commonly experienced by adoptees or birthparents. Ask questions. Has the counselor worked with other adoptees or birthparents? Is he or she familiar with papers being published on this subject? Can the counselor recommend someone who has experience with emotional trauma related to adoption or relinquishment? Many search and support groups will recommend a counselor used by a group member. This might prove an excellent way to locate one who can help you.

WHAT IF I DON'T GET THE MORAL SUPPORT I'M LOOKING FOR?

There is virtually always a source of moral support available to you, especially in light of the search movement's spread across the country. But it is possible you'll be refused support from a source you feel is essential to you—a spouse, parents, friends. Then what do you do?

You ultimately have to make your own decision here. Dig deeper. Look back on your life. Did your spouse, parents, friends always give you the support you felt you needed in all situations? Probably not. Your answer at times has no doubt been to accept the disappointment and go on. Your sense of priorities led you to continue. And on other occasions you may have given in and discontinued whatever you had hoped to pursue. What made the difference? Does it make the difference now? If you receive no support from your spouse, family, or friends, weigh how important your search is to you. The answer may be that it is important enough to continue without support—in some cases without further mention of it. Only you can provide that answer.

However, don't get discouraged and think that no source of support exists for you. You may find that those close to you will eventually respond more positively. Even if they don't, you won't need to search alone. The existence of specially established groups makes it virtually certain that there is a source of support within your reach. Once you recognize the avenues by which support can be obtained, you will find that it is available to you. You only have to turn in the right direction to get it.

NOTES

1. Katrina Maxtone-Graham, *An Adopted Woman* (New York: Remi Books) 1983, pp. 26, 27.
2. Ibid, p. 27.
3. The willingness to deal with any findings a searching adoptee or birthparent uncovers is expressed by Marilyn Louise Beck in an affidavit filed in support of the ALMA lawsuit in New York before the U.S. District Court for the Southern District of New York on May 23, 1977, and reported in the *ALMA Searchlight*, Autumn 1977, p. 10.
4. The effect of the death of an adoptive parent and its ramifications to an adoptee's search are expressed in the affidavit of Roberta van Laven, filed in support of the ALMA lawsuit before the U.S. District Court for the Southern District of New York on May 23, 1977, and reported in the *ALMA Searchlight*, Autumn 1977, p. 12.
5. The statistics estimating the numbers of adoptee searchers in the United States come from "Adoptees and Their Quest," *Washington Post*, February 6, 1978, p. a8.

CHAPTER 3

What Will It Cost Me?

et out your paper and pencil or turn on your computer. Gather together your envelopes, stamps, and library card; and you have the basic search tools at hand. That sounds awfully simple for getting into a process that has such great potential for complication. After all, on many levels you're undertaking to play the role of private investigator, tracking down one or two people lost to you somewhere among millions. How can it be anything but a complex, expensive experience?

There are those within adoptee/birthparent circles who will readily tell you of the great amount of time and money they spent on searching, especially on the Internet. It's true that one can spend thousands of dollars on search efforts. But in most instances that isn't necessary, and you should realize that a good deal of the talk you may hear of great sums spent will fall into the category of one-upmanship. For some there seems to be a sense of status attached to how much money was required to conclude a search. I would like to show that great expenses need not necessarily be the case.

To begin with, it is simply not true that the solution to a complex problem involves spending great amounts of money. Attention to detail and organization are more important here. The truth is, without attention to detail and organization, a large part of any money expended is very likely to be wasted. The organized person working on a shoestring budget has a better chance of success than the disorganized person who deals with complexity by throwing money at it.

With the basic search tools mentioned above, and a careful approach to circumstances requiring an outlay of funds, you can be sufficiently thorough as a searcher to assure yourself an excellent chance of success.

BUDGETING

Only through organization can you assure control of search costs. A fundamental organizational tool is the establishment of a search budget. International conglomerates, local businesspeople, and families all work within a budget, reviewing monies available and setting limits to expenditures in a diversity of areas, depending on money available and the sense of priority that attaches to whatever a particular budget item may be. You can and should do the same. Only you know how much money you can afford to set aside for this project. Don't be discouraged if your resources seem modest. Do not assume a small budget rules out completion of your search. With careful planning, you can often achieve the same results and in the same time as a person with unlimited funds.

Let me give you a simple example of how this can be done. Searcher A sends away for a birth certificate, marriage certificate, and death certificate on a given person. At this point, what he is really looking for is military information. He pays $5 for the short-form birth certificate, $10 for the marriage certificate, and $5 for the death certificate, plus $.32 postage for each letter.

Searcher B, looking for the same information, sends a letter to the Vital Statistics Office in her state. She asks for copies of forms used in requesting the same three certificates and also asks for whatever form is used to request divorce records. Her cover letter asks what information will be given on each certificate, the charge for searching out whatever information is not completely given, and what other records the office holds on file.

When the Vital Statistics Office replies, Searcher B discovers that she need only apply for the death certificate to receive the desired military information. However, she has the additional forms for possible use at a later date and also a summary of what information the other certificates will provide.

Searcher B sent two letters, plus $5 for the death certificate. Searcher A sent three letters, plus $20 for three certificates, only one of which he really needed for his present purposes. While the difference in this instance may seem modest—$15, plus one first-class stamp—multiplied over the course of a series of instances, the difference can mount substantially.

Note also that Searcher A spent money with no certainty of getting the information sought. Searcher B submitted a fee only when she knew it would win the desired information. In another circumstance, Searcher A might spend money without getting anything of substance in return. Searcher B, by virtue of a more organized approach, would lose only the cost of a first-class postage stamp.

Be like Searcher B. Organize yourself to hone in specifically on the information you require. Follow through with one try rather than with random efforts to obtain whatever seems as though it might be useful some time. Meanwhile, keep a file of notes or information that will be useful later when following up on other leads.

Searchers with limited funds will need to spend more time planning. Wait until you have some reliable information before jumping in and sending away for every booklet offered or every certificate you can lay your hands on. Why spend even $.75 for a pamphlet on divorce records when you're still searching for a marriage certificate or even a birth name? Just make a note that the pamphlet is available. Then if you find you need the information later, you'll know how to get it. In the meantime, conserve your resources.

I would like to present an example of how far you can go with about $23 when starting your search. The list is general and would need to be adapted to suit your own needs. However, it is a reliable indication of what can be done with limited funds. Please understand that this $23 represents only a start, but see for yourself what a good start it is. Note that the fees and charges indicated are those that applied in my state at the time this book was published. The telephone rates vary depending on the service you use. Your charges may differ somewhat, but the difference is not likely to be substantial.

Recording family information	-0-
Collecting documents on hand	-0-
Cost (fee plus postage) to obtain the long form birth certificate	$10.32
Cost to notarize 3 request letters at my bank: birth certificate, court records, hospital records	-0-
Cost (fee plus notarized letter) to obtain court records (3 pages)	$ 4.32
Cost (fee plus postage) to obtain hospital records ($.45 per page)	$ 1.22
Letter sent to acquire state adoption laws	$ .32
Letter of inquiry to genealogical library (with SASE)	$ .64
Letter to register with index match-up (with SASE)	$ .64
Waiver of confidentiality sent, certified mail, return receipt requested	$ 2.52
Telephone call to adoption agency, out of state (20 minutes, reduced rate)	$ 2.99
Total	$22.97

You may have only a given amount of money you can set aside each month. Perhaps that amount will be as little as $15. You can still search, but you must plan your search carefully.

Of course there are no guarantees that your search will not eventually involve more money than you wish to spend. Some searches are difficult and go from state to state. Some require a mass mailing to all persons with a given surname in a large city. Some lead from one dead end to another. But even so, an organized approach taken with an attentive eye regarding budgetary limitations will prove most cost effective.

It is generally thought that once you buy a computer your costs are over, but for the adoption searcher using the computer, that's not true. To access all the resources available, you will need to subscribe to a service provider and go online to the Internet. Service providers charge a fee to connect you to the Internet, and this can range from a flat fee to a fee based on the amount of time spent online.

There are many valid reasons for buying a computer and subscribing to an online service provider, but if you are considering doing this only for your adoption search, you should rethink your decision.

While there is no guarantee any search will end as easily as writing one or two letters, there is also no guarantee your quest will end as easily as searching online on the Internet. Take a hard look at what you will be getting for your money. (See Chapter 9, "Searching on the Computer," for more information about online companies.)

You will probably realize that budgetary limits aren't only set by what you can financially afford. If you have a family, you may have to deal with the fact that your values and ways of seeing things often aren't the same as those of your spouse. Besides considering just how much money might be available for your search, you should review priorities with your partner. What value does your spouse put on this search? What other wants and needs exist that might lay claim to shared resources? Some compromise may be necessary when deciding on budget limits, depending on how perspectives coincide or differ. Of course, these can be reviewed periodically. And with the information in these pages, you can demonstrate to a partner concerned with costs that they are manageable. You don't have to keep pouring money into a deep, dark hole in your efforts to reestablish a connection broken so many years past.

EXPENSE FACTORS

Are there necessary further expenses to be aware of? Yes. There will be unavoidable expenses. To a great extent your search will hinge on the unearthing of records kept in official and private files. You will have to pay fees for copies of some of these. Postage expenses can run beyond the roll of first-class stamps you have on hand. You may find yourself making long-distance telephone calls. There are possible membership dues for groups you may feel impelled to join so as to have group support resources available to you. At times you will have photocopying expenses. Now and again you will need the services of a notary public.

However, the essential expenditures here are all quite modest. If you rely on a sound plan of approach, the costs involved will probably fit easily within your budget.

Now let's look at the various expense categories you'll need to fit into your search plan.

Public and Private Agency Fees

Fees to various public agencies and archives can mount quickly. Some expense here will be unavoidable. You will require at least some documentation to establish or confirm facts of the relationship you are investigating.

You will have to pay for copies of official certificates of record held by state governmental agencies. A death certificate can cost $5 in one state and $15 in another. Some states charge a search fee in addition to charging for the actual certificate. You may also be searching through marriage records, divorce records, birth records, property ownership records, and so on. Depending upon the circumstances facing you, you may need only one of these documents, or you may need several. The key to controlling costs here is to pinpoint only those records absolutely essential to establish a significant item of information. (Note also that at times there is a lower fee for obtaining a copy of records in person than there is for obtaining that same copy by mail.)

State reunion registries charge to enter your name into their files; this cost can range from submitting a notarized application to join your state's registry, to a $50 or more per hour fee to search. Expenses depend on the state and the laws governing its registry. Does your state charge for a search, require counseling fees, have a records duplication cost? State reunion registries can become very costly, and usually with no assurance the information found will be released to you.

Private adoption agencies may charge to open and review your files. To reduce repeated file-opening when requesting information from such an agency on your adoption or relinquishment, prepare a lengthy, thorough, and well-planned list of questions. You will probably have to consider several avenues of questions; dealing with possibilities one at a time in this case will occasion multiple visits that otherwise could be avoided.

Only a few hospitals, from which you'll be seeking birth-related information, will require a fee to release your medical information. Ask for a notification of charges on records when you first write. Here again expenses can run up if you have to pay an additional fee because you neglected to ask all the questions you might have at one time.

Archives and public libraries usually charge a fee for photocopying records and other material in their collections. The cost is usually $.25 per page. If the surname you're researching is Smith, you can imagine the expense of copying phone listings for a five-year time period. Some public record-keeping agencies will charge an extra fee for certain popular surnames. Use your judgment when deciding which information in public records to have photocopied.

Postage

Mail service can run expenses up more quickly than you may realize. For occasions when a postcard is as effective as a letter, use stamped postcards from your local post office. Also consider using the double postcard that has a perforated line, permitting the receiver to detach and reply on a separately stamped, self-addressed section. For example, if you were trying to locate a relative in Los Angeles with the surname Askin, you might need to send out 20 letters to all those with that name listed in the Los Angeles telephone directory; your message might be as short as a line or two, asking anyone with information on the person indicated to contact you. If you are sending many such letters, consider using the double postcard instead of sending a letter with a self-addressed stamped envelope.

Other services provided by the United States Post Office that you will want to be aware of in addition to first-class mail are certified mail, registered mail, and express mail, with return receipts available in each case.

Certified mail provides you a mailing receipt, which constitutes proof of mailing. Upon request you can also obtain a return receipt which will show either (a) to whom and the date your letter was delivered or (b) to whom, the date, and the address where your letter was delivered (important in the event mail is forwarded). Determine the current fees at your local post office.

Registered mail offers maximum security and protection against loss of your letters. This service is usually recommended only when mailing items of value. The cost varies according to the value listed. Return receipt services are available, as for certified mail, at the same additional charge, and restricted delivery service is also available.

If you wish an address correction for letters forwarded by the post office, a small charge will be made at the time the letter is sent. This service can be very valuable to searchers when a person sought has moved.

On rare occasions you may want to use express mail service, ensuring delivery of a letter or package the next day. This is an expensive service not available in all areas. Rates vary according to zone and size of package. Return receipts will add another small cost. Restricted delivery service is not available with express mail.

Some post offices will provide a general delivery service at no charge. This service enables you to receive mail addressed to you care of General Delivery, the post office, and the address of the post office. When corresponding with agencies and individuals, list your address as general delivery, the post office, the city, and the state. Mail will be kept at the post office for 30 days and then returned to the sender. You may stop by the post office at your convenience and pick up any mail you may have received. There are no restrictions to where you receive your mail; you do not need to live in the town where you receive mail through general delivery. This is the easiest way to assure privacy and avoid being detected if you have chosen not to tell others of your search. Check your local post office to locate an office with general delivery service.

Each of these special services can be valuable to you. Awareness that they are available from your post office is important whenever it seems advisable or necessary to establish proof of mailing, proof of receipt, name of receiver, and/or address correction. Control your expenses by a realistic evaluation of needs in these areas.

Electronic Mail (E-mail)

E-mail is a cross between your post office and your telephone company. This is the way an online user can send messages to anyone else with an e-mail address. This can be a sister living in another country, a search and support group located in another state, or your best friend who lives around the corner.

If they can be found on the Internet, you most likely can e-mail them. In the Bookmark section in Chapter 9, "Searching on the Computer," a number of e-mail addresses are given along with their Internet address.

Check with your online provider to learn the costs involved. Some allow unlimited e-mail per month while others have a restriction on the number that may be sent free. Keep this in mind when you are considering subscribing to a service.

Telephone Service

To the extent practicable, use the mail instead of telephoning long distance. This is particularly advisable when requesting information that will take time for someone to get together. Keep in mind as well that the mail offers some advantages when you want or need documentary proof that you've been in communication with any agency or person.

If you've tried to elicit information via the mail without success, it can prove worthwhile to make a phone call. You can sometimes get information this way when a letter or series of letters was ignored, or when the reply returned was that the agency to which you were writing is not allowed to give out the information requested. But remember, this can work to your disadvantage. A reply by an agency receiving your letter requesting information on the basis of "judicial need" is based on the information provided only in your letter. If you call, the agency personnel can ask you to explain, and doubts existing in their minds may not be resolved in your favor.

Take advantage of time-zone differences and special rates whenever possible. If you live on the West Coast and are calling the East Coast, call early in the morning. People in New York and Atlanta are busy at work at 9:30 A.M., but at your time of 6:30 A.M. your phone company may offer a reduced rate. If you live in the East, calling just after 6:00 P.M. will find people on the West Coast still at work—it's just after 3:00 P.M., their time. Check the services and reduced rate times for calling with your telephone service. Whenever you call, try not to call at a time when the person you wish to speak to is likely to be at lunch or just getting ready to leave the office.

As with the post office, your telephone company has a variety of services to offer. If you are searching out of state, check into several phone services to learn which has the best rates for your needs. Your knowledge of what services exist and how best to make use of them will help you keep telephone costs to a minimum.

Although person-to-person rates are higher than station-to-station rates, calling person-to-person can, in many cases, be less expensive when seeking to locate someone specific. Here is an example of how this can work: You have reason to believe your birthmother came from New York City. Your birth name is Askin. There are five families listed in the New York area with that last name. However, your birthmother probably no longer goes by that name. You don't know if any of the five listed individuals are family members; you have no way of knowing if your birthmother is still living. You can narrow down the possibilities by calling each listing person-to-person, asking to speak to the name you have for your birthmother. The receiver's reaction can provide a clue of relationship. Statements such as "Operator, that was another family that lived here years ago," "Operator, that's my sister's name," or "Operator, she's no longer living" will all be cause to thank the operator and immediately call the person back using unassisted, station-to-station rates. (Or, if you'd feel more comfortable doing so, write a letter instead.)

Under all circumstances, keep track of each person you call and speak to. In the case above, the person receiving the call might be a teenager or the spouse of a relative. An unexpected call requesting information on someone from the past might not immediately jog the memory or might catch someone off guard. When dealing with agencies, keeping track of whom you've spoken to provides you with a record that makes it possible to refer to that individual in any future exchange. That can often save you the time of having to re-explain yourself in every detail to a second or third person to whom you are a completely new experience. Even when you have to deal with a second or third person, the mention of information or a promise of information provided by an individual helping you previously may prompt this other person to be more forthcoming.

If you are searching out of your immediate area, your local telephone directory will not list the numbers you need. Your telephone business office can give you the telephone number to call to learn the prices of telephone directories in other cities. If the telephone directory for the city you wish is published by your phone company, or if they have a reciprocal arrangement, you may order one or more for your use. (The prices for phone directories range from $7.95 to $25.) You may also want to request a directory for your state capital; it will be an aid for any calls you may need to make to state governmental agencies.

If telephone books are not available from your telephone company, or the charge is more than you wish to spend, check with your local library or the largest branch in your library system so you may photocopy the pages needed. Those searching on the Internet may access current phone books from a variety of Web sites. Look through Chapter 9, "Searching on the Computer," to learn of several online phone books.

The telephone company also makes it possible for customers to list their name and phone number in a city directory outside of their own city of residence. This service is billed to you from the business office in the city where your new listing will appear. Call your local telephone office to subscribe or to determine the name, address, and phone number of the office you need. Ask about the charges and payments. My phone company calls this service a "foreign listing" and charges $1.50 a month plus an $8.50 listing payment. Your listing can appear under your present name, maiden name, or a birth name, whichever would allow recognition by birthparents or their famiily.

Searchers invariably check the telephone directory first when trying to locate a missing relative. How nice to provide this listing in the town of your adoption or relinquishment, in case you also are being sought. This can be especially useful to birthparents as an aid in searching for a relinquished child.

A searcher will find his or her telephone to be an instant source of information. Today, in addition to the telephone directory, there are hundreds of 800 numbers you can call. Once you obtain the telephone number, you simply dial 1-800 or 1-888 and then the seven-digit phone number.

Unlike 800 or 888 telephone numbers, which are free, 900 telephone numbers have a per minute charge. These charges can range from a relatively small amount to $25 a minute. Charges are required to be published on all literature that advertises 900 services. Searchers should know and understand the charges before placing any 900 calls, and have a clock or stopwatch handy.

Two books serve the same purpose as the telephone yellow pages and offer the searcher thousands of fax numbers and Internet addresses: *FaxUSA* is updated each year and offers readers thousands of fax numbers while *The Internet Yellow Pages* (Harley and Stout) presents Web site addresses for Internet users.

Membership Dues

If you decide to join an adoption, genealogical, or historical group, there will undoubtedly be a membership fee. Membership dues vary. Concerned United Birthparents (CUB) charges a $50 membership fee for new members; annual renewals are $35. The Adoptees' Liberty Movement Association (ALMA) has a charge of $65 for new members, with a $45 annual renewal charge. (See Chapter 7, "Search and Support Groups, Researchers/Searchers, Consultants, Intermediaries, and the Courts," for more information.)

Some groups charge $5 for membership while others charge $100. Some memberships are annual; others are a one-time charge. Keep in mind that these fees are subject to occasional revision. You will need to decide if a group fits your needs. The costs to join must be justified by the rewards to be gained. Attend a meeting as a visitor—virtually all groups allow this—to determine what the groups in your area have to offer, how you can benefit, and whether you wish to join.

There are also a number of private and state-run reunion registries, which may or may not charge a fee for you to register with them. Basically, these services maintain a record of adoptees, birthparents, or other blood relatives who have indicated their desire to be listed in a reunion registry. Once someone is listed, a cross-check is run to ascertain whether the party being searched for has also registered with this service. As the reunion registry network expands, the potential for establishing contact in this fashion increases. Even if no immediate match is found, your name remains on file.

In general, membership fees for private search and support organizations— for example, Adoptees' Liberty Movement Association and Concerned United Birthparents—include a listing in the reunion registries they maintain.

Newspapers and Magazines

If you've narrowed your search down to a particular area, you may decide you want to subscribe to a local newspaper to catch any possible notice of persons who may prove to be related by birth or who may be likely to provide you a lead to contacts in the area. This is generally not practical in large cities, but in many rural and suburban areas a local newspaper carries reports of births, deaths, weddings, and other doings of established residents. However, you should think carefully about monies spent on newspaper subscriptions until you are quite certain you've pinpointed the correct area of search and have some clear indication of names to be on the lookout for.

Newspapers can be helpful in another fashion. Some searchers have had success running an ad and have found information from unusual or unknown sources. The cost of such an ad varies widely from locality to locality. When you have the name of a newspaper in your area of search (see Chapter 4,

"Reference Resources"), write and ask for ad rates, days published (not all newspapers publish on a daily basis), geographical area covered, and costs to subscribe. When writing to any newspaper always ask where their old editions are stored. This may save you time when at a later date you wish to review past newspapers from a given area.

Your ad can ask for any information you wish. Some searchers run ads asking for information about births at a particular hospital on a particular day; others use a more genealogical approach, stating they are looking for a missing family member. One searcher asked to receive information on the where-abouts of old school friends, and yet another asked for information regarding births at a particular maternity home.

The wording and placing of ads should be very carefully thought out, to eliminate any embarrassment to the person sought. Try to imagine what actions may result from your ad. The idea, for example, is to find information, not to expose a birthmother's past to her community if she does not wish this.

Everton's Genealogical Helper is a magazine published to provide genealo-gists communication with each other and to answer questions relating to research on family backgrounds. Ads can be placed in their classified section or in the "Missing Folk Finder" column for approximately $.35 a word. At the time of this writing, an average cost runs from $9.10 (26 words) to $9.80 (28 words). The ads make contact possible between individuals who may be researching the same family name. Current subscription costs are $21 for one year (six issues), or $4.50 per copy. Information on "Missing Folk Finder" can be obtained by phone at (801) 752-6022 or by fax at (801) 752-0425.

Heritage Quest is another magazine for genealogists and those seeking information and services to help find a missing or lost relative. Several prices are given to run an ad in this magazine, ranging from $12.50 per column inch to full-page rates. Query submittals are $.30 cents a word. For information on magazine ads, phone (800) 658-7755, ext. 574. Subscription rates are $28 a year for six issues. (More detailed information on these and other genealogical resources can be found in Chapter 4, "Reference Resources.")

Reunions Magazine and *People Searching News* are publications directed to searchers. At this writing, *Reunions Magazine* charges $1.00 per word for their search ads with a minimum of 25 words. *People Searching News* charges $1.77 per line; each line contains 33 spaces, with a four-line minimum. Each ad runs twice. Chapter 10, "Search Resources and Services," contains more informa-tion about both publications. Note that there may be other publications periodically issued in the area of genealogy or adoption research that will provide some information helpful to you. Some are published only within a limited local area. Your state archives, library, or search and support group can tell you what publications are offered and what areas they cover. You can then contact them directly for a clarification of information offered and the costs of subscription or purchase.

Note that your expenses in this area are largely optional. It may be that at one point in your search you find that using ads placed in a newspaper or a periodical is advisable. If you are working on a limited budget, wait until other sources have been used before you take a course of action that requires such an outlay of money.

Consultants

Although the word *consultant* immediately brings to mind professionals hired at considerable cost, the fact is that adhering to a strict budget will not exclude turning to consultants. For one thing, every search and support group has volunteer consultants to aid you in your search. And I have yet to see a group of genealogists that doesn't include at least one kind and helpful person who is willing to share information and advise you on refining your search techniques.

Be aware that your public library has an entire staff of consultants you can refer to at no cost. Your reference librarian will be invaluable as a source of information and aid on the use of the many research resources available through either your local library or interlibrary loan. Think of your local library staff first when you reach out for consultants' assistance.

Keep in mind that you can also refer to your state government for free information on state laws relating to adoption. Your state legislator can serve as a consultant to inform you of any bills pending, in committee, or recently passed in this subject area. State legislatures commonly have a reference service that will provide gratis copies of laws, as well as information that explains the purpose and specific applicability of laws and leads to other government literature in any particular subject area.

Notaries and Photocopying

You *will* need to have papers notarized. Many states will not release your birth certificate without a notarized letter of request. As a rule, hospitals require a notarized letter before they will release medical information that pertains to you.

Your local telephone directory will offer a listing for notaries. These individuals will charge a fee for each letter notarized. However, many banks and savings and loan societies will provide notary service free of charge to their customers. Check with your bank or savings and loan to discover whether such complimentary service is available to you. You can also check with your local real estate offices.

Documents, newspaper articles, pages from telephone directories, and so on will need to be photocopied. As mentioned previously, most archives and libraries have facilities for photocopying material in their collections. Often they have a photocopying machine available for general public use, but rates will usually be higher than through outside photocopying services. (If the material to be photocopied can't be checked out of the library, naturally you'll have to pay the library's charge.) The charges for independent photocopying services vary. Copy services tend to be more available, with more competitive rates, in more populated areas.

CHAPTER 4

Reference Resources

Any search for information no matter how "high" or "low" the purpose—whether it is baseball statistics or philosophy—is valid because it is a search for truth. [1]

Western society is highly records-oriented and has been so for many, many years. The practice of maintaining records is so long-established that in some cases people have been able to trace family history back hundreds of years. Virtually everyone born in North America or Europe (and in many areas of Latin America, Asia, Oceania, and Africa, too) is immediately put on record at birth and a host of life situations and events affecting each person is routinely entered in some ledger or file: medical records, marital records, educational records, property and tax records, voter registration records, military records, passport and travel records, licensing records, litigation and court records, membership records, death records, inheritance records, or computer Internet records. Depending on the individual, some or all of these—or others not included in this broad list—will exist somewhere, a web of information defining the position the person holds or has held in the community. Adding further detail are the individual's own records, either held as letters and documents in personal files or scattered among family and friends, depending on the circumstances. There's hardly a person alive for whom some sort of documentary record does not exist, at least in this part of the world.

When you begin your search, you may be convinced that you face an impossible task. Tracking down one person out of millions may seem like trying to find a needle in a haystack. But each existent record serves as a thread leading back to that figurative needle and dozens of threads radiate out through the haystack, some extending out beyond the haystack's perimeter. If you can locate one or another of these through sharp-eyed research, that can eventually lead you to your needle. Because the nature of our society is such that we tie numerous record threads to each person, separating the needle from the haystack often proves a much more manageable task than you might imagine.

Consider also that you probably have some threads in hand—the records of your own birth and adoption or of your child's birth and relinquishment. These indicate dates and places that tie into the life history of the person you're seeking. They may be very fragile threads, but there is an excellent chance they will at least start you in a direction toward others that may be more securely tied to the object of your search.

A wide variety of reference resources can help you develop and track down leads to the relinquished son or daughter or to the birthparents you're trying to locate. In this chapter, I will introduce you to those resources that searchers have repeatedly found valuable and to some that searchers have occasionally found useful.

LIBRARIES

If I were able to give but one point of advice on tuning in to reference resources, it would be this: Get to know your local reference librarian. More than anyone else, this person will serve as a ready source of aid as you locate and search through various directories and other reference guides and materials you'll need to consult in the course of your investigations. Explain what you are doing and ask what information she or he might have or be able to direct you to. Librarians are characteristically staunch fighters of information censorship. As a rule they welcome and enjoy the challenge of tracking down and isolating desired points of data that together build into a solution to a puzzle that's presented to them.

You can consider yourself lucky if you have access to a large city library, a good college or university library, or to the Library of Congress, where you will find much material available. But even if you live in a rural community and must rely initially on a modest county or branch library, you will probably find it a surprisingly fertile source of information. Also, many library catalogs are now available on the World Wide Web.

Before your first visit, compile a list of what information you will need and of books you may wish to check out or order through interlibrary loan (see next section). Then spend a day or afternoon gaining as complete a sense as possible of what information services are available at your library.

A sample list of considerations might include the following:

1. The reference librarian's name and hours of availability.
2. Maps, old or current, for your area of search.
3. Address of your or your child's adoption agency (if you know the agency involved).
4. Address of the birth hospital (if known) or of hospitals in the city of birth (if specific hospital is not known).
5. The name and address of your local or nearest genealogical society and the date and time of their next meeting.
6. The name and address of any special libraries you might need to refer to—law, genealogy, religious.
7. The name and address of past and current newspapers published in your area of search.
8. A copy of your state's adoption laws.
9. The name and address of an adoption/search and support group in your area.
10. The name and address of a historical association in your area of search.
11. Availability of telephone directories from your area of search, and useful numbers contained in them.
12. Books on adoption that are available.
13. Magazine articles on adoption listed in the *Reader's Guide to Periodical Literature*. Which are available in the library? Can your librarian help you get copies of others?
14. Availability of photocopying services at the library for duplicating material you can't check out.
15. Computer resources available at the library.
16. Additional suggestions the librarian may have.

Your search will lead you in many directions. You alone are in a position to know what you will need, so always remember that you must draw up your own list of considerations when exploring your library's resources.

If you feel the need for better research guidance than your librarian is able to provide you in one or two visits, turn to one of the several excellent library-use guides that are available. Two titles that I have found helpful are The *New York Times Guide to Reference Materials, Revised Edition* and *A Guide to Library Research Methods* (Mann).

When using a library (or any other) resource, make it a habit to note exactly where you found any information and the type of information the source you've used offers. Record the exact book or article title and the author's name, the publisher, the date of publication, and the page(s) where you located useful data. Also jot down in what library you found the book or article. In doing research you may not always immediately recognize the importance of some information you've read and, as a result, you may find the need to go back to a reference source you've previously reviewed. It can be frustrating to look again for a fact you once came across but now can't recall where. Good notes make it possible to pinpoint information quickly a second or third time and save you hours of aggravation.

Interlibrary Loan

Even though your local public library may be small, it will generally have access to a wide range of material not contained on its shelves. This is because public libraries, almost without exception, are part of an interlibrary loan system. This means your local public library can request material not held in its collection from any of a host of other libraries. Some libraries offer this service to lenders at no charge, but most will request you pay a small fee. Ask your librarian about your library's policy.

It's easy to order materials through interlibrary loan. In a matter of minutes you can order photocopies or microfilmed data from the Library of Congress or National Archives. Some libraries will loan the actual book while others will photocopy at the requester's expense. Your librarian will supply you with the forms and help direct you to the proper source. Inquire whether your nearest law library, genealogical library, or other special interest library participates in the loan system. To find out precisely what libraries exist in your area, refer to the *American Library Directory* for the addresses of national, state, county, and city libraries in the United States; refer to the *Directory of Special Libraries & Information Centers* (Young) to locate university, genealogy, law, religious, public administration, and state libraries. Your library probably has a copy of both these volumes in its reference section.

The Library of Congress

The Library of Congress, created in 1800 when President John Adams signed legislation authorizing its establishment, now serves as a central information source serving the needs of the whole country. Today it is the largest library in the United States and among the largest in the world. Its holdings include more than 97 million items. In its own words, "The Library of Congress stands ready to lend to libraries for your serious research much of the material in its general and highly specialized collections when needed items cannot be located at the local, state, or regional level." Although this is but one function of this great library, it is the one that will most concern you. Don't let the lack of reference resources at your local library deter you. All public libraries have access to the Library of Congress and through them you will have access to information you require for your search.

The Library of Congress can be valuable to you for its thousands of indexed items relating particular family histories and recording family members. If you are using genealogy in your search, contact the Library of Congress to see if there is a book published on your birth family. If it is under copyright, order the book through interlibrary loan from your local library. If not, ask the Library of Congress to duplicate it for you. (But be aware of the expense involved—find out the number of pages and the duplicating cost per page before you place a duplicating order.) Ask if the book has an index. If it does, request only those pages relating to the name you are interested in. You will need to submit form #25-15 to the Library of Congress Photoduplication Service, The Library of Congress, Washington, DC 20540-5234. Ask for this form when you send a first letter inquiring what references this great library can make available to you in the area of family history.

For more information on the holdings of the Library of Congress, for microfilm copies of material on file, or for details on general services available to you, write to the Information Office, The Library of Congress, National Reference Service, 101 Independence Ave., SE, Washington, DC 20540-4720; Fax (202) 707-1771. The Library of Congress catalog holdings can now be searched on the Internet at <lc.web.lc.gov/catalog>.

Law Libraries

The *Directory of Special Libraries & Information Centers* can help you locate the law library nearest you where you can get information on past or presently practicing attorneys in the United States. You will be looking for the attorney(s) involved in your relinquishment/adoption. Ask the librarian to direct you to the *Martindale-Hubbell Law Directory*. You may find a current edition of this reference at your local library, but past editions must generally be sought at law libraries. Each edition lists practicing attorneys for a given time period.

Naturally, you're looking to discover your attorney's current address. If there is no present listing, check back editions to find the most recent listing. See if perhaps another attorney now occupies the old address or served as a partner with the previous (your) attorney. In this manner, you may be able to discover where the records on your case are kept or where to write your attorney privately, if he or she is now retired. If a firm refuses to release current address information, ask if it will forward a letter from you to the lawyer's residence.

There are other things to check for at the law library. It's an obvious place to find all you can about state adoption laws. You can check books that provide sample legal forms of the sort you may want to use. If, in reviewing the record of your court proceedings from years ago, you need to have a legal term defined or explained, what better place to discover the definition and to review its implications? One valuable reference book generally found at law libraries is *Adoption Law and Practice* (Hollinger). This reference book contains a chapter on "The Aftermath of Adoption: Legal and Social Consequences" and an appendix on "Inheritance Rights and State Provisions Allowing Access to Confidential Adoption Records Upon Consent."

Many law libraries charge a fee to become a member. These fees vary, but in my case I found it less expensive to photocopy information I needed at the law library than to join it and obtain full borrowing privileges. Ask what the membership charge is and what qualifies a resident borrower. If you live near a law school, find out what use privileges you can obtain from the school's library. Customer service provided to users in these special libraries or collections will not be the same as the customer service provided in public libraries.

BASIC REFERENCE GUIDES

Your library may well use a system that has several computer terminals around the library. These terminals allow you access to periodical literature, business news, news releases indexed under subject matter, or telephone books listed on microfiche. Keep in mind when reading this section that your library will have its own system and you will need to familiarize yourself with its use. The reference librarian will assist you in learning to use the computer, indexes, microfiche, microfilm, and printers that may be found within the library.

When you are trying to discover what books are available in any subject area or what books are available by a particular author, or if you are trying to track down a book for which you have only a title, your best reference resource is *Books in Print*, published annually by R.R. Bowker Company and organized in separate volumes by subject, author, title, and publisher. These volumes are updated by interim supplements that appear regularly during each year. Back volumes will help you discover books previously published that may now be out of print. (The fact that a book is out of print means that it is no longer available from the publisher; it may be readily available for borrowing at a library.) In addition to being available at virtually all libraries, *Books in Print* is also available at larger bookstores.

Today libraries are becoming more and more computerized. If you are lucky enough to have a computerized library there are several things you should know before you begin your search. It used to be you would check through the listings in a hardbound book, but today many libraries have *Books in Print* on computer. To locate books by subject you will need to use "keywords," and for the adoption searcher those might be: adopt, adoptee, birthparent, non-fiction (or fiction). Again, your reference librarian will be your best help in locating the type of book you are looking for and the kind of text you need.

The *Cumulative Book Index* is a single-volume author-subject-title international bibliography of books published within a given year in the English language. Published annually by the H.W. Wilson Company, it can be used for the same purpose as *Books in Print*. Your reference librarian should be able to help you use it.

The *Reader's Guide to Periodical Literature* is an index listing magazine articles. It is organized by subject, author, and title, so that you can locate articles of interest in any of these three ways. The *Standard Periodical Directory* can also direct you to magazine articles of interest. More and more libraries are using electronic periodical databases to provide information on magazine articles. *Info Tract*® and *News Bank*® are two of these databases.

For articles published in academic or professional journals, check the *Social Science Index*. Such articles tend to go into more depth on whatever aspects of a subject they treat than would a comparable magazine article written for a popular audience. Through review of an adoption-related article in a law journal, you could well learn more of the nuances in the law or of new trends in court rulings than you would through general-listed periodicals. The possible disadvantage for you in turning to academic or professional journals is that they frequently use academic or technical terms the average reader is not familiar with. They also often assume familiarity on the reader's part with the subject matter covered.

The *New York Times Index* can direct you to any article published by the *Times* since before the turn of the century. For a report of major news developments, this is probably your best source of information. Most large libraries and college or university libraries will have back copies of the *New York Times* available on microfilm. Other newspaper articles may be available at your local library through DIALOG or other similar computer programs.

However, searchers more usually find themselves trying to locate local or regional newspapers from their area of search. To discover what newspapers are in existence, consult *Editor & Publisher International Year Book*, the *Ayer Directory of Publications*, or *Ulrich's International Periodicals Directory*. These reference books will give you the address, when publication began, and who to contact for newspaper information. Online computer searchers can find a list of many newspapers published in the United States by going to The Largest Newspaper Index at <www.concentric.net/~stevewt/>. Naturally, you have to deal with the possibility that a newspaper published in your area of search, at the time of your adoption/relinquishment, is now out of business. In that case, you will have to seek out back volumes of one or another of these references. It may be worthwhile to contact a newspaper serving your search area now for information on what happened to a competitive or predecessor publication that has since disappeared. You might also try contacting libraries in your area of search to learn if they store old copies of now-defunct local newspapers.

Once you've tracked down a newspaper you want to check, you'll have to inquire whether and where back issues are available for review. If they are available, you'll have to pinpoint the time period for which you want to review issues and then try to arrange access to copies on file. It's highly unlikely you'll have the benefit of an index to work with. There's a good chance you'll have to refer to county or state archives for possible issue availability. Many local newspapers are very haphazard about keeping a complete file of back issues.

The *Encyclopedia of Associations* is a very useful guide that lists religious organizations; labor unions; sororities and fraternities; and trade, business, and commercial organizations. Each of these usually maintains a roll of memberships, current and past. One of your search leads may point you toward one or another such organization. If you want to obtain an out-of-state chamber-of-commerce address, this is also the place to look. Most searchers will find sooner or later that they need information on some social welfare, cultural, veterans', athletic, or genealogical organization. These too are listed in the *Encyclopedia of Associations*. Take the time to become familiar with this book. You might want to photocopy the table of contents for reference should future clues direct you to an area in which one of the organizations listed is operative.

If you're on the trail of a business, industrial, or commercial concern, or if you're trying to track down a professional reference, the *Guide to American Directories* can prove helpful. This lists the hundreds of directories published to provide information for businesses and professionals in almost all areas of commerce, service, and manufacturing.

As I've said before, utilization of available reference resources starts you on the track of a lead that connects to your past at the point of separation from your child or birthparent(s) (or sibling, if you're searching for a lost brother or sister). And there are still more places to investigate.

GOVERNMENT INFORMATION SOURCES

You may feel that since it's government policy that keeps your adoption/relinquishment records sealed there's no point in looking to government agencies for help in your search efforts. Well, the government won't help you search as such, but there *are* various government reference resources that you can use freely. One or more of these can prove important in developing or pursuing a lead to the person(s) you're seeking.

The United States has three layers of government: national (federal), state, and local. Those laws governing adoption or relinquishment procedures and mandating how records shall be administered are state laws. By and large, the federal government does not concern itself with specifics in these areas, although naturally all state law must be consistent in intent and administration with the fundamental principles laid down in the Constitution of the United States. However, because the federal government does interact directly with citizens on many other levels, which results in records being filed on individuals in one context or another, the federal government is often as valuable a source of information as any state office might be.

Basic Reference Aid

A number of good reference books are published to help you through the maze of government bureaucracy. The *United States Government Manual* lists the names, addresses, and departmental affiliations for all federal government agencies. The *Official Congressional Directory* lists the names, addresses, and responsibilities of all who work in or for the United States Congress. These are just a few of the many references available at your library.

Sometimes just identifying the proper agency or department to direct yourself to can be a problem. In that case, ask your librarian for help in locating the appropriate government address. For assistance, you can also call the U.S. Government Information number, which you'll find in your local telephone directory. Keep in mind that a call to the office of either your state's United States senators or of the representative for your district can also win help in the task of orienting yourself to the complexities of the federal bureaucracy.

To find your way through the state government, refer to *Carroll's State Directory* (Harris) which lists executive, legislative, and judicial personnel and their addresses, or ask your reference librarian to direct you to a source in their holdings. For those online, <www.lib.umich.edu/libhome/Documents.center> will offer you information plus much more.

Again, ask your reference librarian for assistance in tracking down a state agency if necessary. If you're still having trouble locating a particular address or official, it may be helpful to call the office of a state senator or assemblyperson for assistance.

Since local government is structurally dependent on the state government, guides to state agencies will generally provide you an eventual lead to a local agency. It may be a matter of having to direct a first inquiry to a state agency. However, your local telephone directory will be a prime source for county/ municipal agency references. Just look in the white pages under the name of your county or municipality. (Some telephone directories have a separate "blue pages" section for government listings.) For local offices of state or federal agencies, check the listings under the name of your state or under United States government, respectively.

The National Archives

The National Archives is the central repository (storage agency) for all public government documents on the federal level. The material held on file dates back to the days of the American Revolution and every day more material is added: census records, military records, government reports/studies, indexes of all kinds, and innumerable other types of records.

This great archive is administered by the National Archives Trust Fund (NATF), and has two central repositories. Archives I is at the National Archives Building, 7th Street and Pennsylvania Avenue, NW, Washington, DC 20408. Archives II is located at 8601 Adelphia Road, College Park, MD 20740-6001. In addition, there are 15 record centers, 13 regional archives, and 12 presidential libraries. The most complete explanation of services is contained in the free pamphlet *Guide to the National Archives of the United States.* A second free pamphlet, *Regional Branches of the National Archives,* details which records are held in common and which are specifically maintained by the individual branch archives. Both pamphlets are issued by the National Archives and can be obtained through them or from a Government Printing Office bookstore. The Internet address is <www.nara.gov>.

The branches of the National Archives are located at the following addresses:

Anchorage, Alaska Region
654 West Third Avenue
Anchorage, AK 99501-2145
(907) 271-2441, fax (907) 271-2442
<www.archives@alaska.nara.gov>

Boston, New England Region
380 Trapelo Road
Waltham, MA 02154-6399
(617) 647-8100, fax (617) 647-8460
<www.archives@waltham.nara.gov>

Chicago, Great Lakes Region
7358 South Pulaski Road
Chicago, IL 60629-5898
(312) 353-0164, fax (312) 353-1294
<www.archives@chicago.nara.gov>

Denver, Rocky Mountain Region
Denver Federal Center, Bldg. 48
P.O. Box 25307
Denver, CO 80225-0307
(303) 236-0817, fax (303) 236-9354
<www.archives@denver.nara.gov>

Fort Worth, Southwest Region
501 West Felix Street, Bldg. 1
P.O. Box 6216
Fort Worth, TX 76115-3405
(817) 334-5525, fax (817) 334-5621
<www.archives@ftworth.nara.gov>

Georgia, Southeast Region
1557 St. Joseph Avenue
East Point, GA 30344-2593
(404) 763-7477, fax (404) 763-7033
<www.archives@atlanta.nara.gov>

Kansas City, Central Plains Region
2312 East Bannister Road
Kansas City, MO 64131
(816) 926-6272, fax (816) 926-6982
<www.archives@kansascity.nara.gov>

Los Angeles, Pacific Southwest Region
24000 Avila Road, 1st Floor East
P.O. Box 6719
Laguna Niguel, CA 92607-6719
(714) 360-2641, fax (714) 360-2644
<www.archives@laguna.nara.gov>

Massachusetts, Pittsfield Region
100 Dan Fox Drive
Pittsfield, MA 01201-8230
(413) 445-6885, fax (413) 445-7599
<www.archives@pittsfield.nara.gov>

New York, Northeast Region
201 Varick Street
New York, NY 10014-4811
(212) 337-1300, fax (212) 337-1306
<www.archives@newyork.nara.gov>

Philadelphia, Mid-Atlantic Region
900 Market Street, Room 1350
Philadelphia, PA 19107-4292
(215) 597-3000, fax (215) 597-2303
<www.archives@philarch.nara.gov>

San Francisco, Pacific Sierra Region
1000 Commodore Drive
San Bruno, CA 94066-2350
(415) 876-9009, fax (415) 876-9233
<www.archives@sanbruno.nara.gov>

Seattle, Pacific Northwest Region
6125 Sand Point Way NE
Seattle, WA 98115-7433
(206) 526-6507, fax (206) 526-4344
<www.archives@seattle.nara.gov>

National Archives (NSA) I, Washington, DC
7th Street &
   Pennsylvania Avenue, NW
Washington, DC 20408
(202) 501-5340, fax (202) 501-5759
<www.nara.gov/nara/dc/ArchivesI_directions.html>

National Archives (NSA) II, College Park, Maryland
8601 Adelphia Road
College Park, MD 20740-6001
(301) 713-6800, fax (301) 713-7205
<www.nara.gov/nara/dc/Archives2_directions.html>

You are most likely to refer to records in the National Archives if you are pursuing your search through genealogical records. (These are explained below.)

If you plan to visit the National Archives or one of its branches, be prepared. Your visit can result in total confusion if you don't plan ahead. Each branch has an archivist and volunteers to assist you and answer questions you may have, but because of the many people using the archives daily, the time that the archivist/volunteers will be able to devote to you will be limited. Some knowledge of what records exist, of what indexes are in print, and of how to use the Soundex coding system (explained at the end of this chapter), together with a list of questions you need the most help with, will work to make your visit productive.

Each region will have a pamphlet explaining what the archives have to offer. *Regional Branches of the National Archives* details which records are held in common and which are specifically maintained by the individual branch archives. Pamphlets can be obtained from your branch archives.

Two pamphlets that will help you understand how to get to what the archives have to offer are *Information About the National Archives for Researchers* and *Select List of Publications* (free upon request). Order directly from the National Archives Trust Fund, NECD Dept. 735, P.O. Box 100793, Atlanta, GA 30384, (800) 234-8861, fax (202) 501-7170. Both publications can be obtained at a nearby Government Printing Office bookstore. The National Archives and Records Administration has a Web site <www.nara.gov> that includes: *The Genealogy Page, Historical Records, Guide to Federal Records in the National Archives,* and more.

United States Government Printing Office

The United States government, through its hundreds of agencies, departments, and offices of every description, generates a tremendous volume of printed materials, all of which are available through the United States Government Printing Office (GPO). The GPO is run by the government to inform the public on its many undertakings; thousands of pamphlets are supplied to private citizens each year. Many of these can be had just for the asking. All can be ordered through the Superintendent of Documents, U.S. Government Printing Office, Washington, DC 20402. They are also available at or through the several GPO bookstores located around the country (see below). You can find products for sale by the GPO, the hours and locations of GPO bookstores, as well as other information on the Internet at <www.access.gpo.gov/su-docs/sale.html>.

Several excellent sources of reference help locate material printed by the government. One of these is the *Index to U.S. Government Periodicals*, which lists magazines, newsletters, monthly reports, and other publications issued on a regular, periodical basis.

You can now use MasterCard and Visa credit cards when ordering books and other items from the National Archives and Records Administration or the regional GPO bookstores. To order directly from Washington, phone (202) 512-1800 between 8:00 A.M. and 4:30 P.M., Eastern Time, Monday through Friday. Or you can call the number given for a nearby regional GPO bookstore.

If you live near a GPO bookstore, it may be of interest to browse through what is available to you. You could come across a publication that may be helpful. One I found valuable was *Where to Write for Vital Records* (Births, Deaths, Marriages, and Divorces), which costs $2.25. This booklet lists, state by state, the addresses of vital statistics offices, the fees charged for searching records or providing duplicate copies, and an indication of dates for which records exist. (You might note, however, that you can call your nearest U.S. Government Information number to receive the same information or view one at your public library.)

GPO bookstores, listed on the Web at <http://www.access.gpo.gov>, are located at the following addresses:

Atlanta, GA 30309-3964
First Union Plaza
999 Peachtree Street NE, Ste 120
(404) 347-1900, fax (404) 347-1897

Birmingham, AL 35203
O'Neill Building
2021 Third Avenue, N
(205) 731-1056, fax (205) 731-3444

Boston, MA 02222
Thomas P. O'Neill Jr. Federal Bldg,
10 Causeway Street, Room 169
(617) 720-4180, fax (617) 720-5753

Chicago, IL 60605-1225
One Congress Center
401 S. State Street, Room 124
(312) 353-5133, fax (312) 353-1590

Cleveland, OH 44199
1240 E. Ninth Street, Room 1653
(216) 522-4922, fax (216) 522-4714

Columbus, OH 43215
200 N. High Street, Room 207
(614) 469-6956, fax (614) 469-5374

Dallas, TX 75242
Federal Bldg., Room 1C50
1100 Commerce Street
(214) 767-0076, fax (214) 767-3239

Denver, CO 80202
1660 Wynkoop Street, Ste 130
(303) 844-3964, fax (303) 844-4000

Detroit, MI 48226
Federal Bldg., Suite 160
477 Michigan Avenue
(313) 226-7816, fax (313) 226-4698

Houston, TX 77002
Texas Crude Building
801 Travis Street, Suite 120
(713) 228-1187, fax (713) 228-1186

Jacksonville, FL 32202
100 W. Bay Street, Suite 100
(904) 353-0569, fax (904) 353-1280

Kansas City, MO 64137
120 Bannister Mall
5600 E. Bannister Rd.
(816) 765-2256, fax (816) 767-8233

Laurel, MD 20707
U.S. Government Printing Office
Warehouse Sales Outlet
8660 Cherry Lane
(301) 953-7974, fax (301) 498-8995

Los Angeles, CA 90071
C Level, ARCO Plaza
505 S. Flower Street
(213) 239-9844, fax (213) 239-9848

Milwaukee, WI 53203
Ste 150, Reuss Federal Plaza
310 W. Wisconsin Ave.
(414) 297-1304, fax (414) 297-1300

New York, NY 10278
26 Federal Plaza, Room 2-120
(212) 264-3825, fax (212) 264-9318

Philadelphia, PA 19103
100 North 17th Street
(215) 636-1900, fax (215) 636-1903

Pittsburgh, PA 15522
1000 Liberty Avenue, Room 118
(412) 395-5021, fax (412) 395-4547

Portland, OR 97201-5801
1305 SW 1st Avenue
(503) 221-6217, fax (503) 225-0563

Pueblo, CO 81003
201 W 8th Street
(719) 544-3142, fax (719) 544-6719

San Francisco, CA 94107
303 Second Street, Room 141-S
(415) 512-2770, fax (415) 512-2776

Seattle, WA 98174
915 Second Avenue, Room 194
(206) 553-4270, fax (206) 553-6717

Washington, DC 20401
U.S. Government Printing Office
710 N. Capitol Street, NW
(202) 512-0132, fax (202) 512-1335

Washington, DC 20005
1510 H Street, NW
(202) 653-5075, fax (202) 376-5055

State Archives and Libraries

Every state, like the federal government, has a central location for storing historical records of all descriptions. These records include state documents, county records, local and state histories, newspapers published within the state, even old telephone books for past listings in the state. And there's more.

Write to the address given in Appendix 1 of this book for your state's archives (or those in the state of search), asking what material is available, whom to contact for different types of material, whether there's a historical society located in your area of search, and so on. You may be dealing with several states. Keep in mind that each may have different policies and procedures.

One word of advice: In writing for assistance, indicate that you are undertaking genealogical research, rather than searching for a relinquished child or a birthparent. (This applies when seeking aid at virtually all government levels, except when you are working directly to open records sealed to you.) State archives have been helping genealogists for years. Their staffs are experienced in this area and know where to find needed references; they know where to locate whatever state census records exist and they'll be able to direct you to old voter registration lists.

State archives are a prime source of information for searchers. It's likely you'll have occasion to refer to this source at some point in your search.

GENEALOGY RESOURCES

Genealogy is the study of family history, of tracing one's roots. Obviously, the search for a relinquished child or a birthparent is in a very real sense a form of genealogical research, although a distinction of sorts is commonly maintained

between search and genealogy. Genealogists and adoptee/birthparent searchers have the same goals: reconstructing the past, locating missing relatives,
and completing a family line. Many searchers find that genealogy in the
broader sense provides an added dimension to their search, as well as aids in
development of general search techniques.

Several years ago, an article was published by the New England Historic
Genealogy Society titled "Adoption Secrecy Laws Threaten Death of Genealogy."

> You reflect that, even assuming you weren't adopted yourself, there is
> a pretty good chance—almost 45 percent—that at least one of your
> new ancestors was. You need to know which one or ones. While an
> adopted ancestor may have quite reasonably considered the people
> who brought him up as his emotional "parents," you didn't know those
> folks, and you certainly can't claim descent from their ancestors. What
> you are after is genealogy, which means biology. . . . If change is to be
> sought, a good forum with which to start is the National Conference of
> Commissioners on Uniform State Laws, whose members, appointed by
> the state governors, draft model laws on many subjects which have
> great influence with legislatures . . . .The Conference is at this moment
> engaged in a complete overhaul of its Uniform Adoption Law, which it
> recognizes is obsolete in many respects. The old uniform law includes
> the secrecy rules mentioned above which, if maintained, will make
> genealogy itself obsolete within a few generations.[2]

This is encouraging news for searchers because it proves that others are
concerned with secrecy and "sealed records," but very discouraging news for
the adoption movement that genealogists are looking in the wrong place for
direction.

Then consider this: If you are a birthparent, what nicer gift to give your
found child (now an adult) than a detailed biological family tree? You might
have information available from family members that would prove impossible
for your child to obtain.

Consider also spending time collecting background data on your child's
other birthparent. This does not mean you have to open direct contact with
that person if he or she is someone with whom you no longer maintain any
relationship. Pursue this task via public records. If you were an unwed
birthmother, you may be the only one who knows your child's birthfather—his
name may not even appear on the original birth certificate. In this case, you
will be the only person who can lead your child to a discovery of his or her full
birth heritage.

Adoptees can begin to construct a family history once they have just one
birthfamily member's name—a birth name of their own, a birthparent's name,
or a grandparent's name. Few people can imagine the feeling an adoptee

experiences the first time he or she enters a name on the birthfamily tree. I recall the tremendous joy and encouragement I got from even the smallest notation on a work sheet or family history chart. What inner excitement when, for the first time, listening to others discuss their cultural background, I could smile and refer to my Irish-Scottish birth heritage.

There are already a number of good reference sources you can turn to for a comprehensive overview of this field. *The Handy Book for Genealogists* (Everton), *The Researcher's Guide to American Genealogy* (Greenwood), *The Source: A Guidebook of American Genealogy*, (Szucs and Luebking), *Discover Your Ancestors: A Quest for Your Roots* (Peskett), and *Searching for Your Ancestors* (Doane and Bell) are five books that serve as good introductions. The *County Courthouse Book* (Bentley) provides useful data on records in over 3,300 county courthouses, the place from which you will usually be requesting information.

The *Oryx American Family Tree Series* contains 12 books: African American, British American, Japanese American, Polish American, German American, Scandinavian American, Italian American, Native American, Chinese American, Jewish American, Irish American, and Mexican American. Each book offers an abundance of genealogical information as well as adoption literature, adoption support organizations, and adoption reunion registries. To learn more about this series visit the Oryx Web site at <www.oryxpress.com> or write Oryx Press, 4041 North Central at Indian School Road, Phoenix, Arizona 85012-3397, (800) 279-ORYX, fax 800-279-4663.

Several periodicals are specifically aimed at those interested in genealogy. *Heritage Quest*, a magazine published bimonthly by Heritage Quest, Ltd, maintains an Adoption Research Department that produces articles that can provide searchers with helpful information on genealogical records. For more information write *Heritage Quest*, P.O. Box 329, Bountiful, UT 84001-0329, e-mail: sales@agll.com, Web site: <www.agll.com>.

Everton's Genealogical Helper is a bimonthly magazine issued by Everton Publishers, Inc. One feature of this magazine is a regular column called "Missing Folk Finder." The editor describes this column as a section "devoted to modern genealogical families. It includes pleas for help and requests for information on persons presumed still living." And isn't that what you want? Contact *Everton's Genealogical Helper*, 3223 S. Main Street, Nibley, UT 87321, (801) 752-6022, fax (801) 752-0425 or view their Web site: <www.everton.com/>. Costs for running ads in *Heritage Quest* and *Everton's Genealogical Helper* can be found in Chapter 3, "What Will It Cost Me?"

Ask your local librarian when and where the nearest historical or genealogical society meets, or have him or her point you to the *Directory of Historical Organizations in the US & Canada*. Once you learn the meeting time and date, attend a meeting and find out what the group's focus is when it comes to historical or genealogical research activities. You may find a group very helpful to you. I have always found genealogists very cooperative and willing to share advice. Most genealogy groups periodically present beginning genealogy workshops. These will help you with research techniques that will prove of use in your present search as well as equip you to become an amateur genealogist. If you are using the Internet to search, check out the various genealogical Web sites listed in Chapter 9, "Searching on the Computer."

You can also contact the American Association for State and Local History, 530 Church Street, Suite 600, Nashville, TN 37219,   (615) 255-2921, fax (615) 255-2979, for the name of a historical society near you.

Census Records

Most searchers will not have to use extensive genealogical research to locate current relatives, but some will have to go quite far back in time to arrive at a present name and address. One adoptee I know discovered the name of a great-grandfather, who was a minor celebrity in a small town. She searched through census records to discover his children's names and through more current records to trace her birthfamily to its living members.

Before you try to review census records, learn something about them. Check out several books on genealogy and read through the sections explaining census records. Your local historical/genealogy society may also have material that can help here.

Federal census records are housed in the National Archives, with copies in each of the branch archives. Anyone may examine these records after a 72-year time lapse. Census records have been maintained for every decade since 1790. Except for the 1890 Census records, which were almost completely destroyed by fire and water damage in 1921, all are still on file. Copies are also available from state archives in many cases and at libraries or Family History Centers established by the Church of Jesus Christ of Latter-day Saints (the Mormon Church). A list of the 1890 records that were saved can be found in *The Researcher's Guide to American Genealogy* (Greenwood).

Many genealogists and states have published indexes to sections of the federal censuses (and to censuses on the state level). Check your genealogy library to see if there are any available for the state and time period sought. Genealogical magazines will advertise individuals who have indexed certain records and will provide you that information at a slight charge.

An index for the federal census record will list the roll of microfilm needed for a given person in a given town. Some indexes will list all information found on the film. You may view these films at many state archives, all federal archives, or at Latter-day Saints (LDS) Family History Centers. You can even purchase copies of film from the National Archives. Write to Publication Services Staff, National Archives and Records Administration, 7th Street and Pennsylvania Avenue NW, Washington, DC 20408 for your census record costs. If you have the roll number you need, include this information in your letter. The single entry from a roll of film can be ordered for $6 using NATF Form 82.

You can also send in an Application for Search of Census Records (Form BC-600) to the Bureau of the Census, P.O. Box 1545, Jeffersonville, IN 47131. The fee to search, at this writing, is $40 to search one census for one person only.

Do not neglect state census records. Many states have compiled these in years between federal censuses. For a record of state censuses, check your local library, genealogical library, or federal archives.

The Church of Jesus Christ of Latter-day Saints (LDS)

The emphasis that the Church of Jesus Christ of Latter-day Saints (the Mormons) places on the documentation of family lines has resulted in vast genealogical holdings. The Salt Lake City headquarters of the LDS Church contains the largest collection of family histories in the world.

There are also Family History Centers in every state. These centers are genealogical libraries that are open to everyone, LDS Church members and nonmembers alike. You may visit and use materials kept there at no charge. There will be a volunteer ready to help you make effective use of the library's resources. I have yet to hear of any discriminatory treatment between LDS Church members and nonmembers, either at a Family History Center or in correspondence with their headquarters.

Your local Family History Center will have rolls of film and sheets of microfiche of genealogical records available for review. These will only partially duplicate the massive collection housed at Salt Lake City. However, any roll of film or sheet of microfiche available at their headquarters in Salt Lake City can be ordered on loan at a current cost of $3.75 per roll for film or $.15 per microfiche sheet (plus postage). When the item you request arrives, you can view it at the LDS Family History Center through which you ordered it. Family History Centers will also order census records from federal or state archives for you. The current cost to order these is also $3.75 per roll of film or $.15 per microfiche sheet (plus postage). The Family History Center will have microfilm and microfiche order cards for you to complete when requesting the above.

Each Family History Center will also have Family Organization Registration and Research Coordination Registration forms available. These forms provide information for the International Genealogical Index files, the computer file index, and family group archive records. You can receive any information held by the LDS Church. You might receive details on census records, family histories, or references occurring in any published book or survey. Whatever information is forthcoming, it may provide you a useful lead.

If you find you need or want to conduct your search at least in part via genealogy, the resources of the LDS Church can prove enormously useful. Their vast collection of names and multiple indexes and resources can offer a wealth of genealogical knowledge. One helpful source that is not part of the International Genealogical Index files is the Social Security Index (see Chapter 6, "As the Search Progresses: Alternate Sources of Data").

In addition to the above, each Family History Center has a specialized collection. To learn your Center's specialty, phone or ask in person. Unfortunately, Family History Centers do not participate in interlibrary loan with public libraries, so you will have to visit the FHC to make use of its resources. To locate a Family History Center near you, call (800) 346-6044. A list of current Family History Centers can be found on the Internet at USA LDS Family History Centers <www.flexnet.com.uk/~detatango/fhcusa.html>.

Special Sources for Native Americans

When Native Americans are adopted, they do not lose their tribal rights, which the United States government recognizes as their right of inheritance. Membership in a tribe is established by an individual's lineage. Eligibility varies from tribe to tribe, but persons of Native American descent, and this includes Aleuts and Eskimos, should check their tribal roll.

For the purpose of establishing tribal affiliation, Native American adoptees come under federal jurisdiction. U.S. Public Law 95-608, Title III, Record-keeping, Information Availability, and Timetables, clearly states that adoption decrees shall show tribal affiliation and name of tribe of the adopted child. Section 107, Title I, of this same law declares, " . . . any Indian who has reached age 18 who was the subject of an adoptive placement, [is entitled] to find out his or her tribal affiliation and any other information that might be necessary to protect any rights flowing from that affiliation." Further, U.S. Public Law 95-608, Title III, Section 302(a),

> requires the State court to provide the Secretary [of the Interior] with a copy of the final decree or order of adoption of an Indian child plus information about the tribal affiliation of the child, the names and addresses of the biological parents and adoptive parents and the identity of any agency having files or information relating to the adoptive placement. This information is not to be subject to the Freedom of Information Act.

The National Archives and Records Administration provides several records relating to Native Americans. Most of the records are arranged by tribe and are dated 1830–1940. These records include annuity payrolls, 1841–1949; annual census rolls, 1885–1940; application for enrollment and subsequent allotment of land to individual tribal members of the Five Civilized Tribes;

Eastern Cherokee claim files; and lists of Indians who moved west during the 1830–46 period. These are listed in a free pamphlet (#5) titled *Using Records in the National Archives for Genealogical Research.*

A catalog of National Archives Microfilm Publications offers a softcover booklet (#200027) called *American Indians* at a cost of $2.00. To learn more about records, lists, and documents held at the National Archives or one of its regional branches, write, phone, fax, or check the Internet address listed earlier in this chapter under the National Archives.

To become aware of your rights as a Native American, you should contact the Bureau of Indian Affairs, Interior Building, C Street, Washington, DC 20240. Ask for a copy of the Indian Child Welfare Act of 1978 and any amendments or other laws which may have been enacted since this writing. A wealth of Internet connections for Native American searchers can be found in Chapter 9, "Searching on the Computer," as well as at theWeb site of the U.S. Department of the Interior, Bureau of Indian Affairs <www.doi.gov/bia/aitoday/aitoday.html>.

Special Sources for Black Americans

Many books and catalogs aid blacks with genealogy. In the past, searching through genealogical records was difficult for blacks because materials were hard to obtain or information had not been compiled.

The National Archives publishes a catalog, *Black Studies*, which includes actual letters, educational reports, land titles, marriages, and much more. Many names and families are listed in this study. A book titled *Black History: A Guide to Civilian Records in the National Archives* contains accurate, concise information about civilian records held by the National Archives (#ISBN 0911333312, soft cover, $15.00). Contact the National Archives and request information about the following pamphlets: *Records of the Bureau of Refugees, Freedmen, and Abandoned Lands; Documents Pertaining to Black Workers Among the Records of the Department of Labor; Black Servicemen;* and *List of Free Black Heads of Families in First Census of the United States.* Also request any other related documents.

Depending on what information you seek, *Index to the Compiled Service Records of Volunteer Union Soldiers Who Served with the U.S. Colored Troops and Negroes in the Service of the U.S. 1639-1866* may be of interest to you.

Your library will have several genealogy books with chapters devoted to black Americans. Certainly Alex Haley's *Roots* would be a valuable and interesting text to read. *How to Find Your Family Roots* (Beard and Demong) lists several societies devoted to black genealogy. *The African American Genealogical Sourcebook* (Byers) and *Black Genealogy* (Blockson) are both valuable to the searcher.

Special Sources for Mexican Americans

State census records can be of special value to Mexican Americans. Contact your state archives to discover the years censuses were taken and if Spanish and Mexican censuses were compiled in addition to state censuses.

Federal and state census records use the Soundex Coding System. This is especially valuable to Mexican Americans because it provides a solution to the problem of variant spellings and similar-sounding names. A more complete guide to understanding the Soundex Coding System is given below.

In addition to the information sources mentioned throughout this book, Mexican Americans should take special note of Catholic Church records. These records were often well kept and can be easily found by today's searchers. If you know the area of your search, it would be advisable to make church contact on a local level. Your private, state, or governmental agency can provide you with the church affiliation of the birthparents and the adoptive parents.

Soundex Classification

The Soundex classification system is used by the National Archives and numerous genealogical libraries. It is also used by a number of reunion registries, notably the International Soundex Reunion Registry (see Chapter 8, "Reunion Registries").

The Soundex system codes names alphabetically by initial letter and by sounds following. The code comes out as one letter followed by three numbers. The letter is the first letter of the surname (last name); the numbers represent the sound combinations of the following letters in the name. This system provides a way around the often confusing problem of variant spellings and similar-sounding names. Many libraries will require you to code the name(s) you are looking for before material is given to you. A guide to Soundex coding is presented below or can be found at <www.genealogy.org/soundex.html>.

Soundex Coding Guide	
Code Number	**Key Letters and Equivalents**
1	b, p, f, v
2	c, s, k, g, j, q, x, z
3	d, t
4	l
5	m, n
6	r

The letters a, e, i, o, u, y, w, and h are not coded. The first letter of the surname is retained; it is not given a number code. A name yielding no code numbers is coded with three zeros following the initial letter. If the name yields only one code number, then two zeros follow; if it yields two code numbers, one zero follows (see examples below). Prefixes to surnames (such as Van, Von, Di, De) are frequently disregarded in alphabetizing and coding.

Regardless of length, each name has one letter followed by three numbers. For names with more than three codable letters following the first letter, only the first three are coded (see examples below). When double letters appear— or letters bearing the same code number appear together—the two are coded as one letter (see examples below).

Sample coded names are given below.	
ASKIN	A225
BAXTER	B236
CARON	C650
DAVIES	D120
DAVIS	D120
LEE	L000
PATRICK	P362
REINHARDT	R563
WHALEY	W400

As you can see, the number of reference resources you can call on in your search is considerable. During the course of your efforts, you will find that some do not provide you assistance in developing or tracking down a lead. But as you sharpen your search techniques and follow the leads that do develop, you'll almost certainly find reference resources that are immensely useful.

Each search takes its own path. Except in rare instances, there's inevitably a trace or several traces that you can follow back, and then across intervening years, to some present connection. There's no guarantee you'll be reunited with a joyous, expectant, relinquished child, birthparent, or lost sibling, but the odds are excellent that through your efforts you'll gain more of a sense of connection than exists for you now. And odds are in your favor that you will at least learn the identity of the person or persons separated from you who are your closest blood kin.

NOTES

1. Mona McCormick. *The New York Times Guide to Reference Materials, Revised Edition,* New York: Dorset Press 1985, p. 3.
2. "Adoption Secrecy Laws Threaten Death of Genealogy," *New England Historic Genealogy Society Newsletter,* vol. 16, no. 5, 1990, pp. 133, 134, 138.

CHAPTER 5

Beginning to Search: Primary Sources of Data

T hroughout this book, it may appear as though particular attention is paid to the location of birthmothers by adoptees, and the location of birthfathers may appear to be treated incidentally. The problem that exists in many cases is that it proves possible to locate a birthfather only after locating the birthmother—and sometimes it's impossible. The fact is that the birthmother had the baby. Her name may appear on hospital records, the original birth certificate, and court records. She necessarily, unavoidably played a part in the relinquishment proceedings. The birthfather, on the other hand, may not be identified in these records. He may not even be aware that he has fathered a child.

Because of the differences between the situation of the birthfather and birthmother at the time of birth, it's easier for the birthfather to escape or miss being identified in the records. Since this is so, if you are searching for your birthparents, you will probably find that there are more leads to your birthmother than to your birthfather. Sometimes your birthmother will prove the only birthparent you can locate. However, where the records on birth and relinquishment and related information give as complete an indication of the birthfather's identity as of the birthmother's, it may be easier to locate the birthfather, as his name will not have been changed by marriage. The general process of search is the same for both.

SETTING GUIDELINES

Where do you start your search? First, consider what guidelines to follow in pursuit of information. Second, consider how to organize the information you will assemble.

I believe all searchers should enter into the search with guidelines individually set. Your plan must begin with an idea of how you will conduct yourself during the entire search. You are undertaking a process where you will inevitably face some conflict of rights. You will have to weigh respect for others' rights of privacy against your own right to know. Setting moral guidelines enables you to balance priorities when you are confronted with this conflict.

GETTING ORGANIZED

It is very important that you be organized in recording and collecting information during your search. You want to take maximum advantage of each fragment of information obtained. There is excitement and frustration in searching. Almost everything comes in bits and pieces. Some information may eventually provide only a part of the whole picture. The more organized you are in recording and collecting these bits of data, the sooner some kind of picture will begin to emerge.

One important organizational tool is a diary of your search. Naturally, you ought to record every piece of information you obtain. This recording is best done in a single notebook in which you enter every detail of your search and the results of your discoveries. Make note each time of the date you speak to someone; identify the person clearly by name and position and write down what this person tells you and what he or she refuses to tell you. Jot down what specifically it is that you are asking, whether the person is helpful, and whether this source might be tapped again later. Don't immediately make judgments on what is or is not significant. Although you may not immediately realize it, sometimes the most unlikely fact will provide a meaningful lead later. Also make notes of research you do (this is described in Chapter 4, "Reference Resources").

Your search is likely to be a months-long process and it's through your search diary that you'll develop a sense of direction on where to turn for the next piece of information you feel you need. Periodic review of seemingly unrelated bits of fact can reveal some kind of pattern. Keeping all papers together in one convenient diary minimizes the risk that important details will be overlooked in any such review. And being as detailed as possible about dates, names, addresses, and positions facilitates re-establishment of contacts or development of alternate contacts. It's frustrating to be unable to recall how to get in touch with someone you have already contacted and would like to speak to or write to again.

Maintain a complete, organized document file. This will save you many hours of rummaging through scraps of paper kept here and there; you'll be able immediately to locate documents needed for further reference.

Make copies of all letters written. Use your copy to make notes about the reply or about a follow-up letter or later telephone conversation. Use a section of your diary for a calendar of correspondence, noting the date, name, and purpose of each letter. This provides you a convenient checklist of sources solicited and of responses still pending. When a letter is answered by another letter, file the reply together with your original letter and enter the date, name, and substance of the response on your checklist. When dealing with an organization or agency, be alert to the name of the party responding. Is that person's title or address different from the one you used?

In addition to letters, you will be dealing with official documents. When you obtain certified copies of these for yourself (as opposed to photocopies that are not certified), treat these with the same care you give to other official documents in your possession (birth certificates, stock certificates, deeds of title, and so on). I recommend storage in a secure location, such as a safe-deposit box. Make photocopies to hold in your home files. You can annotate, underline, or otherwise highlight information on these without risk of defacing a document you may later need to produce for official purposes.

Virtually all official documents include an identifying docket, file, case, or record number. Get in the habit of noting such numbers for your records. The same numbers may tie into another relevant document at a later date, serving as the crucial data that link you to an important name or person.

Much of the correspondence you initiate will relate to locating and obtaining documents that provide vital leads to the person you wish to locate. Your attention to organizational details can to some extent ease gaining access to these documents. Certainly your approach to bureaucrats and others charged with administering or safeguarding documentary sources should be carefully considered as well. Throughout this and other chapters, I have provided sample letters and forms to be used as guidelines in composing letters specifically directed to serving your information-gathering needs. Recognize that these must be adapted to your particular situation; you will have to alter elements of content to reflect what you know or what you hope to learn. Simply copying the letters provided here, omitting changes that would make them apply more specifically to you, can defeat the purpose for which they are intended. This is a time to be creative. More than one person has used these form letters, so add your own personal touch to make them different and to some extent unique.

Always write your letters, even to hospitals, courts, and agencies, with the idea of finding a helpful source. The same holds true when phoning. When you locate a sympathetic person, ask if he or she knows anyone else who may prove helpful. Leave an opening for individuals to contact you. This means spending time on your letters, making the effort to anticipate reactions, and considering all circumstances. Would a clerk be more helpful if asked for aid in a naive or knowing fashion? Do you need to have your letter notarized? Should it be sent by certified mail, return receipt requested? Is a check or money order necessary? Would a typewritten letter appear too formal or a short, handwritten letter too informal?

Rochefoucauld once said, "Some disguised falsehoods represent the truth so well that it would be bad judgment not to be deceived by them." Keep this in mind. Most of your letters will be written with the intention of proving a relationship with a member of your birthfamily. You may want to include in your letters meaningless statements that appear to affirm such a relationship: "I had three brothers and one sister"; "We were all born in another state"; "My grandmother said she came from Virginia"; "My mother would never tell us her age, so I don't know the year of her birth." Statements along these lines aren't required for obtaining certain records, but they may serve the useful purpose of presenting an impression that you know more than you do.

At times, it can help to play dumb. When you are asked for a date of death and insert the response "not living," a clerk may laugh and comment to a colleague on your ridiculous answer, but may then also provide the information.

When writing to a private, religious, or governmental agency or individual, try to put yourself into the position of the person receiving the letter. You know that person will feel somewhat constrained by the limits the law imposes on release of information. Consider whether a generalized request for information may gain you more than one that is narrowly specific and leaves less room for interpretation. Also keep in mind that some letters may win more attention if typed and put in proper form, while others may be more effective if kept brief. These are the only guidelines I can offer. If your letter is requesting only information, keep it simple and write it by hand. More formal or notarized letters should be typewritten and include all the information you need. Try not to mention searching unless you have to. When asking for nonidentifying information, ask for more than you plan to get, ask for everything you can think of.

If a letter doesn't produce the information desired, you may wish to try again at a later date with a different type of letter. Perhaps the same letter addressed to a different person or title might achieve more results. Try to get a feel for the policies of the private, religious, or governmental agencies you will be contacting in your state. Use your instincts. Consider whether it's best to push with a demanding inquiry or to back off a while. Will you get further

claiming an urgent medical need-to-know, or would a chatty, informal genealogical search request be more productive? In most cases, there is no one right
letter. The sample letters are only departure points, pointing you in a general
direction for obtaining records and needed facts.

When it comes to following up leads or making a second or third try at
obtaining information that isn't readily forthcoming, your search diary and
document file will prove invaluable for clues on which way to turn next. In any
case, the degree to which you organize yourself, coupled with persistence and
imagination, will prove important in obtaining records and other needed data.

RECOLLECTIONS

Once you've organized yourself—set your guidelines, developed a systematic
approach to information gathering and evaluation, and alerted yourself to the
problems that can arise when seeking information—you're ready to begin the
actual search. That beginning is best made with a concentrated effort to recall
and sort out any information that may be stored in your own mind. Sit down
and list any bits of information you can recall. What were you told over the
years? What possible telltale comments do you remember having been made to
you or within your earshot?

Since you do not know at this point what information will help you and
what won't, list *everything*. Trying at the beginning to separate fact from fiction
can only be speculative. There is no guarantee that any recollection will
produce the lead to the individual(s) you are seeking, but you have to start
somewhere, so begin by using the scraps of data you already have.

What kind of recollections should you tune into? Anything that possibly
relates or refers to a connection with the person sought. You may, for example,
have heard casual remarks along the following lines:

- Your mother was a college student.
- Your father worked for the state highway department.
- You came from a good Baptist home.
- Your birthchild went to a couple with a college education.
- The birthchild's adoptive father was a doctor.

These can all be clues. Work to recall simple and seemingly unconnected
statements. Even if they don't immediately put you on the track of a substan-
tive lead, they can be useful as pieces of the puzzle you're working to solve.

Look back also into your memory and impressions of what was happening at
the time of adoption or relinquishment. Do you remember names of people
around you that were in any way involved? Would friends you are no longer in
touch with or family members you've lost contact with have some memory of
events at that time? Naturally, if you were adopted as an infant, you won't
have a personal recollection of the circumstances surrounding your adoption,

but dig in your memory for family friends and relatives that were part of your life as a child, whom you've since forgotten. When were you last in touch? Is it possible to contact them? Birthparents or adoptive parents, in addition to turning to their own memories, will want to take the same approach to relocating key people from the past. Try to reconstruct events and conversations. Besides family and friends, was there any involvement on the part of a doctor, attorney, social worker, nurse, or member of the clergy?

If you were adopted as a young child rather than as an infant, you may retain some impression of events at the time, even if there are no focused memories. You may recall some image of a person you can't fully identify or associate with a specific event or place. Make note of your impressions. Complementary details may come to mind subsequently to fill in a vague image more clearly. You may be able to validate an impression as others provide you related pieces of information. Do you remember a hair color? A scent of perfume? Singing or music?

Of course, the more others can help you with their recollections, the more of a foundation you have for developing a sense of direction in your search. Again, note all details, whether they seem immediately valuable or not. Chance remarks about something recalled may come only once, particularly since that something is a part of a chain of events that may be decades past. As an adoptee, if your adoptive parents are to be told of your search, you should have a long talk with them. If you are a birthparent, perhaps your parents will recall important details. Record any names they might remember. Ask specific questions. (I've provided a list later in this chapter of questions you might want to ask when speaking with a social worker. You can use that same list here.) Help jog their memories. Adoptive parents are frequently given some information about the home their child came from, and birthparents about the home their child went to. Much of the information given at the time was correct. The problem may not be in the information given; it may be in the information not given.

Often, adoptees find their adoptive parents reluctant to remember the past. Only when the adoptee comes upon information do the adoptive parents suddenly remember. In one case reported to me, the adoptive parents were left alone for a few minutes by a social worker coordinating the adoption formalities. During his absence, both quickly scanned the relinquishment papers left lying on the desk, discovering the name of the birthmother. Once outside, they both separately wrote down the name, then compared them to be sure they had the exact spelling. Both had copied the same name. They kept the vital information and never mentioned it until their son had initiated his search and began asking questions.

Most adoptive parents will not have this information, but some do and many will have other pieces of useful information. One searcher discovered a name given and changed in court proceedings on her adoption. It turned out to be the last name of the birthmother. The searcher then learned her adoptive parents were told at the time of adoption that the birthmother was attending a local college just before the birth. By checking past student records of this last name for several years, the birthmother's full name was discovered. It proved simple to locate the birthfamily, who still resided in a nearby community. Through the birthfamily, the birthmother was located.

As a rule, recollections from the past provide the most leads to learning a name. For that reason, it's important to gather all recollections available to you. If you or someone in your family has saved correspondence from the past, it may be worthwhile to review those old letters for mention of people who could be of further aid. Do you or does someone else have a diary from previous years that may record an impression or details now forgotten? The more you can learn from an effort to recall the past, the more surely you are on the road to the identity of your relinquished birthchild or birthparent.

ADOPTION/RELINQUISHMENT PAPERS

The process either of adoption or relinquishment is an important one to the parents involved. It may be that adoptive parents have somewhere retained a copy of the court proceedings finalizing adoption. Or you as a birthparent may have retained a copy of your relinquishment papers—or, if you were a minor at the time, your parents or guardian may have these records. If these documents are not in your possession, ask whether your parents have them. (They may also have copies of correspondence with an attorney, hospital, or maternity home; a copy of your baptismal certificate; or, on very rare occasions, even original birth certificates.) Ask for whatever they have.

As an adoptee, your adoption papers will be the official court proceedings about your case. In many states, the copy that is available to you will have sections blacked out to conceal "identifying information." In others, there is a chance that your birth name may be indicated. For example, some proceedings include a legal change of name, in which case the name at birth may have been recorded in the proceedings. There's a slight chance that it may not have been blacked out or has been only partially blacked out. In other instances, however, the change of name may be recorded as from "baby girl/boy" to the name given by the adoptive parent. Still, you should ask for a copy, as there are instances where highly valuable information will be disclosed. If your court proceedings do list your birth name, you can then write for your birth certificate in that name. A few adoptees have, in this way, by mistake—that is, in spite of official obstacles—received their original certificates identifying the birthparents.

A note of warning on birth names: Under law, you may give your child any name you wish, whether you are giving the child up for adoption or not. Usually, the first name is given for sentimental reasons and the last may be either the birthmother's family name or the birthfather's family name, even if they are not married. It can also be a variation on the spelling of either parent's last name; it can even be completely made up.

One adoptee was told by her adoptive parents that her birthmother came from a small town outside Tulsa, Oklahoma. This searcher had also obtained her birth name from the adoption papers. She searched through telephone books and old city directories for all outlying areas during the years immediately preceding and following her adoption. The indicated family name was not listed, but she picked up on a variant spelling of it that always appeared where the spelling she was looking for should be. She took a long shot and contacted several people with that name and was, as a result of this clever deduction and with the admitted aid of luck and a sympathetic blood relation, able to track down her birthmother.

Besides the slight possibility that a critical name reference will be given, you *will* find other important information in adoption papers. You will be able to note a docket or case number, which can tie in with other records held elsewhere. You will see the lawyer's name who was involved with the adoption; the name of the presiding judge; and an identification of any private, religious, or governmental agency involved as intermediary in the adoption, which will include reference to any private, religious, or governmental agency that may have had custody of you in an interim period between relinquishment and adoption. Each of these references is a potential link to the individual you are hoping to identify.

In addition to the actual adoption decree, the courts may have a separately filed petition to adopt, an interlocutory decree, or an independent petition for name change. Consequently, you may in your request for court records want to indicate your desire for obtaining all records available relative to your adoption and change of name. (In the case of a private adoption, there may also be a court investigator's report or home study.)

Relinquishment papers do not usually prove as helpful a source of new information as adoption papers. They will not have any information on the child's new name or about the adoptive parents. They are signed and filed *before* the adoption takes place and what information is given is almost always exactly what the birthmother or birthfather knew and told the agency. But relinquishment papers do list names and dates and docket/case numbers that are helpful for cross-reference. Only birthparents have a right to request copies of the relinquishment papers. Adoptees/adoptive parents, who would be the most served by the information given, do not have access to them.

When writing for copies of adoption or relinquishment papers, always send notarized letters. Each state will have a charge for providing the documents(s), so you will probably need to write or call to find the fee amount. Note that sending a certified check subjects you to less delay than sending a personal check. Never send cash. The appendix at the back of this book indicates the court of jurisdiction to address in your state (or in the state of jurisdiction, if you've since moved) for requesting court documents.

BIRTH RECORDS

Birth certificates are valuable documents for searchers because they specify all the particulars of birth, most importantly the names of the parents. But it gets complicated for adoptees because all adoptees have an altered birth certificate (called an altered registration or given some other official name in certain states). The original certificate is sealed away when the final order of adoption is issued. Until then, a birthparent may routinely request a copy of the child's birth certificate. After relinquishment, the birthparent will find it difficult to obtain this because the original copy is separated from the general registry file and sealed. The birthparent will rarely have any idea of the name on the new, altered certificate replacing the original in the general file and is not entitled to a copy of the altered certificate.

In spite of the difficulty, birthparents should be aware that they are entitled to a child's original birth certificate. If they did not request it at the time of birth, they can do so now. If they are initially refused by the vital statistics department, as more than likely they will be, they should appeal to the court of jurisdiction (see state reference list in the appendix). Sample 1 provides a letter that birthparents can adapt for requesting an original birth certificate.

The original birth certificate will not be particularly helpful in providing leads to the relinquished child, but it is an essential proof of parentage that a birthparent may at some later date be required to supply. It proves a link exists, even if it doesn't locate the individual sought.

One additional note to birthparents: Even if a reunion takes place and all parties are legal adults, many states require a court action to obtain an original birth certificate. Adoptees may be unable to open their records and thus obtain their original certificate. What nicer gift to the adoptee than a certified copy of the original birth certificate? One birthmother received a copy of her relinquished birthchild's original certificate and, along with a letter explaining the circumstances surrounding the birth, sealed this information in a letter. She then wrote to the adoption agency, including a waiver of confidentiality along with the sealed letter addressed to her relinquished birthchild. In this way, she hoped that if any inquiries were made, the agency would pass on the necessary information.

As an adoptee or adoptive parent, you are in most states legally entitled to receive only a copy of the altered birth certificate. Altered means exactly that. The birthparents' names will have been deleted and replaced by the adoptive parents' names. However, you can rely on certain facts of your birth to be accurate in most cases: sex, race, date of birth, hospital, place of birth. But it is not unheard of for adoptees to discover a two-, three-, or four-day difference between the actual birth date and that recorded on the altered certificate. Keep this in mind if, in relying on a date correlation with other records, you find yourself dead-ended. Also familiarize yourself with the applicable state laws, as the practice of alteration varies among them.

SAMPLE 1
LETTER FOR BIRTHPARENT REQUESTING
CHILD'S ORIGINAL BIRTH CERTIFICATE

Date

Court of Jurisdiction
Judge (if known)
Address
City, State, Zip Code

Regarding: Release of original birth certificate of relinquished child

Your Honor:

I did not request a birth certificate at the time of the birth of (give name listed on original certificate). I would now like to request a full transcript of this document.

I am not asking for the amended birth certificate, nor for any identifying information—only the original certificate. If I am refused, please cite the specific law that prohibits the release of this certificate. (1)

Birthparent: (Give name used on relinquishment papers.)
           Relationship to relinquished child.
           Date of relinquishment: (if known)
Birth child: (Give name listed on original birth certificate.)
           Date of birth:
           Hospital (or maternity home):
           City, State, and Zip Code: (2)

Sincerely,
(Your signature)
Address
City, State, Zip Code

Have a notary public certify your signature.

Other Possible Inclusions:
1. *Add*: I am requesting this document for judicial needs. I am in the process of making out a will and need this information. (You may list any reasons you find acceptable.)
2. *Add*: Any other identifying information you have.

Note: This letter must be personalized to fit your particular case.

If you've tracked down your birth name, you can make a stab at sending away for your birth certificate in your birth name. As much information as possible should be included in your letter of request. This is true whether you are requesting an original or altered certificate. States will want an indication of your full name (adoptive or original, depending on the circumstances), sex, race, parents' names (adoptive or original), date of birth (month, day, year), community of birth, hospital, statement of purpose for which the certificate is needed, and your relationship to the recorded person. Sample 2 is a letter for those who are writing in their birth name and have very little information. Obtaining the altered certificate should be routine for the adoptee. In either case, when writing always ask for a certified, full copy of your certificate.

SAMPLE 2
LETTER FOR ADOPTEE REQUESTING ORIGINAL
BIRTH CERTIFICATE USING BIRTH NAME

Date

Department of Vital Statistics
Address
City, State, Zip Code

Records Clerk:
   I need to obtain a copy of my birth certificate. I was born as (give birth name) at (name and address of hospital) on (give date of birth). (1-4)
   I am enclosing a check (or money order) in the amount of (amount stipulated by the state).

Sincerely,
(your signature, using birth name)
Address
City, State, Zip Code

Other Possible Inclusions:
   1. *Add:* My mother's name was (if known).
   2. *Add:* I was born at (give time if known).
   3. *Add:* I weighed (give weight if known).
   4. *Add:* Due to a separation in our family, I am unable to supply you with all necessary facts.

Note: This is one letter you do not want to present in a legal or formal style. It is a "shot in the dark" and more than likely will not produce the desired results. It is used in the hope that your birth certificate was not sealed. Keep it simple and insert only the information needed. You may want to consider writing this letter by hand rather than typing it.

Many states, if not most, require the individual requesting a birth certificate, whether altered or original, to be the person listed on it, with some allowance made for parents. A notarized signature must be presented. When I and my husband, who is not adopted, applied for a copy of our birth certificates to obtain a passport, we both had to request the certificates in person or have our signatures notarized (for Tennessee and California, respectively). However, when I requested the birth certificates for my children, then both minors, I did not have to present their signatures (California).

Because it is occasionally possible for an adult to request a birth certificate for a parent, I've provided a sample letter for that eventuality (see Sample 3). The birth certificate in this case will be useful in confirming birth name and birth date of the parent, two pieces of information that are often essential when working to trace an individual via other officially maintained records.

SAMPLE 3
LETTER FOR ADOPTEE REQUESTING
BIRTH CERTIFICATE FOR A BIRTHPARENT

Date

Department of Vital Statistics
Address
City, State, Zip Code

Dear Registrar:

I need to obtain a full copy of the birth certificate for the following. (1) Name: (full name, plus race and sex). Born: (month and day if known), City of _____, County of _____, State of _____.

Mother/Father: (include this information if known) Residence: (include this information if known)

Relationship to the above: (as it is) Reason for request: Judicial need (2, 3)

Enclosed is a money order (or certified check, personal check) to cover the amount stipulated. (4)

Sincerely,
(your signature)
Address
City, State, Zip Code

Other Possible Inclusions:
1. *Substitute:* My sister and I require a *full transcript* of the record of birth of our (mother/father).
2. *Substitute:* I am starting a genealogical search and need the aforementioned certificate as part of my family record.
3. *Substitute:* I am documenting my genealogical family tree for membership in the Daughters of the American Revolution.
4. *Precede this line with:* I am unable to supply exact data with respect to the above birth, due to family separation in my early infancy.

Note: Many states will require this letter to be notarized and some will require that you establish proof of relationship.

When writing for birth records, address yourself to the bureau of records or vital statistics indicated in the appendix for your (or your relinquished child's) birth state. (You can also request the pamphlet *Where to Write for Vital Records* published by the U.S. Department of Health and Human Services and available from the Superintendent of Documents, U.S. Government Printing Office, P.O. Box 371954, Pittsburgh, PA 15250-7954, or from a U.S. Government Printing Office bookstore in your area. The code reference number is PHS 90-1142 and the charge, as of this writing, is $2.25.) States will indicate a charge for providing the birth record, which you should pay by cashier's check, money order, or personal check.

AGENCY RECORDS

If your adoption/relinquishment was handled by a county agency, private agency, or religious agency still in operation, your records should be housed at that agency. If you know the name of the private, religious, or governmental agency, you should be able to locate the address and telephone number through the local telephone directory or long-distance directory assistance. You can also contact the appropriate state agency (see appendix) for information on where your files are kept and whom you should contact regarding information contained in those files. Your local library may contain, or be able to order through interlibrary loan, *Adoption Agencies, Orphanages and Maternity Homes: An Historical Directory* by Reg Niles. This large reference book is written in two volumes, Alabama through New York and North Carolina through Wyoming & Canada. There are 9,262 entries that include adoption agencies, orphanages, children's homes, maternity homes, maternity hospitals, public welfare departments, adoptive parents' groups, and adoptees' rights groups.

If your adoption/relinquishment was handled by a state agency, a private agency that is no longer in business, or privately through a doctor or attorney, your files will be at the state level. To direct your letter of inquiry to the individual in charge of the proper state department or bureau, check a current *National Directory of State Agencies* or other state informational reference available to you in your local library to discover the name and title of the person to contact. You can also call whatever information number is listed in your local telephone directory, either for the state government as a whole or for the particular department. It is not necessary to address your letter to an individual; if you use the state agency address given in the appendix, the information will be directed to the adoption counselor in charge. Sample 4 is a letter requesting assistance from a state department to get in touch with whatever agency actually holds your records.

There will be many questions you will want to ask of your private, religious, or governmental agency, or of the state adoption records administrator. After all, you've been wondering about your adoption or your birthchild's post-relinquishment history for a long time. Organize your approach to getting the information you want. Are you really concerned only about medical information, or do you want to know everything—names and dates if possible and whether anyone else has been in contact with the agency regarding your file?

SAMPLE 4
LETTER FOR ADOPTEE REFERRING TO A STATE AGENCY FOR AID IN LOCATING LOCAL OR PRIVATE AGENCY RECORDS

Date

Post-Adoption Consultant
State Agency
Address
City, State, Zip Code

Dear Consultant:
    I need to discover the name and location of the agency that handled my adoption. Please include information if this agency is still in operation and, if not, where my files may be found.
    Name: (give adoptive name)
    Date of birth: (as you know it)
    Sex and race:
    Name of adoptive parents:
    Court record number: (if known)
    I appreciate your time and effort on this matter.

Sincerely,
(your signature) Also known as: (list maiden name if married female)
Address
City, State, Zip Code

Note: You may wish to enclose a photocopy of your amended birth certificate.

Most private, religious, or governmental agencies follow the policy of prohibiting release of what is termed *identifying* information. This, as we've observed in Chapter 1, is any specific information that leads directly either to a birthparent or to a relinquished child, particularly names and addresses. However, there's considerable room for interpretation on what amounts to *identifying* information, with some agencies or individual social workers holding back information as "identifying" that others will more routinely release.

What's the best approach to use when first contacting the private, religious, or governmental agency? My feeling is that you should take an open approach, stating that you wish all information in their records. If you are making your request in writing, you should indicate in your letter what you want to know, but be general. Ask for all information. Identify yourself as you are now known. Since the files will be cross-indexed, not knowing your birth name or your birthchild's adoptive name—and you probably won't—should present no problem.

Start out slowly; let yourself get a feel for your social worker. Most likely you will have more than one contact with this social worker, so it's essential you not alienate him or her at the beginning. You don't have to mention any ultimate plan for reunion; start with specifying that you want all information. Put the social worker in the position of making the decision on what is or isn't identifying information—don't make it quick and easy for him or her by self-censorship.

If you do not receive everything you want, write again. This letter should ask for everything you can get. Of course, some of your questions will be denied. Try a variant. Ask for names. If you are refused, ask for initials. Is R.A. identifying information? Is there only one R.A.? Couldn't this apply to thousands of people? Ask your social worker to remain silent if a question is true and reply if it is false. A lot can be learned from refusals to answer questions. Be as reasonable in tone and attitude as possible; you want to keep your relationship with your social worker as friendly as you can. But be persistent.

You may need to request this information on a form provided by your state department of vital statistics. If so, write and request this form and any that may be needed to request information on marriage, divorce, or death.

A friend of mine was born in a private maternity home in Los Angeles. Her adoptive mother could not remember the name of the maternity home, so she requested it in a letter to the state agency holding her files. The agency refused her this information, citing it as "identifying." My friend's adoptive mother (her adoptive father was dead) then wrote again, similarly requesting the name of the maternity home. Again a refusal. Finally, my friend sent a "demand letter," asking the agency to cite the applicable law forbidding release of the requested information and restating a request for access to all medical information. At long last the information was released. This indicates to what degree the subjective interpretation of "identifying" can block a searcher, and provides an example of how persistence and standing up for one's rights can be important in obtaining data.

The following is a list of questions that can prove valuable in themselves or for stimulating more pointed questions of your own. Be sure you list your own questions. Be guided by what you know and what you want to know.

Adoptees

- What were my birthparents' first names?
- Were they both living at the time of my adoption?
- What was the reason for the relinquishment?
- Were my birthparents married to each other?
- Was either of them married to someone else?
- Has there been any update on the file?
- What medical information is listed?
- What was the age of my birthparents?
- Were there any full or half siblings?
- What state were my birthparents from? What city?
- What was their educational background?
- What were their occupations?
- Was my birthfather in any branch of the service?
- What branch?
- What rank?
- What was the order of birth of my birthmother and birthfather?
- Were my birth grandparents alive at the time of my birth?
- What was their attitude?
- Did they participate in the relinquishment/adoption proceedings?
- Was either of my birthparents still a minor?
- What was the coloring of my birthparents' eyes? Hair?
- What were my birthparents' nationalities?
- What were their religious preferences?
- Do you have a state revision registry?
- Do you accept a consent to release identifying information?
- Do you have a state reunion registry?
- Will you accept a consent to release identifying information?
- Is there anything else you can tell me?

Birthparents

- What name—first and last—was given the child?
- What type of home did he or she go to?
- What was the occupation of the adoptive parents?
- How long had they been married?
- Were they from the local area?
- Were there other children in the family?
- Has there been any update on the file?
- Were other children adopted by this family? When?
- Was the adoption finalized? When? In what court?
- Was the child ever in a foster home? When? How many homes?

- Were there any other court actions taken regarding this child?
- What reason did the adoptive parents give for wanting to adopt?
- Have they contacted the agency since finalization of the adoption?
- Do you have a state reunion registry?
- Will your agency or the state recognize a waiver of confidentiality?
- Will the state effect a reunion if the adoptee also requests one?
- Is there anything else you can tell me?

The list can be virtually endless. When you ask these questions and others, whether by telephone or in person, keep notes. Ask for spellings of names and towns. This will be an emotional time for you; by recording all facts, the likelihood of forgetting or confusing information is minimized. Even if the answering social worker adheres to a narrow interpretation of regulations on identifying information, you stand a good chance of learning something that will prove valuable to your collection of data. Your search diary is important for keeping an organized record of your visits or calls to the involved agency.

Birthparents are traditionally given much less information about their relinquished children than adoptees are about their birthparents. But it is still, if not more, important for birthparents to be persistent. For example, you can indicate that you wish a letter to be placed in your birthchild's files in the event that as an adult he or she decides to research the circumstances of relinquishment. Wouldn't you naturally want to address the child by name?

One birthmother persisted on that course: The letter would be much nicer and more personal if addressed to a person rather than to "baby boy" or to a name given at birth to which the now adult person would have no connection. She was able to obtain the first name—John. The social worker's reasoning was that John by itself wasn't identifying information. The mother later obtained the last initial from the social worker in compliance with a request to remain silent when a statement was true. Valuable information, and yet clearly nonidentifying, for first name and last initial are still only pieces of the puzzle to the identity of one individual out of the many John X's scattered almost anywhere.

In seeking answers to questions, many searchers have learned to ask for assistance from alternate social workers when the person they begin with proves unsympathetic and insists on a rigid interpretation of identifying information. Agencies are aware of this, and some have responded by trying to be more specific—and, in consequence, usually more narrow—in guidelines set for determining what is or is not identifying information. Nevertheless, if the first social worker proves difficult, ask for a different social worker to assist you. Maybe that other social worker will be more sympathetic. Attitudes are changing. Note this comment from former social worker Annette Baran:

> I sat behind the desk facing adoptees scores of times during the past years, and I honestly admit that I cringe now as I recall my attitude and behavior with them. That they remained polite and controlled is an indication of how pitifully eager they were for even the little I told them. I know now because of the many adoptees I have spoken with during my research. They have described their intense anger at that woman, me, who had the power to keep their records from them. The stranger, me, sitting there deciding what facts of their lives she would permit them to know.[1]

Naturally, as long as the laws are restrictive, any social worker or civil servant concerned with established regulations—and each must be—will be constricted. And though some attitudes have very noticeably changed within the past few years, most of the law hasn't. Therefore, general policy of administration hasn't changed either.

The question of whether information is identifying or nonidentifying will still determine whether individuals get answers to their questions. Requiring that questions be submitted in writing eliminates a lot of the flexibility that is possible in telephone conversations, although I recognize that allowing submission of questions in writing is still an advance over allowing no out-of-state questions at all.

Whether your private, religious, or governmental agency proves forthcoming or not, there is one very positive step that you can take to break through the wall of secrecy around your files: Supply the agency involved with a waiver of confidentiality to its records as they pertain to you in the event the birthchild or birthparent you hope to contact is also trying to contact you (see Samples 5 and 6). As the adoption search movement spreads, there is a growing possibility that the person you are seeking will be trying to find you. In your waiver, you can specify what information is to be released and to whom. Be aware that insertion of the waiver into your private, religious, or governmental agency file will not always guarantee that information will be passed on to your birthchild or birthparent, should he or she also contact that agency. Many states have laws that may fail to make any provision for recognizing the legal effect of a waiver in this situation, so some agencies may not honor it either. Research the situation as it applies to the agency of your adoption/ relinquishment. However, as there is a growing awareness of the rights of searchers, there is increasing reason to hope these obstacles will soon disappear.

SAMPLE 5
**WAIVER OF CONFIDENTIALITY AUTHORIZING RELEASE OF
INFORMATION FROM AN ADOPTEE'S AGENCY FILE**

This Waiver of Confidentiality Applies to the Following: (1)

Birth name: (if known)
Adoptive name: (list both married and adoptive name if applicable)
Date of birth:
Hospital of birth:
City, State, Zip Code

To Whom It May Concern:
    I wish this letter to be placed in any file(s) by your agency concerning my adoption and used as authorization to waive the confidentiality guaranteed me under law. This includes the release of any agency records, hospital records, court records, and records surrounding my birth and adoption, including "identifying information." (2)
    Further, upon request from either of my birthparents (or siblings, birth grandparents, or other requesting relatives), I wish a photocopy of this letter sent or given to (him/her/them) and recognize this letter to be my consent and authorization thereto. (3)
    Please send a letter informing me of your agency's intent to recognize this waiver and, if I am refused, please cite the state law that prohibits such recognition. (4)

Signed
(your signature)
Address
City, State, Zip Code

Have a notary public certify your signature.

Other Possible Inclusions:
    1. *Add:* This Waiver of Confidentiality applies to the following information as I know it to be true.
    2. *Add:* ...but excluding any papers listing my adoptive parents' names.
    3. *Add:* I request notification should one or both of my birthparents request this information.
    4. *Add:* If your state requires a specific form for this waiver, please include all necessary information.

Note: This letter may be written to state that you wish for notification of your birthparents' names but you exclude release of yours by the agency if a contact is made from any interested party. You might want to consider sending this letter certified, return receipt requested.

SAMPLE 6
WAIVER OF CONFIDENTIALITY AUTHORIZING RELEASE OF INFORMATION ON BIRTHPARENTS TO AN ADOPTEE FROM HIS OR HER AGENCY FILE

This Waiver of Confidentiality Applies to the Following: (1)

Name: (given name used on relinquishment papers)
Present name: (if name changed by marriage)
Relationship to relinquished child:
Date of relinquishment: (if known)
Court record number: (if known) (2)

Concerning:
Name: (give name listed on original birth certificate)
Date of birth:
Hospital or maternity home and address:

To Whom It May Concern:

I wish this letter to be placed in the adoption file of the above mentioned relinquished child and used as authorization to waive the confidentiality guaranteed me under law. This includes the release of any agency records, hospital records, court records, and records surrounding the birth and relinquishment, including "identifying information." (2) (3)

Further, upon request from the relinquished child, I wish a photocopy of this letter sent or given to (him/her/them) and recognize this letter to be my consent and authorization thereto. (4)

Please send a letter informing me of your agency's intent to recognize this waiver and, if I am refused, please cite the state law that prohibits such recognition. (5)

Signed
(your signature)
City, State, Zip Code

_____

Have a notary public certify your signature

Other Possible Inclusions:

       1: *Add:* This Waiver of Confidentiality applies to the following information as I know it to be true.

       2: *Add* any information you may have that will help identify the relinquishment.

       3: *Add:* . . . upon request from the relinquished child or the adoptive parents.

       4: *Add:* I request notification should a request be made for this information by the birthchild or the adoptive parents.

       5: *Add:* If your state requires a specific form for this waiver, please include all necessary information.

Note: You might want to consider sending this letter certified, return receipt requested.

HOSPITAL RECORDS

The hospital records you are primarily concerned with here are those relating to birth. These records serve to confirm a stated date of birth; they should indicate relevant information on medical background of the birthparent(s) and some medical information on the newborn child's state of health; they routinely identify the doctor in attendance during delivery or subsequent complications that may have arisen; they will also contain incidental information on the birthparents that may help in any effort to locate either or both of them. The name(s) will, of course, be indicated in the hospital's records, but you may not be allowed to know them, as they constitute "identifying information." Naturally, the records will be more complete on the birthmother. There may be little if any information on the birthfather in cases where the child was born out of wedlock.

For birthparents seeking to trace a relinquished child, there is little information contained in hospital records that might contribute to identification and location of the birthchild in his or her adoptive environment. As with birth certificates, these records will tell you what you essentially already know. However, I encourage all birthparents to obtain a copy of the hospital records relating birth particulars of the relinquished child. There is a slim chance the records will contain a fact relating to the circumstances of relinquishment that you've forgotten. Whether or not this is the case, these records, together with medical information on any health condition affecting you that may be genetically influenced, will be important to your relinquished child. Even if you have no lead toward the identity of that child, you can ask to have the information inserted into his or her agency files in the event he or she seeks information there.

If you are a birthmother, you should request the records pertaining to the birth of your child in the name you used at that time; the birth is, after all, a part of your medical history. Since hospital records are only released to the individual to whom they pertain, birthfathers will find it difficult to obtain them.

For the adoptee, hospital records can provide both important leads to the identity of birthparents and valuable health-related information. Obtain any health-related information you can to alert you to possible health problems to which you may be genetically predisposed. The name of the hospital where you were born should be listed on your altered birth certificate or in the private, religious, or governmental agency papers. In most cases, the name of the hospital will be released to you.

Most hospitals will have your records listed only under your birth name. Your adoption, after all, took place after the fact of birth. If you have your birth name, send a letter requesting hospital records in that name (see Sample 7). Your letter will need to be notarized because the hospital may not release records to anyone other than the patient or his or her designated agent (see Sample 8). If the hospital where you were born proves reluctant to release the information, ask your doctor to request the records. If all else fails, you can send a letter to the hospital administration which, when signed by the hospital, serves as formal confirmation of the refusal to provide you with your birth records. Include in the letter a statement that says: "I take full responsibility for not releasing medical information to (your name) and am aware that, if I withhold this information and the aforementioned suffers health problems, I am open to legal action." Send this letter via certified mail, return receipt requested. Keep in mind that this is a letter of last resort. You should not include any threats in your first request. I've prepared an alternate sample letter you can also adapt to your use in the event your hospital refuses you any cooperation (see Sample 9).

Don't assume a hospital will have only one record file on you. Many keep separate nursery, delivery, admission, or discharge records. Be sure you ask for all records, under whatever classification they are held.

Your altered birth certificate (if you are an adoptee) or your hospital records or memory (if you are a birthparent) may provide you the name of the attending physician. Many doctors stay in the same area for their entire practicing life, but others relocate. One way to find a current location is to contact the licensing board in the county you are searching. It will release information on the current address, if he or she is deceased, or any relevant information it may have. Another source for locating a practicing physician is the American Medical Association. The local offices will supply you with the same information as the licensing board. Check your local phone book or ask your information operator for the telephone number needed.

If you were adopted as a young child rather than as an infant, check whether there are other medical records on you. Did you undergo tonsillectomy prior to your adoption? Were you treated for any childhood or other disease? Remember that only you can obtain this medical information.

SAMPLE 7
LETTER FOR AN ADOPTEE REQUESTING
RECORDS FROM THE HOSPITAL OF BIRTH

Date

Hospital
Address
City, State, Zip Code

Attention: Medical Records

I need to have *all* my medical records forwarded to me as soon as possible.

Please include the following: nursery, admission, discharge, and delivery room records, and any other records kept by your hospital recording my birth.

What types of records do you keep and what are they called? Please list them so that my doctor may review the list and, at a later date, ask for more detailed information.

Name: (give birth name if possible)
Born: (give date)
Thank you for your time and consideration.

Signature: _____ Dated: _____

This letter will need to be notarized.

Note: You may wish to include any personal questions that pertain to your search—time of birth, weight at birth, length at birth, parents' names, name(s) of doctor(s) in attendance, or any other facts that may be on the record.

SAMPLE 8
FORM AUTHORIZING RELEASE OF MEDICAL INFORMATION

I, (give name), hereby authorize my attorney, (give attorney's name), or his agent to inspect, copy, or Photostat any and all of my hospital and medical records, and I authorize you or any hospital, doctor, or nurse to supply (him or her) with all information concerning treatment for injury or illness or reexamination for determination of my general state of health or any other information related to my state of health or that may be contained in my medical record. (1)

_____
(Signature)
Address
City, State, Zip Code

_____

This form will need to be notarized.
Other Possible Inclusions:
  1. *Add:* This authorization shall be in effect from (give date) and remain valid through (give date).
Note: If you are designating someone other than an attorney as your agent, your form should reflect authorization to that person as your agent.
Source: From the *Handbook of Law Office Forms* by Robert Sellers Smith, 1974. Published by Prentice-Hall, Inc., a Division of Simon & Schuster.[2]

SAMPLE 9
LETTER TO A HOSPITAL ADMINISTRATOR REGARDING
NONCOOPERATION ON RELEASE OF MEDICAL RECORDS

Date

Hospital Administrator
Hospital
Address
City, State, Zip Code

Regarding: Release of medical information

Dear (give administrator's name if possible):

Your hospital has refused to release to me any medical information pertaining to my birth. As you are the person responsible for policy, I am hereby requesting you to alter the previous decision and release *all* medical information kept by you in order to ensure that my future medical treatment will be handled with full facts available.

If you authorize the withholding of *any* records, please note that your refusal to release such records could cause damage to my future health and may result in legal action against you and this hospital.

I am hopeful that this letter will lead to the release of the needed records so that no further difficulty need arise between us.

Signed: _____   Dated: _____

Title: _____   Witness: _____

_____

Have a notary public certify your signature.

Note: If you prefer, have an attorney draw up this letter. Use it only if information is withheld, not as a first attempt at trying to elicit records.

You may wish to include in the letter a reference to copies sent to your attorney, doctor, or the state attorney general.

FOREIGN BIRTH RECORDS

For adoptees who are United States citizens through their parents' citizenship, but who were born outside the United States, the birth may have been registered with a United States embassy or consulate in the country of birth. To obtain a copy of the birth registration, write to the Passport Services, Correspondence Branch, U.S. Department of State, Washington, DC 20522-1795 and ask for the Consular Report of Birth, Form FS-240. You will need to submit a signed statement identifying the person whose birth record you are requesting. The cost, at this writing, is $10.

Adoptees who were born outside the United States, of foreign parents, and who have been adopted by United States citizens can obtain copies of their altered birth certificates from the Immigration and Naturalization Service (INS), U.S. Department of Justice, Washington, DC 20536. Birth information is required to be kept on file with the INS for your adoption to be legal.

Request INS Form G-641. At this writing, a $15 check or money order must accompany the completed form before you can receive a copy of your birth certificate.

If you require a birth or death certificate from a foreign country, write to the closest embassy or consulate of that country for information on how to go about obtaining these documents.

For additional information on births or deaths abroad or for information regarding births or deaths occurring aboard a vessel at sea or on an aircraft, you will need to obtain form HRA 77-1143. This form requests records of United States citizens who were born or died in foreign countries. It can be obtained from the National Center for Health Statistics, 6525 Belcrest Road, Hyattsville, MD 20782-2003. For information on individuals abroad who aren't (or never were) United States citizens, you must rely on records being made available to you by the foreign government having jurisdiction. The Correspondence Branch of Passport Services, is again your best first reference for an indication of whom to contact and what procedures you should follow.

Adoptees who were born in a United States territory or dependency can direct inquiries to the proper government agencies there for obtaining birth information and/or confirmation of death.

Here is a list of addresses for the appropriate agency in each case:

American Samoa
Registrar of Vital Statistics
Government of American Samoa
Pago Pago, American Samoa 96799

Former Canal Zone
Panama Canal Commission
Vital Statistics Clerk, APO, Miami,
  FL 34011

**Former Trust Territory of the
  Pacific Islands**
Clerk of Court of the district in
  which the birth or death oc-
  curred. To discover the district,
  write to:
Office of Vital Statistics
Superior Court
Saipan, Mariana Islands 96950

Puerto Rico
Department of Health
P.O. Box 11854
Fernandez Juncos Station
San Juan, Puerto Rico 00910

Virgin Islands (U.S.)
St. Thomas: Registrar of Vital
  Statistics
Charlotte Amalie, St. Thomas
  Virgin Islands 00802
St. Croix: Registrar of Vital Statistics
Charles Harwood Memorial Hospital
St. Croix, Virgin Islands 00820

For searchers trying to locate information on persons in Australia, New Zealand, Canada, Scotland, or England, the search and support groups in those countries may be of assistance. Direct your inquiries as follows.

Australia

The Victorian Freedom of Information Act 1984 provide for adult adoptees and birthparents to obtain birth certificates, identifying information and other information and assistance to help them locate family members and relinquished children (18 years of age or older). This act has other sections that may be of interest to the searcher.

Adoption Information Service
29 Coventry Street
South Melbourne, Australia 3205
(03) 9695 3888

Adoption Jigsaw S.A., Inc.
P.O. Box 567, Prospect East
South Australia 5083
Phone 08 344-7529
Fax 09 344-7529

Adoption Jigsaw-Tasmania
G.P.O. Box 989K
Hobart, Tasmania 7001

Adoption Jigsaw WA
P.O. Box 252, Hillarys
Western Australia 6025
(08) 9388 1922, fax 08-9382-3915
e-mail: slj@onaustralia.com.au

Adoption Triangle
P.O. Box 96
Jesmond, New South Wales 2299
(049) 65 588888

Association for Adoptees
Queensland
18 Wain Avenue
Woodridge, Queensland 4114
(07) 3808 3126

Association of Relinquishing
Mothers
20 Beauvorna Ave.
Keysborough, Victoria 3331
(03) 9803 3311

Association of Relinquishing
Mothers
P.O. Box 60, Tuart Hill,
Western Australia 6060
(08) 9336-1337

Australian Relinquishing Mothers
Society
51 North Terrace
Hackney, South Australia 5069
(08) 8362 2418

Jigsaw Queensland
P.O. Box 55
Roma Street, Queensland 4003

Origins Inc.
P.O. Box 33
New South Wales 2203
Phone/Fax (02) 9560-8808

VANISH
199 Cardigan Street, Carlton 3053
Phone (03) 9348 2111 or
1800 334-043
Fax 03-9349 4853
e-mail: vanish@vicnet.net.au

New Zealand
Adoption Support Link
Patricia Stroud
G.P.O. Box 4164
Auckland, New Zealand
Phone 09-424-1035

Birth-Search
27b Ranui Road
Stoke, Nelson
New Zealand
Phone 03-547 3248
e-mail: BirthSearch@xtra.co.nz

Jigsaw Inc.
Josie Hendry
PO Box 38681
Howick, Auckland
New Zealand
Phone/Fax 09-533-9191

Movement Out of Adoption (NZ)
(this is a lobby group)
PO Box 7162, Wellesley Street
Auckland, New Zealand

Canada
A new adoption law in British Columbia (the B.C. Adoption Act) now allows thousands of adoptees to receive their original birth certificates. For additional information, contact one of the Canadian groups listed below.

Adoption Reunion Searchline
Joan Marshall, ISC
Merivale, P.O. Box 65043
Nepean, Ontario, Canada K2G 5Y3
(613) 825-1640, Fax (613) 825-7479
e-mail: reunion@istar.ca

Adoption Roots & Rights
187 Patricia Avenue
Dorchester, Ontario
Canada NOL 1G1
(519) 268-3674, fax (519) 268-7239

Adoption Roots & Rights
3 John Davies Drive
Woodstock, Ontario
Canada N4T 1M99
(519) 421-0581, fax (519) 421-0572

Canadian Adoption Reunion
  Registry
Joan E. Vanstone
3998 Bayridge Ave.
West Vancouver, B.C., Canada
  V7V 3J5
e-mail: reunion@portal.ca
Web site: <www.portal.ca/~reunion/>

Parent Finders, National Office
Joan E. Vanstone
3998 Bayridge Avenue
W. Vancouver, B.C.,
  Canada V7V 3J5
(604) 980-6005,
  fax (604) 926-2037
e-mail: reunion@portal.ca
Web site: <www.portal.ca/~reunion/>

Triad, Calgary
P.O. Box 5114, Station A
Calgary, Alberta, Canada T2H 1X1

TRIAD, Regina
Mrs. Marlus Kulas, Box 33040
Regina, Sask. Canada S4T 7X2
(306) 586-4782, fax (306) 757-9880
e-mail: triad.society@dlcwest.com

TRIAD, Saskatoon
Bob & Sophie Pearson
#84 - 3 Columbia Drive
Saskatoon, Sask., Canada S7K 1E3
(306) 665-3109

See Chapter 9, "Searching on the Computer," for several Canadian search Web sites.

Scotland
Family Care & Scotland
Birth - Link Register
21 Castle Street, Edinburch EH2
   3DN
Scotland
031 225-6441

England
NORCAP
Lind Savell
112 Church Road, Wheately
Oxfordshire, England OX33 1LU
01865 875000

War Babes
15 Plough Avenue
South Woodgate
Birmingham, England B32 3TQ

Listed below are some organizations in the United States that provide assistance to people conducting searches in other countries.

- Association of Korean Adoptees, SG, 1208 N. Brand Blvd., Glendale, CA 91202
- Leonie Boehmer, ISC, Germany, Austria, Switzerland; see Appendix 1 under New Mexico
- Pearl S. Buck Foundation, P.O. Box 181, Green Hills Farm, Perkasie, PA 18944
- C.E.R.A. foreign search in any country; see Appendix 1 under New York
- Daniel J. Duffy, Ireland, 850 Mission Hills, St. Louis, MO 63141
- Family Search Services, Italy; see Appendix 1 under California
- Gari-Sue Greene, Central America, England, Ireland, Germany, Mexico, Puerto Rico; see Appendix 1 under Arizona
- Alberta Sorensen, Italy; see Appendix 1 under California

United States search and support groups with a national membership will be able to advise and direct you toward help when searching outside the country. Refer to Chapter 7, "Search and Support Groups, Researchers/ Searchers, Consultants, Intermediaries, and the Courts," for those addresses.

The *International Vital Records Handbook* is published by the Genealogical Publishing Company, 1001 N. Calvert Street, Baltimore, MD 21202. This book is an excellent source for obtaining application forms and ordering information from countries all over the world. Check your local library to learn if a copy is available or can be ordered through interlibrary loan. You can purchase a copy from most genealogical bookstores for $29.95.

SURROGATE MOTHERS

Over the last decade a new method of adoption has taken place in small, but highly publicized, numbers. An infertile woman married to a fertile man wishes to have a child. Rather than adopt through conventional means where neither is the birthfather or birthmother, they choose to obtain a surrogate mother who will receive the father's sperm through donor insemination and then carry the child to term. After birth, the surrogate mother relinquishes the child for adoption. The wife of the birthfather adopts the child. In so doing, the wife, in all respects, assumes the same position as that of any other mother.

Several cases involving surrogate mothers have been widely publicized, most notably the "Baby M Trial." While I am no expert on surrogacy, I do know that there should be much alarm and concern over this process, as it differs little from the black-market adoption. It involves the selling of a child, or at least the selling of parental rights, which is illegal in all states and in all other circumstances.

If the searcher is a surrogate mother, looking back can be disturbing and frightening. She may, however, have the advantage of knowing the birthfather's and adoptive mother's names when seeking records. As for the restrictions on records involving surrogacy in the future, I doubt that anyone can make that prediction or foretell the reactions to a surrogate mother's relinquishment 5, 10, or 20 years from now. One surrogate mother related the following from an article in the New York Times, printed during the "Baby M Trial":

> Until Mary Beth's [Baby M's surrogate mother] case came to light, none of us knew who we were and none of us was willing to talk about it, because giving up a baby is not something we're proud of . . . . I have lost a baby and I don't say that out of pity for myself, but for the hundreds and maybe thousands of other surrogates who will reach that point of understanding some day, just as I did. Then they will look in the mirror and say, "My God, what have I done?"[3]

If the searcher is an adoptee, discovering the circumstances of his or her relinquishment will be painful. The adoptee has the advantage of a genetic link to the birthfather but must conduct a search for the birthmother the same as other adoptees.

Daniel Callahan, director of the Hastings Center, wrote the following in an article for Newsweek: "We are wandering into all kinds of new parental relationships. I don't think we have the faintest idea of how it's going to work out. It's a social experiment."[4]

Lawmakers are learning that "sealed records" and confidentiality are not viable, just as they have known for years that black market adoptions do not work. Will a time come when lawmakers consider this "social experiment" unworkable?

DONOR INSEMINATION (DI)

There are no precise figures stating the numbers of births from donor insemination (artificial insemination) because this procedure requires no record keeping, except those records showing information needed for tax purposes. Few states reported to me laws on their books pertaining to donor insemination, yet many reported laws regarding surrogate mothers. But surrogate mothers and donor insemination are in essence very much alike. They both perform a task that leads to the birth of a child and generally they both do it for money.

Some men donate their own sperm to a doctor or sperm bank to increase their chances of fathering a child. A product of this type of insemination produces a child from both genetic parents. Record keeping or proceedings are not necessary. Other men donate their sperm to a sperm bank in exchange for money.

Sperm banks have their own forms which they use to compile information received from the donor. Whether any checking is done on the information is strictly up to the sperm bank. These facilities are like blood banks in that they may advertise for or seek out donors within their own guidelines.

In many cases, a couple discovers they cannot conceive a child due to the husband's infertility. They contact a sperm bank and Mrs. Jones is injected with sperm from an anonymous donor. She bears the child. The birthfather is the donor, yet Mr. Jones is assumed to be the father. No one, including the hospital, asks Mr. Jones if he is the father. The results are that all records for the child are as if he or she were a genetic descendent of both Mr. and Mrs. Jones.

A most interesting book titled *Lethal Secrets* has brought to light many of the problems that come with donor insemination. While the book is well worth reading, several comments stand out for those considering a search:

> We [the authors] feel that a primary objective is to take the concept of insemination out of the laboratory and to impart the necessary human quality to the giver of the sperm . . . . No more anonymous donors or mixed sperm for insemination means that we eliminate the reservoir of anonymous and mixed sperm in sperm banks. All sperm must be received from known volunteers who agree to share total identifying social and medical information. The donor must agree to be available on a lifetime basis as the genetic parent.[5]

Typically, the laws surrounding donor insemination include statements like: "The name of the putative father shall not be entered on the certificate of birth without the written consent of the mother and the person to be named as father" and "Any child or children born as the result of heterologous artificial insemination shall be considered at law in all respects the same as a naturally conceived legitimate child of the husband and wife requesting and consenting in writing to the use of such technique." These laws clearly show the feelings of the lawmakers, the courts, and the adults involved in donor insemination. The emphasis is to create a "natural family" by ignoring genetics and medical need-to-know.

A vast number of children are born using donor insemination and the most frightening aspect of this type of conception is the ability to keep the birthfather a secret, even from the child. This child grows up, marries, has children and grandchildren, and eventually dies without ever knowing that the medical information used throughout the years is incorrect or that there ever was a donor insemination.

Since there is no record keeping and no adoption process, donor insemination leaves everyone with a sense of uneasiness. The child must rely totally on the honesty of his or her parents to know if they are actually birthparents. Parents who place their need for privacy ahead of their child's need for factual medical information completely disregard "the best interest of the child."

Where is it written that responsible, honest people who consider a legal act, plan to execute the act, and then put the act into operation would then believe it should be kept a secret about all else? And if when the secret is revealed it causes shame and some disgrace; what does that say about the act?

> The donor offspring who knows the truth may be relieved to know it, but accompanying this knowledge is the suggestion that he is really only half a person. Nowhere is there a record that would authenticate him. Even in a life-and-death emergency, where knowledge of the genetic father or his whereabouts might save the donor offspring's life, there is no help to be had; all of the bridges have been burned, and the road is closed."[6]

I am aware of one group, Donors' Offspring (see Chapter 7, "Search and Support Groups, Researchers/Searchers, Consultants, Intermediaries, and the Courts") which concentrates on those who were products of donor insemination. This might be a start for those searching and needing this type of reference. International Soundex Reunion Registry (see Chapter 8, "Reunion Registries") has a separate method of listing those who were products of donor insemination and are now seeking more information.

Possibly the sperm bank or the doctor who performed the insemination might have some records. Your best approach would be to contact your family physician to see if any facts regarding the insemination are known to him or her.

Outside of the few sources mentioned above, I have little advice or suggestions to offer, although a search and support group would be highly recommended.

RECORDS FOR BLACK MARKET BABIES

It's a tragic fact that a black market has long existed to supply babies to childless couples who are desperate for children in their lives and homes. Different motives lead such childless couples to resort to illegal rather than legal channels.

There are several books and articles that discuss baby selling at more length that I can here. In these few pages, I simply want to point to the difficulties that arise for searchers adopted under such circumstances and to suggest a line of approach for pursuing a search.

As an adoptee, you have commonly experienced the same sense of disconnectedness that other adoptees report. The problem that arises for you, in addition to possible emotional shock, is that you may find yourself unable to pursue a search with assurance of any likelihood of success. Information you were told about your background, if you were told anything, might be the same story related to your adoptive parents to place a premium value on your adoption. What records do exist may have been falsified. What chances might otherwise have existed for you to learn eventually your birth heritage may have been obliterated. There may be no way to trace back to the desired connection.

In some cases, however, it happens that the adoption of a child for money took place between people who knew each other. Only your adoptive parents can provide the key and, in this situation, they will understandably be reluctant to encourage inquiry into the circumstances of your adoption. You may be able to identify and locate an intermediary to your adoption, but his or her cooperation is hardly to be expected. The person—possibly an attorney or doctor—will usually prefer to keep any involvement in this kind of transaction unknown.

Corrupt agencies may be involved in arranging black market adoptions. Where that is the case, it remains possible that important agency documentation of your birth identity remains unfalsified. But the opposite is just as possible. A notorious agency in Tennessee, the Tennessee Children's Home Society, operated on a "commercial basis" for 14 years before being shut down by the state in 1951. One state investigator's report noted that TCHS made no investigation of the background of the children. Often, they destroyed what information they did have and in many cases falsified the child's background to adopting parents. A *Good Housekeeping* article printed two startling facts about this agency:

> Over time, Georgia Tann [during the 1940s she was the agency head], comfortable by birth, accumulated more than $1 million (that would translate to at least $5 million today) from her illegal adoptions. She would describe the child of a tenant farmer as the daughter of a debutante; Protestant babies were passed off as Jewish.[7]

The task facing the adoptee searcher with that kind of agency background is considerable.

Dr. Thomas Jugarthy Hicks was a doctor who practiced at the Hicks Clinic, Toccoa Street, McCaysville, Fannin County, Georgia. His abortion trade was very lucrative, but at some time he realized there was more money to be made by selling babies also. The following facts are known:

- Between 1955 and 1964, 56 babies were born at the Hicks Clinic. Of those, 49 babies went to people living in Sumit County, Ohio, 2 to Michigan, 1 to Illinois, and 1 to Pennsylvania. The fathers worked at Akron Tire Companies except for a Cuyahoga Falls doctor who bought two.
- All the birth certificates listed the people buying the babies as the birthparents.
  All sales were arranged by an Akron woman, who bought 4 babies. All paid up to $1000 to Dr. Hicks.
- There were no questions asked, no home visits, no background check, no paperwork, no legal fees, no adoption. The new parents had the option of telling the baby they were not the birthparent OR NEVER TELLING THEM. It is unknown how many babies were sold in this fashion.
- Dr. Hicks died in 1972, and no records have been found for the "Hicks Babies" to date. In the last 25 years, a dozen "Hicks Babies" have contacted Margaret Brown, the only survivor of Dr. Hicks' immediate family, to learn about their relinquishment.

A registry for Hicks Babies, "Silent Legacy," was started to provide a means for contact between the birthmothers and adoptees born at this black market clinic (see Chapter 8, "Reunion Registries," for information on this registry). It is hoped that more and more people will hear about the Hicks Babies and the birthmothers will come forward and identify themselves so the relinquished children (now adults) may be allowed the opportunity to learn about their birthparents, obtain knowledge of any siblings, and be provided correct medical information.

The Hicks Babies and the Tennessee Children's Home Society are two examples of black market operations run for profit. We can only wonder how many more black market babies are out there.

As a birthparent who relinquished a child to the baby black market, you also face a nearly impossible task. Records have probably been deliberately falsified or destroyed. You may have dealt with an intermediary who never divulged where your child went. However, since you know the identity of the intermediary, it may prove worthwhile to try to trace the transaction. As in the case of the adoptee, the intermediary is not likely to provide details voluntarily. And you, the birthparent, are usually in an awkward position too. Who really wants to admit, even years later, to having been involved in an illegal, potentially scandalous set of circumstances of this nature?

However, not all adoptions in which money changes hands are black market adoptions. Some are termed gray market adoptions, and are carried out perfectly legally. Fees may legitimately change hands as long as they fall into allowable categories, are properly documented, and stay within any limit prescribed by state law. Gray market adoptions may take place within an extended family or between unrelated families. They may be arranged by the birthparent(s), a family doctor, a private attorney, or a friend of the family, always, of course, according to law.

Black market adoptions work *outside* prescribed laws such as this and are arranged expressly for the purpose of making money. The best interests of the child are not a consideration.

If you find you are a black market baby and nevertheless wish to pursue a search, what could you find that would be so terrible, assuming you can determine your origins? Many adoptees have long suspected that their birthparents were not happily married and might not have come from ideal backgrounds. Black market transactions may involve children who were never freely relinquished, babies born in prisons and institutions for the insane, or babies born as the result of rape or incest. None of this is a reflection on the now-adult child's integrity, and to be such a child should not be seen as any reason for loss of self-esteem. Even so, this knowledge will probably still require a difficult emotional adjustment on your part.

If you decide to go through a search despite a black-market-baby background, you will undoubtedly be concerned to know where you can turn for support and assistance. The best first contact in this context will be a search and support group or one of the adoption resource libraries identified in later chapters. They can direct you to information or persons with experience in this situation. There are search and support groups established with the sole purpose of helping adoptees and birthparents involved with a specific problem agency. Maybe you'll locate such a group to help with your search; maybe you'll be led to a consultant who specialized in black market adoptions. Just to discover a fellow searcher who shares your situation may be enormously helpful to you.

If you are a black market baby who is determined in spite of all these problems to trace your birth heritage, you have made a difficult, courageous decision. My hat is off to you.

FOUNDLINGS

We have all read stories about the baby found on the doorstep, in a park, or even in a trash container. These are foundlings, with the most difficult of all searches to complete. You may not know you were a foundling, and it's possible you may not uncover this fact. However, if you are told, here are a few suggestions to help you conduct your search:

- A visit to the local newspaper that carried the story might be useful. Possibly there is someone still working there who would remember the event and add some fact to the few published.
- Another possible source of information will be police records. Abandoning a child is a crime, and a record of involvement by the police force will be kept.

Foundlings, along with black market babies, will need much help in tracking and tracing their birthfamilies. Birthparents who are searching for an abandoned child will also find little cooperation and few facts to aid them. I strongly recommend seeking help from one of the many groups across the country that offer search help.

GROUP SUPPORT

A number of search and support groups have been established in the United States. These search and support groups aid you in your quest for information that can lead to identification and location of birthparents or relinquished children. The appendix at the back of this book lists groups operating in each state. You'll find a fuller discussion of group support in Chapter 7, "Search and Support Groups, Researchers/Searchers, Consultants, Intermediaries, and the Courts."

KEEPING BUSY

The process of search is an extended one and the fact that so much time is involved frequently leads to discouragement. You will have sent off letters asking all the questions you want to know. You will have made some initial contact, perhaps with a private, religious, or governmental agency. You will have compiled all the recollections available to you. It may seem that most leads have trailed out to a vague nowhere, except in instances where they run into an obstacle, such as an agency or individual who will not provide you with information they hold on you. At times you may be discouraged. Don't give in to this discouragement. But don't expect that your first round of search activity will be rewarded if you just sit back and wait for answers to flow in. While there are times when you will have to wait for a particular response before you can pursue a related lead, you can constructively direct your energies in other directions. It may prove helpful for you to take the time to read the account of another's search; several good ones have been published (see Chapter 10, "Search Resources and Services"). You may want to familiarize yourself with genealogy, a very related interest for searchers. You may want to attend a meeting on adoption search or get in contact with other individuals who are engaged in this process. Direct yourself to one of the national organizations for information about your area.

You can also begin plotting out further areas for research. Check your library for a map of your county of birth. Locate the newspapers published in the area of your birth. A good many adoptees have found a record of their birth through old newspaper archives. A local newspaper may have reported the birth of four baby girls and six baby boys on a given day. This could provide a lead to tracking down your birth name. If you have your birth weight and length, look to see if that is given for an infant reported born on a particular day. The *Ayer Directory of Publications* or *The Standard Periodical Directory* will give you current names and addresses to contact at particular newspapers. Editions of these same reference books from around the time of your birth will alert you to what newspapers have since gone out of business. Old copies of those newspapers may be housed at the state archives.

You get the idea. As a searcher you can to some extent depend on good fortune, but the informed, persistent searcher who seeks out all the options for obtaining information is ahead of the searcher who is haphazard and uninformed in pursuit of this goal. During any period when you are waiting for responses to queries you've sent out, make the effort to become more informed. If you seem blocked on all sides, unable to get beyond basic scraps of information you cannot organize, avoid dwelling on what you don't have. Concentrate instead on how you might get what you need. Take the time to look for additional moral support.

Just a few years ago, the average search took from one to three years. Now, the search organizations tell me, the average length of search is from several days to three months. Of course, there is no guarantee that your search will be concluded within that time period. But your chances of achieving your goal are better than they were before. Even so, your success is largely dependent on your determination and the amount of thought and energy you invest. You must take full responsibility for your search. You will get out of it what you put into it. Certainly there will be times when you'll feel the need to take a break, and you will probably find that the concerns of day-to-day living on occasion force you to direct yourself toward other priorities. There is no reason for self-recrimination in either event. If you are truly a dedicated searcher, you will find that your momentum continues on a certain level anyway and building back to full momentum will occur naturally.

The bottom line in your search project is you. How much thought are you willing to invest? How clever can you be? Can you develop an aptitude for picking up on leading statements? Can you sharpen your instincts on how best to deal with people and situations? As you enter into the search that you've decided you want to pursue, learn to be as good a listener as you can be. Organize yourself so as to maximize the benefit of any piece of information you obtain. Persist in following the leads that open up to you. With the sources of information, the tools of research, and the support networks that have developed within the past few years, there is more reason than ever for optimism that you will locate that important missing link to your past that has eluded or puzzled you for so long.

NOTES

1. Former social worker Annette Baran's recollections of dealing with adoptees and birthparents seeking information are detailed in *A Time to Search* by Henry Ehrlick (New York: Paddington Press, 1977), p. 17.
2. The sample form authorizing release of medical information is based on form 712 in the *Handbook of Law Office Forms* by Robert Sellers Smith (Englewood Cliffs, NJ: Prentice-Hall, 1974).
3. Surrogate mothers and the issues surrounding the "Baby M Case" are discussed in the *New York Times*, March 2, 1987, p. B1.
4. "After the Baby M Case," *Newsweek*, April 13, 1987, pp. 22-23.
5. Annette Baran and Reuben Pannor, "Lethal Secrets: The Shocking Consequences and Unsolved Problems of Artificial Insemination," New York: Warner Books, 1989, p. 155.
6. Ibid., p. 73.
7. Barbara Bistanz, "The Woman Who Stole 5,000 Babies," *Good Housekeeping*, March 1991, pp. 140-41, 180-86. This article describes Georgia Tann and the Tennessee Children's Home Society.

CHAPTER 6

As the Search Progresses: Alternate Sources of Data

Y ou may find that a determined effort to uncover information opens up enough leads to put you securely on the track of the person you hope to locate. However, you may find this doesn't fill in enough of the blanks. Recollections are vague. Birth records are unavailable. Agency and hospital records remain sealed. No one seems interested in helping you develop the leads you need to achieve your goal.

Perhaps you find yourself in this situation. Despite energies spent getting yourself organized, and after a variety of efforts along lines recommended for approaching individuals and agencies, you still have only an altered birth certificate and a short letter notifying you that your adoption agency closed its doors years ago. It may have taken you two months to learn virtually nothing. One option is to call off your search. But if your decision to search came after years of agonizing questioning and doubt, giving up now condemns you to living with those unresolved feelings. The truth is, there are still many avenues of inquiry you can follow to learn who and where your birthparents are or where your birthchild is. Even with a limited budget, but with a bit of imagination and a lot of persistence, chances are good you can achieve your goal. To help you to that end, this chapter pulls together information on alternate sources of data that you can turn to when the primary sources covered in the previous chapter prove inadequate for whatever reason.

One word of caution before going into these alternate sources: You're unlikely to get all the information you hope for from any one of these. Rather, you will probably find that you can only get bits and pieces of information at a time. It's not until you've assembled enough of these pieces of information, relying on a variety of sources, that an entire picture begins to emerge.

One of the great frustrations you may encounter is that sometimes it seems that the only way to find someone is to first know where he or she is. It's a real "catch-22" situation. You may not be able to make the best use of some potentially helpful sources of information until you have at least a few facts to work with. That is why imagination and persistence are so important. You may find sharing the experiences of people who have searched or are searching valuable at this time.

You find yourself missing the one key detail you need to take advantage of a source to uncover another key detail. View this as only a temporary setback. Occasionally you may find that, even though you're missing a seemingly essential piece of information, you can finesse another bit of information without it. Unfortunately, there's no rule of thumb I can offer to guide you here. You need to cultivate a certain intuition, taking a chance on things occasionally. How you get to a certain record and what you can obtain from it vary according to the state you're searching in, how you express yourself, and how cooperative a clerk or social worker is willing to be. When you first begin your search, you will inevitably be awkward or unaware at times. Gradually, however, you'll find yourself developing a feel for what you're doing and how you should go about doing it.

PRIVILEGED INFORMATION

This is often one of the first sources of frustration you'll encounter. Although you might spend days arguing the justice of it, the fact is that certain people have easier access to information about you than you do yourself. Fortunately, in a few cases you may be able to use that fact to your advantage.

Hospital and medical records may very well be released to your doctor even though refused to you. Consider asking your doctor to write for all hospital and medical records pertaining to you if you are having difficulty getting them on your own. Your doctor is not bound by law to keep them confidential from you. Often psychiatrists and psychologists are willing to provide aid in this manner as well.

Insurance companies often require medical and family history records to determine whether or not you are an acceptable risk. Approach your insurance agent and ask that your insurance company request your medical and hospital records. After all, it's logical for the company to need those records. Your agent may only need to consult the company's computer memory bank if the information was already routinely gathered. Take heed when using this resource, as the information received can be used against you by the insurance company when requesting coverage.

Many times people who seem to have some official authorization are granted privileges denied to an average citizen. Some searchers have found that a document designating someone else to act as their agent or granting another a limited power of attorney can impress a records administrator into releasing information that was refused earlier. Although there is no binding legal distinction here from a third party's point of view, the officialness of the document can prompt more ready cooperation. Most stationery stores carry a form for use in granting a power of attorney. I've also provided a sample form here for your reference (see Sample 10).

SAMPLE 10
FORM GRANTING LIMITED POWER OF ATTORNEY

I,_____, of _____, do hereby appoint
_____, of _____, my agent, for me
and in my name to (1,2) _____
_____
_____

and generally to do and perform all things necessary in or about the premises as fully in all respects as I could do if personally present. (3,4)

Signed this _____ day of _____, 19_____

_____
(signature)

_____

Sample Inclusions:
  1. ...apply for and receive any vital records of my birth, my health, and hospital records, or court records that pertain to me.
  2 ...apply for and receive any official or personal record of medical information that may have any bearing on my health and well-being.
  Other Possible Inclusions:
  3. *Add:* The date of this limited power of attorney shall begin on (date) and be valid until (date) and on that date shall end.
  4. *Add:* No other powers than those mentioned shall be empowered to (name).

Note: A printed form of this document can be purchased at most stationery stores for $2 or less.

Suppose you're an adoptee who wants to search old probate records. If you come in and just express a vague need to review records available, the clerk may point to an area of the room and say: "The records are over there." And with that, you're on your own. You have to figure out how records are coded and organized. You may miss an index that could give you a quick overview of what is contained in them. Now suppose you come in with a grant of power of attorney. (You may have made out the power of attorney to yourself, using your current name over your birth name.) You show the clerk your "credentials." The clerk may very well respond by taking you in hand, leading you to the index, even actually searching the records with you. Your review of the records is accomplished more speedily and with greater assurance that you've gotten all you can out of them.

MARRIAGE RECORDS

Once your search uncovers a name or an estimated date of marriage, you may be able to develop further leads through publicly kept marriage records. Marriage certificates will provide you with the names of the couple, the site of the intended ceremony, indication of the type of ceremony, and the name of the person officiating at the marriage. The exact form of the certificate varies from state to state and in some states even from county to county.

Many states have indexed past marriage records. The indexes are open to the public and very easy to use. Depending on the practice in your area of search, you may be allowed direct access at no charge or be required to pay a search fee and have a clerk pull the records for you. For more individual state information, consult the appendix at the back of this book.

Other sources to check for marriage records include newspaper announcements and church files. In the event the ceremony was performed by a justice of the peace, he or she will have a record of it. Check with a clerk at the county or municipal hall of records to discover where records of civil ceremonies are maintained if these are held separately from the actual marriage license/ certificate.

An adoptive mother helping her son to search recalled that she'd been told the birthmother was to marry after she left the hospital. Although the marriage was not to the birthfather, knowing the married name could make it possible to contact the mother. The son knew his own birth name. He went to the hall of records and searched marriage records, starting with those for the day his birthmother was released from the hospital. After searching through only 15 days, he found her name and that of her new husband. He went to the local library and found a report of the marriage in the area newspaper's vital statistic's section. From that he learned his birthmother's age, her hometown, and the names of attendants at the wedding ceremony.

Birthparents on the trail of a relinquished child can also make much use of marriage records. The primary prerequisite is having a name to work with, together with some sense of the dates to check. For example, if you were told at the time of relinquishment that your child was going to a young Catholic couple who married two years before, you might at one point find it possible to check marriage records as an aid to tracking down the present identity and location of your child. You will usually need a name, but remember that other facts combined may give you an opportunity to locate the names.

Using the example above, list what information you have. You already know the couple has been married two years and that they are members of the Catholic Church. In addition, the agency has given you a physical description of both adoptive parents and told you the husband was a pharmacist in his father's drugstore. With a little luck and some time spent researching newspapers in outlying areas to your agency, you may locate the missing couple. You know the persons' ages. Will your agency tell you if they live in a rural or city area? Use your imagination and piece your puzzle together. Ask a search group for advice. You have valuable information; now you must learn to use it.

DIVORCE RECORDS

The failure of a marriage, leading to separation and divorce, also occasions official record keeping. Divorce records will list names of the couple involved, date and place of marriage, date and place of divorce, names of children (including adopted, but not relinquished children), residence, and a description of property held by the couple. Most states have an index to divorce records and they will generally be kept with the other vital statistics records. There may or may not be a charge to view them or have them searched. Consult the appendix at the back of this book for individual state information on divorce records.

Divorces filed will be listed in local newspapers. Check this source as well to obtain information. You may also find that church records include data on divorce of any member of the congregation or parish.

DEATH RECORDS

Adoptees and birthparents can find that records of death in a birth or adoptive family prove useful as a source of leads to the person sought. The official document recording a person's death is the death certificate. A death certificate can be a gold mine of information. It will indicate the name of the deceased, last place of residence, date of death, age at time of death, and cause and place of death. It may further indicate surviving family members, military service history, occupation of the deceased, or other data. Each state differs somewhat from others on what is included; some states release a lengthy certificate, while others issue certificates listing only a few necessary particulars.

If you know the approximate date of death and the state in which the death occurred—or if you suspect a certain state has the records—you can write to obtain a copy of the death certificate. If you're not sure of the actual date of death, request a search of the records over a period of time during which you think the person died. You will have to indicate your relationship to the deceased as it is known to you. In citing a reason for the records search, you can note medical need-to-know or judicial need relating to questions of inheritance, or you can indicate that this is a genealogical inquiry. To write for the death certificate, use the address listed in Appendix I in the back of the book under the state you are searching. Sample 11 provides a form letter you can adapt for this purpose. Chapter 9, "Searching on the Computer," provides their Web site address.

SAMPLE 11
LETTER REQUESTING A DEATH CERTIFICATE

Date

Department of Vital Statistics
Address
City, State, Zip Code

Dear Registrar:

Would you please search for and provide a full transcript of the Certificate of Death for:

(name of person on certificate)
Sex and race:
Date of death: (approximate if unknown)
Born: (give approximate dates if exact date is unknown)
Name of spouse:
Residence at time of death:
Please advise who received the ashes of the deceased if cremation occurred.

My relationship to the above is (list as it actually is) and my reason for this request is judicial need.

Enclosed is a certified check in the amount required for a search and a copy of the record.

Sincerely,
(your signature)
Address
City, State, Zip Code

Note: You may need to request this information on a form provided by the department of vital statistics. If so, write to request the form and ask to receive forms needed to obtain birth, marriage, and divorce records.

At a search and support group meeting I attended, a birthmother told of receiving information that her relinquished child had gone to a lovely family (a common reassurance). In asking lots of questions, including questions about other members of the adoptive family, she learned that the maternal grandfather had died just prior to the adoption. She had already determined the area where the family was located and a lengthy search of the death records for that area produced several possible leads. By following through systematically, she was able to discover the family she sought.

There are other death records you can turn to as well. You can check an area newspaper for an obituary notice. (Keep in mind that it will run a day or two after the date of death.) The obituary customarily lists surviving children and provides other leads you may wish or need to pursue at some point: church membership, lodge membership, birth date, hospital or other location where the person died, the funeral date, and the name of the funeral home involved. The names of surviving children and/or other relatives are customarily accompanied by a note of each person's town of residence. Married names are given for the women in the family. Adopted children are routinely treated as integral members of the surviving family.

Just exactly what you learn that benefits you depends on your or your birthchild's relationship to the deceased. If the record is of, say, your birthmother, those surviving could include siblings as well as a surviving partner, possibly your birthfather. If the record is of a member of an adoptive family, the survivors could include the adoptive parents as children of the deceased or, if one of the adoptive parents died, your relinquished birthchild as a child of the deceased.

You may be able to pursue an aspect of your search via mortuary or cemetery records. Of course, you need to have a reasonable idea of which mortuary or cemetery to direct yourself to. Once you have that, you may upon request be able to obtain a copy of the obituary notice, a copy of any printed matter given out at the funeral service, indication of the type of service and the date, information on whether the deceased was buried in a family plot, names of other family members buried there, when and whether there is perpetual care on the grave site, and, if so, who is keeping up the payments. (Sample 12 is a form letter for requesting mortuary results.)

SAMPLE 12
LETTER REQUESTING MORTUARY RECORDS

Date

Name of Mortuary
Address
City, State, Zip Code

Dear Sir:

I am an active genealogist and have been tracing my family background and relationships for many years. A service was held at your mortuary on (date) for (name of deceased). I would appreciate any help you can provide with respect to the following:

1. A copy of the obituary. If this is not available, do you know what newspaper it was printed in?
2. Any surnames involved.
3. Relatives' names and addresses.
4. The deceased person's religious affiliation.
5. Any printed material distributed at the funeral. If there was such material, can you send me a copy?
6. Is the burial plot kept on a perpetual basis? Who is maintaining it?
7. Is there a family plot? What other members of this family are buried in the same area?
8. Any newspaper clippings or other information kept in your files.

Thank you very much for your time and consideration. I am enclosing a stamped, self-addressed envelope for your convenience in replying and a check for ____ to cover any photocopying expenses.

Sincerely,
(your signature)
Address
City, State, Zip Code

Note: You should include at least $.50 per page to be copied. It can be difficult to estimate how much material may be available. Be assured you will be notified if the amount you remit is not enough.

This same basic letter could be used for cemetery information.

Mortuaries and cemeteries routinely deal with genealogists and will not be surprised or disturbed by your inquiries. You will not need to prove relationship nor send your inquiry via certified mail. Ask for all information in their files. For their convenience, include a self-addressed, stamped envelope to facilitate reply. If you decide to call, the best time to contact a funeral home is early in the morning or on Sundays, when services are usually not held. You might call to ask what the most convenient time is to visit the mortuary or cemetery if you decide to go in person to request and review records on file there.

If there's no indication the person you're searching for has died, why would you want to go through mortuary or cemetery or other death records? Suppose no one has even mentioned death, much less the name of a specific funeral home. You don't even have a full name to search. Let me illustrate with a set of circumstances how bits and pieces of information, including death records, can be fitted together to help locate someone who's living. I will use the example of an adoptee searcher who has learned the following particulars:

- You have a change-of-name record from the court handling your adoption. Your indicated birth surname is Reinhardt.
- Your agency has informed you that your grandparents (by birth) played no role in your adoption. In fact, your birth grandfather had recently died. (Your birthmother was unmarried at the time she relinquished you, so this is your maternal birth grandfather).
- Agency records indicate your birthmother was born in Hancock County, Illinois.
- A call to the agency which handled your adoption has elicited your birth grandparents' first names, Jim and Barbara. The surname was refused you as identifying information, but you obtained that through another source.
- You have discovered through hospital records that your birthmother was 20 years old at your birth.

With these facts, this is what you can do: Send a letter to the Illinois Vital Statistics Department requesting a copy of the death certificate for Jim Reinhardt. The estimated date of death is in the months or year prior to your adoption. Using your mother's age as a rough guideline, you estimate your grandfather's date of birth. If you were adopted as an infant in 1957, he was probably from 40 to 50 years of age, which would give a birth date somewhere about 1907 to 1917. So, in your letter you ask for a search of the records for a death certificate for Jim Reinhardt who died in 1956 or 1957, probably in Hancock County. You note his birth date as falling in or about the decade between 1907 and 1917.

Provided all your previous discoveries are accurate, you stand a good chance of obtaining a death certificate listing the full name of your grandfather and particulars as to last residence. Also given will be the name of the mortuary handling disposition of the remains. Now you can write a letter to the mortuary requesting a copy of the obituary, which should provide the names of all surviving children. One of these will be your birthparent. The town of residence will likely be given for each surviving child.

One adoptee, in working to locate her birthmother, was able to make some use of mortuary and cemetery records. All she knew at the time was the date of death for her maternal birth grandmother, the approximate date of death for her maternal birth grandfather, and the town they lived in. A check of the telephone directory for that town gave her the name of local funeral homes. She wrote a brief letter to the indicated addresses, asking for information and citing a legal need to know. The result was that the mortuary handling funeral arrangements sent back a copy of the obituary for her birth grandmother and copies of the interment order to the cemetery for both her and the birth grandfather. In the cover letter sent with these was a note that one son was in charge of payments for care of the grave and his current address was indicated. That son, of course, was a brother to her birthmother.

What do you need to know before you can take advantage of these death records? That depends. Different pieces of information can fit together in various combinations to provide you a sense of direction to pursue. It can also depend on whether you are writing for information or are able to check files in person. If you go in person, you may be able to search the records even though you have only a date of death and no name, or a name and no date of death. You will have to have a good or reasonable idea of locality.

If you are writing for information, you will need to provide more specifics. Of course, it also depends on where you are writing. It's easier to check records in a small town than in a major city. Has a private, religious, or governmental agency worker mentioned a death in the adoptive or relinquishing family at or about the time of adoption or relinquishment, or at any other fairly identifiable period of time? You may be able to uncover the corresponding record by relying simply on the date and a relative certainty about where the deceased lived or died.

If you have a name, you can also turn to probate records, which relate the disposition of any estate a deceased person may have left behind. These indicate all people receiving money or property from a person's estate, with addresses of the property involved and addresses for all persons named.

Probate records are open to the public. You can walk into any county courthouse or hall of records and look through the index to these records. When you see a name you want—even if you choose one at random—you fill out a card with the name and case number, hand that to the clerk, and you will be brought that probate file to review. You can go through as many of these files as you want. Sample 13 provides a form letter for requesting probate records.

SAMPLE 13
LETTER REQUESTING PROBATE RECORDS

Date

Probate Department
Hall of Records, (name of county)
Address
City, State, Zip Code

Dear Records Clerk:

Please send me photocopies of information held by your office on (name of person). (His/Her) death took place on (give date) in the county of (name of county).

I have a judicial need for these records. (1) My relationship to the above is (state as in fact it is).

Please include all information held in the probate packet.

I am enclosing a check for _____ to cover any photocopying expenses.

Sincerely,
(your signature)
Address
City, State, Zip Code

Other Possible Inclusion:

1. *Substitute:* I need these records for genealogical purposes.

Note: See the preceding sample letter for requesting mortuary records for a suggestion about determining photocopying costs.

You may need to have this letter notarized and to prove relationship.

Older records are frequently stored separately from those that are more recent. My county's index of records immediately available covers the most recent 15 years. If your situation is such that you are researching a death that occurred previous to a cutoff date for recent records, you will have to inquire about arranging access to the older files.

Adoptees who have learned their birth surname can check probate records in that name. To check the records in person, that surname would be enough, but if you are writing, you need to specify, in most cases, a first name as well. Birthparents would need a knowledge of the adoptive family's surname, which is often difficult to come by.

SCHOOL RECORDS

If you have reason to believe the person you seek attended an institution of higher learning, write to colleges and universities in the area of your search.

The state archives can provide you a list of schools operating within the state during the years you want to review. *Patterson's American Education,* a book that can be found in the reference section of your library, will list the addresses of all colleges, universities, junior colleges, high schools, grammar schools, and private schools in the United States. These are given by state and city.

Colleges generally keep a library copy of the student yearbook for each year. If you know the college the person you seek attended, then you should certainly ask for a photocopy of the yearbook pages listing him or her. A letter to the school's library requesting a photocopy of pages listing the surname you are seeking can supply you with important leads. The yearbook will list clubs, associations, major area of studies, and achievements. Fraternity or sorority affiliations will be noted and maybe religious association. These provide further avenues for potential clues. The yearbook will most likely also have a photograph of the person you seek, especially if he or she was in the graduating class for that year.

Sometimes yearbook information points in the direction of a subsequent career. Say the person you're seeking majored in metallurgical engineering. That's a fairly directed major, suggesting he or she has a specific career goal in mind. Chances are good that the person established some professional association once out of school. In this case you would check your library's copy of the *Encyclopedia of Associations* to see if you can identify a professional or trade association of metallurgical engineers. Just as the American Medical Association includes the vast majority of medical doctors, so many other professionals and trade specialists have their own special-interest group or association. You can direct inquiries to whichever of these is appropriate for a list of active members.

Unfortunately, you can't always count on this line of approach working out. Many college and university graduates, particularly those obtaining a liberal arts degree, go on to careers that have no direct bearing on the major area of study. A student who graduated as an English major and served on the college literary review may now be working in publishing, but he or she could just as easily be anything from a schoolteacher to a travel agent to a homemaker.

Sample 14 provides a sample letter of request to a college library for yearbook information. Let me caution you against using adoption search as the reason for your request. The information you're requesting is not private information, but a librarian disapproving of adoption search could refuse your request if he or she so chooses.

SAMPLE 14
LETTER REQUESTING YEARBOOK INFORMATION
FROM A COLLEGE LIBRARY

Date

Library
College
Address
City, State, Zip Code

Dear Librarian:

Would you please send me a photocopy of all students in attendance with the last name of_____ from your yearbook for the years of _____. (1,2,3)

I am enclosing a check in the amount of _____ to cover photocopying expenses. The stamped, self-addressed envelope is for your convenience in replying.

Sincerely,
(your signature)
Address
City, State, Zip Code

Other Possible Inclusions:

1. I am currently putting together a surprise album for a friend's birthday and would like to include several photocopied pages from (his/her) college annual.
2. I have so few pictures of my (mother/father) from (her/his) early years that I would appreciate copies of any photos taken from (her/his) college annual.
3. Since the death of my (mother/father), I realize we have no pictures from (her/his) college days. Please send me a photocopy of any pictures from (her/his) college yearbook.

A letter to the college's alumni association, to the past student records office, or to the admissions office may also prove worthwhile. Samples 15 and 16 provide letters for contacting these offices. You might also ask who the president of the graduating class was for the year(s) your relative might have been in attendance. When will the next class reunion be? Who's the class coordinator for reunion or alumni affairs? It's possible you will be put in touch with the president or class reunion coordinator for your birthparent's or birthchild's class. He or she may know the person you seek and release a current address, or at least prove ready to forward a letter from you. Sometimes it's possible to purchase a copy of a class reunion pamphlet. This may include photos and current address information for class members.

SAMPLE 15
LETTER REQUESTING INFORMATION
FROM A COLLEGE ALUMNI AFFAIRS OFFICE

Date

Alumni Affairs Office
College or University
Address
City, State, Zip Code

Student Activities Director:
    I am trying to contact a friend from the class of _____. The last known address I
have is _____. Will you please check your alumni files for a past
student named _____ and send me a current address reference? (1)
    Your time and help is much appreciated. I am enclosing a stamped, self-addressed
envelope for your convenience in replying.

Sincerely,
(your signature)
Address
City, State, Zip Code

Other Possible Inclusion:
    1. *Add:* Please let me know the name and address of the Reunion Coordinator for
       the year(s) I've indicated.

You need at least a surname, approximate dates of attendance, and, of course, some idea of what school to address yourself to before you can make use of school records. You will probably have to piece this information together from two or more other sources of detail. Obviously, you should get as much information as possible from private, religious, or governmental agency records. Press for as much detail on educational background as you can get—most of it is unquestionably from two or more other sources of detail. The agency may give you useful school information that could provide leads. Statements such as "Your birthmother was vice-president of her college graduating class" or "Your father was active on his college basketball team" might bring about the following. You can estimate the year of graduation from the age given you by the agency. You've learned there are three colleges that cover the area your birthparents lived in at that time. Old yearbooks provide you the names of class officers, thus giving you a list to work from. If you have your birth name, this list may provide a clue. You may have the surname of one of the basketball team members or one of the class vice-presidents. Even a first name may provide you with a lead.

SAMPLE 16
LETTER REQUESTING PAST STUDENT RECORDS

Date

Registrar
Past Student Records
College
Address
City, State, Zip Code

Dear Registrar:

Please review your student records and forward to me information on a past student by the name of _____. (He/she) was in attendance at your school about (list several years if unsure of dates).

I understand some information cannot be released, but I have been advised the following will be made available to me.

Full name of student
Dates of attendance
Birth date and age at entrance
Major field of study
Degrees earned
Social Security number
Last school attended
Address upon entrance
Next of kin
Fraternal organizations

Thank you for your consideration and help. If you have any additional information, please supply me with that also. If your records do not list all of the above information, please send me what you have. (1)

I am enclosing a check in the amount of _____to cover any photocopying expenses. Also enclosed is a stamped, self-addressed envelope for your convenience.

Sincerely,
(your name)
Address
City, State, Zip Code

Other Possible Inclusion:

1. *Add:* If you will not release the information, but have a current address, will your policy allow you to forward a letter written by me?

Note: This is a very formal letter and one that will be considered with care. A more personal letter can sometimes win cooperation from a small school.

If school records can't give you a clear fix on where the person you seek is now, through school records, perhaps you can contact a classmate. Classmates, especially in more rural areas, can often prove helpful in tracing the movement of fellow alumni. Think of yourself. If an old friend of one of your classmates asked for your aid in locating that person, wouldn't you be inclined to help?

Don't despair if indications are that your birthparent or birthchild never attended a college or university. You can take much the same approach in searching through high school records. High schools conventionally issue yearbooks too. Many high school classes hold reunions at five- or 10-year intervals. Some school districts have conducted follow-up surveys on former students. Contact the superintendent of schools in the city or county where your search indicates the person you seek attended high school to find out if these and other records were kept, for what years they were kept, and where they are now housed.

Local newspapers commonly print the names of graduating high school seniors. Check with the newspaper or write the state archives in the appropriate state to see if you can get a photocopy of the list of graduating students in the appropriate town. You may need to check the lists for several years if you don't know the exact graduation year. Learning a particular class year for your relative makes it easier to request other school records. When writing to high school officials, married women will probably do best to sign letters with their married name. This eliminates the chance that school officials might double check to find if the letter of inquiry originated with someone who attended the school or not. Married men might consider writing in their wife's name, if the impression they wish to convey is that they writing for information on a school chum.

CHURCH RECORDS

It's possible to discover vital information through church records. If you have information on your birthparents' religious affiliation and have some idea if and when you were baptized or christened, you may be able to pursue these leads. Birthparents who learn that the adoptive family has had their child baptized or christened can follow much the same route of inquiry.

You should keep in mind that churches also have general membership records, as well as confirmation records, Sunday school records, marriage records, and death records on members. Sometimes a church will also have a record of a marriage performed there that was not of active church members.

Church records may exist on a central or regional (diocese, synod, and so on) level or be maintained locally. If you know the denomination with which your birthparent or birthchild was or is associated, call a local church of that denomination to find out what is kept locally and what is kept in the denomination's regional or central archives. Three books list addresses for local churches, dioceses, synagogues: *Handy Book for Genealogists* (Everton), *A Survey of American Church Records* (Kirkham), and *International Vital Records Handbook* (Kempt). Sample 17 offers a sample letter you can adapt when writing for church records.

Again, sometimes you may have to backtrack through a birth grandparent's religious records to get on the trail of more current information. In that case, you may well have to rely on church records that are kept in centralized archives. Here are the central records sources I've located for several denominations:

American Baptist
Samuel Colgate Baptist Historical
  Library
1106 South Goodman Street
Rochester, NY 14620-2532
Ask for state Baptist historical
  collections

American Jewish Archives
Hebrew Union College
3101 Clifton Avenue
Cincinnati, OH 45220-2488

**Catholic records are kept at the
  parish level.**
Consult the *Official Catholic Directory* for information on parishes.

Concordia Historical Institute
The Lutheran Church-Missouri
  Synod
801 De Mun Avenue
St. Louis, MO 63105
(314) 505-7900, fax (314) 505-7901
e-mail: chi@lrucom.com
Web site:

Congregational Historical Society
Congregational Library
14 Beacon Street
Boston, MA 02108
(617) 523-0470, fax (617) 523-0491
e-mail: lplato@tiac.net
Web site: <www.tiac.net/users/
  lpato/>

**The Church of Jesus Christ of
  Latter-day Saints**
Family History Library
Genealogical Society of Utah
35 North West Temple
Salt Lake City, UT 84150
(801) 240-2331

Archives of the Episcopal Church
606 Rathervue Place
P.O. Box 2247
Austin, TX 78768
(512) 472-6816, fax (512) 480-0437

Friends Historical Library
Swarthmore College
500 College Avenue
Swarthmore, PA 19081-1399
(610) 328-8496, fax (610) 328-8673
e-mail: friends@swarthmore.edu
Web site: <www.swarthmore.edu/
  Library>

**Lutheran Archives Center at
  Philadelphia**
7301 Germantown Avenue
Philadelphia, PA 19119-1794
(215) 248-6383, fax (215) 248-4577
e-mail: lutthelibeltsp.edu

Mennonite Library & Archives
Bethel College
300 E. 27th Street
North Newton, KS 67117-0531
(316) 284-5360, fax (316) 284-5286
e-mail: jthiesen@bethelks.edu

Reformed Church Archives
21 Seminary Place
New Brunswick, NJ 08901
(908) 246-1779, fax (908) 249-5412
e-mail: rgasero@aol.com
Web site: <www.rca.org>

Presbyterian Church (USA)
Department of History (Montreat)
318 Georgia Terrace
P.O. Box 849
Montreat, NC 28757
(704) 669-7061, fax (704) 669-5369

United Methodist Archives Center
Beegly Library
Ohio Wesleyan University
Delaware, OH 43015
e-mail: SJCOHEN@cc.owu.edu
Web site: <www.owu.edu>

Some church records have been published—the Works Progress Administration records taken on churches during the Depression can still prove very useful. Look in your library for a copy of the *Genealogist's Address Book* (Bentley) or the *Yearbook of American & Canadian Churches* 1990 if your church archives is not listed. Some churches, such as the Baptist Church, keep their records at the local level. If this is the case, contact your local church or the church in the area you are searching for information. Ask your local reference librarian or local genealogical society if they have a list of church archives.

The Daughters of the American Revolution (1776 D Street, NW, Washington, DC 20006-5392) has an excellent library of church records and will share information with nonmembers. As mentioned in a previous chapter, the Church of Jesus Christ of Latter-day Saints has a network of Family History Centers that are particularly good in genealogical collections.

There's no guarantee a local church will prove as cooperative as you'd like. Some will be very helpful, while others do not allow individuals to make use of their records. However, at meetings of search and support groups I've attended, numerous birthparents and adoptees have testified to the value of church records, particularly baptismal certificates. I'd say you have at least an even chance of winning access to these.

SAMPLE 17
LETTER REQUESTING INFORMATION
FROM CHURCH RECORDS

Date

Church Archives
Address
City, State, Zip Code

Dear Records Department:

I am trying to locate the church records on a family member (give full name if possible).

Please send me the following from your archives and any additional information you may have that will enable me to document fully (his/her) church activities, with the dates indicated for those. (1)

    1. Date of membership

    2. Church marriage records

    3. Branch church attended

If your records are not centralized, please send me the name of the local church/ parish functioning in the city of (name of city) during the years from (give estimated date of relative's birth) to (present/estimated date of relative's death).

I've enclosed a stamped, self-addressed envelope for your convenience. Also enclosed is a check for ___ to cover any photocopying expenses.

Thank you for your time and consideration in this matter.

Sincerely,
(your signature)
Address
City, State, Zip Code

Other Possible Inclusion:

    1. *Any of the following:* Death records, confirmation records, offices held in the church, information from letters of transfer to other branches.

Note: As set up here, this would go to a church archives. You can easily modify it for a branch (local) church. In that case, ask for all records kept and if they may be reviewed by you.

An adoptee who did not know her birth name or the names of her birthparents was told that she had been baptized four days after her birth. She knew her parents' religious affiliation and the city of her birth. She contacted the appropriate churches in her city of birth to trace all baptisms for the day indicated. There turned out to have been only one. She questioned the minister of the church where that baptism had been conducted and discovered her own birth name, her birthmother's name, the names of her birth godparents, and the circumstances of her birth.

Individuals who are searching records of Jewish congregations will find that the same considerations govern obtaining records from those. For other non-Christian congregations, such as the Baha'i, refer to an area center known to you, or to the national headquarters for direction on what records are kept and where. Whenever writing for religious records, keep your letter brief. Ask for the name of a clergyperson or other spokesperson you can refer to in your search area if the records you need are not centrally kept.

MILITARY RECORDS

Do you have reason to believe a missing relative served in any branch of the military? Was there a war or draft registration during this period? Then there's some chance you may be able to win information from military records on that person, although these can be difficult to obtain.

Military records from the period prior to World War I are open records. These would be of use to you if you were pursuing an aspect of your search through genealogy (see Chapter 4, "Reference Resources"). Subsequent military records are subject to very strict controls that limit access. The standard General Service Administration form "Request Pertaining to Military Records" states:

> Release of information is subject to restrictions imposed by the military services consistent with Department of Defense regulations and the provisions of the Freedom of Information Act (FOIA) and the Privacy Act of 1974. The service member (either past or present) or the member's legal guardian has access to almost any information contained in that member's own record. Others requesting information from military personnel/health records must have the release authorization in Section III of this form signed by the member or legal guardian, but if the appropriate signature cannot be obtained, only limited types of information can be provided. If the former member is deceased, surviving next of kin may, under certain circumstances, be entitled to greater access to a deceased veteran's records than a member of the public. The next of kin may be any of the following: unremarried surviving spouse, father, mother, son, daughter, sister, or brother.

You are actually next of kin to the service person you seek, but you will have to be able to prove that. If he or she is deceased, you may be able to get information through this channel. Write for the "Request Pertaining to Military Records" (Form #180) at one of the addresses listed below or to the National Personnel Records Center (Military Personnel Records), 9700 Page Blvd., St. Louis, MO 63132-5100. There is a fee, plus a service charge for the records search, which can vary, depending on the effort the search requires.

The request form asks a range of quite specific questions: full name, Social Security number, date and place of birth, branch of service, dates of active duty, and service number. You will probably not be able to answer most of them, as they include information that you as a searcher are not likely to know. Unfortunately, the odds are probably against your being able to use this information source to your advantage. However, if you have some combination of the requested details, it's worth a try.

If you know the branch of service in which your relative served, you can try writing the records center for that service branch. You may get nothing more than the standard GSA form, which is used by all the services. But you may get a response that includes the name of a records administrator you could contact for a clearer sense of what other types of military records might be made available to you. You might find that a partially completed request form wins more response from the service branch than from the National Personnel Records Center. You might also want to try addressing the Military Archives Division of the General Services Administration in Washington.

Here are the addresses for the various military records centers:

The Adjutant General
(of the appropriate state, DC, or Puerto Rico)

Air Force Manpower and Personnel Center
HQ AFPC/DPSRP
550 C Street W., Suite 19
Randolph Air Force Base, TX 78150-4721

Air Reserve Personnel Center/ DSMR
6760 E. Irvington Place, #4600
Denver, CO 80280-4600

Army National Guard Readiness Center
NGB-ARP
111 S. George Mason Dr.
Arlington, VA 22204-1382

Bureau of Naval Personnel
Pers-313D
2 Navy Annex
Washington, DC 20370-3130

Commandant CGPC-Adm-3
United States Coast Guard
2100 2nd Street, SW
Washington, DC 20593-0001

Commander, United States Army
Enlisted Records and Evaluation Center
Attn: PCRE-F
8899 E. 56th Street
Indianapolis, IN 46249-5301

Commander, United States Army Reserve
Personnel Center
Attention: ARPC-VS
9700 Page Avenue
St. Louis, MO 63132-5200

Department of Veterans Affairs
Records Management Center
P.O. Box 5020
Washington, DC 63115-5020

Headquarters, U.S. Marine Corps
Personnel Management Support
   Branch
(MMSB-10)
2008 Elliot Road
Quantico, VA 22134-5030

**Marine Corps Reserve Support
   Command**
(Code MMI)
15303 Andrews Road
Kansas City, MO 64147-1207

Military Archives Division
National Archives & Records
   Administration
Archives I Textural Reference
   Branch
Washington, DC 20408

**National Archives & Records
   Administration**
8601 Adelphi Road
College Park, MD 20740-6001

**National Personnel Records
   Center**
(Military Personnel Records)
9700 Page Boulevard
St. Louis, MO 63132-5100

U.S. Total Army Personnel
Command
200 Stoval Street
Alexandria, VA 22332-0400

Although the service records for the individual's term in whichever branch of the military he or she served are hard to come by, there are two other sources of military data to which you have somewhat freer access. Some Selective Service (draft registration) records are open to the public, but to make any headway here, you will need a full name, an indication of the local Selective Service Board and where the person registered, and, probably, a birth date. For registration information, write to Selective Service System, P.O. Box 4638, North Suburban, IL 60197-4638 or phone (708) 688-6888.

The Veterans Administration's Freedom of Information Act, Section 1.503, specifies information that must be released to persons about veterans:

> The monthly rate of pension, compensation, dependency and indemnity compensation, retirement pay, subsistence allowance, or educational allowance to any beneficiary shall be made know to any person who applies for such information.

Of course, in this case you have to be able to provide the name reference and enough service data so that the Veterans Administration can locate the records for the person you're tracing. And you'll note that the information you get won't include anything that amounts to identifying information—you're supposed to provide that.

The Veterans Administration provides extensive medical services through its network of VA hospitals. If you know or think the person you're seeking received medical treatment from the VA, you may get some information via that route. The person's name will be entered in the VA computer as having received medical treatment benefits.

I learned that the VA will release information that is not detrimental on any deceased officer. In working to trace my birthfather, I called the VA three times and each time I received different answers on what information I might be able to get. I never had enough information identifying my birthfather to be able to pull further information out of the VA computer, but I was at least able to induce an officer to run what I had through the computer. Name and service number would have produced the desired results, but what searcher will ever have a service number? I always told VA spokespeople that my father was ill and wanted to get in touch with an old navy friend. (The "old navy friend," in this case, would have been my birthfather.) I knew the branch of service, had a partial name, and battalion number, and knew where he fought and with what company, but this information was not sufficient for a computer check. A Social Security number and a full name, or a full name and date of birth, would be more valuable. Finally, my birthfather must have received medical treatment from the Veterans Administration to be listed and I did not know that he had received treatment. I was just trying.

The address of your local Veterans Administration, Benefits and Assistance Division, will be listed in your telephone directory under United States government. The VA will not release a current address for any veteran their records show still to be alive. However, I've found the VA will help you by forwarding a letter to a relative or "buddy." Write or ask your local VA office for details and the forms needed.

There are lesser-known sources of information on military personnel, but these are not easy to use. For example, each branch of the service has a book listing the officers serving in that branch. The book gives a lineal number (which indicates seniority), name, date of achieving the indicated rank, sex, and year of birth. The actual name of the book is different for each branch of the service, but a reference to the Lineal List or the Blue Book will be enough to make clear what you are after. For example, the Navy calls its book *Registry of Commissioned and Warrant Officers of the U.S. Navy and Reserve Officers on Duty.*

Before giving up on military records, check your local library or genealogical library for Lt. Col. Richard S. Johnson's *How to Locate Anyone Who Is or Has Been in the Military.* Ask your librarian if there are other books listing military resources.

For those of you using the computer to help with your search, the Internet has Web sites devoted to finding missing military buddies. Chapter 9, "Searching on the Computer," will list several of these resources.

Some time ago, I met a birthparent who had learned that her birthchild had gone to a family with a military background—the adoptive father was a career officer. She knew the date of the adoption and also where the family had originally come from (another state). She also knew that the family had adopted two other children. Through a long and arduous process that is too complicated to relate here, she was able to use a service Blue Book to locate the name corresponding to this information and a few other particulars that she knew. She went through three years of Blue Books—each with more than 52,000 names—before she was able to match a name and the particulars given for that person with information she knew about her birthchild's adoptive father.

Often a searcher will not even know for sure whether or not the missing relative ever served in the military. How would you know whether it could prove worthwhile to check out the possibility that he or she did? Here you'd work on the basis of probabilities. Was draft registration required about the time the person came of age? Were these war years? Was enlistment high during the years you're concerned with? The answers to these questions can give you a sense of whether a stint in the military is a reasonable assumption. Naturally, all these remarks have greater pertinence for men than women.

If you've learned that your birthfather or your birthson fought in World War II or another conflict, there's an outside chance his name appeared in a report filed by a war correspondent. Ernie Pyle, probably the most famous of war correspondents during World War II, eventually compiled and edited his reports in book form. At the end of his books are listings of the servicemen's names given in the book text. There are a fair number of books with this type of listing—*Guadalcanal Diary* by Richard Tregaskis, *Battle Report* by Walter Karig, and *Bloody Buna* by Lida Mayo are just three examples. Ask your reference librarian if she or he knows or has record of other books with this type of information. Check *Books in Print* (the subject index) and/or the library catalog under headings for a conflict in which your birthfather or birthson might have served.

PROPERTY RECORDS AND CITY DIRECTORIES

If you learn or guess that the person you seek owns or has owned home or other real estate, you may want to review property records maintained in and for your area of search. Property records are public records accessible to everyone. They are kept at the county courthouse or hall of records, where title searches on the part of individuals and businesses are a routine occurrence.

To use property records for a home owner, you would need to know both a name and a county of residence. If you have this information, you can refer to a general index of property records that will direct you to the specific document detailing acquisition or transfer of any property held in the name you have. Here, for example, is how a past entry for my family's home read in the Orange County (California) General Index of Grantors.

Title*	TR DD
Grantors Defendants*	Askin, Charles R. & Ida J.
Grantees & Plaintiffs***	Home S&L Assn. BFC
Number of Document	13238
Date of Filing	4/18/69
Book	8932
Page	44 *

* Nature of Instrument. The key explains this to mean Trust Deed.

** The full and exact title: Grantors & Defendants—also mortgagors, lessors, vendors, assignors, appointers, parties releasing, judgment debtors, wills bonds, parties against whom liens are claimed or attachments issued, mining locator, name of mine, proof of labor, and so on.

***The full and exact title: Grantees & Plaintiffs—also mortgagees, lessees, vendees, assignees, appointees, parties whose mortgages are released, and so on.

This reference pinpoints location of the actual title or deed to the property, which you can then have photocopied.

If the person you're tracking down continues to reside at the address given, from this point on it's a simple matter of making contact there. However, often it will turn out that the property has been transferred to new ownership. In that event, the new owners will be indicated, together with a record of the date of transfer. Your next step in this case would be to get in touch with the new owners. They may have some indication of where the previous owners moved.

For example, you've traced your birthfather to a county in a neighboring state. You have his name, but you can't find a current telephone listing. A check of the property records for the county shows he sold his home, and through the records you find out who purchased the home. You contact the current owners and ask if they have any information on where the previous owners are now living. They respond, "His company transferred him to San Diego." You can now follow the same process to establish an address reference in San Diego if there's no telephone listing given for him there.

The limitation here is that property records list only property owners. Those who rent or lease property will not be indicated. However, there is an alternate reference source that can be used as a supplement or in place of property records to locate persons living in a given locality, whether or not they own property there. This reference source is the city directory.

Not all cities have directories, and individuals who have unlisted telephone numbers may not be listed in a city directory. On the other hand, it is at times possible to locate an address reference for someone who isn't listed in a local telephone directory. City directories are published by companies—or sometimes by a chamber of commerce—primarily as a service to area businesspeople. They generally include lots of advertising in addition to address information. They are similar to telephone directories in many respects, but commonly provide more personal information than does a telephone directory. Of course this varies, depending on the directory referred to.

You will find city directories kept in state archives, in the office of the local chamber of commerce (but usually for that locality), or in public libraries. To discover what directories, if any, were kept for your area of search, ask your reference librarian for assistance. You may also find it helpful to refer to a local search and support group for information on available directories.

The two most widely used directories in past years have been *Cole Directory* (published by Cole Publications, 901 W. Bond Street, Lincoln, NE 68521) and the *Polk Directory* (published for many years by R.L. Polk & Company, 37001 Industrial Road, Livonia, MI 48150-1146).

Cole leases its directories to businesses, libraries, professional agencies, and certain individuals. Their directories are divided into several sections that include zip code, street address, and telephone. They offer a National Look-Up Department that charges $3.00 for the 1st minute and $2.00 for each additional minute. Subscribers to the service can request any information contained in previously issued directories. If your library leases a present directory, you may find this a valuable service.

The *Polk Cross-Reference Directory* has four types of listings: Alphabetical, Street Guide, Telephone Key, and Demographic Summary. From this directory, you can determine not only who resides at a given address, but neighbors as well. Names are also given. That may be of benefit if the person sought has moved since publication of the particular directory referred to. A subsequent directory, if there is one, should also provide an indication of who currently lives at an address previously given for that person. This directory often indicates the name of a spouse, place of employment, occupation, and whether the individual listed owned or rented property at the address given. Your state archives or a large public library should have past Polk directories. When referring to these, again use a range of years when requesting photocopies for listings of a given surname or for a street address.

Suppose you found a 1955 listing in a Polk directory. How would you use the information? If the person listed owned his or her house, you know there have to be property records—deeds and transfer-of-title papers when the person sold the residence. The indicated occupation could provide a useful clue in correlation with other information. What company did the person work for? Maybe this person was transferred by the company. Maybe employment records that exist indicate other address references for family members or show that the person left to work for another company. Possibly neighbors still in the area know where he or she moved to. Maybe one or another of them is still in touch on a regular or occasional basis.

There are a number of other directory publishers established in and serving different parts of the country. To learn the addresses and areas served, ask your local librarian or city chamber of commerce the name of the company in the city you are researching. They should be able to provide you with the information. Several books can be found in your library that list directory publishers. *Directories in Print* is one such book.

Write to the publishers who serve your area of search and ask what cities they print directories for, where their archives are located, and how you can receive a photocopy of any listings from years past. Ask the cost of providing photocopies. Enclose a self-addressed, stamped envelope for the publishers' convenience in replying to your inquiry.

VOTER REGISTRATION RECORDS

If you have a name and a probable or certain county of residence for the person you're seeking, you may be able to use voter registration records to your advantage. These can supply you with an address reference, indication of political party affiliation, and month and day of birth. (The year of birth is commonly not given, but this can be estimated with no great difficulty because a social services department will almost always release the age of your birthparents at the time of your birth.)

Current voter records are kept at the county level. These can generally be viewed without charge or proof of relationship. They may be called precinct books, rosters, or voter registrations. Older records may be kept at local libraries or possibly in the state archives. State law governs disposition of these records. Ask the appropriate county registrar of voters whether old records have been preserved and where they are kept.

One adoptee used voter registration records in this way: She was searching in the state of her birth, although she now lived hundreds of miles away in another state. She had learned the first names of her birthparents from the social services department that had administered her adoption. Her adoptive parents had been told the birthfather was from a small farming community in the state and had learned his last name from a social services clerk. She figured the community must lie close to the city where she was adopted, or her birthparents would have dealt with another large city's social services department. (This is the sort of deduction that can lead to valuable information or to a complete dead end. You sometimes have to take a chance.) She obtained a map of her home state and drew circles around areas with large cities and those with the largest social services departments. That left the primarily rural areas. Now she observed which of those lay closest to her city of adoption. She then wrote letters to the voter registration offices in the several counties included, asking for a record listing the first and last names of her birthfather as she knew them. Most did not respond, but one sent back a letter stating the information could not be released before payment of an indicated fee. The searcher quickly sent a certified check, assuming this response would not have come without good reason. The information that was returned gave the name, month, and day of birth; party affiliation; voting precinct number; and home address.

Another adoptee I know of traced her birthmother to a city in the South. But when she searched through the telephone directories for that area, she could not find the name she had listed. However, a visit to the voter registration office turned up the needed address. It turned out her birthmother had an unlisted telephone number. (A hint: If you suspect that someone you're searching for has an unlisted telephone number, call directory assistance and ask for the listing. Although the operator will not give you an unlisted number, the reply given will generally confirm whether there is an unlisted number for the party, which means at least you're searching in the right area. Otherwise, you will be advised that the records show no listing whatsoever.)

As you can see, reliance on voter registration records may require only a full name and a reasonable idea of the area of residence. But while the searchers in the above examples were rewarded with success, they might as easily have met with failure, since there is no compulsory voter registration in the United States.

MOTOR VEHICLES DEPARTMENT RECORDS

The vast majority of adult Americans have a driver's license, and driver's licenses have become one of the primary documents of identification for people in this country. Businesses routinely rely on them to verify addresses. Individuals also can use driver's license records to trace people, although you will need a good reason for doing so. Many searchers have found the most acceptable reason to be that they are trying to locate someone who passed a bad check. In most states, there are statutory limits on who may apply for and receive personal address information through the motor vehicles department, but these limitations are rarely stringently enforced. To find out what the rules and procedures are for your state, refer to your local motor vehicles department office, or write to the state address given in the appendix of this book. If there is a fee, the informational material you receive will indicate that.

In order to make use of these records, you will already need to know a full name and birth date, or a full name and address. (As a rule, searchers are working to obtain a current address.) You will have to fill out a request form that is forwarded to the state motor vehicles department office. The information that is returned to you, assuming the person holds a currently valid driver's license from that state, will be all that is listed on the driver's license itself. You may even receive an exact photocopy of the license. In any event, you will be given a current address reference. This avenue of search can be especially helpful for locating individuals who maintain unlisted telephone numbers.

SOCIAL SECURITY ADMINISTRATION

If, in fact, a loved one (once the name is known) can be located simply by tapping into this terrific resource that we, as a country/government, have created—then why not use it for the purpose of reuniting families? Some will immediately tout the privacy laws, but if you read the privacy laws, you will find that they were initially established to protect the citizens from government interference into out lives—NOT to protect us from simply finding and/or knowing our kin.[1]

The Social Security Administration (SSA) has a policy authorizing it to forward mail from one individual to another for "humanitarian purposes." Obviously, this is in cases where the first individual has no clear address reference for the person he or she seeks to contact. Since most adults have a Social Security number and file, chances are good that the SSA has at least a relatively recent employer's address reference, and may very well have a current home address, particularly if Social Security benefits are being paid.

I have not personally heard of any instances of search efforts pursued through this channel, but Hal Aigner, author of *Faint Trails*, does relate one experience. Mr. Aigner used the SSA to locate his half brother. He had his half brother's name, the approximate year of birth, the approximate years he served in the military, and his birthmother's name. It would have been very helpful to have a Social Security number, too, but that was out of the question. Mr. Aigner forwarded what information he had and gave the reasons he had for wanting the SSA to forward a letter he'd written to his half brother indicating a desire for contact.

The SSA, on receipt of this request, carefully worked to locate the half brother through its extensive record files. Once identification was made, the SSA wrote a letter to the half brother, giving the reasons why Mr. Aigner desired contact, pretty much as he had expressed them in his correspondence with the SSA. The SSA letter added that, even though the message was being forwarded by a government agency, there was no legal obligation to reply. A second letter went to Mr. Aigner, indicating that the SSA had identified his half brother and that an agency correspondence had been mailed, including the letter to be forwarded. The SSA added that there was no way to provide assurance that the letter would be received or that any response would follow; in any event, the SSA would send no follow-up letters.[2]

Essentially the same procedure applies for anyone hoping to make contact through the Social Security Administration. You should recognize that the desire to establish contact with a birthparent or a relinquished child may not be sufficient "humanitarian" reason of itself to prompt the SSA to work for you in search efforts. I suspect health problems, a legal need-to-know, or inheritance would be the most acceptable reasons for contact. I would not give genealogical inquiry as a reason.

If you want to try the SSA, write a letter to the Social Security Administration, Location Services, 6401 Security Blvd., Baltimore, MD 21235, saying you want to contact an individual. The best information to give is a complete name and Social Security number, but, as already observed, it's unlikely you'll have the latter. If you can provide a place and date of birth, however, that will usually suffice. Enclose in your envelope a letter to the person you want to contact, but *do not seal that letter.* The SSA must verify that it qualifies under the "Humanitarian Purposes" rule. Only after that verification has been made will they forward it. It gets sent to the person's last known employer, if the records do not show the person is currently drawing benefits that are sent directly to him or her. The employer then hands the letter to the person or, if he or she has since moved on, may forward it to a subsequent employer.

The Church of Jesus Christ of Latter-day Saints has a Social Security Index that lists many deceased persons who were issued a Social Security number. To use the index, you must have a name. This could be a grandfather, distant relative, or any birthfamily member believed to be dead. The information provided for a given name is: the Social Security number issued, date of death, state of residence at death, and zip code. From the zip code, you can determine all possible towns and cities within the designated code, one of these being the last residence of the person for whom you are seeking. Don't neglect this valuable source when you are using genealogy or searching for the location of family members. For Internet online Social Security Index records see Chapter 9, "Searching on the Computer."

NEWSPAPER AND MAGAZINE ADS

Local newspapers can prove a valuable source of information, especially if your search is concentrated in an area served by a newspaper that routinely reports births, weddings, and deaths among local residents. Your reference library can help you determine what newspapers exist or have existed in your area of search.

Earlier in this chapter, I made note of how reports of births, marriages, deaths, graduations, and so on can provide leads to the person being sought. In addition to that, you may find it worthwhile to run a personal ad in a newspaper in your area of search to generate information or enable contact.

Should you wish to pursue this possible route to information, there are one or two points particularly to keep in mind. First of all, there are laws that protect a person's rights of privacy. Your ad should not be so worded as to amount to an invasion of privacy. Remember, too, that when you run an ad naming someone, you can put the person named in the position of having to explain to people in the community. Identifying someone by name as the birthmother or birthfather of a relinquished child would be ill-advised for reasons related both to rights of privacy and to potential embarrassment. Discretion is always the basic rule to follow.

How you word your ad should be decided by the information you have and the information you need. Provided below are several examples of good ads that have been run; ads designed to win information without focusing unwelcome, curious attention on the personal affairs of the party sought.

> Genealogist needs information on the (name) family in the (specific area of search) area. Any information will be appreciated (your name and address).

> (Your married name) looking for old school friend (name of the person you are seeking). Anyone with knowledge of present address write (your name and address).

> Looking for lost relative (person you are seeking). Anyone with information please contact (your name and address).

If you find this sort of ad produces no information, you might try another approach, assuming you remain convinced there is information to be won in this community. You could offer a cash reward. You might simply add an element of greater interest. An ad like the following would certainly pique the interest of most people.

> Inheritance information needs to be forwarded to (person you are seeking). Anyone with information about the above, or other family members, please contact me or forward my address to same (your name and address).

Your inheritance information may be as little as informing your relative that your rights of inheritance were waived by the courts—check your state's laws, as in some states adoptees retain inheritance rights—or as much as stating you wish to include the missing person in your will. Again, whenever placing an ad in which you name another person, keep in mind that you don't want to embarrass or expose the person you are seeking. The chances of a satisfying future meeting can be jeopardized by thoughtless advertising and careless disclosure of facts.

If you still do not have a name to work with, you may wish to try a different approach. For example:

Information needed on babies born (date) at (name of hospital). Please contact (your name and address).

Anyone with information regarding children adopted from (name of agency) during (year) please contact (your name and address).

Genealogical magazines, in particular *Everton's Genealogical Helper* and *Heritage Quest* also take ads for information on missing family members (see Chapter 4, "Reference Resources"). Your ad in one of these would be slanted toward fellow genealogists rather than to someone who might be directly acquainted with the person you're seeking, so it would read differently:

(Your name and address) seeking information on (list full name if possible). Born in the state of (list state) on approximately (list several years). Is (he/she) in your city directory or phone book? Need address and married name. Please help.

Naturally, the particulars would vary according to whom you're seeking and what you already know.

THE SALVATION ARMY

The Salvation Army maintains a Missing Persons Bureau that: attempts to reunite immediate family members who are mutually interested in seeking one another. When a missing person is found, their whereabouts are never disclosed without their consent. We do not enter into legal matters, such as recovering child support or alimony, inheritance or estate matters, closed adoption cases, or parental kidnapping. Our large caseload does not permit us to handle requests involving tracing one's family tree.

The above is presented to illustrate the Salvation Army's aim as well as its restrictions for those seeking a missing person and wishing to use its service. To obtain a Missing Persons Inquiry Form, write Missing Persons Inquiry Form, The Salvation Army, 2780 Lomita Blvd., Torrance, CA 90505-5215, (800) 698-7728, fax (310) 534-7157. There is a $25.00 nonrefundable registration fee.

WHAT ELSE?

I've already mentioned genealogy in my discussion of reference resources. You may find that a study of genealogy will help you identify and locate information sources you had not previously recognized as available. This will prove especially helpful if you have leads that require tracing an extended family relationship.

I've also noted that under the Freedom of Information and Privacy Acts you can obtain information held on you by any agency of the federal government. Some of that information might provide previously unknown leads to your relative.

You may find an employment record you can use to good effect. Or you may uncover a record of association with a club, professional organization, and so on, that you can contact for membership information. School records are an excellent example of how your general request for information may produce records that contain additional sources that help complete the picture.

Whatever source of information you utilize, whether one of those listed in this book or known only to you, exercise imagination, common sense, and consideration for others in working to achieve full advantage from it.

There's no precise recipe to follow for guaranteed search results. You have to adjust to the unique circumstances that affect you in your search. Keep an open ear, an open eye, and an open mind; those will prove the most useful in assuring that you move toward your search goal.

NOTES

1.   This appears to be too logical to ever be adopted into policy. See pages 109-10 in *To Prison with Love* by Sandy Musser, available from Awareness Press, 162 SW 48th Terrace, Cape Coral, FL 33914.
2.   The account of one searcher's use of the Social Security Administration to locate another individual is chronicled by Hal Aigner in *Faint Trails* (Greenbrae, CA: Paradigm Press, 1980).

CHAPTER 7

Search and Support Groups, Researchers/Searchers, Consultants, Intermediaries, and the Courts

This chapter is broken down into several different types of help and support systems. As a searcher, you will need to decide which type of help you are looking for and this decision will be based upon several factors.

The first and most important factor is how involved do want to be in your search. Do you wish to conduct your own search or have someone else conduct the search for you?

The second factor is cost. For those searchers working on a budget, or those wishing an active part in their search, groups may be most effective because they are less expensive than search consultants and invite more active participation.

The third factor is your state's laws and the difficulty of your search.

Read through this chapter, along with Chapter 8, "Reunion Registries," and Chapter 10, "Search Resources and Services," then check your state's laws. This will give you an idea of what is available to you in your state and help in determining how to conduct your search. Throughout this chapter I have highlighted several groups and one intermediary organization which has provided me with their membership information, addresses, and costs. This should give the reader an idea of the variety of services available to those searching.

Only you can decide the type of help or service you need. Before beginning your search, it is important to think the above questions over carefully; it will greatly influence the way in which your search is conducted.

SEARCH AND SUPPORT GROUPS

Adoptee/birthparent search on a widespread scale and conducted openly is a recent phenomenon. For years individual men and women, with only their personal sense of determination and persistence to keep them going, explored previously untried sources and experimented with unproven methods in efforts to reestablish the broken connection that troubled them. In doing so, they experienced frustrating encounters with a broad range of people who could not or would not understand their motives. Fortunately, many also came into contact with others like themselves, who expressed understanding, who were willing—eager, in most cases—to share their own search experiences with them.

It is out of this kind of sharing that search and support organizations were born. Now there are groups spread across the country to which you can turn for understanding and encouragement of the sort that only other searchers can provide you.

A word of caution, however. You may believe groups will conduct the actual search for you, expecting that they are professionals who have all the right answers and can direct you to a single, simple solution. You may think that after one meeting you will be able to return home, write and send off one prescribed letter, then sit back and wait for all the desired information to come in by return mail.

If this is what you're looking for from a group, you're looking in the wrong place. Groups will help you establish a sense of direction; they will offer useful advice based on the experiences of group members. But they won't do your searching for you, and they are not in possession of some secret formula that will guarantee your search will suddenly become as simple as sending off an order to a mail-order catalog house. If you want someone else to do the work for you, there is generally only one way to accomplish that: Hire a professional.

Also, don't confuse your search and support organization with the reference section of your local library. You may hear about a publication of interest or a source of information that proved useful to one or another member of the group. But when it comes to looking up address references or locating a newspaper published in the area of your search—that is, generally learning to identify and hone in on the scattered sources of information you must often rely on in pursuit of leads—the appropriate source of aid is your reference librarian.

So, what benefit do you get from a group? You get reinforcement of your hopes. You get encouragement in pursuit of an intensely personal goal that many others around you will not understand and may not support. You get advice on possible directions to take in your search. You get a perspective on your attitudes toward yourself in your search and toward others reacting to you during this period—a perspective that comes from people who have been or are where you are now.

Your attitude, how you define your needs, and how the local chapter of the search and support group to which you turn is run, all determine what you can and will receive from the group. The potential is considerable.

Understanding Friends

To begin with, groups provide you a source of new friends who understand what you are doing. Here is a place you can come to and not have to explain why you are searching. You won't be put into a defensive position on a controversial social problem; you won't continually find yourself having to restate your right to know. And these people understand the problems you are or will be facing during your search.

If you've decided to search, conducting the search will assume a very important part of your life. For those who find few members of their family willing or able to understand and few friends who give genuine support, groups offer a place to keep your sanity. Don't we all feel the need to talk about our accomplishments in life? Our hopes? Our fears? When we set out to do a difficult task and find we had more strength and courage than we thought, isn't it pleasant to have friends who recognize and acknowledge that difficult task well done? When your search hits a snag or dead end and you have no other leads to follow, nowhere else to turn, supportive friends may be the impetus that enables you to dig deeper inside yourself, to start anew in another direction.

The friends you meet will have much in common with you and each other. At the same time, they will come from varied backgrounds, so that each has a personal line of experience and viewpoints to share. You will fit in, both for the goals and motivations you share with other group members, and for the individual differences that exist between you and each of the others.

Every variety of adoptive situation is likely to be reflected among group members. Here, more likely than anywhere else, will be people you can talk to about your own situation and find an open, listening ear with an understanding, sympathetic mind responding directly to what is common or uncommon in your circumstances. No other group of friends can be supportive in quite that fashion.

That is not to say that your search and support group will or ought to replace friendships you have developed over the course of the years. In a great many instances, the opposite will happen. Because you have available to you the interest and encouragement of members of the group, you may well find it easier to forgive and tolerate what you see as the failings of personal friends who don't understand your need to know. The organization is set up to be an added support resource for you, not to supplant previous relationships to which you had looked for support.

Like individuals seeking guidance, groups also need to find support, encouragement, and a place to share new ideas and information. The American

Adoption Congress (AAC) offers groups this type of help (see Chapter 10, "Search Resources and Services").

Search Workshops

Many search and support groups conduct search workshops on a regular basis. These are special meetings, featuring no speakers or films, to which members bring all documentation of their search efforts to date. The entire session is given over to reviewing work in progress and discussing new directions to follow.

How the workshop specifically operates depends on the group's membership and organization. In a small, rural area, your group workshop may consist of only three or four members, each possibly at a different stage of search or involved in a different type of search. In a large urban area, your group may be set up so that certain members are designated to act as search assistants. An occasional group will have trained specialists as search assistants. You may work with a single member or a search assistant. In large groups, you may join together in small subgroups with others searching in the same area of the country you're concentrating on.

Regardless of the group's size or organization, you can substantially benefit from a search workshop. You get the opportunity to present your search work to others who have had search experience. Their questions and suggestions can provide you with new alternatives to explore or give you the courage to carry on a difficult line of approach. Someone may have had a similar experience in an area of search that's proven troublesome for you. Someone whose search focus is quite different from yours may nevertheless have an insight into your situation that can throw things into clearer perspective for you.

Don't underestimate your value to the other group members during these workshops. You may have tapped a source of information others have overlooked. You may simply have organized your search effort in a fashion that makes search manageable for you; another group member without that capacity for self-organization can benefit through your sharing of your experience in that area. Such sharing also benefits you. Your suggestion may prove the key to another member's further progress in searching. Your contribution may be just a simple statement of understanding and shared frustration that helps someone else through a difficult moment. To know you can make that kind of contribution provides you with a source of strength in an endeavor that can make heavy demands on your emotional strength.

There is no exact formula for solving search problems. Any insight, information, or advice on new methods to consider can prove of use to you and those in the workshop with you. As a beginning searcher, you may feel you have nothing but questions to raise, when in fact you may be voicing questions others need to consider. There is no demand that you contribute any minimum benefit to the others in the group. All you need bring to the group is a record of your own experiences for review and a willingness to share your interest in and thoughts on the search work of fellow members.

Search and Support Newsletters

Many groups publish a newsletter for their members. These will be printed monthly, bimonthly, or simply as funds allow. The usual listings include announcements of meetings, with dates, times, and speakers indicated. Other upcoming events of interest will be noted as well. In addition, each newsletter will make an effort to keep you abreast of changes in state law that affect adoptee/birthparent search, progress on class-action lawsuits in the courts, and new search-related information from whatever source. Reviews of books and magazine articles will provide a useful service, directing you to discussions of adoption and search considerations you may be interested in reading, or to new Internet Web sites you might want to connect to on your computer

Your group's newsletter may contain announcements of television or radio programming you will want to know of. Is there an interview scheduled with a legislator or other government spokesperson on the subject of changes (or no changes) in current adoption laws relating to search and reunion possibilities? Look in your newsletter. Have you received advance notice of such an interview? Recognize that through the newsletter you have the opportunity to keep other members abreast of what is going on around them. Call your group's newsletter coordinator to suggest mention of it for the benefit of other members. You can receive and pass on notice of conventions or other public forums of interest to searchers in the same way.

One part of any newsletter will be reports of other searchers' successes. It is exciting to read about how a member located a birthparent, a relinquished child, or a lost sibling. News of happy reunions of course provides a welcome note of encouragement to all searchers. However, the value of these articles often goes further. A review of methods used in a highlighted successful search can be a source of new ideas for you. A word of caution on a search technique that backfired can alert you to a mistake you may unwittingly be duplicating. Reading of difficulty in a search, or of nonreceptivity on the part of an individual located through search, can help keep you grounded in reality.

HOW TO FIND A SEARCH AND SUPPORT GROUP

Search and support organizations are volunteer groups that usually do not have an established, permanent office. Meetings are held in libraries, public halls, or private homes. It can take some effort to locate the group in your most immediate area, but chances are you will be able to.

Those active in the search movement continually meet people who say, "If only I had known of your group when I did my search." It is a genuine problem for the search movement that many people who want and need to be reached simply do not know how to make contact. Search and support group members strongly encourage other searchers to seek out the support that is available.

By reading this book you have been alerted to the existence and work of many search and support organizations. Knowing they exist, that there may be one in your area or nearby, is half the battle. Now, to locate a group.

As with so many volunteer organizations on a local level, a group's address often changes with the installation of each president. The organization per se has no fixed address. Some groups have solved this problem by renting a post office box. Others simply direct mail to be forwarded to the new presiding officer's address. A few may drop from sight after a period of time or be replaced by a new group with a new membership.

Perhaps you've been given an address for a group and received a reply that the group has ceased to function. Do not assume that all adoptee/birthparent groups have gone out of existence.

Review the listing of highlighted groups which follows this section. A nationally established organization may be able to direct you to a nearby affiliated group you are not aware of. An organization functioning primarily in your state may be able to help you also. Chapter 10, "Search Resources and Services," offers services that can provide you with the current address of groups functioning within a given area.

Search Triad, Inc., a group in Arizona, provided me with their 1997 Contact Report showing new contacts, the action taken on those contacts, and the sex of those requesting information.

New Contacts (Female = 273, Male = 80):

Adoptees	202
Birthmothers	54
Birthfathers	14
Siblings	30
Other (professionals, etc.)	44
No Information Given with Request	9
	353

Action Taken:

Sent membership sheet & International Soundex Reunion Registry form	332
Information given on the telephone	21
Referred to other groups	78
Referred to Independent Search Consultants (see later in this chapter)	65
	496

The above report shows the cooperation between this group and other support systems.

Once you've located a group, allow yourself the opportunity to check out whether you'll feel comfortable in it. Most groups will permit you to attend a meeting as a guest. This makes it possible for you to learn something about the group's workings and to meet those with whom you'd be in contact as a member. Find out both what programs the group has had in the past and what activities are scheduled and projected for the future. Your questions will generally be welcomed; members will appreciate your interest in their work and organization. Call ahead to express your desire to attend a meeting as a guest-observer and learn the group's policy on visitors.

In the state-by-state reference lists in the appendix, you will find address information on groups active in each state and on groups involved in different types of search activities. (Some groups focus primarily on helping birthparents, while others are more oriented to adoptees. Here and there are groups that aid both adoptees and birthparents but concentrate on those involved with a particular agency.) Since the number of groups functioning today is large, the list is not all-inclusive.

In choosing groups to highlight here, I have considered how long a group has been functioning; whether it has been recognized by state agencies (recognition, while not a formal sanction, does indicate some degree of informal cooperation between state agencies and the search group); whether it has served as a particularly good source for specialized search information; and whether it has a strong national or state headquarters. Some of the groups and resources included in the following section are more limited in scope of operation than others. However, these organizations seem to take the lead in offering a sense of stability and permanence to the movement, although your needs may be still better served by a local or regional group not included among those highlighted here. As a general rule, there is a commitment to cooperation among groups. They will direct you to another group that may fit your needs better if you are not wholly comfortable with the one you've chosen or do not feel its focus fits your needs. (In fact, be leery of any group that displays evident jealousy or hostility toward other search groups.)

There are several important points to remember when reading the information that follows:

1. Membership fees listed are accurate at the time of publication; these fees may change due to increasing operating costs.
2. Always include a self-addressed, stamped envelope with all your correspondence.
3. As is common among many volunteer groups, the addresses and phone numbers listed may be of the residences of the groups' current office holders and as such are subject to change. This information is being included to offer you a starting point for contacting these groups. If the addresses and phone numbers prove no longer current, perhaps your letter will be forwarded, or a new phone number can be obtained.

4. Search consultants/searchers working in groups will generally charge a
    fee to do your search or help you obtain information, while researchers
    work at no cost except out-of-pocket expenses.

Adoptees-in-Search (Maryland)

Adoptees-in-Search (AIS)is located in the metropolitan Washington, DC,
area and has a nationwide membership. Chartered in 1975, this group and
continues to operate while addressing the 2500 inquiries a year from those
searching.

This unique group offers searchers a choice: They can do their own search
with expert help, they can have their search done for them with AIS taking the
primary role, they can seek a court order to "break the adoption seal" with AIS
doing a confidential intermediary search.

AIS also maintains a Mid-Atlantic States Search Registry (see Chapter 8,
"Reunion Registries").

Membership is open to anyone 18 years of age or older. (Adoptees under 18
are allowed membership with the written consent of the adoptive parents.)
The $75 tax-deductible membership donation entitles the new member to
inclusion in its search registry, to an individual search orientation, an evaluation conference, a newsletter, and more. AIS is funded by tax-exempt donations, membership fees, and fees for services.

Office hours are 9:00 A.M. to 5:00 P.M., Monday through Friday. To receive
information by mail, write Adoptees-in-Search, P.O. Box 41016, Bethesda,
MD 20824, or call (301) 656-8555, fax (301) 652-2106. Please enclose a
stamped, self-addressed envelope with all correspondence.

Adoptees' Liberty Movement Association (ALMA)

On March 21, 1971, Florence Fisher, now president of Adoptees' Liberty
Movement Association (ALMA), ran the following newspaper ad:

> Adult who was an adopted child desires contact with other adoptees to
> exchange views on adoptive situation, and for mutual assistance in
> search for natural parents.

I'm sure Ms. Fisher had no idea this ad would generate the response it did and
prove to be the seed that led to the establishment of one of the largest search
and support groups in the country. ALMA would go on to reunite thousands of
its members.

ALMA is a nonprofit, tax-exempt agency based in New York. The organization currently has chapters and satellite groups nationwide, and active,
working members in nearly every state. All ALMA staff members are volunteers.

The following statement from an ALMA brochure well illustrates the organization's aims:

> As ALMA has grown over the years the objectives have expanded to encompass the changing needs of its members. Thousands have united to raise the consciousness of the country to the injustice of "sealed records." Mutual assistance in search still remains a priority. A network of understanding, compassion and information exists to remind members that they are not alone. The RIGHT TO KNOW is an emotional issue, but also a legal one.

ALMA offers many services to its members. One such service is a national network of "search buddies," individuals working through ALMA to offer advice and mutual assistance to other members. Each chapter has coordinators and search consultants, all of whom have completed their search and are now willing to volunteer time, advice, and moral support to any active member. Various groups offer "rap sessions" where members may meet to discuss their experiences and receive support.

Searchlight is ALMA's national newsletter. Local newsletters are distributed to members in each chapter, and these provide information about meetings and other events at the local level, indicating meeting places, times, and speakers. Both *Searchlight* and the local newsletters offer articles about progress in legal actions, reviews of publications of interest, stories about those who have found the one they are seeking, and new search techniques.

Registration in ALMA is $65 and includes free membership in their registry for the year in which you join. Membership dues are $45 annually which includes registration in the International Reunion Registry Data Bank (see Chapter 8, "Reunion Registries"). No additional fees are ever charged. ALMA welcomes any interested person into its groups but will not actively engage in search activities for those under 18 years of age.

Check your local telephone directory white pages for mention of a possible nearby chapter, or write to ALMA, National Headquarters, P.O. Box 727 Radio City Station, New York, NY 10101-0727, (212) 581-1568, fax (212) 765-2861, e-mail: ALMAINFO@aol.com, Web site: <www.almanet.com/>. Please enclose a stamped, self-addressed envelope with all correspondence.

Adoption Crossroads

In 1986, Joe Soll, C.S.W., founded Adoption Crossroads to offer search help and adoption education to all members of the Triad: adoptee, birthparent, and adoptive parent. A second purpose is to "educate all those whose lives are affected by adoption and thereby protect them from ignorance and inappropriate and unnecessary fear and paranoia and from unwitting manipulation by others."

This group went on to organize The Council for Equal Rights in Adoption (see Chapter 10, "Search Resources and Services") and the New York State Task Force on Adoption, which includes 35 adoption agencies working to change the sealed records law.

Each branch holds a monthly meeting offering a search workshop. In addition to the monthly search workshops, members may receive help by phone from the Adoption Crossroads headquarters office which is open 18 hours a day. Rap groups are held weekly, no reservation is needed. Significant others are welcome if space is available. Before each rap group meets, an orientation for newcomers is held. Nonmembers may only attend one rap session.

Adoption Crossroads maintains a computerized reunion registry with over 5,000 names of adoptees and birthparents listed. Since it is an affiliate of International Soundex Reunion Registry, an ISRR form is given to all those requesting information kits. Annual membership fees are based on a sliding scale from $0 to $75. Adoption Crossroads currently has approximately 300 active members.

The group's newsletter, *Access*, provides articles on adoption rights, reprints of related subject matter, and guest submissions. Its columns include an *Access* calendar, new locations, letters, and a list of other area groups, along with meeting times and individuals to contact.

A library is located in the Adoption Crossroads headquarters for use by all members. Adoption-related books may also be purchased. A wide variety of other services are offered, including a speakers bureau, list of referrals, and "soft shoulders" support program.

Adoption Crossroads is headquartered in New York City, with chapters located throughout New York, New Jersey, and Vermont. Information or membership forms may be obtained by writing Adoption Crossroads, 356 E. 74th Street #2, New York, NY 10021, (212) 988-0110, fax (212) 988-0291, e-mail: cera@mail.idt.net, Web site: <www.adoptioncrossroads.org/>. Please enclose a stamped, self-addressed envelope with all letters.

Adoption Network Cleveland

Betsie Norris founded this extremely active group in 1988. Their mission statement reflects both their purpose and beliefs:

> Recognizing that adoption is a lifelong process and that a unified voice is a strong voice, the mission of Adoption Network Cleveland is to advocate for truth and honesty on behalf of all members of the adoption triad (adoptees, birthparents, and adoptive parents). We pursue personal empowerment, community awareness and social change through support, education and promotion of openness in adoption practice, policy, and law.

As of this writing the group's membership is 700 plus. Four support/ discussion meetings are held each month (each in a different location in the Greater Cleveland area), along with monthly search workshops. Their newsletter, *Adoption Network News*, comes out every two months and offers members current news from the Cleveland area as well as national adoption news. Adoption Network Cleveland is both a member of AAC and an affiliate of ISRR. Membership dues are $30 for individuals, $40 for family, and $75 for organizations.

Information or an application to join can be received from Adoption Network Cleveland, 291 East 222 Street, Cleveland, OH 44123-1751; (216) 261-1511, fax (216) 261-1164, e-mail: bln2@po.CWRU.EDU, Web site: <pages.prodigy.com/adoptreform/anc.htm>.

Adoption Triad Midwest

In 1979, Sandy Johnson began the Adoption Triad Midwest which has remained an active and vibrant search group through the years. They are considered an excellent resource to groups in other states and demonstrate the value of experience and perseverance.

The following statement is included in their newsletter to remind old members and illustrate to prospective members the purpose of Adoption Triad Midwest.

> Actively networking with more than 300 support groups, the Adoption Triad Midwest is non-profit and dedicated to providing search assistance, emotional support and education to its members and the community on the subject of adoption searches. We are aggressively involved in making sealed records available to adoptees and birth parents who want access.

Informal monthly meetings are held in Omaha and revolve around the search issues of those in attendance. The *Adoption Triad Midwest Newsletter* is published every two months and include notices of upcoming events, member updates, meetings, Internet Web sites, and a warning section to alert members about information and services that are costly and provide no real results.

Adoption Triad Midwest cooperates with AAC and ISRR. Their membership is $25 yearly, and no search fee is charged for the help provided. Contact should be made at Adoption Triad Midwest, P.O. Box 45273, Omaha, NE 68145-0273.

Concerned United Birthparents (CUB)

Concerned United Birthparents (CUB) was incorporated in October 1976 as a nonprofit mutual help organization providing support for mothers and fathers who had lost children to adoption. In addition to CUB's original purpose of providing member-to-member support, its goals are to assist adoption-separated people in locating their missing relatives; to encourage legislative and social policy changes; to promote honesty and openness in adoption and offer education about separation and adoption issues; and to prevent unnecessary family separations.

One way CUB extends education is through the publication of books and pamphlets. These include *Thoughts for Newly Searching Adoptees*, *Thoughts for Birthparents Newly Considering Search*, *Understanding the Birthparent*, *The Birthparent's Perspective on Adoption*, *Child Abuse & Adoption*, and *The Social Worker's Role in Adoption*.

A monthly newsletter, *The Cub Communicator*, provides a list of "Soft Shoulders Available." These "soft shoulders" are adoptees, birthparents, or adoptive parents, along with their phone numbers, who are available "when you need to talk to someone who really understands."

A Reunion Registry is offered to all members. CUB encourages members to also register with International Soundex Reunion Registry (see Chapter 8, "Reunion Registries").

Concerned United Birthparents has representatives in Alaska, Arizona, California, Florida, Illinois, Michigan, New Mexico, New York, South Dakota, Tennessee, and Vermont. Branches can be found in California, Colorado, Illinois, Iowa, Kentucky, Maryland, Massachusetts, Minnesota, Nebraska, Ohio, and Washington, DC. If your state is not listed here, write to the National Headquarters to learn of new representatives or groups. There are members in all 50 states and several foreign countries.

CUB branches conduct monthly support meetings and search workshops that welcome birthparents, adoptees, adoptive parents, and members of the community. Current annual membership dues are $50 for new members and $35 for renewals.

If you wish to join or receive more information, write to Concerned United Birthparents, National Administration Headquarters, 2000 Walker Street, Des Moines, IA 50317, (800) 822-2777, fax (515) 263-9541, e-mail: cut@webnations.com, Web site: <www.webnations.com/cub/>. Please enclose a stamped, self-addressed envelope with all correspondence.

Donors' Offspring

Donors' Offspring was formed in May 1981 by Candace Turner. Its purpose is "to give support to all involved with high-tech conceptions, including search support to donor and recipient families who wish to exchange information or make contact."

This unique group has a national membership and meets approximately four times a year via a conference telephone call. To participate in this conference call, send a $20 check, along with your phone number, to the address listed below. These conference calls take place on a Friday evening. Members who reside near one another may meet more often.

A newsletter is printed quarterly and can be received for a subscription fee of $20 per year. Membership dues are $5, plus $20 to contact other members. This group is affiliated with International Soundex Reunion Registry. To obtain more information or to submit your membership, write to Donors' Offspring, P.O. Box 37, Sarcoxie, MO 64862; (417) 673-1905, fax (417) 673-1906, e-mail: Candace@usa.net. Please enclose a stamped, self-addressed envelope with all correspondence.

Kansas City Adult Adoptees Organization (KCAAO)

This organization, incorporated in the state of Missouri in 1978, explains its purpose in the following statement: "To increase the education and knowledge of members of the corporation in family history, genealogical and adoptive records."

Kansas City Adult Adoptees Organization (KCAAO) holds monthly meetings offering help and information to its 1,200 members. There is a one time membership fee of $35.

Training and assistance is limited to persons searching for an adult, unless an urgent health problem exists. Applications for membership from those who are of minority age will be filed and brought forward when the person reaches the legal age of majority.

For more information or an application to join, send your inquiry to Kansas City Adult Adoptees Organization, P.O. Box 11828, Kansas City, MO 64138; (816) 229-4075 before 10 A.M. or (816) 363-2810 after 6 P.M.; e-mail: Whassler@Prodigy.net. Please enclose a stamped, self-addressed envelope with all correspondence.

Operation Identity

This group was founded in 1979 by Sally File and describes itself as "a nonprofit organization embracing all facets of the adoption triad, adult adoptees, adoptive parents and birth parents." It is involved in search and support activities, offers speakers to local groups, and is working to motivate change in state laws on sealed adoption/relinquishment records. The organization is located in New Mexico and is recognized by the New Mexico Human Services Department.

Membership is open to searchers 18 years of age or older and the group requires that the person(s) who is the object of search also be at least 18. Membership dues are $20, which includes registry in the International Soundex Reunion Registry; an application for ISRR will be sent to you when you receive the Operation Identity membership brochure.

This group has approximately 250 members, meets monthly, and sends out a quarterly newsletter to all members. Members are provided search advice and taught procedural techniques at no additional fee. Sally File stated in a letter to me, "I personally will see to it that if we can't help we will refer on to someone who can." Searchers should place great value on this personal commitment. Operation Identity has a search coordinator who is certified through the New Mexico Courts as a Confidential Intermediary.

For additional information, or to receive a membership application, write Operation Identity, 13101 Blackstone Road NE, Albuquerque, NM 87111, (505) 293-3144. Please enclose a stamped, self-addressed envelope with all correspondence.

Oregon Adoptive Rights Association (OARA)

This is an extremely active group both in search and in dealing with local and national issues. Their brochure says the following:

> OARA is a volunteer, non-profit organization incorporated under the laws of the State of Oregon in 1979 to provide support to those involved in the adoption experience. To advise and assist in searching for separated family members. To educate the public about adoption issues. To advocate legislative reform of adoption records.

OARA seems to thrive on member involvement, as they provide regular monthly meetings, search workshops, and support groups. A Web site allows members to contact all board members as well as to reach out to the ever-growing Internet population.

The *Oregon Adoptive Rights Association Newsletter* is sent quarterly to all members and includes dates and times of meetings along with articles, poetry, new studies, and announcements. This is an informative newsletter covering issues not just in Oregon, but those that affect the movement overall.

New members are automatically placed in OARA's large computerized registry. This registry has made many matches and is an excellent resource. To ensure an even larger search base, members are also encouraged to join the International Soundex Reunion Registry.

OARA has continually reached out to the adoption movement and general public, offering help and information. This group has been involved with American Adoption Congress conferences and works with other groups to the benefit of the searcher. Much to their credit, OARA was selected to represent the open records/equal access position on the *News Hour with Jim Lehrer*, "Adoption Reform Debate." Membership dues are $40 with renewals at $25. Currently there are 155 members. For more information, contact OARA, P.O. Box 882, Portland, OR 97204, (503) 235-3669. Enclose a stamped, self-address envelope if material is requested. They can also be contacted at their Web site: <www.oara.org>.

Organized Adoption Search Information Services, Inc. (OASIS)

Organized Adoption Search Information Services, Inc. (OASIS) is a nonprofit group chartered in Florida in 1980 by Rachel S. Rivers. The group's purpose is described on its General Information Sheet.

> OASIS knows the need for personalized assistance for each individual searcher since no two searches are alike and we pride ourselves in our ability to provide this type of help to everyone who comes to us. We are also very proud of the reputation we have earned over the years through our work in bringing about hundreds of reunions.

This group is open to all individuals who have reached their 18th birthday and to adoptive parents searching for a child under 18, as long as it is evident that such a search is for the well-being of the child. OASIS has excellent resources and offers a worthwhile vehicle for networking and exchanging valuable contacts.

For each member, a search file is created, updated, and kept at OASIS headquarters. A birth date match-up registry, known as the OASIS Birthdate Index, is available to members free of charge with their membership and for a $5 one time fee for nonmenbers. In addition, all members are provided with an International Soundex Reunion Registry Form (see Chapter 8, "Reunion Registries," for both reunion registries).

Dues are currently $70 for searching members. Other costs include any out-of-pocket expenses connected with the search, including telephone calls, duplicate records, or costs to obtain vital documents. Each member is required to provide one book of first-class stamps which will go into the postage fund.

To receive more information or a registration form, write OASIS, Inc. Headquarters, P.O. Box 53-0761, Miami Shores, FL 33153. Please enclose a stamped, self-addressed envelope with all correspondence.

Orphan Voyage

This is the oldest search and support group in the United States of which I am aware. Founded as the Life History Study Center in Philadelphia on September 19, 1953, it has survived several changes of name and address. Founder Jean Paton has amassed literature, newspaper accounts, and papers on adoption from around the world; this collection is probably the largest of its kind in existence.

Some Orphan Voyage groups offer search and support while others offer search services. Their workers and volunteers are scattered across the country.

There are branch groups located in various states, but the organization prefers working with searchers on a one-to-one basis rather than in groups. Meeting schedules, membership dues, and services can be obtained from one of the Orphan Voyage groups listed in the state-by-state section of this book.

You can address correspondence or direct telephone inquiries to any of the individual affiliates mentioned in the state lists in the appendix to learn of meeting dates, membership dues, and services offered. Groups are located in Alabama, Arizona, Florida, and Texas. Please enclose a stamped, self-addressed envelope with all correspondence.

Search Triad, Inc.

Search Triad, Inc., founded in the spring of 1976, describes itself as "an independent organization offering a free service of idea exchange, volunteer support and educational guidelines in the adoption triangle." This group has grown to be an extremely active search and support group with current membership between 125 and 150.

Members are offered monthly meetings, a quarterly newsletter, guest speakers, panels, videos, and use of the organization's reference library. Meetings are open to adults in search. Search Triad, Inc. does not advocate birthparents searching for minors or minors searching for birthparents. Counseling referrals are made. Membership dues of $45 per year include registration in the International Soundex Reunion Registry. Membership renewals are $30 per year.

Each new member is assigned a "volunteer" search assistant. Search Triad attempts to present the searcher with a complete package. New members are "required to attend meetings, read books & be prepared for their reunion. We [Search Triad, Inc.] care about not only the searcher but the person found as well."

Those interested in this group should write Search Triad, Inc., P.O. Box 10181, Phoenix, AZ 85064-0181, or call (602) 834-7417. Please include a stamped, self-addressed envelope with all correspondence. Web site: <home.att.net/~kehgchu>.

Tennessee's the Right to Know

To say that Tennessee's the Right to Know is a hard-working, productive search group is an understatement. This group was founded in late 1980 by Denny Glad and Nancy Kvapil (who were soon joined by Jalena Bowling and Debbie Norton) with the purpose of offering search help and guidance to all adult members of the adoption triad.

The vast majority of those assisted by TRTK live out of state. To deal with this problem, a few highly dedicated members spend hours working with letters, computers, and phone calls. There are no regularly scheduled meetings and no fees are charged other than such incurred expenses as postage, telephone calls, parking fees, copying fees, etc.

Those adopted through the old Tennessee Children's Home Society (and birthfamily members searching for anyone who was placed through that agency) should contact Tennessee's the Right to Know as one of their first search steps. As should anyone who was born in Memphis, or who relinquished a child for adoption in Memphis. All others should contact the support group closest to the place of birth of the adoptee (as shown on the amended birth certificate) or closest to where the child was relinquished.

A reunion registry is maintained by Tennessee's the Right to Know, in conjunction with the Tennessee Coalition For Adoption Reform, which currently has in excess of 4,000 entries from all parts of the country. Upon request, your name will be entered into this reunion registry at no charge. While searches are not conducted for minors, their names may be entered into the group's reunion registry.

All of Tennessee's various search and support groups (see Appendix I under Tennessee) provide dedicated volunteer services to persons who contact them. However, because of the groundswell in recent years of national publicity about the illegal activities of Georgia Tann, who headed up the Memphis branch of the old Tennessee Children's Home Society, this group probably has one of the highest volumes of requests for search assistance of any such group in the country.

Tennessee searchers may write Tennessee's the Right to Know, P.O. Box 34334, Bartlett, TN 38134, (901) 386-2197 or (901) 373-7049, e-mail: FFMJ26B@prodigy.com. Please enclose a stamped, self-addressed envelope with all correspondence.

Wichita Adult Adoptees

Kansas records were opened in 1951 that allowed adult adoptees to obtain their birth certificate. This certificate provides the name given at birth and the name of the birthmother at the time of birth; it may or may not list a birthfather. While this may be enough for some searchers, most of those seeking a connection to the past are just beginning. In May 1981, Wichita Adult Adoptees was founded. Currently, they work with over 100 members, living in or out of Kansas, to offer support and help to complete each search whether it be a reunion, updated medical information, or genealogy.

WAA membership is $25 yearly. Monthly meetings (except July and August) are held for all adult members of the triad. Their newsletter, *News 'n Views*, comes out every other month and offers members local and national information. Several pages of the newsletter present search ads submitted by members that include any basic information the searcher has acquired.

This group is affiliated with the American Adoption Congress and International Soundex Reunion Registry. For searchers wishing help with their search, Rochelle Harris will assist for a nominal fee, generally $20, to cover the costs involved.

For more information or an application to join, contact Wichita Adult Adoptees, 4551 S. Osage, Wichita, KS 67217, (316) 522-8772, Web site: <www2.southwind.net/~1peters/waaindex.html>.

ENLISTING ASSISTANCE

Having read the information presented so far in this book, you may find yourself thinking that search seems too complicated a process for you to manage. Perhaps you've been searching already, but no leads seem to be developing. Maybe you feel you simply haven't the inner resources to undertake the weeks or months of looking, hoping, and waiting that search appears likely to entail. Isn't there another way to go about it?

Alternatives to undertaking search efforts on your own do exist. You can follow any one of these three approaches: (1) line up someone who can and will help you with difficult aspects of your search; (2) find someone who will actually conduct the search for you; (3) initiate court action in an effort to unseal the adoption or relinquishment records that hold the identifying information you want to know.

No one has to undertake a search alone, without any kind of assistance. As already noted, search and support groups exist in every state and these provide the most readily available source of practical advice and ideas on how to manage a search. But even then, you still have to do most of the actual work yourself. Reunion registries can simplify things considerably, but only if the person you seek is on file with the registry you refer to; if not, you still have to go on searching. However, there are other sources of assistance available to you.

RECORDS SEARCHERS

A records searcher does just that—searches census, birth, death, or any other records pertaining to an individual or family. Ideally, a records searcher is thoroughly aware of what information is available at municipal, county, and state offices or archives, and knows how to use these records and other documentary sources to your best advantage. A records searcher can check through more record sources with greater understanding and speed than you can. While you might find yourself spending hours pouring over a given record file, the records searcher would know if there was an index to those records and be able to check through the file with greater efficiency. Don't engage a records searcher just because you see one advertised as such; ascertain what experience and references he or she can offer and determine if he or she has been involved in your kind of search and is familiar with your area of search.

Records searchers may be part-time enthusiasts or full-time professionals, who will most likely charge for their services. Fees will probably be charged according to the needs in your case and depending on the difficulty of access to the records you want searched. Be certain you know what the charges will be before you allow any records searcher to search. Make sure to ask if the fee quoted is all-inclusive or whether expenses will constitute an additional charge. Keep the question of expenses in mind. Many states charge a fee to view certain records; if you will be charged expenses in addition to a basic service rate, be sure you know all the expenses that may be involved. For example, will there be travel expenses for which you're expected to reimburse the records searcher? How will these expenses be computed? When working with someone who charges an hourly rate, you may also want to agree on a maximum fee, so that the charges do not exceed your budget. If making a flat fee arrangement, determine specifically what the records searcher will be doing for that fee.

SEARCH ASSISTANTS

A records searcher is obviously a form of search assistant in the sense that he or she meaningfully assists in your search. However, among searchers there is a distinction drawn between records searchers and search assistants. A records searcher commonly limits work to records search only. A search assistant works on a broader level, counseling on search techniques and helping you apply them to your individual needs.

Many search and support groups are associated with volunteer or professional search assistants trained to aid you in your search. Charges can range from nothing for someone who volunteers his or her time to as much as $50 per hour for a professional. Obviously, you need to know what any charge would be before you have a search assistant work with you. Contact a local group for the name of a recommended search assistant if you want this kind of help.

Once you are in contact with such an individual, be careful to outline the type of help you hope to have provided, and any fee arrangement. Any professional arrangement you make should be in writing and should spell out the type of help you are seeking and the charge for this help.

SEARCH CONSULTANTS

In the past, working with search consultants was a hit-or-miss process for searchers. Usually consulting services were available only through a few search and support groups, and matching the consultant's experience with your particular needs was difficult. Today, there are consultants working alone or within a group. Their fees range from moderate to outrageous, so searchers must make sure all charges are discussed before entering into an agreement. Family Search Services, a consulting firm in California, provides an information sheet to all prospective clients that lists educational background and search experience qualifications for all the firm's consultants, as well its affiliations with other groups, consultants, registries, and associations. The information sheet includes the following fee information:

> Full Search—$ _____ —A $ _____ non-refundable retainer fee is required and the balance is due upon completion of the search. At completion of the search, the client is provided the name, current address, and telephone number, if available, of the person for whom we are searching. Phone calls to the client will be collect.

Independent Search Consultants, Inc. (ISC)

Independent Search Consultants (ISC) is an organization founded in the fall of 1979 and incorporated as a nonprofit, tax-exempt company in 1980 by Pat Sanders. It has established a reliable training and certification program for those wishing to become adoptee/birthparent search consultants. ISC has a standardized program of education and training leading to certification, which includes a personal apprenticeship. All applicants for certification must present three personal recommendations (at least two must be written by certified ISC consultants), document 500 hours of training, attend a regional or national conference, agree to abide by the ISC Code of Ethics, take a qualifying examination, and spend a one-year period as an "associate consultant" before being eligible for full certification.

Independent Search Consultants has drawn up a code of ethics to be followed by all of their consultants.

ISC CODE OF ETHICS

A search consultant realizes that he has moral obligations to the client, to the profession and to society as well. His honesty must be above suspicion, his skill and reasoning ability well developed, and his competency of the highest degree. Understanding all of this, I make the following commitments:

To the Client:
I will use all resources available to me to acquire information beneficial to the client.
I will obtain from the client all information so far assembled, so as to avoid duplication.
I will keep accurate and complete records of the client's search.
I will not promise success on any level, but will enter into and carry on the search with every expectation of success.
I will communicate directly and clearly with my client and will keep him fully informed on the progress of the search.
I will consider each client's case confidential.
I will not make any personal contacts other than at the client's specific request and with his permission.
I will be discreet and will advise the client to use discretion in his search.
I will remember that the search is the client's.

To the Profession:
I will not knowingly act in a manner detrimental to the best interests of the profession.
I will unhesitatingly refer my client to another consultant or other professionals when I can no longer be of help to him.
I will not injure the professional reputation, prospects, or practice of another consultant.
I will not use my position or influence within an organized adoption search and support group to recruit clients.

To the Public:
I will maintain professional integrity at all times.
I will be aware that search consultation as a profession is relatively new and must earn a reputable name for itself.
I will remember that the area of adoption search is often a delicate one and must be handled with care and thoughtfulness.

ISC also can aid searchers directly through consultant referrals. When someone in search contacts ISC with a specific request for help, he or she is sent the name(s) of one or more ISC consultants who specialize in the area of the search. Each consultant sets his or her own fees and guidelines for conducting a search. Searchers are advised to ask for a contract and to discuss all charges and parameters which may apply to the search before hiring a consultant.

ISC publications range from reference guides of state records to an *ISC Calendar of Adoption Fantasy Reality*. Books published by ISC and by ISC consultants are listed in Chapter 10, "Search Resources and Services." ISC consultants are listed in Appendix I.

ISC also sponsors conferences in different areas of the country. These are search oriented and are of special interest to adoption triad members, genealogists, private investigators, heir searchers, researchers, as well as adoption triad members

To receive more information or to request the services of a consultant, send a self-addressed, stamped envelope with your inquiry to Independent Search Consultants, P.O. Box 10192, Costa Mesa, CA 92627, e-mail: ISC@rmci.net, Web site: <www.rmci.net/isc>.

GENEALOGICAL CONSULTANTS

You may find that your search necessarily leads you into genealogy, because sometimes only through tracing extended family lines across several generations does it seem possible to locate a missing relative. You can, if need be, call on the services of professional genealogists who will do genealogical research for a fee. Such consultants are trained and experienced in searching records, using indexes, and applying techniques for tracing relatives. The usual distinction between genealogical consultants and consultants more specifically concentrating in the adoption search area is that the former deal mostly with records on persons now dead, while the latter concentrate on those living, or at least presumed to be living.

A local genealogy group can usually direct you to a qualified genealogical consultant or provide you with a list of such consultants. A local historical society may be able to do so as well. Your reference librarian may be able to provide direction here; state libraries and state historical societies will send you a listing of recommended consultants. The Church of Jesus Christ of Latter-day Saints will send you a list of genealogists accredited by them; these individuals will be highly trained and skilled in genealogical techniques. The church list will carry names from all over the United States and from various foreign countries. Chapter 9, "Searching on the Computer," lists several Web sites that are beneficial to the adoption searcher.

Note that genealogical magazines commonly carry ads for specialized assistance or information sources (see Chapter 4, "Reference Resources"). An individual genealogist may have searched through census records from a particular area and compiled an index for that area. For a nominal charge, sometimes as low as $2.25 per surname, he or she will provide you a one-line family listing from those census records. Or perhaps he or she is offering information from area birth or probate records. It is possible that such a person could in a limited sense be considered a consultant. More to the point, that person might have information helpful to you.

LEGAL CONSULTANTS AND RESEARCHERS

There may be times when you feel the need for legal counsel during your search. You may not feel entirely at ease adapting the sample forms given here to assign a limited power of attorney or to draw up a waiver of confidentiality. You may feel it desirable to have correspondence with state agencies, hospital administrations, and so on, in which you assert your rights to information held on you, issued under an attorney's letterhead, or at least reviewed by an attorney.

If you have your own attorney, then it's a simple matter of consulting with him or her when questions arise that involve legality or legal form. If you do not have your own attorney, look in your telephone directory for your county's bar association and ask for assistance in obtaining the legal counsel you require. Of course, you should discuss fees for whatever services are to be performed. These can be substantial, and you want to know in advance what kind of financial burden you will incur as the result of any work your attorney does for you. Your county bar association may provide a relatively inexpensive legal clinic for county residents. You can also refer to a local branch of the Legal Aid Society, which provides free or inexpensive legal advice to eligible persons. Contact your local society to find out what the rules are that determine eligibility for legal assistance.

Legal researchers may search for missing heirs or persons involved in mineral rights or they may seek old friends or neighbors. The list of those being sought is as varied as those requesting the search. Legal researchers offer searchers their services for hire and may be found in your telephone directory or they may advertise in genealogical and search newsletters or magazines. Beware, many will charge a fee for each listing found. Thus, a listing for John Smith or Mary Jones can produce hundreds of names from various regions around the United States.

INTERMEDIARIES

An intermediary is someone who acts for you in contacts with other parties. To many searchers think "intermediary" is a dirty word. That is because adoption agencies act as intermediaries, too often without regard for search-ers' needs or feelings. Courts, too, act as intermediaries—or appoint them—also frequently with results that are not satisfactory to a searcher. In these situations, the intermediary makes decisions for you that do not depend on any instruction from you or that do not take your search goals into sympathetic consideration.

However, you can make arrangements on your own, whereby you designate someone to act on your behalf. If you feel that someone else can speak for you better than you can speak for yourself, or if your emotions and sense of involvement are too overwhelming or conflicting to allow you to deal with a situation as thoughtfully as is necessary, it makes sense to consider using an intermediary.

Who will act as your intermediary? The possibilities are numerous. You may ask your spouse or someone you trust to act for you. You may ask a fellow searcher to act for you. Another alternative is to hire a professional consultant or private investigator (see below) to serve as intermediary.

Weigh the advantages of employing an intermediary against the possible pitfalls in relying on someone else to speak for you. Will that person represent you and your interests capably? There may be times when you have only one opportunity to win the cooperation of someone who has access to or holds information valuable to you. In the sensitive situation of establishing actual first contact with the person you're seeking, will a subsequent meeting between you and your relative be easier or harder if you use an intermediary? Here, it's advisable to rely on an intermediary only if you're convinced it's absolutely necessary because you know right now you cannot handle it well yourself.

If you have decided to use an intermediary in your search, you will have to provide him or her with a waiver of confidentiality. Individuals will not be allowed access to personal records kept on you without explicit authorization from you. Your waiver may be specifically directed to one record or file, or it may be broadly stated to include all records and files. The scope of your waiver depends both on what you are looking for and on the intermediary involved. A private investigator or other professional consultant may ask that you sign a waiver of confidentiality prepared as a standard form. Exercise caution; be aware of what you are signing. If there's a chance that any of your private records may come to be held by an intermediary, make sure you'll get them back when the search work done for you is concluded. See Sample 18 for a waiver of confidentiality that you can adapt for use with an intermediary.

Some consultants may ask you formally to assign them a limited power of attorney so that they can obtain personal documents in your name. Be extremely careful here. State clearly and specifically what limited powers you are delegating, to whom you are delegating them, and what time limit is set on exercise of them. Be sure you don't foolishly grant unlimited power of attorney. An unlimited power of attorney would enable your intermediary to take control of all your affairs, including disposition of property you own and committing you to contractual obligations without first consulting with you. You may want to get legal advice if you're faced with a request for a grant of power of attorney to an intermediary.

SAMPLE 18
WAIVER OF CONFIDENTIALITY FOR USE BY AN INTERMEDIARY

To Whom It May Concern:

I, (give present name), also known as (give name by adoption/at time of relinquishment if different, or give name at birth if known), residing at (give current street, city, county, and state address), do state the following:

Permission is given to (name of agent or consultant) to maintain private records on me and to keep certain files on me as listed below. This permission is granted starting (month, date, year) and shall extend to (month, day, year).

Those records covered by this affidavit waiving confidentiality in respect of the person herein named are: hospital records, court records from (list court of jurisdiction), agency records (list agency or private adoption intermediary), birth records, and any other documents or information pertaining to (adoption or relinquishment). (1)

It is clearly understood that all records and information obtained under this waiver of confidentiality shall be forwarded intact to the undersigned upon the final date herein indicated.

Signed: _____ Dated: _____

_____
Have a notary public certify your signature.

Other Possible Inclusion:
1. *Add:* The person herein named shall not undertake any personal or written contact with individuals named in the documents indicated, other than officials or records administrators whose cooperation is necessary to assure obtaining of the documents themselves.

Note: This letter should be very clear on what records and rights you wish to grant. You may wish an attorney to draw up the waiver for you.

COURT-APPOINTED INTERMEDIARIES

Several states have passed legislation that provides a court-appointed intermediary for all those requesting the court to "unseal" records or conduct a search for birthparents or a relinquished child. Currently, Alabama, Arizona, Arkansas, Colorado, Illinois, Indiana, Kentucky, Maryland, Michigan, Mississippi, New Mexico, North Dakota, Oregon, Texas, Washington, Wisconsin, and Wyoming are states having this confidential intermediary system, although legislation is being considered in several more.

Many search and support groups strongly oppose the use of court-appointed intermediaries. These opponents are in principle against the interposition of any agent or person between the individual adoptee/birthparent and his or her records. Others feel state-appointed intermediaries provide a useful means of doing what needs to be done in order to aid searchers.

Searchers should make sure they understand what is required and what is forbidden by the courts: what records will be released, what records require the consent of both the adoptee and the birthparent before release, and what will be the total cost for the search.

Highlighted below is one such Confidential Intermediary Program. Each state has a slightly different approach but this should give a basic idea of their workings.

Washington Adoption Rights Movement (WARM)

The state of Washington, through its judicial system, passed a law in 1990 that adopted a policy of using court-appointed intermediaries to aid adoptees, birthparents, siblings, cousins, birth grandparents, etc. with their searches. This arrangement has its origins in a proposal made in 1976 to the King County Superior Court, the Washington Adoption Rights Movement (WARM), and adoption agencies to use WARM volunteer workers to aid adoptees and birthparents in their efforts to contact each other. All 39 counties in Washington participate in this intermediary system.

For those with sufficient facts to conduct a search on their own, WARM will provide search advisors to help utilize the information. For those born or adopted in Washington State with little or no data, WARM will petition the court to appoint a confidential intermediary (CI). The CI has access to the court's sealed documents and works with the information contained there but is sworn to secrecy by the court and faces a contempt-of-court violation if subsequent procedures are not carried out in accord with secrecy requirements. Once all facts have been gathered, the CI begins tracing the individual you seek.

If that person is located, the CI makes a discreet contact in an effort to obtain a signed consent. Generally, the court will set a time limit of one year on the CI's efforts to locate a person, but this may be extended on approval of the court. If a direct contact is desired and the appropriate release statements have been obtained, the parties may be reunited. Where it is discovered that the birthparent sought is deceased, the court may grant a request for opening the heretofore sealed records.

WARM, which publishes a newsletter called *Warm Journeys*, holds support group meetings across the state, is a member of the American Adoption Congress, and participates in the International Soundex Reunion Registry. WARM also communicates and exchanges information with similar organizations in the U.S., Canada, Mexico, and other countries.

Search membership in WARM is open to everyone over the age of 21. Each member agrees to use an intermediary for the initial contact with their birthparent(s) or relinquished child. Searches are not conducted for children under the age of 21 unless ordered by the court, or the adoptive parent petitions the court.

This group widely publishes information about receiving "non-identifying information" and "uncertified copies of an original birth certificate" by the birthparent. Both of these services are offered at a minimum cost.

WARM has approximately 2,000 members at the present time. The annual membership fee is $25. The current Confidential Intermediary Service is $350, which includes (1) service for legal access to sealed records if you were born or adopted in Washington, (2) locating the birthfamily member(s), and (3) contacting them. The current Search Advisor Service is $250. This service was designed for those with documented identifying information on their birthfamily. Both of the above include a one-year membership fee. Time spent by WARM volunteers in search for you is donated. A portion of this fee will go to the intermediary to cover out-of-pocket expenses incurred during the actual search. Only very rarely does the intermediary need additional fees to search. Everything is documented, and you are kept advised of the costs. The $350 fee is based on an average search, but 95% never exceed that amount. Since out-of-pocket expenses can mount substantially, discuss all financial arrangements and method of payment before proceeding with the search.

For more information or an application to join this group, write to Washington Adoption Rights Movement, 5950 Sixth Avenue South, Suite 107, Seattle, WA 98108, call (206) 767-9510, fax (206) 763-4803. Office hours are 9:30 A.M. to 4:00 P.M., Monday through Wednesday, Thursday and Friday by appointment. The voice mail is on 24 hours a day, and telephone calls are answered promptly during normal business hours. General Support Group meetings are held around the state. Telephone or write for the current address and times for a meeting near you (e-mail: warm@wolfenet.com).

CONTACTS

The word *contact* conjures up images of espionage activity, with illegal information surreptitiously passing from hand to hand. It's a fact that in adoption search there are contacts who are paid for their services of obtaining information. I have heard of adoptees paying as much as $1,000 for their birth name, obtained through an "agent" with access to sealed files. And then I know of another adoptee who paid only $25 for the name of her birthmother. In either case, it's doubtful the name was obtained by legal means.

Are you the kind of person who would use a contact to obtain information illegally? Only you know the answer to that question. Some searchers make this distinction: no—to obtaining information on others that might be used against them; yes—to obtaining information on oneself or one's family that is freely available to the average person who is not part of the adoption triangle. It is a fact that laws exist about the passing of certain types of information. You should be aware that you expose yourself to risk whenever you participate in illegal activity, whatever your motives.

If you use a contact, be wary when paying cash to a source unknown to you. If your source is reliable, payment is often made after you're satisfied the information received is correct, with only a partial payment made before then.

Many contacts are not the person actually obtaining the information. Contacts often are the individuals who know a sympathetic source whose identity they protect. They are, in effect, another form of intermediary. You may not be able to ascertain whether the source is a legal one or not; it may simply be someone in your area of search who has genealogical/search resources and experience that go far beyond those you have. You only know information is being promised you that you very much want to have.

Before dealing with contacts, make every effort to ascertain their reliability. Can other searchers attest to their reliability? Ask yourself what you stand to gain for the price you must pay. Recognize that there are risks to be faced: the risk of possible involvement in illegal activity, even the risk that you are being victimized in a cruel confidence hoax.

PRIVATE INVESTIGATORS

You may hire a private investigator to search for you. A good private investigator can frequently find whatever information you need. I've found professional investigators as a group to be highly professional and particularly adept at locating missing persons. And, of course, this is essentially what you're working to accomplish in your search.

Private investigators work in mysterious ways, at least from a layperson's perspective. They seem to have superior access to records and reliable, established contacts to provide needed information in any of a number of areas. They have the means to get hold of information you would find difficult to obtain on your own.

The greatest value I see in hiring private investigators is the relative speed with which they get results. Most often, you submit all your information to them, and before long you have the additional information you want. No, it does not always work out that way, but it does happen regularly. You'd spend months collecting and sorting through material that a good private investigator gets hold of and evaluates quickly. One private investigator who has undertaken a number of search assignments told me that in one case his search took only 15 minutes. The longest took several weeks.

How do you go about hiring a private investigator to work for you? You can obtain addresses from listings in area Yellow Pages of the telephone directory. You can check with an attorney you know for a possible recommendation. Many search and support groups will provide you the name of a private investigator used by other members. A check with the local Better Business Bureau would turn up any complaints lodged against a particular private investigator or private investigative agency. Start by contacting at least three who work in your area of search. That will give you a good idea of the rates charged and the services offered. Find out how much information you are likely to obtain for the amount you have to spend. Ask what types of missing person searches they specialize in and whether they are familiar with your type of search. Ask how long they have been in business.

In making a determination to hire, you should exercise the same good judgment you would exercise in hiring anyone. Stress what you want done and what limitations you are setting. If you use a private investigator in a supplementary fashion, be sure you both understand and agree on what the range and cost of service will be. Do you want the private investigator to have any contact with the person sought? State that clearly. Do you want the private investigator to undertake the entire search for you, or do you wish that he or she handle a particular aspect of your search only? In either event, be sure the private investigator meets your needs.

Most private investigators like to work on a retainer, if not on payment of a full fee in advance. It works something like a checking account: You deposit a given sum of money with the private investigator, and he or she draws on that until the balance reaches zero. If you decide there's more you want done, you can deposit more money into "the account."

It's customary for the private investigator to alert you whenever your "balance" approaches zero. Suppose you've provided a $100 retainer for a private investigator charging $25 an hour plus expenses. He will probably contact you after three hours of searching. If you choose not to continue once the retainer account reaches zero, the investigator will send you all the information obtained to that point. If you want to continue, you send an additional $100 check, or whatever the amount is. It will depend on your budget, on your satisfaction with what the private investigator has been able to discover, and on your feeling about whether this is the best way to proceed with your search. Time can also be an important consideration. Included here is a sample retainer agreement (Sample 19) that you can adapt for your purposes.

SAMPLE 19
RETAINER AGREEMENT

The undersigned, (your name), of (your home address), hereinafter called "the client," does hereby retain and employ (list name, business, or assigned agent) as (agent, attorney, consultant) in connection with (state nature of business to be undertaken).

Payment for services rendered shall be on the basis of:

A. A total fee (including expenses) _____ or retainer received _____.

B. An estimated fee which shall be no less than _____ and no more than _____.

C. Fees plus expenses. It is understood and agreed that the agent herein indicated shall be due monies for the following expenses: (list as specifically as possible).

No additional expenses shall be incurred and charged the client without express written consent from the client. The fee shall be computed on a(n) (hourly/flat) rate of $ ____. The total charge to the client of fees and expenses shall not exceed a total sum of $ ____.

Likely expenses are estimated at $ _____. The agent hereby agrees to advise the client at such time as it is evident that this estimated figure will be exceeded and will not incur further expenses on the client's account without the client's express consent.

Client: (your signature) Dated: _____
Assigned Agent: (signature) Dated: _____

Note: Many agents, private investigators, and consultants have their own retainer forms. Read through them carefully. Insist that everything you wish to have spelled out be included.

You may turn to a private investigator in order to ensure privacy. You may not be able to receive letters or make calls freely. You may not be able to withstand the emotional conflicts raised by pushing and probing for information related to your adoption or relinquishment. By turning your search over to a professional, you are removed from these problems. But remember, you run a risk of your confidentiality being compromised or your search goal being endangered if you take on a private investigator who is not familiar with adoptee/birthparent search. You run even greater risks if you do not communicate a clear understanding of how you want your search conducted. Hiring a private investigator is a step that should be taken only after careful consideration of your needs and resources and a thorough discussion of these with the professional involved.

GOING TO COURT

As an alternative to searching, you can try initiating a court action to unseal adoption/relinquishment records. You should recognize, however, that this can be as time-consuming and emotionally draining as the most difficult search. While it's evident that public attitudes are slowly changing and that the laws in some states are beginning to reflect this change, existing laws, on the whole, are still weighted against you.

Each state has its own set of procedures to follow. In some states, it's possible to file a request to unseal your records without an attorney having to be present. An appearance before a judge in the appropriate court of jurisdiction is all that is required. This informal hearing may result in release of all the sealed information upon your presenting an affidavit (to the court, not just to you) need-to-know. In other states, a more formal procedure must be followed, with an attorney pleading your case. Restrictions on release of information may be so stringently worded and observed that not even the best-pleaded case could get any records released to you.

If you're contemplating a court action, the first thing to do is to find out what the process is for petitioning to have records unsealed in the state in which your adoption or relinquishment took place. Call or write the appropriate court of jurisdiction for the necessary details. You'll need the answers to many questions before proceeding. Do you need an attorney to plead your case? If so, do you need to be present as well? What papers or forms must you present to start the action? How long will the case take? If you now live in another state, is it possible to have the proceedings conducted there? (Some states will allow the hearing to be held in your state of residence.) What court costs will there be?

Costs will be a major consideration. Chances are you will need or want legal counsel representing you. Perhaps you can locate legal clinic services or are eligible for Legal Aid Society assistance, but you'll probably have to retain your own attorney. If you employ an attorney, how many hours of legal work are likely to be required? You have to decide how much money you're both willing and able to spend to start an action. There are other cost factors to take into account also. Is your court in another state? Does this action involve travel expenses and/or time off from work? Remember, regardless of the outcome of your case, you will have to pay the burden of the expenses involved.

What will you use as a reason for insisting that your records should be opened to you? You need to prove good cause, that is, a substantial, legally sufficient reason that will prompt the court to do as you ask. Consider carefully what reasons the judge will recognize as valid. Study past cases fought in your state. If you discover that four cases have recently been won on grounds of a medical need-to-know, while three have been lost that cited a psychological need-to-know, take this into account. For a sense of what other compelling arguments you may be able to raise, return to Chapter 1, "Deciding to Search." Unless your state has provision for an informal hearing without counsel before a judge, I urge you to consult with an attorney before taking any action.

While court action may be an alternative to search, it is rarely an easy alternative. It often proves more difficult and more costly. If the case is decided against you, as it very well may, then you're back where you started. The decision again is whether or not to search. At present, search affords a greater likelihood of success than court action.

CHAPTER 8

Reunion Registries

Reunion registries are designed to provide a means by which relatives separated by relinquishment or adoption can locate each other. They are files maintained by private groups or public agencies holding on record the names, addresses, and other identifying information of searchers, like yourself, who are hoping to locate a relinquished child, a birthparent, or a sibling from whom they've been separated. It is not unusual for adoptees, birthparents, or siblings to discover each other though a listing in one or another reunion registry. It is, in all likelihood, the easiest route to a successful search. That does not mean it is one you should wholly count on.

HOW DO REUNION REGISTRIES WORK?

The first reunion registry was established in 1952 by Jean Paton, founder of Orphan Voyage. Since that time, other registries have been established, most within the past decade. New ones are appearing more and more frequently. Many small search and support groups now maintain their own registry, usually with listings from the specific area in which they operate. They generally supplement one of the larger registries, to which they will have established a link.

Group (private) registries have for the most part been set up and are maintained by private search and support groups. The process of application to these registries is relatively informal. Sending in a complete application form is taken as implicit consent to release of information by the registry at any time that a link is established to you via a contact made with the registry.

State registries are maintained by the respective states in which they have been established, and are growing each year. These registries function on a more complex level than private group registries. As a general rule you must apply via a notarized letter, and an affidavit of consent is required before information is released. In some states, registries provide adoptees and birthparents with the explicit option to request that they not be listed. States usually charge a fee to register. Some will actually do a search, but most have a waiting period because a large number of adoptees/birthparents have applied. As a rule, states will not give out any identifying information unless both the adoptee and birthparent(s) sign a waiver. Check with your state registry to learn of the rules for applying. The names and addresses for existing state registries are listed at the end of this chapter.

Group reunion registries work on the simple principle of matching up information on file. In each case—whether you're an adoptee, birthparent, or separated sibling—you send away for an application form, complete as much information as you have, then return the form, with whatever fee is required, to the address indicated.

Certain information that can contribute to an identification will be needed to make a match possible and that information will be requested on the application. You may feel you do not have enough information—you may not know your birth name, for example, if you're a searching adoptee—but you generally have more useful information on hand than you think. You can at least indicate sex and you probably know the date of birth. Well, that's a beginning. Do you know the state of relinquishment? The court in which it was handled? The hospital where you were born? What was the name of the adoption agency involved and what information did it give you? Parents' religion? Occupations? Do you have a change of name filed with the court overseeing your adoption? What is the docket or case number indicated on any court proceedings?

If you are a birthparent, what did the agency tell you about the home your child was going to? The adoptive parents' occupations? Other children in the family and their ages? Birth dates, hospital names, court case numbers, and the like are other items you can probably provide without too much difficulty. From either side of the adoption situation, you can probably provide more facts to list for eventual match-up than you may at first think.

Once your application is received by the reunion registry, your responses on the application form are coded. Any previous or subsequent referral to the registry that lists substantially similar or identical particulars in a number of areas will automatically be checked against yours. When the match is close enough to assure the two searching parties are actually searching for each other, the reunion registry moves to make contact possible.

As awareness of the services of reunion registries grows, it can be expected that more and more birth families will be reunited this way. In fact, search and support groups report more and more reunions effected through both parties locating each other by means of these registries. There is, however, no guarantee that you will benefit from joining a registry. In order for a match-up to occur, two persons have to be searching for each other. Increasing state involvement, particularly where the state mandates an immediate records search by the administering agency, may improve chances when only one person registers. But keep another fact in mind. Joining a registry puts you on permanent file. Your search is put on record, so that two years from now, five years from now, even ten years from now, another party initiating a search for you will be able to locate that record and thereby eventually locate you. Even if your search comes to a halt on all other fronts, joining a reunion registry keeps it alive at least to some degree. No, there's no guarantee of a match, but you will certainly want to consider the possible benefits of registering.

INDEPENDENT (GROUP) REUNION REGISTRIES

Which reunion registries should you look to? Below is information about group registries. Don't overlook the possibility of benefit from the many other, small reunion registries that exist. As mentioned, these frequently function within a limited geographical area. Contact a search and support group in your area of search—particularly where your adoption or relinquishment took place—and ask if the group maintains a reunion registry.

In addition to the numerous registries listed below, others should be noted. These may be located in your area of search and provide the exact resource you require. Several excellent registries can be found in Chapter 9, "Searching on the Computer." Other registries can be found by contacting a local search and support group in the area of your search.

> **Adoptee/Birth Family Registry,** Trudy Helmlinger. Information about this national registry can be found in Chapter 10, "Search Resources and Services."

> **Adoptees & Birthparents in Search,** Karen Connor, P.O. Box 5551, West Columbia, SC 29171, (803) 791-1133, fax (803) 791-1133. A valuable registry for South Carolina searchers with 1000-plus people registered. There is a $25 fee to join. Please enclose a stamped, self-addressed envelope with all correspondence.

> **Adoptees Identity Doorway, Reunion Registry of Indiana,** Betty Heide, P.O. Box 361, South Bend, IN 46624, (219) 272-3520. This free registry has over 9,000 people registered. It is primarily for, but not limited to, Indiana searchers. Please enclose a stamped self-addressed envelope with all correspondence. E-mail: bheide@mvillage.com.

The ALMA International Reunion Registry Data Bank, (see high-lighted registries listed below).

Adoption Crossroads Reunion Registry, 356 East 74th Street #2, New York, NY 10021, (212) 988-0110, fax (212) 988-0291. A large reunion registry with 5000 plus names. More detail is presented in Chapter 7, "Search and Support Groups, Researchers/Searchers, Consultants, Intermediaries, and the Courts," under Adoption Crossroads. E-mail: cera@mail.idt.net; Web site: <www.adoptioncrossroads.org/>.

Adoption Information Center at Daniel Memorial, Robert Rooks, 134 East Church Street, Jacksonville, FL 32202, (800) 96-ADOPT for in state, out of state (904) 353-0769, fax (904) 353-3472. Mainly receives calls from Florida searchers but refers others to ISRR. No fees are charged. E-mail: geriryan@aol.com.

Adoption Reunion Registry, Linda Cecil, P.O. Box 1218, Nicholasville, KY 40340, (606) 885-1777, (800) 755-7954, fax, (606) 885-1778. Over 8000 registered in this Kentucky registry. No fee's are currently charged but a reimbursement of cost is asked if a reunion made. Please enclose a stamped, self-addressed envelope with all correspondence. E-mail: LCECIL@aol.com.

AmFor Reunion Registry, P.O. Box 401, Palm Desert, CA 92261. $5 registration fee plus two stamps. Please enclose a stamped, self-addressed envelope with all correspondence.

Concerned United Birthparents (CUB) Reunion Registry (see high-lighted registries listed below)

Iowa Reunion Registry, Doris Smith, P.O. Box 8, Blairsburg, IA 50034-0008. Approximately 2000 people are enrolled in this free registry. Please enclose a legal-size stamped, self-addressed envelope with all correspondence.

International Soundex Reunion Registry (see highlighted registries listed below)

Lost Loved Ones, Bob Mulvehill, 621 W. Crawford Street, Ebensburg, PA 15931, (814) 472-7525. This free registry deals primarily with Pennsylvania searchers but receives more and more listings from out-of-state. Please enclose a stamped, self-addressed envelope with all correspondence.

Maternity Home Reconnection Registry, The Adoption ReConnection Directory, Birthparent Connection. Curry Wolfe, P.O. Box 230643, Encinitas, CA 92023-0643, fax (760) 753-8073. E-mail: ccwolfe@worldnet.att.net. Registry to reconnect others from the same maternity home. There is a one time fee of $5. Please enclose a stamped, self-addressed envelope with all correspondence.

The Mid-Atlantic States Search Registry (MASSR), Adoptees-in-Search, P.O. Box 41016, Bethesda, MD 20824, (301) 656-8555, fax (301) 652-2106. This registry is primarily for those adopted or relinquished in the Mid-Atlantic states. There is a $75 fee to join. Please enclose a stamped, self-addressed envelope with all correspondence.

National Adoption Registry Inc., 6800 Elmwood Avenue, Kansas City, MO 64132, (800) 875-4344. This registry covers the United States & Canada plus limited foreign countries. There is a lifetime registration fee of $54 + $5. A $25 reunion fee is also charged. Web site: <www.searchint.com>.

NC Adoption Connections, P.O. Box 4153, Chapel Hill, NC 27515-4153, (919) 967-5010. A free registry dealing with North Carolina adoptees and birthparents. Please enclose a stamped, self-addressed envelope with all correspondence. E-mail: NCCAAE@aol.com

Organized Adoption Search Information Services, Inc. (see highlighted registries listed below).

Origins, Inc., Jim McDonald, P.O. Box 13134, Des Moines, IA 50310-0134, (515) 277-7700, fax (515) 277-9811. This is mainly an Iowa registry with 2500-plus names. There are no charges to join. Please enclose a stamped, self-addressed envelope with all correspondence. Web site: <www.originsinc.com>.

Silent Legacy, The Hicks Clinic Birth Registry, Jane Blasio, P.O. Box 134, Green, OH 44232. This is a new and very important registry for searchers born at the Hicks Clinic in Fannin County, Georgia (see Chapter 5, "Beginning to Search," for more information). Please enclose a stamped, self-addressed envelope with all correspondence.

Tennessee's the Right to Know, P.O. Box 34334, Bartlett, TN 38134, (901) 386-2197 or (901) 373-7049. This is a free registry for Tennessee Children's Home Society babies. E-mail: FFMJ26B@prodigy.com.

In the case of highlighted group (private) registries, the information given here reflects what was provided to me in response to a request for details. This is not to say that in the case of any particular registry, you would not be well served as an individual on file. What it does mean is that you should consider the use of a registry with your own situation in mind. Be sure to ask for information to supplement that which is given here so that you can determine how the registry will work in your particular case. Check Chapter 9, "Searching on the Computer," for reunion registries on the Internet.

The ALMA International Reunion Registry Data Bank

The Adoptees' Liberty Movement Association (ALMA), (see Chapter 7, "Search and Support Groups, Researchers/Searchers, Consultants, Intermediaries, and the Courts") also maintains a large reunion registry, which has been set up for the benefit of its members. This large registry provides many opportunities for a potential searcher match-up.

ALMA describes its registry as "a multi-level cross reference file system located at the national headquarters, utilizing data to match birth dates, names, etc., to facilitate a reunion."

You must be an ALMA member to register with the ALMA Reunion Registry. The annual membership fee is $65. You can apply for membership by writing ALMA, National Headquarters, P.O. Box 727 Radio City Station, New York, NY 10101-0727, (212) 581-1568, fax (212) 765-2861, e-mail: ALMAINFO@aol.com, Web site: <www.almanet.com>. Please enclose a stamped, self-addressed envelope with all correspondence.

Concerned United Birthparents (CUB) Reunion Registry

The Concerned United Birthparents (CUB) Reunion Registry was formed in 1976 and is operated by the largest birthparent support group in the world (see Chapter 7, "Search and Support Groups, Researchers/Searchers, Consultants, Intermediaries, and the Courts").

Applicants are placed in the registry under the birth date of the offspring. If two applicants submit the same birth dates, a check is made into sex, state of birth, and additional facts known. If all information matches, the applicants are contacted.

Services are offered to any individual who has been separated from a family member due to any number of circumstances, including adoption, relinquishment, family feud, kidnapping, or divorce.

All applicants must be members of CUB to register. There are no restrictions for applying; all those searching for lost family members are welcome. CUB encourages all members to also register with International Soundex Reunion Registry (see below).

Those interested in this registry should write for more information or request an application to join Concerned United Birthparents, National Administration Headquarters, 2000 Walker Street, Des Moines, IA 50317, or call (800) 822-2777, fax (515) 263-9541. Please enclose a stamped, self-addressed envelope with all correspondence. You can contact CUB by e-mail at cub@webnations.com or visit their Web site at <www.webnations.com/cub/>.

International Soundex Reunion Registry (ISRR)

The International Soundex Reunion Registry (ISRR) was established in 1975 by its founder, the late Emma May Vilardi to provide a centralized reunion registry to meet the needs of the adoption community. While there are many reunion registries now functioning, search groups use ISRR solely or in coordination with other registries to offer their members the best chance of "making a match." This is by far the largest reunion registry.

The following statement, provided to me by ISRR, shows the purpose and direction of this registry:

> ISSR is a non-profit, humanitarian service to serve and promote through the reunion registry, the interests of any adult persons desiring and seeking a reunion with next-of-kin by birth. Serving the needs of birth family members who have been separated from each other by many causes . . . ISRR provides a confidential and voluntary identification on a national and international scale. ISRR processes the information its registrants provide to determine if the person(s) they seek had previously registered and when a "match occurs, the ISRR Registrar will contact the registrants and exchange information to the registrants of the match."

Registration is open to (1) any child/adoptee, 18 years of age or older; (2) birthparents; (3) adoptive parent of adoptees who are still under the age of 18. Files of adoptees under 18 years are brought forth on their 18th birthday.

ISRR has a service for people with special needs: those searchers with a pressing medical need. In an effort to help searchers with medical problems, or possible medical problems, ISRR has established a MEDICAL-ALERT Service. If you have a medical need, you should obtain a registration form from the address listed below. Mark your form, in bold letters across the top, MEDICAL-ALERT. Include a brief letter of explanation with your registration to insure it will receive priority processing. ISRR files will be checked to learn if the person you seek is registered; if so, you will be contacted immediately.

Although the registration ratio is currently five to three in favor of adoptees over birthparents, it is interesting to note the tremendous increase in birthfamily registrations. This is an encouraging revelation for birthparents as it reveals a growing concern for "the best interest of the child." Birthparents should register their relinquished children as soon as possible. Consent is made when the adoptive parent(s) register on behalf of the minor child.

ISRR is a registry, not a search service, but referrals to organizations will be made upon request. Groups wishing to become affiliated with this unique registry need only submit information about their group and request a master copy of the Soundex registration form to be used for listing present and future members with ISRR. Individuals only need to request and fill out an application. To receive information and a registration form, contact International Soundex Reunion Registry, P.O. Box 2312, Carson City, NV 89702-2312; (702) 882-7755. There are no membership fees, but all letters must include a self-addressed, stamped letter-size envelope for reply. This is a unique registry that charges no fees or costs. ISRR is maintained solely by individual donations. Web site: chariott.com/~schmidt/spiel/general/issr.html.

Organized Adoption Search Information Services, Inc. (OASIS)

Organized Adoption Search Information Services, Inc. (OASIS) maintains its own birth index match-up registry in its offices in Florida. Membership is not a requirement to be placed in OASIS' registry. While paid members of OASIS are placed in this working registry, nonmembers may pay a one-time fee of $5 to be included. This group routinely provides an International Soundex Reunion Registry form so that members' information will be included in both registries.

To receive more information or a registration form, contact Organized Adoption Search Information Services, Inc., P.O. Box 53-0761, Miami Shores, FL 33153; (305) 757-0942. Please enclose a stamped, self-addressed envelope with all correspondence.

STATE REUNION REGISTRIES

In the state-by-state listings in Appendix I, each state that offers a state registry will be listed. Each state's registry is more or less formal in its organization. While the state in which you are searching may not have a state reunion registry, legislation may have passed allowing a registry in the near future. Check your current state laws to learn of any recent changes which may have taken place.

In July 1990, the American Adoption Congress (AAC) announced a nationwide boycott of 22 state adoption-reunion registries (see Chapter 10, "Search Resources and Services"). In the AAC newsletter, Kate Burke, then current AAC president, said the following:

> America's adoptees, birthparents and adoptive parents remain enslaved by the institution of adoption. We can no longer cooperate with state-run registries that serve only to hinder the efforts of those who wish contact with biological relatives. A registry is not a solution to the problems created by sealed records; it's like giving a menu to a starving man instead of feeding him a meal.

Individuals should be aware of the many restrictions placed on state reunion registries. In addition to the conditions, states charge a fee to participate in their registry with no guarantee that the information found will be revealed to the searcher. Each state has different rules and guidelines, but generally the following apply:

> To enroll in a state registry, a fee must be paid. This fee is set by the state and must be provided when an application to join is sent.

> Other restrictions may include a requirement for psychological counseling or the consent of the adoptive parents, regardless of the searcher's age.

> Generally, the state has a mutual consent registry. This means that *both* parties, the searcher and the one searched for, must agree to the release of identifying information. The one registering, the searcher, pays all fees.

Beware of states that allow "Affidavits for Identifying and Non-Identifying Information Forms" or "Irrevocable Consent Forms." Such forms indicate that the person sought has refused to sign a consent form and therefore no release of identifying information will be given by the agency during the individual's lifetime or after their death. The fees, however, must still be paid.

When you join a private or group reunion registry, you receive any information found from a match. You have the opportunity and the right to make contact.

As of this writing, 32 states maintain some form of a registry or have registry legislation pending. Listed below are the addresses of state registries; you can write to them to obtain information on prices, registration, restrictions, and other policies.

Arkansas

Arkansas Mutual Consent
  Voluntary
Adoption Registry
P.O. Box 1437, Mail Slot 808
Little Rock, AR 72203-1437

California

California Department of Social
  Services
M.S. 19-67, 744 P Street
Sacramento, CA 95814

Colorado

Colorado Department of Public
  Health and Environment
Voluntary Adoption Registry
4210 E. 11th Avenue
Denver, CO 80220

Connecticut

Connecticut Reunion Registry
505 Hudson Street
Hartford, CT 06106
Each agency is also required
to maintain a registry

Florida

Florida State Reunion Registry
Department of HRS-CYF
Adoption Reunion Registry
1317 Winewood Boulevard
Tallahassee, FL 32399-0700

Georgia

Georgia State Reunion Registry
State Adoption Unit
2 Peachtree Sttrry NW
Suite 13-400
Atlanta, GA 30303
(404) 657-3555

Hawaii

**Hawaii State Reunion
Information:**
Those adopted/relinquished in the
state of Hawaii may submit a
"Request to Inspect Confidential
Adoption Records of the Family
Court." Check your phone book for
the Family Court in your district.

Idaho

Idaho State Reunion Registry
Voluntary Adoption Registry
Idaho Department of Health &
  Welfare
Center for Vital Statistics and
  Health Policy
450 W. State Street,
  P.O. Box 83720
Boise, ID 83720-0036
(208) 334-5990

Illinois

Adoption Registry
Illinois Department of Public Health
605 W. Jefferson
Springfield, IL 62702-5098
(217) 782-6553

Indiana

**Indiana State Department of
  Health**
Indiana Adoption History Registry
Indiana Medical History Registry
P.O. Box 1964
Indianapolis, IN 46206-1964

Kentucky

Kentucky Sibling Registry
Cabinet for Human Resources
275 E. Main Street, 6th Floor West
Frankfort, KY 40621

Louisiana

Louisiana State Reunion Registry
Voluntary Registry
Department of Social Services
Office of Community Services
P.O. Box 3318
Baton Rouge, LA 70821
(800) 259-2456, (504) 342-9922

Maine

Maine State Reunion Registry
Office of Vital Statistics
Maine Department of Human
  Services
Adoption Reunion Registry
221 State Street
State House Station 11
Augusta, ME 04333

Maryland

Maryland Mutual Consent
Voluntary Adoption Registry
Social Services Administration
311 W. Saratoga Street
Baltimore, MD 21201
Web site: <www.GL.umbc.edu/
  ~HICKMAN/adopt.htm>

Michigan

Michigan State Reunion Registry
Adoption Central Registry
P.O. Box 30037
300 South Capitol Ave.
Lansing, MI 48909
(517) 373-3513, fax (517) 335-4019

Missouri

Missouri State Reunion Registry
Division of Family Services
Adoption Information Registry
P.O. Box 88
Jefferson City, MO 65103

Montana

Montana Adoption Resource Center
P.O. Box 634
Helena, MT 59624

Nevada

Nevada State Reunion Registry
Nevada State Adoption Registry
Welfare Division
Department of Human Resources
711 E. 5th Street
Carson City, NV 89710

New Jersey

Division of Youth & Family Services
Adoption Registry Coordinator, Central
1 South Montgomery Street
Office Adoption Unit, CN 717
Trenton, NJ 08625-0717
(609) 292-8816
State agency adoptions only

New York

The Adoption and Medical Information Registry
New York State Department of Health
Empire State Plaza, Corning Tower
Albany, NY 12237-0023
(518) 474-9600

Ohio

Ohio State Reunion Registry
Ohio Adoption Resource Exchange
30 E. Broad Street
Columbus, OH 43266-0423

Oklahoma

Oklahoma State Adoption Registry
Volunteer Adoption Reunion/Registry
Department of Human Services
P.O. Box 25352
Oklahoma City, OK 73125

Oregon

Oregon State Reunion Registry
Department of Human Resources
State Office for Services to Children & Family
Voluntary Adoption Registry
500 Summer Street NE
Salem, OR 97310-1017

Pennsylvania

Pennsylvania's Adoption Medical History Registry
Hillcrest, Second floor
P.O. Box 2675
Harrisburg, PA 17105-2675
(800) 227-0225

Rhode Island

Reunion Registry
State of Rhode Island
Family Court, Juvenile Division
One Dorrance Plaza
Providence, RI 02903

South Carolina

South Carolina Reunion Registry
SC Department of Social Services
P.O. Box 1520
Columbia, SC 29202-1520
fax (803) 734-6285

South Dakota

**South Dakota State Reunion
  Registry**
Child Protection Services
Voluntary Registry
700 Governors Drive
Pierre, SD 57501
(605) 773-3227, fax (605) 773-6834

Tennessee

Department of Children's Services
Post Adoption Unit
8th floor, Cordell Hull Building
436 Sixth Avenue North
Nashville, TN 37243-1290

Texas

**Texas Department of Protective
  and Regulatory Services**
Voluntary Adoption Registry
Mail Code Y-943
P.O. Box 149030
Austin, TX 78714-9030
(512) 834-4485, fax (512) 834-4476

Utah

Utah State Reunion Registry
Bureau of Vital Statistics
Voluntary Adoption Registry
P.O. Box 16700
Salt Lake City, UT 84116-0700

Vermont

The Vermont Adoption Registry
103 S. Main Street, Osgood Building
Waterbury, VT 05671
(802) 241-2122

West Virginia

**West Virginia Department of
  Health & Human Resources**
Mutual Consent Registry
State Capitol Complex
Building 6, Room 850
Charleston, WV 25305
(304) 558-7980

CHAPTER 9

Searching on the Computer

By now, the Internet had grown far beyond a research experiment. As more people discovered its utility, it was becoming a household word. The Net promised to be to the twenty-first century what the telephone had been to the twentieth.[1]

As a resource, the Internet can be a valuable tool to help unlock the secrets that have been sealed away since the time of your adoption or your relinquishment. When the Internet first began it was not with the idea of helping the adoption searcher, it was to provide a free flow of information—the type of information you may need to use in your search. Every day, new resources and Web sites are added to the Internet as it grows towards becoming the Library of the World.

GETTING READY FOR THE INTERNET

This section is written for novice adoptee/birthparent/sibling searchers who want to use the Internet to help them in their quest to find a reconnection to the past. If you already have a computer and are familiar with online services, skip to the "Searching Alone" section later in this chapter. If you are just beginning, what is written below will show you how to become a part of this new world and as the above quotation indicates that new world—the Internet— is vast and constantly growing.

The Internet (the Net) is a group of networks freely exchanging information. Once you decide to be a part of the Internet and sign up with an online service (see Internet Service Providers), you will be able to send and receive information to and from others both in the adoption movement and in a wide variety of other areas of your life. "What the Internet does, basically, is transmit data [information] from one computer to another."[2] Isn't that what you want to do? Discover what others have learned and what "data" they have amassed so you too can use these valuable resources.

The Internet has its own terminology. Some terms are used for "information only" and are offered to help you understand a phrase or topic while others are necessary to know before you can travel around the Internet. To assist you, I have compiled a brief list of definitions to start you on your journey of discovery. Those terms preceded by an asterisk (*) are presented in more detail later in this chapter.

Definitions

*BOOKMARK: This is a way to save Web sites you find valuable. Your Bookmark will allow easy return to those sites when later needed.

BROWSER: A software application used to locate and move around Web pages.

BULLETIN BOARD SYSTEM (BBS): Most are subscriber services that deal with specific subject matter. Some Web pages offer a free bulletin board for their guests.

DATABASE: A collection of information organized in such a way that, when prompted by a user, a computer program can quickly select pieces of data (information). Database sometimes appears as two words: data base.

DOWNLOAD: This is the process of receiving information. This information will be downloaded (copied) from a resource and sent to your computer, where it may be read.

*E-MAIL: Electronic mail is generated on one computer and sent through a network to another computer. Every user has a unique e-mail address.

FAQs: Short for Frequently Asked Questions.

HTML: Hypertext Markup Language. The authoring language used to create documents on the WWW.

HOME PAGE: This is the main page of a Web site. Usually, it contains a table of contents or index to the site.

HOST: The system that houses the data is the host, while the computer at which the user sits is called the remote terminal or guest.

HOT SPOT: An area on a Web page that activates a function. When selected, it takes you to another Web page. Also called a hot link.

http: Hypertext Transport Protocol: This is the official name indicating that you are asking for information. Some Web browsers do not require you to type in the http://; they add it automatically.

INTERNET: Also known as "the Net." The Internet is a series of networks that are interconnected.

*INTERNET SERVICE PROVIDER (ISP): A company that provides access to the Internet. It may be a large national company or a small local company. Sometimes called a service provider.

*KEYWORDS: These are subject terms used to find the information you are seeking. General keywords for adoption search could include: adoptee, birthmother, birthfather, search, reunion registry.

*LINK: A reference to another document, Web site, or Web page. Some links are called hot links because they take you to another document, site, or page when you click on them. Called a hyperlink.

LOG ON: When you type your username to gain access to your Internet Service Provider, you log on to begin the connection process.

MODEM: The device that connects your computer to your telephone line.

ONLINE: You are considered "online" when connected to a service provider through a modem. Online may also be written as on-line.

*SEARCH ENGINE: A program used to search for information using keywords and then to return a list of Web pages where those keywords were found.

URL: Universal Resource Locator. The global address of documents or resources on the World Wide Web.

USERNAME: A name used to gain access to a computer system, like a password. This is the first part of your e-mail address.

WORLD WIDE WEB: A system of Internet servers that support specially formatted documents. For your purpose, the terms WWW and Internet can be interchanged.

WEB PAGE: A document on a World Wide Web site.

WEB SITE: A location on the World Wide Web that is owned and maintained by an individual, company, or organization. Within a Web site there may be numerous Web pages.

Some people are more comfortable learning in the classroom and should check with their local junior college or computer store to see what classes are offered to learn about the Internet. Be sure to look around and find a class that suits your needs, as the costs vary greatly.

Other people learn best by having a few books handy and sitting down at their computer to take a look at the Internet. There are hundreds of books that will help you understand how to use your computer and how to discover the resources that exist on the Internet. My best advice on finding a good book to serve your needs is to talk to a salesperson at your local computer store. Discuss what you need and what you wish to accomplish. Don't be afraid to ask a question for fear you might sound foolish; after all, this is new to you and no question should go unanswered.

GETTING STARTED

As with anything new, you will need certain basic tools. First, you must own a computer and a modem, and have a telephone line. Second, you need to call an Internet Service Provider (see below) and register with their service so you will have a connection to the Internet. I am assuming you are using a single computer, not one hooked up to other computers in your home or office, so you will need to use your home telephone line to connect to the Internet and begin to "Surf the Web."

Internet Service Providers (ISP)

Internet Service Providers are companies that deliver access to the Internet through a dial-up account. The cost involved with a service provider is generally a monthly service charge (a set amount due each month) or a monthly charge plus an additional fee based on the time you spend online. Once you subscribe, your phone line will connect to their service and enable you to go online to the Internet. It is important to make sure your service provider offers a local or 800 number when they connect. If you are charged for the amount of time spent online and your service provider's number is long distance, your costs will add up quickly, causing your telephone bill to sky-rocket.

While you are "online" on the Internet, your telephone is in use, so anyone trying to call you will get a busy signal until you go "offline." If this becomes a problem, because you find you are spending a great amount of time online, you may need to call your phone company and have a second line installed in your home. It would be wise to wait and see the amount of time you will be spending online and how much it interferes with your personal calls before you request a second line, as this addition requires an installation charge and a monthly service fee.

There are several types of Internet service providers. Some offer only e-mail access like MCI Mail or AT&T Mail, while others are national or local providers that offer a variety of services. Check your phone book, as using a local service provider may be more economical than using a large national service provider, depending on the services you desire. Ask them what service plans they offer and make sure you understand what will be included in your monthly bill. Talk to an employee at your local computer store and see who they use or which service they recommend. If you have access to a computer, contact <www.thelist.com>. This Web database will ask for your area code and then supply you with a list of all service providers within that area code.

Listed below are three national service providers widely known to the beginning Internet user. These are large companies that generally offer an 800 or local telephone number to access their service. The Internet service providers shown below are not to be considered better than others not listed.

America Online: (800) 827-6364

Microsoft Network: (800) FRE-EMSN

Prodigy: (800) PRO-DIGY

Search Engine

A search engine is a database that gives your service provider additional resources and adds power so you may contact different Web sites on the Internet. Listed here are a few of the many search engines offered today. Examples not to be thought better than others you may use: Alta Vista <www.altavista.com/>, Excite <www.excite.com/>, HotBot <www.HotBot.com/>, Infoseek <www.infoseek.com/>, Lycos <www.lycos.com/>, WebCrawler <www.webcrawler.com/>, and Yahoo <www.yahoo.com/>. If you are unable to find a specific address or site with one search engine, try another one. Your service provider may offer some of these or others at no cost to you.

Links

Linking is when one Web site offers to establish a connection to another Web site. Generally, when you go to a site you will be offered several options. One might be to go to another related site that is "linked" to the initial Web page. Suppose you have gone to a Web site and the home page lists "Adoption Links" in its table of contents. If you click this area with your mouse, you will be connected to another Web page where a large list of Web sites is presented. If you look at this list, you will see the Social Security Death Index among the choices. All the sites listed are "hot spots" or "hot links"; they generally appear in a different color from the page's main text. If you click on the Social

Security Death Index with your mouse, you are instantly taken to that Web page. You don't need to type in the address, as this "hot spot" connects to the original site you visited.

Keywords

Your service provider or search engine will prompt you to list "keywords" so they may sort through the millions of pieces of data and select those Web pages that have the information you are seeking. The majority of adoption search Web pages can be reached by listing the keywords *adoptee, birthmother, birthfather, birthparent(s), reunion registry, search*. The keywords you use will determine what Web sites are selected and offered for viewing. If you use the keyword *adoption* instead of *adoptee*, the list presented will generally be about those wishing to adopt, not those adopted. If you only write the keyword *search*, an enormous list will be presented giving information from airline schedules to zoology papers.

As a beginner, you will probably want to look around and see what is on the Internet that deals with adoption search. When you become more familiar with moving around the Web, try other keywords that describe your specific search. You may wish to look at your state laws or join a reunion registry in your state of search while another searcher may wish genealogical information or political action groups that deal with open records.

Take a few moments and note those keywords that describe your search. What kind of information are you looking for? How would you best describe the subject matter needed to conduct your search? What are your goals—medical information only, or contact with a person from your past? Keep in mind that as we search, our aims change, and what began as a casual curiosity may become a desire for a meeting with a relinquished child or birthparent.

Most browsers will list Web sites according to the keywords used. They take the keywords in order of their importance, as they are listed. Regardless of the keywords you use, an unbelievable number of Web sites generally will be presented to you. This is when it is so important to build your Bookmark, so you can eliminate sites that are of no use and build a list of sites that are, or might be, useful to your search.

Electronic Mail (E-mail)

Your e-mail address is separated into three parts. The first part is your name or the way you are addressed on the computer. Many people have difficulty using their name because they are concerned with privacy, so they choose a "nickname" or "username." This username is separated from the second part of e-mail address by an "@," then the name of your computer or the service provider you use. The third part is a three-letter zone name, such as the following:

.com   commercial organizations
.edu   educational institutions
.gov   government bodies and departments
. net   networking organizations
.org   all other organizations

One example of an e-mail address might be: Searcher@aol.com.

SEARCHING ALONE

Searching on the Internet provides a wonderful tool for those who cannot attend group meetings or for the searcher who needs additional help and resources. However, this method of search should not be used *instead* of joining a group, but rather as an *additional resource*. Check Appendix I in the back of this book to learn of search and support groups in your area. Call your local library or look in your telephone directory to learn where groups may be meeting.

I cannot emphasize enough, the value of a group to help you through this difficult time. A search and support group will provide help and direction to aid you in completing your search. They will offer support when you come to a point where you believe all avenues have been traveled. A group will offer discussions on setting guidelines for your search and on recognizing the importance of respect and responsibility. As you go through different stages in your search, group members will recognize those stages and help you maintain focus as you begin to put bits and pieces together. Others who have faced difficulties will help you remember that you are looking for information, and hope that you find someone who will cooperate. They'll help you keep in mind you shouldn't do anything that will prevent a successful contact.

The searcher must spend some time thinking about contact before deciding to make contact. Whether you are looking for medical information only or would like to get to know your birthparent(s) or relinquished child (now an adult), how you make the initial contact is something you need to consider carefully before coming to a decision. The person you are seeking may not want to be found, so if you go barging in without thinking about what you are doing, the information you seek may be withheld from you. Would it be better to write a letter or make a phone call? Does the relinquished child (now an adult) even know he or she was adopted? Has the birthmother ever told anyone about the relinquishment? At this point, it is so important to connect with people in the search movement who will help you understand what you may find, how you may find it, and how you should treat the information you do find. People offer you support and advice. The computer searcher would be well advised to learn from those with years of experience in adoption search.

It is equally important to understand that you are looking for someone who, like you, is a genetic birthparent or relinquished child, and may react to the same things you do and in similar ways. To combine the experience of others with your natural instincts offers you, the searcher, the best chance of a successful contact.

If you find you do not wish to attend a group meeting in person, most service providers offer chat rooms that allow you to talk to other members in the adoption triad. Find a search and support group on the Internet, but make sure it has a reciprocal arrangement for their members, a way of communicating back and forth. Become involved with a bulletin board, newsgroup, or mailing list. Learn what others have done that worked and what didn't work. Talk to people on the Internet who have the same need-to-know. Your contact may be with search group members or chat rooms on the Internet.

Instant gratification may be the friend of the casual or business computer user, but it is the enemy of the adoption searcher. The person who searches on the computer with the idea that they will search, find, and contact all in one day has overlooked a very important part of search. The part that deals with "rights," "exposure," and "privacy." The part that recognizes your needs as well as the needs of person you are seeking.

BUYER BEWARE

In previous chapters, I have cautioned searchers to understand exactly what they are paying for, whether it is membership in a group, the price to hire a consultant, or the fees involved when they enroll in a registry. With the advent of the "computer search," it is more important than ever to know what you can expect from a person or service on the Internet. What began as a free flow of information has also become a source for commercial business. If you think you have been deluged with people trying to get you to use their telephone service, wait until you see the people on the Internet trying to get your business. Like other areas of our lives, when dealing with the Internet we must be alert to unethical business offers or services that we do not need. As we throw away junk mail, we need to throw away junk e-mail.

There are searchers and search services that you should approach with caution. Beware of the "business" that offers to do your search for you. Note I say "business," not a search and support group or an individual offering help for costs only or a small fee to obtain the documents needed to help you meet your goal. It is common to find one business charging $100 for a service while another business charges $500 for the same service. Always make sure you know exactly what the business or individual is going to provide and what the charges will be.

Be cautious of the business or person who charges $1,000, $2,000, or $5,000 to do a search for you before you even know if your search is going to be difficult and whether help will be needed. You might pay $2,000 to someone who simply goes to the Social Security Death Index and learns the person sought is deceased. The business or individual hired has completed the task, the search is over, and you pay the fee. The Social Security Death Index is on the Internet and it is free to you (see The Bookmark Address Book later in this chapter). You could have learned that the person sought was deceased as easily as the person you hired and saved yourself $2,000. Never use a paid searcher until you have exhausted all of your free resources. Then be sure the person you hire is aware of your efforts so they will not be duplicated.

What should be emphatically stressed is how important it is to ignore costly search help. There are so many excellent free researchers and searchers charging only the costs they have incurred. Before you use anyone listed on the Internet who charges to search, get a referral. If you are wondering about using paid search help, go to a Web site bulletin board or chat room and see what response you get from an ad. An example of an ad on a bulletin board or in a chat room might simply say the following:

> Are they legit? I am wondering whether to use John Doe to do a search for me. The charge is $500 and there is no guarantee of success. Has anyone out there used John Doe or does anyone have a better and cheaper resource?

You may be surprised at the response. Give your announcement a few weeks and see what happens.

Another example of abuse is the person online offering a name search service that is totally misleading. The cost of the name search might be $45, $100, or even $2,000. You pay the fee, and the business or individual enters the name into their database of phone directories, just like the ones listed on the Internet. Soon a list of names is found, but because this type of search does not find "a specific person" it provides a list of all names matching the one sought. The list may contain 5, 50, or 500 names depending on the database(s) used and the name sought. If the person's name is Alexicitius Zkorvinski, the list will most likely contain a single entry, but if the name is David Johnson, the list will be voluminous. What isn't said is there is no guarantee the person sought will be found, just that you will receive a list of persons in the United States with that name. There is no mention of the fact that all phone directories in the United States are not listed. The only guarantee is the searcher must pay $45, $100, or $2,000 to start the name search. Why not try to get the name yourself (see The Bookmark Address Book listed below for a phone search Web site).

Again, post an ad on a Web site bulletin board or chat room. You don't need to spend hours fretting about your ad; say something simple like "I want to do a name search and am not sure how to start. Can anyone help me?"

Before you even consider hiring someone, read the previous chapters in this book and learn what you can do yourself and how you can do it yourself. Give serious thought to joining a group so you can learn more about the experiences you will face and more about what you can expect.

Don't automatically think your search should be undertaken and completed in a day or two. Remember, your search will pass through several stages, both in development and in your evolution. No adoption or relinquishment happened in one day as should no search; much time should be spent thinking about what should be done and how to meet that end. Be patient and allow yourself time to catch up to the task you have set.

BOOKMARKS

Once a Web site is found on the Internet that you believe you will want to visit again, you should start to make a list of such sites. Most service providers have a place you can click with your mouse that builds such a list. It may be called "Bookmarks" or "favorite places"; they mean the same thing. Your Bookmarks are devoted to those Internet sites you will be using during your search. Once a site is on your Bookmark, you can click the Web site sought and be taken there without writing the address or Web site name.

It would be impossible to provide you with a complete list of useful Internet Web sites. Not only are there many sites dealing with a given subject matter, but a site may change its address or a new one may appear on the Internet days or hours after this writing. A Web site may cease to exist, or fall out of favor due to inaccuracies or infrequent updates.

You will find a vast array of search groups, information sources, and forums to use when you are trying to put together the few pieces of information you have obtained. Which Web site you select will depend on the area of your search, the information needed, and the services a Web site offers.

Some sites deal with a specific state or type of search like TXCARE, which is a free online search registry for Texas Adoptees; or Bits and Pieces—a charity dealing primarily with NC, SC, GA, MA, VA, and the District of Columbia. Most sites deal with all states.

Highlighted Web Sites

In choosing Web sites to highlight here, I looked at how long the site has been functioning and the number of resources it provides its viewers. I attempted to select free Web sites (some sites require you to subscribe to their service) that updated their material on a regular basis and provided satisfaction to its users.

When selecting Web sites to highlight, the major difficulty was the newness of the Internet and its sites. As the World Wide Web is relatively young, most sites did not have a long-term track record that would provide proof of their value and stability. Each day when you go online there are new sites, and old ones have disappeared. All Web sites presented here are current as of this writing but may not be as of your reading. Do not overlook new Web sites.

A Barrel of Genealogy Links <cpcug.org/user/jlacombe/mark.html>. As of this writing, there are about 400 links listed on this Web site that include information on regions of the United States, countries of the world, Civil War sites, and specific religious and nationality sites. There is a section on directories that includes fast area code look-up; Telephone Directories on the Web; Telephone Directories of Canada, France, and New Zealand; plus Vital Records State-by-State.

While there are numerous genealogy Web sites, I believe this one offers so many resources for the searcher it should be mentioned. This site's e-mail address is jlacombe@cpcug.org.

Adoptees Internet Mailing List (AIML) <www.webreflection.com/aiml/>. I strongly believe searchers need support from the very beginning of their search and that there is a need to talk to others about the feelings you are encountering, to have a place to go to discuss issues that you are now facing (see Chapter 2, "Getting Moral Support"). When a searcher is working primarily on the computer, this type of interaction may be difficult to find.

This Web site is for all members of the Triad, but one Web page, the AIML Mailing List, is for adoptees and adoptee-lites only ("adoptee-lites are people who were raised without one or both birthparents, but who were never legally adopted"). Birthparents, siblings, and adoptive parents should also check out this Web site as it provides links to mailing lists for all triad members. I am including this Web site to show the value of a mailing list for all searchers.

The Adoptees Internet Mailing List began in March 1995 to "provide adoptees with a private forum for the discussion of search and reunion issues." Once you arrive at their site, you may move to Subscription Information to learn the responsibilities of a mailing list member. Upon joining the AIML, you are instantly put in contact with all subscribers, as new e-mail is sent to everyone on the list. Membership is free and subscription is easy. As of this writing, AIML has over 1,000 members.

You may request to receive e-mail from subscribers on all adoption subjects (estimated at up to 100 per day) or request you receive e-mail from any of the six topics offered (Search, Reunion, Media, Legal, Social, Ads). Subscribers may also request their messages come in a few large e-mails or as individual messages.

For many adoptees who are searching, this is the first forum they have ever found in which they feel free to discuss their adoption and topics of special concern. This valuable resource should not be overlooked by the searcher. To join this free mailing list, either visit the AIML Web site at www.webreflection.com/aim/, or send an e-mail to listserv@ maelstrom.stjohns.edu with the words SUBSCRIBE ADOPTEES in the body of your message.

Adoption Law and Reforms <www.webcom.com/kmc/adoption/ adoption.html>. This excellent resource serves a valuable purpose to the adoption searcher as it presents adoption legislation, U.S. and International Law, legal sources, policy resources, and more.

Once a state puts its laws online, this site includes them in their list of codes and statutes. Pending legislation is discussed and information is given that can be useful to you concerning your state of search as well as in the U.S. Congress.

A wide variety of adoption law links are presented, such as Legal Information Institute, American Law Sources Online, and FindLaw. These links allow you to search for the state and type of legal information you are seeking.

This Web site furnishes a useful source of legal information and should be a part of the adoption searcher's Bookmark. Send e-mail to kmc@netcom.com.

The Adoption Ring <www.plumsite.com/adoptionring/>. A ring is a group of similar content sites that are linked together in a ring, a circular fashion. On the Webring's home page they give an excellent description of their purpose: "The Webring provides the Internet community with a different way to organize content on the World Wide Web." You enter their home page, and go around the ring visiting each site or selecting to skip two or five, even viewing the ring on a random basis. This ring includes more than 175 pages and is growing daily.

Some useful sites include: Adoptees Internet Mailing List Home Page, Adoption Information & Direction, Cat's Adoption Links, Cyn's Adoption Stuff, Jim Albertor Adoptee Page, The Homepage for Adoptees & Birthfamilies, Lori's Adoption Page, Adoption Connection, Adoptee & Birthmother, Adoptee Related WWW Library, Welcome to Bastard Nation, Adoption Reunion Registry—world wide, The Adoptees link, The Adoptees Newsgroup, and Adoption Triad's Reading Guide. Do not neglect other sites on the ring as new ones are added with each update. This is a wonderful Web site to add to your Bookmark. Send e-mail to adoption@plumsite.com.

An Adoptee's Right to Know <www.plumsite.com/shea/>. A Web site with all the "nuts and bolts" needed to conduct a search on the Internet. An Adoptee's Right to Know was introduced to the World Wide Web in 1995 by Shea Grimm. Since that time, large numbers of visitors have signed their guest book with questions and comments.

An Adoptee's Right to Know offers a multitude of links that include Current Events, General Adoption Links, the Uniform Adoption Act of 1994, Shea's Search Series, Search and Reunion Support and Resources, Adoption-Related and Reform-minded Organizations on the Web, Transracial and International Adoptions, and an Adoption Law Library.

Since I strongly believe in an organized approach to searching, the Shea's Search Series offers the searcher a strong resource. Visit this Web site and sign their guest book. Once you have seen the wide variety of useful resources, adoption searchers will want to include An Adoptee's Right to Know on their Bookmark. Send e-mail to sheag@oz.net.

Angry Grandma's Adoptees' Resources <www.ior.com/~laswi/ patdubois.htm>.

> None of us would willingly forfeit all rights in perpetuity for ourselves and all our descendants forever to **any knowledge** of our lives, an induced amnesia of all family history; yet society has taken for granted the assumption that adoptees have no right to our own heritage.

This Web site has very moving statements and letters. Five areas are addressed, including the following:

- *General Search Links:* The index to Adoptee's Links provides access to: Where to be Found on the Net, Urgent, Why I'm Angry, Links, Boards, Articles, and Adoption Issues. These links are useful to all searchers.
- *The Senior Citizen and Search:* There is the belief that we search at an important time in our lives. This may be the birth of our first child, on our 21st birthday, or at the death of one or both of our parents. This site recognizes an important time to search may also come when you meet your first grandchild or on your 60th birthday. A chat room and boards are offered to provide the "grandma" or "grandpa" a place to feel comfortable during this time.
- *The Abused Adoptee/Birthmother:* In 1978, I first heard stories about abused adoptees and the birthmother who had relinquished her child because of abuse. Since that time the subject has come up again and again but no figures or data are provided to show the numbers involved. Finally there is a Web site that addresses this issue. Visitors are offered the option of participating in a survey dealing with abuse. The Angry Grandma's Adoptees' Resources and Abused Adoptees' sections of the message boards are also displayed.

This is a wonderful, creative site that every searcher should visit and add to their Bookmark. Send e-mail to 2123605@pager.mirabiles.com.

Bastard Nation <www.bastards.org/>. On the Internet it is thought rude to type in CAPITALS, as that is considered shouting. Bastard Nation is on the Internet and they are shouting "WE WON'T TAKE SEALED RECORDS ANYMORE." While many people are turned off by their name and their aggressive style, I find Bastard Nation refreshing. They believe they have a job to do, and they are not about to let anyone stop them.

Bastard Nation does not meet in homes or at the library, rather it is a Web site with its own home page. Members do not have to live in one city or state to be active, they can live anywhere. Their mission statement is as follows:

Bastard Nation has as its primary goal the opening of all adoption records, uncensored and unaltered, to an adoptee upon request, at age of majority. We respect the diversity of opinion present in the adoption community among adoptees, which is why we advocate that each adoptee have the ability to choose whether he/she wishes to search or access his/her birth records.

Offerings include a variety of committees that have been established including Legislative, Publication/Arts, PR/Media, Events, Education/Training as well as general search information. Also included are USA & Canadian Searches, laws affecting adoptees, international and transracial adoptees, books, adoptee home page, and reunion registries.

One very important service provided by Bastard Nation is their Terminal Illness Emergency Service Program (T.I.E.S.). This impressive professional team has been set up to offer volunteer searches as well as a reunion support network to help search for birthfamily members of adopted individuals with a terminal illness. For details on how to enroll in this service, contact T.I.E.S. at 2269 Chestnut Street, #224, San Francisco, CA 94123, (415) 931-0844, e-mail: DebSPR@aol.com.

Mail may be directed to Bastard Nation, 12865 NE 85th Street, Suite 179, Kirkland, WA 98033, (415) 435-7960, fax (415) 470-3741, e-mail: bn@bastards.org.

The Center for Adoptee Rights <www.netaxs.com/~sparky/adoption/rights.htm>. A "stand up and take notice" site for the politically inclined. Their opening statement is as follows:

The purpose of this site is to collect facts, development [of] arguments, build strategies and promote action for the reform of U.S. adoption law. This site will serve as a reference for activists, lawmakers, adoption professionals and others concerned with human rights and ethics in adoption law and practice.

Several options are presented to the visitor: Immediate Release, Main Menu, News and Legal Events, Essays, Review and Opinion, Reference, Contacts, More Adoption References, Legal Buzzwords, Quote(s) of the Week(s). Two pages offer the reader an opportunity to review conventional thinking: Adoption-speak and Statement of Grievances. There is even a section on Anti-Adoptee Lobby Groups to allow the viewer the opportunity to learn what their opponents' plans are to keep records sealed.

If you want to know what is happening in the adoption movement, put this Web site on your Bookmark. If you don't think you would be interested, think again. This site is a wealth of information. Send e-mail to sparky@netaxis.com.

Doug Henderson's Guide to Adoption Acronyms <www.uwsp.edu/acad/psych/dh/acrony5.htm>. Originally, this Web site was called "The Big Dummy's

Guide to Adoption Acronyms." While the original title may sound whimsical, the information offered is not silly or foolish—it is useful, accurate, and informative.

The adoption movement uses many acronyms like AAC, ISRR, CUB, CERA, and UAA. Each of these acronyms is well known to those who have been around for a while, but for the beginning searcher they may only seem a puzzle. Doug Henderson has made the beginning searcher's job much easier as he presents each group, their acronym, current information about the group, and some of their history.

Both old and new searchers will find this a good choice for their Bookmark. Send e-mail to dhenders@uwsp.edu.

More Adoption Links & Other Stuff <members.tripod.com/~HevensDawn/adoption.html>. It is difficult to imagine a site that offers links to: statistics, surveys, adoption reform, directories, reunion registries, adoption links, state laws, adoption books, vital records information, genealogy resources, Canadian resources, phone and e-mail addresses, plus many other resources. With more than 90 links, More Adoption Links & Other Stuff provides the searcher with many such resources and avenues to pursue.

This site was founded in March 1996 and is updated weekly. At the time of this writing, more than 20,000 people have visited this Web site. Send e-mail to EarlyDawn@worldnet.att.net.

The Seeker—a Magazine Online <www.the-seeker.com/adopt.htm>. *The Seeker* is an online magazine that started their Web site in 1995. All costs are paid for by "off-line" advertisers, as *The Seeker* does not charge the visitor for using their site. At the top of their Web site you will read "An Up-to-the-Second Website for People Seeking People," and that is exactly what you will find.

When you go to *The Seeker*, you are offered a variety of Web pages to view: Generally Seeking, Relatively Seeking, Militarily Seeking, Seeking Beneficiaries. As an adoptee/birthparent searcher, you would select "Relatively Seeking." Once there, you type in the date of birth of the child in common. You don't need a name or even an exact birth date to find who you are looking for or to learn if they have already placed a message for you.

Look around this Web site as there are several areas that might be of value to your search. The Militarily Seeking Site offers a large number of links and will prove most useful to those searching in this area. The Genealogy Site provides links to Telephone Directories on the Web, Vital Statistics, U.S. National Archives, U.S. Library of Congress, and Social Security Death Records. The Factually Seeking Site offers help to locate "friends and relatives if they don't have a computer and can't seek The Seeker."

The "Place Your Own Message" Site lets you write as many messages as you like for your relinquished child/birthparent/sibling. You may place your own message in this section so others can contact you to provide you with information you are seeking. Their classified section can be an excellent way of making contact with someone who is searching for you. The Site Seeking section is a compilation of links to other sites. The Miscellaneous Database Sites area lets people type in the name of whoever they are looking for, like a telephone directory (20+ of them.)

The Seeker is an easy to use and understand Web site that should be on your Bookmark. Send e-mail to seeker@Packet.Net.

Voices of Adoption <www.ibar.com/voices/activism/>. This award-winning site was created by Denise Castellucci in 1997. Since that time, hundreds of people have visited and contributed their stories, poetry, and art, providing a place to express your thoughts and ideas.

Voices of Adoption delivers: features, stories, events, activism, articles, resources, poetry, books, art, chat rooms, FAQs, T.I.E.S., B.E.S.T., Borderlands, Contact, Coming Soon, and Interactive forms.

So many new ideas and resources are yet to come in the adoption movement and this Web site has prepared for those additions. Your Bookmark should contain this innovative, feel-good site. Send e-mail to voices@ibar.com.

VSN (Volunteer Searchers Network) <www.wolfenet.com/~vrummig/vsn.html>. I found the VSN of great value for the adoption searcher. They do not offer meetings or group support; rather this resource offers a "buddy system" on the Internet. When you first visit the VSN Information Page, you will read their purpose statement:

> The Volunteers Network is a nationwide group of Volunteers who have come together to offer our services to people touched by adoption who need search help. We are a diverse group made up mostly of triad members, some have found, some have not, but all of us want to help. We do not make a profit on services, it is at a cost only basis. Our Volunteers charge only for what it costs them to help you. This help is available only for adoptees, birthparents and their family members who are looking for lost loves. We do not locate infants to be adopted.

This Web site offers a unique service to adoptees, birthparents, and family members looking for information in a distant city or state. VSN volunteers do not perform full searches; instead, each does a different specific task such as checking city phone books/directories, visiting the local library city hall, going to the local courthouse to find records, or doing legwork as needed. A few volunteers offer you phone dish and search databases. Some VSN volunteers may search an entire state while others provide help in just one county or city. This group of volunteers charges reimbursement costs for expenses, not for time or profit.

The VSN Information Page is updated most weeks as changes are made and new areas of the country are covered. If you are searching out of your state, VSN should definitely be added to your Bookmark. Send e-mail to vrummig@wolfenet.com.

World Wide Registry Matching Adoptees and BirthParents <www.phoenix.net/~aquarian/davids/birth.html>. This large reunion regis-try has more than 23,000 searchers registered at the time of this writing. It is a Web site that links two sites to provide a free confidential registry for adoptees and birthparents.

As you begin to view this Web site, several choices will be offered: Register, Change, Found, Resources, Right-to-Know, News, Sponsor, Search the Birth Index. Your first choice should be "Search the Birth Index" to see if you are being sought. This simple Birth Index provides a list of those sought by year, month, and day of birth, and includes the state born.

To become a part of the World Wide Registry Matching Adoptees with BirthParents go to "Register." Enter your information by answering the basic questions provided.

One feature that makes this registry stand out is their Resources page. This page gives birthparents and adoptees an opportunity to talk about what they are searching for, what is happening in their search, and sometimes, how their search ended. A wonderful effort, this registry is filled with valuable informa-tion and useful resources. Several reunion registries should be on your Book-mark and this registry is definitely one of them. Send e-mail to ds396@ncf.carleton.ca.

The Bookmark Address Book

Listed below are a variety of useful Web sites you may want to visit and use in your search. Some service providers or browsers locate a site by its name (the Adoption Ring) while others need an address <www.plumsite.com/adoptionring/>.

It is unlikely your browser will need the full address <http://www.plumsite.com/adoptionring/>, but in the event it does, insert http:// before each address given.

- Adoptee's Internet Mailing List (AIML) **www.webreflection.com/aiml/**
Highlighted above.

- Adoptees Liberty Movement Association (ALMA) **www.almanet.com/**
Highlighted in Chapter 7, "Search and Support Groups, Researchers/Searchers, Consultants, Intermediaries, and the Courts."

- An Adoptee's Right to Know **www.plumsite.com/shea/?**
Highlighted above.

- Adoptee's Search Page **members.wbs.net/homepages/q/w/e/qweet.html**
General or specific search help. Links to name, address, and phone searches; Underground Legal Net; Adoption Revolution led by adoptees on the Web; registries; and much more. Good resource for U.S. and Canadian searchers

- Adoption Bulletin Board **www.webstreet.com/cs/orphans/board.htm**
A wonderful site to post or read messages from other searchers.

- Adoption Crossroads **www.adoptioncrossroads.org/**
Highlighted in Chapter 7, "Search and Support Groups, Researchers/Searchers, Consultants, Intermediaries, and the Courts."

- Adoption Help Page **www.kxan.com/~micah/adopt.html**
A suggested Bookmark addition since there are so many adoption links here.

- Adoption in the Computer Age **www.ecst.csuchico.edu./~program/adoption/**
Contains Social Security Death Index, Freedom of Information, and ethical concerns. A very interesting and informative site.

- Adoption Information Exchange **kinsolving.com/locate**
Highlighted in Chapter 10, "Search Resources and Services."

- Adoption Information Clearinghouse **www.calib.com/naic/**
Highlighted in Chapter 10, "Search Resources and Services."

- Adoption Law and Reforms **www.webcom.com/kmc/adoption/adoption.html**
Highlighted above.

- Adoption Links **www.public.usit.net/jmchris/birth1.htm**
A find people, find resource site, and a find free posting and free search site.

- Adoption Network Cleveland **pages.prodigy.com/adoptreform/anc.htm**
Highlighted in Chapter 7, "Search and Support Groups, Researchers/Searchers, Consultants, Intermediaries, and the Courts."

- Adoption Puzzle Pieces—Links **www.geocities.com/EnchantedForest/Dell/5167/adoptionlinks.html**
A must see for its variety and number of links. A definite Bookmark selection.

- Adoption Resources on the Net **psy.ucsd.edu/~jhartung/forums.html**
Information on search links, search and support groups, state laws, lobby organizations, mailing lists, reunion registries, newsgroups, books, and multimedia as well as

a multitude of other Internet resources. Searchers must see this site to believe its depth.

- The Adoption Revolution **www.openadoption.org/bbetzen/adoptee.htm**
  Links and personal stories. Well worth visiting.

- The Adoption Ring **www.plumsite.com/adoptionring/**
  Highlighted above.

- Adoption Search and Reference Web ring **www.geocities.com/Heartland/Meadows/7375/awr.html**
  A new and growing Web ring.

- Adoption Triad Outreach **www.cm-online.net/adoption/**
  Links, Web rings, events, news, chat, BBS, plus more. Their reunion registry allows the searcher to enroll with the exact birth date or an "unknown" date permitting siblings and birthfathers to search.

- The Adoption Triad's Reading Guide **www.wolfenet.com/~oren/adopread.html**
  A reading list of fiction and nonfiction books dealing with adoption. Adult adoptees, birthparents, searches, searching and reunions, children and young readers, and miscellaneous. Some books may be ordered from this site.

- AdoptioNetwork **www.adoption.org/**
  State-by-state adoption laws, books and magazines, newsletters, and much more.

- alt.adoption Newsgroups **www.vcu.edu/news/alt.adoption.html**
  An unmoderated newsgroup for all members of the triad.

- American Adoption Congress **rdz.stjohns.edu/amer-adopt-congress**
  See Chapter 10, "Search Resources and Services" for more information on this umbrella organization.

- American School Directory **www.asd.com/**
  Over 106,000 school Web sites, grades K-12.

- Angry Grandma's Adoptee's Resources **www.ior.com/~laswi/patdubois.htm**
  Highlighted above.

- A Barrel of Genealogy Links **cpcug.org/user/jlacombe/mark.html**
  Highlighted above.

- Bastard Nation **www.bastards.org/**
  Highlighted above.

- BigBook **www.bigbook.com/**
  Yellow pages combining businesses with street-level maps, plus lots more.

- BigYellow **www/bigyellow.com/**
  Here you will find phone, e-mail, Internet, business, and global directories.

- Birthmother's Mailing List **www.eden.com/~belinda**
  A mailing list for birthmothers only.

- Bureau of Indian Affairs **www.doi.gov/bia/aitoday/aitoday.html**
  For more information, see Chapter 4, "Reference Resources."

- CANADopt **nebula.on.ca/canadopt/**
  Resource for Canadian searchers.
- The Cancer Web **infoventures.com/cancer/canlit/des0995.html**
  For more information, see Chapter 1, "Deciding to Search." DES information.
- Carrie's Crazy Quilt **www.mtjeff.com/~bodenst/page3.html**
  Adoption and genealogy links on this Web site.
- Carter's Adoption Search Page **www.armory.com/~cartert/**
  Many links to search sites make this a Bookmark addition.
- Cat's Adoption Page **www.starsysfw.com/meowser/adopt.htm**
  Adoption statues and legislative code by state/province/country. Newsgroups, mailing lists, and many other useful links are provided on this Web site.
- The Center for Adoptee Rights **www.netaxs.com/~sparky/adoption/rights.htm**
  Highlighted above.
- Chain of Life **www.bastards.org/life.htm**
  Progressive adoption newsletter.
- Cindi's List of Genealogy Sites on the Internet **www.oz.net/!cindihow/sites.htm**
  Over 24,950 links. Excellent resource for information.
- Concerned United Birthparents (CUB) **www.webnations.com/cub/**
  Highlighted in Chapter 7, "Search and Support Groups, Researchers/Searchers, Consultants, Intermediaries, and the Courts."
- Council for Equal Rights in Adoption (CERA) **www.adoption crossroads.org/**
  Search help, statistics, a list of missing in adoption, and much more. See Chapter 10, "Search Resources and Services," for more detail on this group.
- Cyn's Adoption Stuff **www.visualimage.com/cyn/Adoption.HTML**
  Lots of links, information, and a useful searching on the Web section.
- The Definitive Adoption Links Page **webreflection.com/pinkerton**
  Patrick Pinkerton has put together a site filled with adoption information.
- Doug Henderson's Guide to Adoption Acronyms **www.uwsp.edu/acad/psych/dh/acrony5.htm**
  Highlighted above.
- Ecola Newsstand **www.ecola.com/**
  Newspapers and magazines from around the world
- The Electronic Activist **www.berkshire.net/~ifas/activist/**
  Provides an e-mail address directory of congresspeople, state governments, and media entities. Those searchers looking for a Web site dealing with magazines, books, or classified ads should check this one out.
- Ellen's Reuniting Families **www.highfiber.com/~leninger/**
  Message boards for adoptees, birthparents, and adoptive parents. Help for new searchers, links, books, and a section on the Internet for adoption searches. A Bookmark must for all searchers.
- Especially for Adoptees **www.adoption.org/adoptees.html**
  National & State Search organizations, articles, online search registry, and books.

- Everton's Genealogical Helper **www.everton.com/**
  A genealogical magazine. See Chapter 3, "What Will It Cost Me?" and Chapter 4, "Reference Resources," for more information.
- Forget Me Not Family Society **www.portal.ca/~adoption/Feedback/mailordr.htm**
  Small selection of adoption search books are offered for sale at this site.
- Four11 Directory Services **www.four11.com/**
  A free telephone, net phone, e-mail, and government address directory.
- Genealogical Hotlinks **www.infouga.org/hotlinks.htm**
  Available on the Utah Genealogical Association Web site. Many useful links.
- Genealogy Is My Hobby **home.earthlink.net/~middleton/**
  A wonderful site for name searches, archives information, magazine articles, and genealogy links.
- Government Printing Office **www.access.gpo.gov/su-docs/sale.html**
  A list of GPO products for sale and their locations. Chapter 4, "Reference Resources," provides more information on their services.
- The Ideal Maternity Home **www3.ns.sympatico.ca/bhartlen/**
  A registry and information about the Butterbox babies.
- Independent Search Consultants **www.rmci.net/isc**
  Highlighted in Chapter 7, "Search and Support Groups, Researchers/Searchers, Consultants, Intermediaries, and the Courts."
- InfoSpace **www.infospace.com/**
  A free address, phone, white and yellow page search.
- International Soundex Reunion Registry **chariott.com/~schmidt/spiel/general/issr.html**
  The world's largest reunion registry. For more information on this free registry, see Chapter 8, "Reunion Registries." A MUST registry.
- The Internet Sleuth **www.isleuth.com/**
  A great site to do searches on business, government, and research. Also genealogical links.
- Irish Genealogical Society, International (IGSI) **www.rootsweb.com/~irish/adopt.htm**
  Irish adoption links.
- Julie's Search and Reunion Site **www.fastlane.net/~jules/**
  Lots of resources on this Web site.
- Kay's Adoption Corner **www.koyote.com/personal/hobb/main.html**
  A must for your Bookmark. Law and law library resources, search engines, mailing lists, phone and address sites, genealogy sites, and poems and writing. A large list of sites to read and post information when seeking an adoptee or birthparent.
- The Largest Newspaper Index **www.concentric.net/~stev.wt/**
  A resource listing many newspapers published in the United States.
- The Library of Congress **lcweb2.loc.gov/catalog/**
  See Chapter 4, "Reference Resources," for more information.

- LINC Online Adoption Reunion Registry **www.reunionregistry.com/**
  A free reunion registry that has more than 15,000 people enrolled at present.
- THE Link Page **members.aol.com/magules96/link.html**
  Registeries, post boards, search pages, phone and address searches, other places of interest.
- The Lost Bird Society **www.montrose.net/users/fouche/zintka.htm**
  A resource for Native Americans. Genealogy links, personal stories, and adoption issues in the United States, Canada, and Australia.
- Mental Health Net—Adoption Resources **www.cmhc.com/guide/adoption.htm**
  A must-see site filled with important information and mailing lists.
- Military City Online Web Outpost **www.militarycity.com/**
  A military resource. Subscription required but you may conduct a free sample search.
- Military Network **www.military-network.com/**
  Contains site search, contents, message center, and Web search.
- Miracle Search Network **www.miraclesearch.com**
  This search service charges a fee. I have included it here as a resource for those needing paid search help.
- Missy McAllister—Adoption and Search Links **dragon-street.com/~missy/alinks/ html**
  Offers links to Web sites for adoptees and birthparents, registries, telephone and addresses, census age search, military, and genealogy. A five star Web site.
- More Adoption Links and Other Stuff **members.tripod.com/~HevensDawn/ adoption.html**
  Highlighted above.
- National Adoption Information Clearinghouse (NAIC) **www.calib.com/naic/**
  A place to receive your state's adoption laws. Send e-mail to naic@calif.com.
- National Archives **www.nara.gov/**
  See Chapter 4, "Reference Resources." for more information on the Archives.
- Oregon Adoptive Rights Association (OARA) **www.oara.org**
  Highlighted in Chapter 7, "Search and Support Groups, Researchers/Searchers, Consultants, Intermediaries, and the Courts."
- Other Online Adoption Resources **www.portal.ca/~adoption/**
  Resources and other Web sites. A large number of links for Canadian searchers.
- Owen's Quick-Links **personal.riverusers.com/~oburt/links.htm**
  Registries, newsgroups, genealogy, legal records, and home pages are just a few links available at this Web site.
- Perspectives Press **www.perspectivespress.com**
  Offers adoption related books
- Post Adoption Center for Education and Research **www. plumsite.com/pacer/**
  Highlighted in Chapter 10, "Search Resources and Services."

- Reconnections in Adoption **www.crashers.com/search/**
  A free registry for women who wish to reconnect with other women who resided in the same maternity home.

- The Reporters Network **www.reporters.net/**
  Maintains e-mail directory of journalists, editors, producers, and freelance writers.

- Reunions Online Adoption Registry **www.absnw.com/reunions/**
  A free reunion registry that is also filled with search and adoption links.

- Reunions Magazine **www.exepc.com/~reunions/adopt.html**
  An on- and off-line magazine. See Chapter 10, "Search Resources and Services," for more information.

- Roots and Wings Adoption Magazine **www.adopting.org/rw.html**
  A magazine offering articles for adoptees and birthparents searching and also for those adopting. Send e-mail to adoption@interactive.net.

- Search Triad, Inc. **home.att.net/~kehgchu**
  Highlighted in Chapter 7, "Search and Support Groups, Researchers/Searchers, Consultants, Intermediaries, and the Courts."

- Searching for People **ddi.digital.net/islander/index.html**
  Links for a variety of resources.

- The Seeker—A Magazine Online **www.the-seeker.com/adopt.htm**
  Highlighted above.

- Social Security Death Index **www.infobases.com/ssdi/query01.htm**
  Resource for Social Security information.

- Surrogate Mother's Online **www.geocities.com/Wellesley/2025/Index.html**
  Web site for surrogate mothers that offers bulletin boards, links, and classifieds.

- Switchboard **www.switchboard.com/**
  A free resource that allows searching the entire United States for a phone number.

- Tapestry Books **www.webcom.com/~tapestry/**
  A small selection of adoption search books are offered for sale.

- Telephone Directories on the Web **www.contractjobs.com/tel/**
  Telephone and fax directories from around the world.

- T.I.E.S. (Terminal Illness Emergency Search) **www.ibar.com/TIES/**
  See Bastard Nation highlighted above.

- The Ultimate Adoption Bookstore **www.burningelectrons.com/adopt/bookstore.html**
  Filled with adoption related books and how to order them through Amazon Books.

- USA LDS Family History Centers **www.flexnet.com.uk/~detatango/fhcusa.html**
  Family History Centers and state-by-state LDS information.

- Voices for Open Records **www.ibar.com/voices/activism/**
  Articles, letters, and opinions.

- Voices of Adoption **www.ibar.com/voices/activism/**
  Highlighted above.

- VSN Info Page **www.wolfenet.com/~vrummig/vsn.html**
  Highlighted above.

- WWW Adoption Resources **www.cyberspacepr.com/adoptfaq.html**
  A useful place to discover sites that range from FAQs, registries, mailing lists, classifieds, and adoption law and reform, to specific search areas.

- Where to Write for Vital Records **www.medaccess.com/address/vital-toc.htm**
  Current information on vital records sources.

- Wichita Adult Adoptees **www2.southwind.net/~1peters/waaindex.html**
  Highlighted in Chapter 7, "Search and Support Groups, Researchers/Searchers, Consultants, Intermediaries, and the Courts."

- World Alumni Net **www.alumni.net/**
  A long shot for finding school records, as you need to know the name, and the school must be included in this site. Lists alumni from university, college, high school directories from around the world.

- World Wide Registry Matching Adoptees and BirthParents **www.phoenix.net/ ~aquarian/davids/birth.html**
  Highlighted above.

- World's Largest Adoptee Related Link Page **www.idir.net/~pbrown/wlarlp.html**
  Over 60 links that include Uniform Adoption Action information, Phone Phinder, Internet Resources, and much more.

- Yahoo!—Society & Culture **www.yahoo.com/Society-and-Culture/Families/ Parenting/Adoption/**
  An excellent place to find a search link.

NOTES

1. From Katie Hafner and Matthew Lyon, *The Origins of the Internet*, New York: Simon & Schuster, 1996, p. 257.
2. Taken from John R. Levine and Carol Baroudi, *The Internet for Dummies*, San Mateo, CA: IDG Books, 1993, p. 55.

CHAPTER 10

Search Resources and Services

As more and more individuals begin and end their searches, new resources and services begin to appear. One of the advantages to the adoption movement is that adoption touches people from all walks of life who possess varied skills. As a search is progressing, or at its completion, searchers will many times combine their search experience with their work or hobby experiences. When a new service becomes available to the general public, someone always seems to ask, "How can I apply that to adoption search?" It may be someone with sympathies for the adoption movement or someone who simply feels adoption search could use their ideas.

This chapter contains a wide variety of reference sources directed solely to the person seeking information on a birthparent or relinquished child. It presents the searcher with a final look at the many services available and offers a clearer picture of the growth the adoption search movement has experienced.

The following resources and services can be of great value to the searcher, offering one more way to network and utilize information to reach your ultimate goal.

EDUCATIONAL AND LEGISLATIVE GROUPS

Most individuals involved in adoption search soon come to realize the value of legislative and educational groups. These groups provide information on pending laws within a state, unite to demonstrate against "sealed records," offer classes or literature to assist the searcher in understanding the legislative progress, distribute newsletters, or a medley of some or all of the above. A few groups have a national membership with a headquarters, while others serve a more regional area or specialized topic.

To give you an idea of the variety of the educational and legislative groups currently active, review the following list:

Adoption Forum, P.O. Box 12502, Philadelphia, PA 19151, (215) 238-1116

Adoption Knowledge Affiliates, 2121 S. Lamar, Suite 112, Austin, TX 78704

Answers, P.O. Box 337, Diablo, CA 93528

Adoptees' Political Action Coalition, P.O. Box 2807, Glenville, NY 12302

Adoption Reform Movement, Bob Schafer, 95 N. Whitesbridge Road, Belding, MI 48809, (616) 897-8342

AdOption Resource Center, P.O. Box 383246, Cambridge, MA 02238-3246, fax (617) 547-5308, e-mail: kinnect@aol.com

Bastard Nation, Shea Grimm-Jones, 12865 NE 85th Street, Suite 179, Kirkland, WA 98033, (206) 833-7293, fax (415) 680-2420, e-mail: sheag@oz.net

In highlighting several groups, I do not wish to imply that others might not better serve your particular needs.

Adoption Information Exchange (AIE)

Adoption Information Exchange (AIE) of North Carolina describes itself as ". . .a non-profit support group composed of adult adoptees, birthparents, adoptive parents, prospective adoptive parents, and supportive professionals in the field of adoptive services."

This group is involved in public education and provides annual forums, classes, workshops, and meetings. AIE informs members, as well as the general public, of current legislation on adoption issues in North Carolina.

Chapters of AIE can be found in Charlotte, Winston-Salem, Boone, Ashville, New Bern, Greensboro, and Greenville. They meet monthly and offer members an extensive list of lending materials from their library.

Members (18 years or older) seeking search assistance will be referred to North Carolina searchers. AIE is a member of the American Adoption Congress and an affiliate of International Soundex Reunion Registry.

Information or a membership form can be obtained by writing to the Adoption Information Exchange, P.O. Box 1917, Matthews, NC 28106, or by phoning (704) 537-5919. Please enclose a stamped, self-addressed envelope with all correspondence. Send e-mail to mzchrislee@aol.com, or view Web site at <kinsolving.com/locate>.

American Adoption Congress (AAC)

In the "President's Message" of the first issue of *Open A.R.M.S. Quarterly*, Penny Partridge (AAC's first president) described the AAC as follows:

> What is the AAC?—The AAC is a coalition—"coalesce" means "growing together"—of individuals and groups across North America who care about making adoption more open. The AAC is an acknowledgment of the many people who, on their own or in groups, are working toward this goal in a great variety of ways. The AAC is a means of educating ourselves about this and a channel through which we can educate the rest of the adoption community and the general public. The AAC allows groups, large and small, to learn from each other, and for individuals, whether in a group or not, to connect up with the larger network.

The AAC was conceived in May 1979. Final bylaws, election of officers, and membership policy were established in Kansas City in 1981. The AAC concerns itself with all those involved in adoption: adoptees, birthparents, adoptive parents, social workers, judges, lawyers, and the general public. It was formed as an "umbrella" organization to bring the various search and support groups together to learn about legislation and common problems within the movement. The AAC holds national and regional conferences. These conferences provide workshops and speakers in addition to the guidance, support, encouragement, information, and sharing of ideas found whenever people of mutual interest meet.

Their major goal is to tackle the problem of sealed records. One of the ways in which it addresses this problem is by sponsoring an annual "March on Washington." The 9th annual "March on Washington" will be held June 13, 1998. Its objective is to pressure individual states to change their laws regarding sealed adoption records.

A new member service is an Internet mailing list for AAC members, AAC Life. This offers "AAC members the opportunity to come together, plan events, exchange information, learn, grow and get to know one another."

The *Decree* is their quarterly newsletter. It is packed with feature articles talking about all aspects of adoption issues. Current information on changes in state laws, new online resources, letters to the editor, book reviews, and "Inside the AAC" are a few of the departments regularly reporting. *Decree* offers a fascinating look at where adoption is going and what is happening in the adoption movement, and presents ideas with a different perspective.

Highlighted groups that have an affiliation with the AAC will have current information on hand for those individuals who wish to learn more about the American Adoption Congress. Membership is on a sliding scale and entitles you to a subscription to *The Decree*, discounts on all conference classes, workshops, AAC activities, events, and services.

For information, write to the American Adoption Congress, 1000 Connecticut Avenue NW, Suite 9, Washington, DC 20036, (202) 483-3399, Web site <rdz.stjohns.edu/amer-adopt-congress/>.

Americans for Open Records (AmFOR)

American for Open Records (AmFOR) is a nonprofit international civil liberties network that has reunited over 10,000 adoption-affected families and others, without charge, since its 1989 founding. AmFOR has been a data reporting source to the United Nations "Rights of the Child" Project and the Hague Intercountry Abduction/Adoption Treaty Conferences.

AmFOR has a national and international network involved in education and legislation. To accomplish this goal, AmFOR's members attend legislative hearings and demonstrations, speak on talk shows and radio/television news programs, send letters to editorial pages, write articles for newspapers and magazines, and prepare legal briefs.

To learn more about this organization or to apply for membership, write to Americans for Open Records, P.O. Box 401, Palm Desert, CA 92261, or see AmFOR's information running on Bastard Nation's Web site www.bastards.org.

Council for Equal Rights in Adoption (CERA)

The Council for Equal Rights in Adoption (CERA) is a political action committee (PAC) formed by Adoption Crossroads. The following is taken from their membership information:

> The Council for Equal Rights in Adoption is a charitable organization; a network of those affected by adoption, and 354 Adoption Search & Support Groups, Mental Health Facilities and Agencies in the United States, Australia, Canada, Holland, New Zealand and South Africa. As a member of C.E.R.A. you will be supporting an international effort to open adoption records, educate the public about adoption related issues and keep families together.

This group is working to raise public consciousness through media exposure, state task forces on adoption, letter-writing campaigns, conferences, marches, and demonstrations. CERA has organized a march in Washington, DC for the past nine years. In 1997, marchers talked with senators from New York, New Jersey, Connecticut, Massachusetts, Michigan, and New Hampshire. As CERA's membership grows, so do the number of senators and states contacted. For those who would like to show their support but cannot participate in the march, CERA supplies a support vehicle with names and birth dates printed on the outside, thereby giving a visual image of those concerned with current adoption issues. As of this writing, the cost is $5 for a birthdate and name listing on the support vehicle participating in the march.

A quarterly newspaper provides information on CERA activities, conferences, retreats, videos, and marches. Membership in this group is $35 a year. For more information on membership, the Washington March, or other CERA services, contact the Council for Equal Rights on Adoption, 356 E. 74th Street, #2, New York, NY 10021, (212) 988-0110, fax (212) 988-0291, e-mail: cera@mail.idt.net, Web site <www.adoptioncrossroads.org/>.

Post Adoption Center for Education and Research (PACER)

The Post Adoption Center for Education and Research (PACER) was founded by Dr. Dirck W. Brown in 1978. This group does not promote search efforts, but concentrates on improving the adoption experience for all those involved in it.

PACER offers support groups, preliminary search information, resources and education about adoption, information on the adoption experience from childhood through adulthood, and information on legal and ethical concerns for adoptees, birthparent, and adoptive parents. In addition to the above, PACER offers workshops, seminars, professional consultation, training for volunteers, and programs for the community. The programs, discussions, and surveys on problems relating to adoption have given this group a special place among active search and support organizations.

A wide variety of support groups are sponsored by PACER and directed to single-focus groups (Birthmothers, Adoptees, etc.) or Triad groups (open to all members of the triad). See the state-by-state listings under California for a list of these support groups.

This unique, information-resource group welcomes the participation of any person or group interested in its activities. There is a $40 membership fee that includes a quarterly newsletter. For more information, write Post Adoption Center for Education and Research, P.O. Box 309, Orinda, CA 94563, (510) 935-6622, Web site <www.plumsite.com/pacer/>.

STop the Act Coalition (STAC)

STAC was formed in 1994 by a group of members from Concerned United Birthparents (CUB), the American Adoption Congress (AAC), and Council for Equal Rights in Adoption (CERA). They began as, and remain, a "grassroots" group working in about half of the states. To a person, their purpose is to stop the Uniform Adoption Act. For more detail on the UAA, see Chapter 1, "Deciding to Search."

Currently, STAC groups are functioning in 22 states: California, Colorado, Delaware, Florida, Hawaii, Idaho, Illinois, Iowa, Maryland, Massachusetts, Michigan, Missouri, New Hampshire, New Jersey, New York, North Carolina, Ohio, Pennsylvania, Texas, Vermont, West Virginia, and Wisconsin. To learn if your state has a STAC group, contact the American Adoption Congress (earlier in this chapter), The Council for Equal Rights in Adoption (earlier in this chapter), or CUB Headquarters (see Chapter 7, "Search and Support Groups, Researchers/Searchers, Consultants, Intermediaries, and the Courts"). Enclose a stamped, self-addressed envelope for all requests. You might want to talk to your local search and support group to learn about your state's legislative actions.

State Legislative Groups

Several states have legislative groups working as watchdogs to insure that any changes being planned or any upcoming votes by state lawmakers are announced to group members. Plans are then made to address these changes.

Active legislative groups are listed below. These do not represent every state or every group working. To learn if a group exists in your state of search, contact a search and support group located in that state.

Colorado Adoption Dynamics
Ronald J. Nydam, Ph.D.
9185 E. Kenyon Avenue, #120
Denver, CO 80237
(303) 741-5588, fax (303) 741-9977
e-mail: RJNYDAM@aol.com

Illinois Coalition for Truth in Adoption
P.O. Box 4638
Skokie, IL 60076-4638
(217) 664-3342
e-mail: ICTA97@aol.com
Web site: <www.tbcnet.com/~andrea/icta/>

Indiana Adoption Coalition
Cheri Freeman or Candy Jones
P.O. Box 1292
Kokomo, IN 46903-1292
(317) 453-4427 or (317) 472-7425,
fax 317-453-7418

Adoption Reform Movement of Michigan
95 N. Whitesbridge Rd.
Belding, MI 48809
(616) 897-5342

New Jersey Coalition for Openness in Adoption
206 Laurel Place
Laurel Springs, NJ 08021
(609) 784-7532, fax (609) 784-7532
e-mail: mgpic@cyberenet.net

North Carolina Center for the Advancement of Adoption Education (NCCAAE)
P.O. Box 4153
Chapel Hill, NC 27515-2823
(919) 967-5010
e-mail: NCCAAE@aol.com

PA Adoption Legislation Coalition
Nancy M. Newman, Esq.
24 North Merion Avenue, #127
Bryn Mawr, PA 19010
(610) 631-2829, fax (610) 520-4552
e-mail: Nanpatch@aol.com

Tennessee Coalition for Adoption Reform
P.O. Box 41808
Nashville, TN 37204
(901) 386-2197, fax (901) 385-5453

MAGAZINES AND NEWSLETTERS

While newsletters from search and support groups are routinely sent to members, several other magazines and newsletters are published that should be considered when undertaking a search. In addition to those highlighted below, several other excellent sources are published including Roots & Wings, Adoption Magazine, P.O. Box 577, Hackettstown, NJ 07840, (908) 637-8828 (online information can be found in Chapter 9, "Searching on the Computer") and American Journal of Adoption Reform, 3821 Tamiami Trail #301, Pt. Charlotte, FL 33948.

People Searching News

People Searching News (PSN) began publication in 1986 and contains information on new books, legislative updates, search services, and classified ads (see Chapter 3, "What Will It Cost Me?" for costs), as well as articles on topics ranging from adoption agencies to search guidelines for specific states or cities.

At this writing, subscription rates are $18 for six issues (published quarterly). Subscriptions may be ordered through PSN's National Search Hotline (305) 370-7100, or by writing to *People Searching News*, P.O. Box 100-444, Palm Bay, FL 332910-0444.

Reunions The Magazine

Reunions The Magazine was started in 1990 by Edith Wagner. In addition to school, military, and family reunions, this magazine has an area devoted to adoption search.

The Autumn 1997 issue included classifieds for adoptions listed by birth, Professional Searchers, Adoption Search & Support Organizations, and Adoption Miscellany (see Chapter 3, "What Will It Cost Me?" for classified costs.)

This well-written and informative magazine offers a place to find information and ask for help. The staff is prompt, professional, and adoption searchers should not overlook their advantages.

Subscription rates are $24 for one year (four issues). For more information, write to *Reunions The Magazine*, P.O. Box 11727, Milwaukee, WI 53211-0727, (800) 373-7933, fax (414) 263-6331, e-mail: reunions@execpc.com, Web site <www.reunionsmag.com>.

ADOPTION-RELATED BOOKS AND PAMPHLETS

Beginning in 1971, adoption search and support groups started to organize in astonishing numbers. Forming these groups were men and women who were fighting for equality and the right to search. These courageous individuals were willing to speak out on what they believed to be the injustice of sealed records.

The next nine years brought new meaning to adoption search, and there developed a "front line" of individuals who conducted their own searches in their own way while contributing to a larger movement. This movement soon began to change adoption laws to improve searcher access to previously withheld information concerning birthparents, relinquished children, and other relatives.

Many of the early search pioneers wrote of their experiences or of methods they had used to search. Others related their personal observations, telling of the barriers that had been crossed and those that would probably have to be crossed again.

A Reading List of Adoption-Related Literature

Many of the books listed below can be found in your library, ordered through interlibrary loan, or purchased in a bookstore. Some search and support groups offer adoption publications for members and nonmembers. These will list the addresses where the books may be purchased along with their current prices.

Several book brokers or publishers sell adoption-related books: Perspectives Press, P.O. Box 90318, Indianapolis, IN 46290-0318, e-mail: ppress@iquest.net, Web site <www.perspectivespress.com>; Morning Glory Press, 6595 San Haroldo Way, Buena Park, CA 90620-3748, fax (714) 828-2049; and Adoption Education Resources, P.O. Box 100-444, Palm Bay, FL 32910-0444.

It would be impossible to learn of all adoption-related books being published today, since many are printed by groups or individuals. If you find a book not listed below, this in no way suggests that it is not an excellent resource.

Aigner, Hal. *Adoption in America Coming of Age.* Greenbrae, CA: Paradigm Press, 1986.

————. *Faint Trails: A Guide to Adult Adoptee-Birth Parent Reunification Searches.* Greenbrae, CA: Paradigm Press, 1987.

Allen, Elizabeth Cooper. *Mother, Can You Hear Me?* New York: Dodd Mead, 1983.

Anderson, Carole. *Thoughts for Birthparents Newly Considering Search.* (Available from Concerned United Birthparents, Inc., 2000 Walker Street, Des Moines, IA 50317. $4.50).

————. *Thoughts to Consider for Newly Searching Adoptees.* (Available from Concerned United Birthparents, Inc. See above listing. $3.50).

————. *Why Won't My Birthmother Meet Me.* (Available from Concerned United Birthparents, Inc. See above listing. $2.50).

Anderson, Robert, MD. *Second Choice; Growing Up Adopted.* (Available from the American Adoption Congress, 1000 Connecticut Avenue NW, Suite 9, Washington, DC 20036. $10.00). 1991.

Arms, Suzanne. *Adoption—A Handful of Hope*. Berkeley, CA: Celestial Arts Publishing Co., 1989.

Baker, Nancy C. *Baby Selling: The Scandal of Black Market Adoptions*. New York: Vanguard Press, 1978.

Barton, Elisa M. *Confessions of a Lost Mother*. (Available from the American Adoption Congress, 1000 Connecticut Avenue NW, Suite 9, Washington, DC 20036. $15.00).

Benet, Mary Kathleen. *The Politics of Adoption*. New York: Free Press, 1976.

Benski, S. *The Missing Pieces: Stories*. New York: Harcourt, Brace, Jovanovich, 1990.

Brodzinsky, David M., Ph.D. and Henig, Robin Marantz. *Being Adopted: The Lifelong Search for Self*. New York: Doubleday & Co., 1992.

Brodzinsky, David M., Ph.D. and Schecter, Marshall. *The Psychology of Adoption*. New York: University Press, 1990.

Brown/Miller-Havens. *Making Contact*. (Available from the American Adoption Congress, 1000 Connecticut Avenue NW, Suite 9, Washington, DC 20036. $6.00).

Buck, Pearl S. *Children for Adoption*. New York: Random House, 1964.

Burgess, Linda Cannon. *The Art of Adoption*. New York: W. W. Norton, 1981.

Busharis, Barbara Esq. *State by State Review of Legislation Affecting Access and Adoption Information*. (Available from the American Adoption Congress, 1000 Connecticut Ave., NW, Suite 9, Washington, DC 20036. $15.00).

Campbell, Lee. *Understanding the Birthparent*. (Available from Concerned United Birthparents, Inc., 2000 Walker St., Des Moines, IA 50317. $4.50).

Carangelo, Lori. *The Ultimate Search Book*. (Available from Access Press, P.O. 401, Palm Desert, CA 92261. $29.95). 1997 Update.

Carlin, Heather. *Adoptee Trauma*. (Available from the American Adoption Congress, 1000 Connecticut Ave., NW, Suite 9, Washington DC 20036. $17.00).

CUB Board, *The Birthparents' Perspective on Adoption*. (Available from Concerned United Birthparents, Inc., 2000 Walker St., Des Moines, IA 50317. $2.50).

Dean, Amy E. *Letters to My Birthmother*. New York: Pharos Books, 1991.

Dusky, Lorraine. *Birthmark*. New York: M. Evans and Company, 1979.

Ehrlick, Henry. *A Time to Search*. New York and London: Paddington Press, 1977.

Ezell, Lee. *The Missing Piece*. Eugene, Oregon: Harvest House Publishers, 1986.

Fararo, Eugene. *You Can Find Anyone*, 5th ed. Madison, IN: Bookstar, 1995.

Fisher, Florence. *The Search for Anna Fisher*. New York: A. Fields Books, 1973.

Gallagher, Helen; Sitterly, Nancy; and Sanders, Pat. *The ISC Searchbook*. (Available from ISC Publications, P.O. Box 10192, Costa Mesa, CA 92627. $10.00). Updated annually.

Gediman, Judith, and Brown, Linda P. *Birthbond: Reunions Between BirthParents and Adoptees—What Happens After*. New Hampshire: New Horizons Press, 1989.

Giddens, Lynn. *Faces of Adoption*. Chapel Hill, NC: Amberly Publications, 1984.

Goldstein, Joseph; Freud, Anna; and Sonit, Albert J. *Beyond the Best Interest of the Child*. New York: The Free Press, 1973.

Hulse, Jerry. *Jody.* New York: McGraw-Hill, 1976.

Jones, Merry Block, *Birthmothers: Women Who Have Relinquished Babies for Adoption Tell Their Stories.* Chicago, IL: Chicago Review Press, 1996.

Kirk, David. *Adoptive Kinship: A Modern Institution in Need of Reform,* rev. ed. Port Angeles, WA: Ben Simon, 1985.

―――. *Shared Fate: A Theory & Method of Adoptive Relationships,* rev. ed. Port Angeles, WA: Ben Simon, 1984.

Krementz, Jill, *How It Feels to Be Adopted.* New York: Knopf, 1982.

Leitch, David. *Family Secrets: A Writer's Search for His Parents & His Past.* New York: Delacorte, 1986.

Lifton, Betty Jean. *I'm Still Me.* New York: Bantam Books, 1986.

―――. *Lost and Found.* New York: HarperCollins, 1988.

―――. *Twice Born—Memories of an Adopted Daughter.* New York: McGraw-Hill, 1975.

―――. *Journey of the Adopted Self.* New York: Basic Books, 1994.

Lindeman, Bard. *The Twins Who Found Each Other.* New York: Morrow & Co., Inc., 1969.

Magnuson, James, and Petrie, Dorothea G. *Orphan Train.* New York: Fawcett, 1978.

Mason, Mary Martin. *Out of the Shadows: Birthfather Stories.* (Available from the American Adoption Congress, 1000 Connecticut Ave., NW, Suite 9, Washington, DC 20036. $15.00).

Maxtone-Graham, Katrina. *An Adopted Woman.* New York: Remi Books, 1983.

McColm, Michelle. *Adoption Reunions.* Toronto, Ontario, Second Story Press, 1993.

McKuen, Rod. *Finding My Father, One Man's Search for Identity.* Los Angeles: Cheval Books/Coward, McCann & Geoghegan, 1976.

McMilion, Doris. *Mixed Blessings.* New York: St. Martin's Press, 1985.

Musser, Sandra Kay. *I Would Have Searched Forever.* 1985. (Available from 162 SW 489th Terrace, Cape Coral, FL 33914. $7.95).

―――. *To Prison With Love.* 1995. (See listing above. $11.95).

Nickman, Steven L., M.D. *The Adoption Experience: Stories and Commentaries.* New York: J. Messner, 1985.

Pannor, Reuben; Massarik, F.; and Evans, B.W. *The Unmarried Father.* New York: Springer, 1971.

Partridge, Penny Callan. *An Adoptee's Dreams: Poems and Stories.* (Available from the American Adoption Congress, 100 Connecticut Avenue, NW, Suite 9, Washington, DC 20036. $10.00), 1995.

Paton, Jean M. *The Adoption Colony.* 1982. (601 S. Birch, Harrison, AR 72601-5911. $2.00).

―――. *The Adopted Break Silence.* 1982. (see Paton's first listing. $7.95).

―――. *The American Orphan and the Temptations of Adoption.* 1971. (see Paton's first listing, $2.00).

―――. *The Character of the Adopted.* 1984. (see Paton's first listing. $4.00).

————. *A Commentary on the Model State Adoption Act—A Proposal*. 1980. (see Paton's first listing, $3.00).

————. *Guide to the After-Adoption Reunion*. 1975. (see Paton's first listing. $1.00).

————. *The Influence of the Sealed Record*. 1987. (see Paton's first listing. $2.00).

————. *Mass Burial in Adoption*. 1974. (see Paton's first listing. $2.00).

————. *My Mother, Lost and Found*. 1980. (see Paton's first listing. $1.00).

————. *The Orphan and Society*. 1973. (see Paton's first listing. $2.00).

————. *Orphan Voyage*. 1968. (see Paton's first listing. $8.95). This book was written under the name of Rutnena Hill Kittson.

————. *Pioneer for Adoption Reform*. 1984. (see Paton's first listing). Reprinted and distributed with permission of Clair Marcus, $3.00).

————. *They Serve Fugitively*. 1959. (see Paton's first listing. $4.95).

————. *What Happened to Adoption?*. 1982. (see Paton's first listing. $2.00).

Powell, John Y. *Whose Child Am I? Adults' Recollections of Being Adopted*. ew York: Tiresias Press, 1985.

Quinlan, Joseph, and Julie. *Karen Ann: The Quinlans Tell Their Story*. New York: Doubleday, 1977.

Raymond, Louise. *Adoption & After*. New York: Harper & Row, 1974.

Rayner, Lois. *The Adopted Child Comes Of Age*. State Mutual Book and Periodical Service, Ltd. New York, 1980.

Reagan, Michael. *On the Outside Looking In*. New York: Zebra Books, 1988.

Riben, Marsha. *Shedding Light on the Dark Side of Adoption*. Detroit: Harlo Press, 1988.

Rosenberg, Elinor B. *The Adoption Life Cycle*. New York: McMillan, 1992.

Rosenberg, Maxine B. *Growing Up Adopted*. New Jersey: Simon & Schuster, 1989.

Sanders, Patricia. *Directory of ISC Consultants*. Annual. (Available from ISC Publications, P.O. Box 10192, Costa Mesa, CA 92627. $15.00).

Sanders, Patricia and Sitterly, Nancy. *Search Aftermath and Adjustments*. 1981. (Available from ISC Publications. See above listing. $6.00).

Schaefer, Carol. *The Other Mother*. New York: Soho Press, 1991.

Schooler, Jayne. *Searching for a Past: The Adopted Adult's Unique Process of Finding Identity*. Colorado Springs, CO, Pinon Press, 1995.

————. *The Whole Life Adoption Book*. 1993. Colorado Springs, CO: Pinon Press.

Severson, Randolph W. *Sibling Reunions*. (Available from the American Adoption Congress, 1000 Connecticut Avenue NW, Suite 9, Washington, DC 20036. $7.00).

————. *Adoption: Philosophy and Experience*. (Available from the American Adoption Congress. See above listing. $22.00).

Silber, Kathleen, and Speedlin, Phyllis. *Dear Birthmother*. San Antonio, TX: Corona, 1983.

Sleightholm, Sherry, and Redmond, Wendie. *Once Removed—Voices from Inside the Adoption Triangle*. Ontario, Canada: McGraw-Hill-Ryerson, 1982.

Smith, Debra G. *Searching for Birth Relatives*. National Adoption Information Clearinghouse, free booklet, Rockville, MD, 1993.

Snodgrass, Ginni D. *Adoption Reality. A Paradox*. Tualatin, OR: G.S. Enterprise, 1990.

Solinger, Rickie. *Wake Up Little Susie*. (Available from the American Adoption Congress, 1000 Connecticut Ave., NW, Suite 9, Washington, DC 20036. $17.00).

Sorosky, Arthur D.; Baran, Annette; and Pannor, Reuben. *The Adoption Triangle*. New York: Anchor Books, 1984.

Stiffler, LaVonne Harper. *Synchronicity and Reunion: The Genetic Connection of Adoptees and Birthparents*. (Available from the American Adoption Congress, 1000 Connecticut Ave., NW, Suite 9, Washington, DC 20036. $10.00).

Strauss, Jean A.S. *The Great Adoptee Search Book*. Claremont, CA: Castle Rock Publishing Co., 1990.

————. *Birthright: The Guide to Search and Reunion for Adoptees, Birth Parents and Adoptive Parents*. New York: Penguin Books, 1994.

Tillman, Norma Mott. *How to Find Almost Anyone, Anywhere*. TN: Rutledge Hill Press, 1994.

Triseliotis, John. *In Search of Origins: The Experiences of Adopted People*. London and Boston: Routledge & Kegan Paul, 1973.

Verrier, Nancy. *The Primal Wound. Understanding the Adopted Child*. 1993. (Available from the American Adoption Congress, 1000 Connecticut Ave., NW, Suite 9, Washington, DC 20036. $15.00).

Waldron, Jan. *Giving Away Simone*. 1995. (Available from the American Adoption Congress. See above listing. $22.00).

Watts, Tim J. *The Right of Adoptees to Know Their Biological Parents: A Bibliography*. Monticello, IL: Vance Bibliographies, 1988.

Wishard, Laurie and William R. *Adoption: The Grafted Tree*. San Francisco: Cragmont Publications, 1979.

Wolfe, Curry. *The Adoption Reconnection Directory* (formerly the *Blue Book*). Annual. (Wolfe Press, P.O. Box 230643, Encinitas, CA 902023-0643. $17.00).

BULLETIN BOARDS—MISCELLANEOUS ADOPTION SEARCH SERVICES

Within every movement, there is a need to announce events directly related to the cause or studies being conducted which require some participation by those involved. Unfortunately, these announcements never seem to fall into any specific category or fit in anywhere when lists are being prepared. Thus they are discarded because of an inability to determine where they belong. This is true regardless of their usefulness to those seeking resources.

This Adoption Bulletin Board will attempt to address those few areas that should be known but do not fall into any category or index.

The Adoptee/Birth Family Registry

Trudy Helmlinger, Ph.D., has compiled a reference book, *The Adoptee/Birth Family Registry*, for all those involved in the adoption triangle but who have no official spokesperson. These are the adoptees, birthparents, or birthfamily members not wishing to search or identify themselves, but feeling a desire to direct a message to someone involved in their adoption or relinquishment— people who would like to share some nonidentifying information. It may be something about their lives, the circumstances surrounding their relinquishment, family background, current medical information, accomplishments, or just some thoughts they may wish to relate to combine the resources of all adoptees and birthfamily members—searchers and nonsearchers alike—for the purpose of sharing information.

In a letter to me, the author expresses the book's purpose as follows: "I believe that people who are trying to connect should have many avenues available to them; and that individuals who would like to share information but do not want to meet should be able to get their needs met as well." *The Adoptee/Birth Family Registry*, a veritable "Who's Who" in adoption, achieves these goals.

Questionnaires are provided at no cost. Listings in the registry are by birth date and birthplace and are restricted to those 21 years of age and older. A guarantee of confidentiality is given and an Authorization for Release of Information is included with each data sheet sent. Names and addresses are not printed in the registry itself, but a separate mechanism outside the registry assists those who would like their names and whereabouts made available to potential birth relatives. Upon completion, the book will list 1,000 people. Should the number of those wishing to be included in the Registry exceed 1,000, a second edition will be compiled. *The Adoptee/Birth Family Registry* will be distributed to libraries and agencies and will be available for sale to groups and individuals

Those who would like more information or wish to receive a data sheet can write to *The Adoptee/Birth Family Registry*, P.O. Box 803, Carmichael, CA 95608. The book's price is not available as of this date. When you write, enclose a business size or larger, stamped, self-addressed envelope. Note if you are requesting a questionnaire for an adoptee, birthparent, or birth family.

The Minnesota Twins Study

If you are a twin separated at birth from your twin sibling and you have completed your search, you may want to consider participating in the next Minnesota Twins Study.

Since 1979, studies of monozygotic (identical) and dizygotic (nonidentical) twins separated at birth have been conducted at the University of Minnesota.

Dr. Thomas J. Bouchard and his associates have written numerous scientific papers dealing with twins and adoption research, ranging in topic from intelligence and personality to chemical and biological bases of individuality.

The Minnesota Center for Twins and Adoptive Research has hosted 133 pairs of twins to date. Most twins have found each other prior to participation but a few have been reunited by the Center. Generally, the twins have met each other before their arrival in Minnesota, but a few are meeting for the first time.

> The primary research objective of the Minnesota Study of Twins Reared Apart is to study the differences and similarities in the medical and social life histories between members of twin pairs, and to determine how they may relate to current medical and psychological differences and similarities between them.[1]

Twins involved in these studies agree to participate in interviews and medical and psychological studies. Participation lasts one week, Sunday noon through Friday afternoon, from 8:00 A.M. to 5:30 P.M. Spouses are invited to participate as well.

Travel, hotel accommodations, food allowance, and compensation from work are provided by research funds. Any twins interested in applying should contact the Minnesota Center for Twin and Adoption Research, Elliot Hall, 75 East River Road, University of Minnesota, Minneapolis, MN 55455-0344, (612) 625-4067, fax (612) 626-2079, e-mail: bouch001@tc.umn.edu.

National Adoption Information Clearinghouse

The National Adoption Information Clearinghouse (NAIC) is operated by Cygnus Corporation under contract to the U.S. Department of Health and Human Services, Administration for Children, Youth and Families. The Clearinghouse can provide a multitude of materials, ranging from individual state laws to names and addresses of search and support groups in any or all states. This is also a source for locating adoption agency addresses throughout the country. NAIC offers a multitude of free articles, essays, and reports, such as "Searching for Birth Relatives," and a number of larger publications that require payment, such as the "National Adoption Directory."

Materials under 50 pages are generally provided free of charge. Materials over 50 pages cost $.10 per page. Since the NAIC is under contract, there is no guarantee that its services will continue indefinitely. Those wishing information from NAIC should contact National Adoption Information Clearinghouse, Suite 1275, 1400 Eye Street NW, Washington, DC 20005, (202) 842-1919. (Also Suite 410, 11426 Rockville Pike, Rockville, MD 20852, (301) 231-6512, fax (301) 984-8527, e-mail: ncia@calib.com, Web site: <www.calib.com/naic/>.

Orphan Train Heritage Society of America, Inc.

One of the Orphan Train Heritage Society of America, Inc. members has said that being an orphan means being a survivor. Regardless of why our parents gave us up, we might remember that they, too, were trying to survive. Perhaps they gave us the genetic material for our own survivorship.

Orphan Train Rider

"Orphan trains" originated in Boston in 1849. Between 1850 and 1929, over 150,000 children rode the orphan trains and were literally "put up for adoption." That is, when the trains pulled into the stations, or at various locations around the towns, children were "put up" onto a stage and viewed by preselected families. These children were to be adopted by families in smaller communities, generally in the Midwest.

Today the Orphan Train Heritage Society of America, Inc. (OTHSA) seeks to preserve information on the children's institutions, agents, railroads, towns, and families involved with orphan train riders. OTHSA is a clearing-house that members may use to access video tapes, books, magazines, audio tapes, and all information in its files.

A quarterly newsletter, *Crossroads*, is sent to all members or can be purchased from the OTHSA office for $6 per issue. Searchers as well as history buffs may ask their local library to subscribe to *Crossroads*.

In addition to providing information and search help to orphan train searchers, OTHSA has reunions, gatherings, and meetings. A typical meeting might include speakers or programs offering search help as well as information on what OTHSA can do for you.

Any searcher who believes he or she was an orphan train rider should request information from OTHSA. Membership is $10 a year for orphan train riders. Non-orphan train riders may obtain memberships for $25 a year. OTHSA is located at 614 E. Emma Ave., #115, Springdale, AR 72764-4634, (501) 756-2780, fax (501) 756-0769, e-mail: mjohnson@jaf.jonesnet.org.

NOTE

1. Nancy L. Segal, "The Nature vs. Nurture Laboratory," *Twins*, July/August 1984, p. 56.

CHAPTER 11

Ending Your Search

You've come so far and finally it's your red-letter day. You'd think this would be the easiest part of your search, but many find it the most difficult. You have the name of your birthparent or child and the telephone number in hand, yet you can't seem to make the call. Friends and family find it impossible to understand why you have reached this point and at the last step seem to falter.

This is an intensely personal moment. The decision to establish the contact you've worked so hard to make possible is strictly yours. I do not believe anyone else is qualified to make the decision for you. If you were my good friend, however, I would provide you moral support, help you in whatever way I could, and acknowledge your decision, whatever it is, as the right one for you.

When you make the decision to contact, if you make that decision, take some time to review how you will go about it. You may decide that putting your thoughts into a letter first is preferable to an immediate telephone call. Think what you will say. Recognize that you may be faced with any number of reactions—surprise almost certainly, but perhaps expressed as shock. You probably hope for joyful acceptance, but you instinctively realize the possibility of rejection. You may get a mixed response, one that is neither clearly acceptance nor rejection.

You want to establish contact in a frame of mind that has you as prepared as you can be for whatever you may discover. You want to be firm in your resolve and in your sense of self-esteem. You must recognize that the moment of contact almost certainly will be a difficult one for your relative too. Fantasies, guilt, and fears exist on both sides. Because of your search, you may have already started to confront many of these feelings, but your relative may not. He or she may need time to adjust to your sudden appearance. A first reaction of bewilderment and confusion is not unlikely. Give your relative, and *yourself*, time to make the adjustment. It may not be until a subsequent occasion that either of you is fully able to accept the other person as he or she is, without the interference of old feelings of resentment or guilt, or with longstanding illusions all dispelled.

Although the tie between you is biologically the closest that exists, as individuals you will at first be strangers to each other. Even under the best of circumstances, it will take time for your relationship to take shape. Contact is the end of your search, but in terms of building a relationship with your child or birthparent, whatever that comes to be, it's only a beginning.

It's possible you may decide, or be forced to accept, that a close relationship with your newly located child or birthparent is impossible. Perhaps you dreamed of something that now evidently will not come to pass. You may be inclined to feel you've failed. Don't. Your search has always been an activity with a double focus: discovering the identity of someone who is genetically linked, and also exploring in depth your own sense of who you are. Regardless of the outcome as far as discovering another's identity goes, you cannot help but have achieved a clearer perspective of yourself. How can that be a failure? Don't let disappointment blind you to the discoveries you've made about yourself—about the courage you've displayed in accepting the challenge facing you, about the determination and imagination you were able to bring to bear in seeing a difficult project through.

If you're reading through this book with the idea of undertaking a search of your own, you'll have your own secret thoughts and fears about what you might learn. Facing those through the process of search will always assure you a worthwhile return on efforts expended. To me there is no such thing as complete failure in a search.

APPENDIX 1

State-by-State Listings

This section contains state-by-state information for your search. In gathering this information I asked the appropriate state agency or department how adoptions and relinquishments were handled. It is a difficult, if not impossible, task to present the information simply by listing the appropriate names and addresses, since state laws in these matters are complex and varied. A report from the Child Services Association's "Information Paper on Issues and Recommendations Regarding Sealed Adoption Records" shows how confusing the subject of state laws is:

> It should be a simple matter to determine which states have open records and which do not. But, it is not. Laws are seldom clear in terms of which records are sealed, who may have access to the records, what information is contained therein and what specific information is considered sealed. In addition, the effect of a law is felt less in its actual wording than in its interpretation and administration which vary not only from state to state but within a state over time. A final problem is that it is difficult to keep up with new legislation in this area across 50 states.[1]

This explains occasional vagueness and some omissions for various states in this appendix. Below are notes that explain the categories found under each state. The importance and use of each category have been explained in the text, but this listing is to help you carry out your search in an efficient, informed, and economical manner. It will save you many hours of looking for addresses and sources and it will define the many options open to you under law.

State Agency: If you know the agency that handled your adoption or relinquishment, contact it directly. If you do not know where your adoption or relinquishment took place (a county agency, a private adoption/relinquishment, or an agency that is no longer functioning), write to the state address given. To locate the address of a private agency still functioning, call your information operator or check the telephone directory in the city where it is located.

Court of Jurisdiction: This is the court that is empowered to act on your adoption/relinquishment. Some states have several courts that are so empowered, depending on the circumstances in the case. Please note: this is the court that holds trials but also the court that in some states allows an adoptee/birthparent a private meeting with a judge to determine access.

Birth, Death, Marriage, and Divorce Records: These are the vital statistics or record holding departments to write to or visit in order to obtain any of the documents indicated. If you know in what city or county these records are held, use the applicable listing.

State Library/Record Holdings: These are state or genealogical libraries that can be contacted to learn if they hold the information you are attempting to find. If the information you seek is not available through the address given, this library will be able to direct you to the proper source, which may be a large public library, a local historical library, or a small newspaper archive.

Department of Motor Vehicles: These are state agencies to contact to discover the codes, costs, and accessibility of automobile records in your state. While the addresses listed were confirmed by the DMV, they were usually vague about the department that would provide the information. A local telephone directory is still your best resource.

Search and Support Groups, Researchers/Searchers, Consultants, Intermediaries: All the groups, researchers, or consultants functioning today are not listed here. I have attempted to represent each state, and most types of search and support available. Some groups or researchers focus on helping adoptees, while others primarily aid birthparents; some help both adoptees and birthparents. Adoption Crossroads, ALMA, and CUB are listed with their national headquarters address only. Check your local telephone directory or the information operator, or write to the headquarters to receive a current local address.

Some groups have a name that clearly identifies their function while others are more general and leave the reader unsure what to expect. To help clarify the functions of a group, a statement will appear on the line with the groups title indicating: search and support group (S&SG), support group only (SG), genealogical help, other names. An absence of clarification means the group's name is self-explanatory. Either in a group or working alone, when an individual is providing a paid search service, they will be identified as a searcher or consultant and their area(s) of search will be noted at the end of their listing. If a search and support group searches only within the state, no mention will be made of where searches are done. This searcher or consultant may work within the group and charge minimal search fees, if any; other consultants or searchers may conduct searches as their business, in which case fees usually are determined case by case. A researcher does not charge a fee except for expenses incurred. Phone/fax numbers and e-mail addresses are provided when given by a group.

State Reunion Registry: Reunion registries are files maintained by independent groups or public agencies, and contain names and addresses of searchers hoping to locate a relative from whom they've been separated. Those states that have established a state reunion registry are noted here. Information on addresses for state and independent (group) reunion registries can be found in Chapter 8, "Reunion Registries."

Age of Majority: Several states will have two or three ages of majority in their adoption laws. The age of majority for obtaining nonidentifying information may be 18, while the age of majority for participating in the reunion registry is 21. Many states have policies rather than laws covering the release of information. Searchers should keep this in mind and recognize the age of majority listed may not prevent them from obtaining some information, the release of which is governed by state law. If there is any doubt, contact the state agency listed.

Laws Governing Opening Records: These laws govern the procedures to open and unseal your records.

Laws Governing Inheritance: A birthparent always has the option of leaving an inheritance to a birthchild and a birthchild to a birthparent, whether recognized by law or not. The laws governing inheritance listed in this appendix are those that refer to the legal rights of adoptees/birthparents/adoptive parents under each state's laws.

Policies: This section explains state policies to the extent that I have been able to determine them, as well as pending legislation, existing laws, or laws that died in committee. The latter are presented to show interest in changing laws or to give a feel for a state's thinking.

Author's Observations: There were several laws, procedures, or statements that I found particularly interesting. The author's observations are just that, my own thoughts.

ALABAMA

State Agency: State Department of Human Resources, 50 N. Ripley St., P.O. Box 304000, Montgomery, AL 36130-4000, (334) 242-1374.

Court of Jurisdiction: Probate Court

Birth and Death Records: Center for Health Statistics, State Department of Public Health, 434 Monroe St., Montgomery, AL 36130-1701. Money order or certified check only. Call (205) 242-5033 for current fees. State office has records since January 1908.

Marriage Records: Center for Health Statistics (see address listed above) has marriage records since August 1936; or contact Probate Judge in county where license issued.

Divorce Records: Center for Health Statistics (see address listed above) has divorce records since January 1950; or contact Clerk or Register of Court of Equity in county where divorce granted.

State Library/Record Holdings: Alabama State Library, Department of Archives & History, 624 Washington St., Montgomery, AL 36130.

Department of Motor Vehicles: Motor Vehicle Division, Department of Revenue, 50 Ripley St., Room 1216, P.O. Box 327630, Montogmery, AL 36132-7630, (334) 242-9000, fax 334-242-0312.

Search and Support Groups, Researchers/Searchers, Consultants, Intermediaries:

Lynn Davis, searcher, 196 Clara St., Webb, AL 36376, (334) 794-7884

Leah Wesolowski, searcher, Orphan Voyage, 164 Maningham, Madison, AL 35758, (205) 464-0506, fax (205) 464-0230, e-mail: Leahwes@ACMEInform.com

State Reunion Registry: Alabama does not currently have a state registry. Refer to Chapter 8 for information on independent (group) reunion registries.

Age of Majority: 19 years or older

Laws Governing Opening Records: Alabama Adoption Code, Section 26-10A-31. (g) "Notwithstanding subsection (f) [the law directing confidentiality of files] of this section, the state department of human resources or the licensed investigating agency, appointed by the court . . . shall furnish, upon request, to the petitioners, natural parents or an adoptee 19 years of age or older, nonidentifying information which shall be limited to the following: (1) Health and medical histories of the adoptee's natural parents; (2) The health and medical history of the adoptee; (3) the adoptee's general family background, including ancestral information, without name references or geographical designations; (4) Physical descriptions; (5) The length of time the adoptee was in the care and custody of one other than the petitioner; and (6) Notwithstanding subsection (f) [the law directing confidentiality of files] if either the natural mother or the natural or presumed father have given consent in writing under oath to disclosure of identifying information, the state department of human resources or a licensed child placing agency shall release such identifying information including a copy of the birth certificate as it relates to the consenting parent to an adult adoptee when that adoptee reaches the age of 19."

Laws Governing Inheritance: Alabama Adoption Code. Section 26-10A-29. *Name and status of adoptee.* (a) "The adoptee shall take the name designated by the petitioner. After adoption, the adoptee shall be treated as the natural child of the adopting parent or parents and shall have all rights and be subject to all the duties arising from that relation, including the right of inheritance. (b) Upon the final decree of adoption, the natural parents of the adoptee . . . are relieved of all parental responsibility for the adoptee and will have no parental rights over the adoptee."

ALASKA

State Agency: Department of Health & Social Service, Division of Family & Youth Services, Adoption Unit, P.O. Box 110630, Juneau, AK 99811-0630, (907) 465-3636, fax (907) 465-3397, e-mail: Smaxson@HEALTH.STATE.AK.US or Sstears@HEALTH.STATE.AK.US.

Court of Jurisdiction: Superior Court

Birth and Death Records: Department of Health and Social Services, Bureau of Vital Statistics, P.O. Box H-02G, Juneau, AK 99811-0675. Money order only. (907) 465-3391 for current fees. State office has records since January 1913.

Marriage Records: Bureau of Vital Statistics (see address listed above) has records since 1913.

Divorce Records: Bureau of Vital Statistics (see address listed above) has records since 1950. Or contact Clerk of Superior Court judicial district where divorce granted. First District—Juneau and Ketchikan. Second District—Nome. Third District—Anchorage. Fourth District—Fairbanks.

State Library/Record Holdings: Alaska State Library, P.O. Box 110571, Juneau, AK 99811-0571, (907) 465-2921, fax (907) 465-2665, e-mail: asi@muskox.aka.edu, Web site: <www.educ.state.ak.us/lam/library.html>.

Department of Motor Vehicles: Department of Public Safety, Division of Motor Vehicles, 5700 E. Tudor Rd., Anchorage, AK 99507-1225, (907) 269-1225, fax (907) 333-8615, Web site: <www.cps.state.ak.us/dmv/dmvhome.htm>.

Search and Support Groups, Researchers/Searchers, Consultants, Intermediaries:

CUB *Respresentative, Anchorage* (Consult telephone directory, check the CUB National Headquarters listed under Iowa for their mailing, e-mail, or Web site address.)

State Reunion Registry: Alaska has a "passive registry" that allows adoptees (18 years and older) and birthparents to submit to the state registrar a notice of change of name or address. This will be attached to the original birth certificate and given to the adoptee or birthparent when requesting information. Refer to Chapter 8 for information on state and independent (group) reunion registries.

Age of Majority: 18 years or older

Laws Governing Opening Records: Vital Statistics Act, Article 5. Access to Adoption Information, Sec. 18.50.500. *Identity of biological parents.* "(a) After receiving a request by an adopted person 18 years of age or older for the identity of a biological parent of the person, the state registrar shall provide the person with an uncertified copy of the person's original birth certificate and any change in the biological parent's name or address attached to the certificate."

Laws Governing Inheritance: Chapter 23. Adoption. Sec. 25.23.130. *Effect of adoption decree.* (e) "Inheritance rights between a child and a biological parent are not voided by a decree terminating parental rights on the grounds set out in AS 25.23.180(c)(3) unless the decree specifically provides for the termination of inheritance rights."

ARIZONA

State Agency Division of Social Services, 1717 W. Jefferson, P.O. Box 6123, Phoenix, AZ 85005.

Court of Jurisdiction: Superior Court

Birth and Death Records: Vital Records Section, Arizona Department of Health Services, P.O. Box 3887, Phoenix, AZ 85030. Check or money order should be made payable to Office of Vital Records. Call (602) 542-1080. State office has records since July 1909 and abstracts of records filed in counties before this date. Applicants must submit a copy of picture identification or have their request notarized.

Marriage and Divorce Records: Clerk of Superior Court, county where license was issued.

State Library/Record Holdings: Arizona State Library, State Capitol, Third Floor, 1700 W. Washington, Phoenix, AZ 85007, (602) 542-5297 or (800) 228-4710, fax (602) 542-4400, e-mail: rerefde@dlapr.lib.az.us, Web site: <www.dlapr.lib.az.us>.

Department of Motor Vehicles: Motor Vehicle Division, Department of Transportation, 1801 W. Jefferson, P.O. Box 2100, Phoenix, AZ 85001, (602) 255-0072.

Search and Support Groups, Researchers/Searchers, Consultants, Intermediaries:

The Adoption Counseling Home, S&SG, Dee Davis, searcher, 11260 N. 92nd St. #1046, Scottsdale, AZ 85260, (602) 614-2882, e-mail: adopdee@amug.org, Web site: <www.amug.org/~adopdee/>

CUB, Representative, Tucson, (Consult telephone directory or contact CUB National Headquarters listed under Iowa.)

Flagstaff Adoption Search & Support Group, P.O. Box 1031, Flagstaff, AZ 86002, (520) 779-3817, fax (520) 779-3817

Gari-Sue Greene, searcher/researcher, Tracers, LTD, P.O. Box 18511, Tucson, AZ 85731-8511, (520) 885-5958, e-mail: Gari8865@aol.com

Kristen Hamilton, searcher, Research Etc., Inc., 6929 N. Hayden Rd., #C4-105, (602) 991-3571, fax (602) 991-5660, Scottsdale, AZ 85250, e-mail: RSearchEtc@aol.com, Web site: <www.destinyink.com/research>

Search Triad, Inc. S&SG, P.O. Box 10181, Phoenix, AZ 85064-0181, (602) 834-7471, Web site: <home.att.net/~kehgchu>

Alice Syman, searcher/researcher, (formerly Orphan Voyage of Arizona), see Florida address

Karen Tinkham, ISC Consultant, P.O. Box 1432, Litchfield Park, AZ 85340, (602) 935-4974

TRIAD, SG, Joy Pantelis, researcher, 8372 N. Sage Pl., Tucson, AZ 85704, (520) 297-4204, e-mail: Joylark@Prodigy.com

Triad, S&SG, P.O. Box 12806, Tucson, AZ 85732, (520) 881-8250

State Reunion Registry: Arizona does not have a state reunion registry. Refer to Chapter 8 for information on independent (group) reunion registries.

Age of Majority: 18 years or older

Laws Governing Opening Records: Arizona Public Welfare Laws, General Provisions, Chapter 1, Article 1, 8-120. *Records; inspection; exceptions; destruction of certain records.* A. "Except as provided in section 8-129, all files, records, reports and other papers compiled in accord with this article, whether filed in or in possession of the court, an agency or any person or association, shall be withheld from public inspection. B. Such files, records, reports and other papers may be open to inspection by persons and agencies having a legitimate interest in the case and their attorneys and by other persons and agencies having a legitimate interest in the protection, welfare or treatment of the child if so ordered by the court."

Laws Governing Inheritance: Arizona Public Welfare Laws, General Provisions, Chapter 1, Article 1, 8-117. *Rights under adoption order.* (B) "Upon entry of the decree of adoption, the relationship of parent and child between the adopted person and the persons who were his parents just prior to the decree of adoption shall cease to exist, including the right of inheritance . . ."

ARKANSAS

State Agency: Department of Human Services, Division of Children and Family Services, Adoption Services Unit, P.O. Box 1437, Little Rock, AR 72203-1437, (501) 682-8462, fax (501) 682-8666.

Court of Jurisdiction: Probate Court

Birth and Death Records: Division of Vital Records, Arkansas Department of Health, 4815 W. Markham St., Little Rock, AR 72201. Checks or money order should be made to Arkansas Department of Health. Call (501) 661-2336 for current fees. State office has records since February 1914 and some original Little Rock and Fort Smith records from 1881.

Marriage Records: Division of Vital Records (see address listed above). Full certified copy may be obtained from County Clerk in county where license issued. Coupons since 1917.

Divorce Records: Division of Vital Records (see address listed above); or contact Circuit or Chancery Clerk, county where divorce granted. Coupons since 1923.

State Library/Record Holdings: The Arkansas History Commission, #1 Capitol Mall, Little Rock, AR 72201, (501) 682-6900.

Department of Motor Vehicles: Revenue Division, P.O. Box 1272, Little Rock, AR 72203. (501) 682-4630.

Search and Support Groups, Researchers/Searchers, Consultants, Intermediaries:

Contact the American Adoption Congress, National Office (District of Columbia), Adoption Crossroads National (New York), or Concerned United Birthparents (Iowa) to learn of search resources for Arkansas.

State Reunion Registry: Arkansas has a Mutual Consent Voluntary Registry. Refer to Chapter 8 for information on state and independent (group) reunion registries.

Age of Majority: 18 years of age or older

Laws Governing Opening Records: An Act to Adopt the Uniform Adoption Act for the State of Arkansas. Section 17. (2). "All papers and records pertaining to the adoption whether part of the permanent record of the court or of a file in the Arkansas Social Services or in an agency are subject to inspection only upon consent of the Court and all interested persons; or in exceptional cases, only upon an order of the Court for good cause shown . . ."

Laws Governing Inheritance: An Act to Adopt the Uniform Adoption Act for the State of Arkansas. Section 15. (a). "A final decree of adoption and an interlocutory decree of adoption which has become final, whether issued by a Court of this State or of any other place, have the following effect as to matters within the jurisdiction or before a Court of this State: (1) . . . to relieve the natural parents of the adopted individual of all parental rights and responsibilities and to terminate all legal relationships between the adopted individual and his relatives, including his natural parents, so that the adopted individual thereafter is a stranger to his former relatives for all purposes including inheritance . . ."

Policies: From a letter from the Adoption Services Unit. "The Department of Human Services, Division of Children and Family Services, Adoption Services Unit, requires that individuals present their requests for information about the registry in writing. All requests will be answered in a timely manner. The unit staff is available to assist persons involved in the registry process."

CALIFORNIA

State Agency: Department of Social Services, Adoption Branch M.S. 19-67, 744 P St., Sacramento, CA 95814, (916) 322-3778.

Court of Jurisdiction: Superior Court

Birth and Death Records: Vital Statistics Section, Department of Health Services, 410 N St., Sacramento, CA 95814. Records since July 1905. Check or money order should be made payable to Vital Statistics. Call (916) 445-2684 for current fees. For earlier records, write to County Recorder in county where event occurred.

Marriage Records: Vital Statistics Section (see address listed above) has records since July 1905. For earlier records, write to County Recorder in county where event occurred.

Divorce Records: Vital Statistics Section (see address listed above) if county unknown; or contact Clerk of Superior Court, county where divorce granted. There is a fee for search and identification of county where certified copy can be obtained. Certified copies are not available from State Health Department.

State Library/Record Holdings: California State Library, P.O. Box 942837, Sacramento, CA 94237-0001, fax (916) 654-0064.

Department of Motor Vehicles: Department of Motor Vehicles, P.O. Box 932328, Sacramento, CA 94232-3280.

Search and Support Groups, Researchers/Searchers, Consultants, Intermediaries:

Adoptee/Birthparent Connections, S&SG, 8820 Kennedy Ln., San Miguel, CA 93451, (805) 467-2707, fax (805) 467-2431, e-mail: tina@tcsn.net

Adoptees' Identity Discovery, S&SG, Neil Kelly, searcher, P.O. Box 2159, Sunnyvale, CA 94087, (408) 737-2222

Adoptees Research Association, S&SG, Missing Persons Search Service, P.O. Box 24393, Ventura, CA 93002

Adoption Connection of San Diego, S&SG, Curry Wolfe, ISC, searcher, P.O. Box 230643, Encinitas, CA 92023-0643, (760) 753-8288, fax 619-753-8073, e-mail: ccwolfe@worldnet.att.net, Web site: <www.crashers.com/search>

Adoption Reality, S&SG, Gayle Beckstead, ISC, searcher, 2180 Clover St., Simi Valley, CA 93065, (805) 526-2289, fax 805-526-2920, e-mail: Beckars@juno.com

Adoption Triad Support Group, SG, Saint Helena, CA, (707) 942-5877, fax (707) 942-2211

Adoption with Truth, SG, 66 Panoramic Way, Berkeley, CA 94704, (510) 845-2927

Americans for Open Records (AmFOR), S&SG, Lori Carangelo, researcher, P.O. Box 401, Palm Desert, CA 92261

Auburn Adoption Support Group, 10583 Rock View Ct., Auburn, CA 95602, (916) 823-5236

Bastard Nation, adult support, Damsel Plum, 454 Las Gallinas Ave., #199, San Rafael, CA 94903, (415) 564-3691, (415) 479-3741, e-mail: dplum@ix.netcom.com, Web site: <www.bastards.org>

Bay Area Birthmothers Association, SG, 1546 Great Hwy #44, San Francisco, CA 94122, (415) 564-3691, fax (415) 564-3691

Patricia Bowers, searcher/researcher, Bookworm Research, P.O. Box 8003, Long Beach, CA 90808, (562) 421-3996, e-mail: patkb@ix.netcom.com

Jan Bowyer, searcher, Sunland Search, 2917 Anaheim St., Escondido, CA 92025, (760) 746-5800, e-mail: JNDiego@aol.com

Martin Brandfon, ISC, searcher, 620 Jefferson Ave., Redwood City, CA 94063, (650) 366-6789, fax (650) 364-6262

Central Coast Adoption Support, S&SG, P.O. Box 8483, Goleta, CA 93118, (805) 682-5250, fax (805) 968-4351, e-mail: Katiedid51@aol.com

Central Coast Adoption Support Group, SG, Tina Peddie, searcher, 8820 Kennedy Ln, San Miguel, CA 93451, (805) 467-2707, fax (805) 467-2431, e-mail: tina@tcsn.net

Central Coast Adoption Support, S&SG, Susan Bott, researcher , P.O. Box 8483, Goleta, CA 93118, (805) 968-4351 , e-mail: ccasg@aol.com

CUB Branches, La Mirada, Carlsbad, Representatives, Terra Bella, (Consult telephone directory or contact CUB National Headquarters listed under Iowa.)

Delayn Curtis, searcher, 270 S. Bristol #101-159, Costa Mesa, CA 92626, (714) 574-0141, e-mail: delayncurtis@juno.com

Linda Davilla, searcher, Tennessee Adoptees in Search, 4598 Rosewood St., Montclair, CA 91763, (909) 621-2442

Mary Anna de Parcq-Goode, researcher, P.O. Box 2575, Atascadero, CA 93423-2575, (805) 460-9663, fax (805) 460-9663

Family Finders Research, S&SG, 5982 Toyon Terrace, Yorba Linda, CA 92886-5383, (714) 779-5719, fax (714) 779-5721, e-mail: MrsIda@JUNO.com

Steve Felix, researcher, 11 Stirrup Rd., Palos Verdes, CA 90275, (310) 548-0335, fax (310) 831-8133, e-mail: SteveFelix@prodigy.com

Pat Fox, searcher, Family Research & Information Services, 19381 Newhaven Ln., Huntington Beach, Ca 92646, (714) 968-8825, e-mail: TTPM47A@prodigy.com

Denise Gray, searcher, California Research, 11804 Tristan Dr., Downey, CA 90241, (562) 869-7988, fax (562) 869-7988, e-mail: dgray92237@aol.com

Norma Gutierrez, searcher, P.O. Box 1004, Baldwin Park, CA 91706-2818, (818) 960-4279, fax (818) 960-0949, e-mail: WGFH85A@prodigy.com

Hand In Hand, SG, 63 E. Ave. de Las Flores, Thousand Oaks, CA 91360-3104 (805) 494-0199, e-mail: PattyB51@aol.com

Independent Search Consultants (ISC), National Headquarters, P.O. Box 10192, Costa Mesa, CA 92627, e-mail: ISC@rmci.net, Web site: <www.rmci.net/isc>

Suzanne Kauffman, ISC, searcher. 1127 E. Del Mar Bl. #232, Pasadena, CA 91106, Fax (626) 440-9755, pager (818) 278-5550, e-mail: RTPP58A@prodigy.com

Ida Knapp, ISC, searcher, Family Finders Research, 5982 Toyon Terrace, Yorba Linda, CA 92886-5838, (714) 779-5719, fax (714) 779-5721, e-mail: MrsIda@JUNO.com

Mary Lou Kozub, ISC, searcher, 2027 Finch Ct., Simi Valley, CA 93063, (805) 583-4306, fax (805) 583-4160, e-mail: mygrandkidsrgr8@juno.com

Christina M. McKillip, searcher/researcher, Bookworm Research, P.O Box 8003, Long Beach, CA 90808, (562) 420-9561, e-mail: chris2u@ix.netcom.com

Marilyn Miller, searcher/researcher, P.O. Box 039, Harbor City, CA 90710, (310) 833-5822, fax (310) 257-1185

Missing Links of Tulare County, S&SG, Karen Ybarra, searcher, 755 N. Terrace, Park, Tulare, CA 93274, (209) 688-3760, e-mail: adopted63@aol.com

P.A.C.E.R., Triad SG, Auburn, (916) 823-5236; Contra Costa County, (510) 939-7547; Elk Grove, (916) 686-8191, ext. 68; Marin, (415) 381-1503; Sacramento, (916) 751-0905; San Francisco, (415) 441-1949; Sonoma, (415) 898-8938; South Bay/Peninsula; (415) 325-9510; Yuba City, (916) 751-0905

P.A.C.E.R., Adoptee SG, East Bay, (415) 868-2355, (510) 215-8008; San Francisco, (415) 931-0844

P.A.C.E.R., Birthmother SG, East Bay, (510) 253-0435; Marin, (415) 381-1503, e-mail: Merhunn@aol.com; Sacramento, (916) 429-6307; Sonoma/Marin, (415) 898-8938

Jeanne Paredes, researcher, Paredes & Paredes, 3461 State St., Santa Barbara, CA 93105-2662, (805) 967-1969, fax (805) 569-0643

Reconnections of CA, S&SG, Sylvia Hill, researcher, 1191 Eastside Rd., El Cajon, CA 92020-1416, (619) 449-1713, fax (619) 449-0605, e-mail: Sylreconn@aol.com

Research Unlimited -LACASA, S&SG, Vikki Schummer, ISC, searcher, P.O. Box 1461, Roseville, CA 95678, (916) 784-2711, fax (916) 784-0796, e-mail: NMMF66A@prodigy.com,

Gina Ricca, searcher, Friends Forever Searching Specialist, P.O. Box 2829, Capistrano Beach., CA 92624, (714) 496-2030 or (714) 802-5588, e-mail: griccafriends4evr@prodigy.com

ROOTS, S&SG, P.O. Box 40564, Bakersfield, CA 93384-0564, (805) 832-2429, e-mail: ROOTSCA@aol.com

Search-Finders of CA, S&SG, Doreen Alegrete, ISC, searcher, 1537 Calle de Stuarda, San Jose, CA 95118, (408) 365-6711, fax (408) 356-2711, e-mail: KFDT48A@prodigy.com

Search-Finders of CA, S&SG, Dorothy Yturriaga, ISC, P.O. Box 24095, San Jose, CA 98154, (408) 356-6711, fax (408) 356-6711, e-mail: KFDT48A@prodigy.com

Searchers Connection, S&SG, Sherrie Railsback, researcher, 1335 N. LaBrea Ave., Suite 2200, Los Angeles, CA 90028, (562) 946-8545, fax (562) 946-8745

Alberta Sorensen, ISC, searcher, Family Search Services, P.O. Box 587, Camarillo, CA 93011-0587, (805) 482-8667, fax (805) 482-8608

Ann Spanel, ISC, searcher, Lost and Found, 4212 Starling Dr., Bakersfield, CA 93309, (805) 832-2429, fax (805) 832-2429, e-mail: SearchCA@aol.com

Terminally Ill Emergency Search T.I.E.S., S&SG, 2269 Chestnut St., San Francisco, CA 941233, (415) 931-0844, fax (415) 931-2404, e-mail: DebSRP@aol.com, Web site: <www.ibar.com/TIES/>

Triad Support Group, SG, 2175 W. 236th St., Torrance, CA 90501, (310) 325-0552, fax (310) 325-5078, e-mail: peggy_wolff@toyota@,com

Triple Hearts Adoption Triangle, S&SG, P.O. Box 84, Vacaville, CA 95696, (707) 447-9898, e-mail: Kurtz3@aol.com

Triple Hearts Adoption Triangle, S&SG, P.O. Box 52017, Riverside, CA 92517, (909) 864-3240

Ann Wren, searcher, 14040 Barrymore St., San Diego, CA 92129, (619) 484-2134, fax (619) 780-0764, e-mail: annwren@aol.com

State Reunion Registry: California has a state registry. Refer to Chapter 8 for information on state and independent (group) reunion registries.

Age of Majority: 18 years or older

Laws Governing Opening Records: Chapter 7. *Disclosure of Information.* Family Code 9200. Inspection of documents; authorization; fee; deletion of identification of birth parents; certificate of adoption. "The petition, relinquishment or consent, agreement, order, report to the court from any investigating agency and any power of attorney and deposition filed in the office of the county clerk pursuant to this chapter shall not be open to inspection by any other than the parties to the action and their attorneys and the department, except upon the written authority of the judge of the superior court."

Laws Governing Inheritance: Civil Code Section 221.76. *Effect on former relations of child.* "The parents of an adopted child are, from the time of adoption, relieved of all parental duties towards and all responsibility for, the child so adopted and have no right over it."

COLORADO

State Agency: Department of Human Services, Adoption, 2nd Floor, 1575 Sherman St., Denver, CO 80203-1714.

Court of Jurisdiction: Denver, Juvenile Court; all others, District Court

Birth and Death Records: Vital Records Section, Colorado Department of Health, 4210 East 11th Ave., Denver, CO 80220. Check or money order should be made payable to Colorado Dept. of Health. Call (303) 320-8474 for current fees. Death records since 1900 and birth records since 1910. There is a state office that also has birth records for some counties for years before 1910.

Marriage Records: Vital Records Section (see address listed above); or contact County Clerk, county where license issued. Statewide index of records for 1900-39 and 1975 to present. Fee for verification.

Divorce Records: If county unknown, contact Vital Records Section (see address listed above); otherwise contact the Clerk of District Court, county where divorce granted. Index of records for 1900-39 and 1968 to present. Fee for verification.

State Library/Record Holdings: Denver Public Library, Western History/Genealogy Dept., 10 W. 14th Ave. Parkway, Denver, CO 80204, (303) 640-6291, fax (303) 640-6298, Web site: <www.denver.lib.co.us>.

Department of Motor Vehicles: Motor Vehicle Division, 1881 Pierce St., Lakewood, CO 80214, (303) 205-5613, fax (303) 205-5830. Mail to Motor Traffic Records, Denver, CO 80261-0016.

Search and Support Groups, Researchers/Searchers, Consultants, Intermediaries:

Adoptees in Search, S&SG, Susan Friel-Williams, researcher, P.O. Box 24556, Denver, CO 80224, (303) 232-6302, e-mail: LazyLady@aol.com

CUB Branch: Boulder (Consult telephone directory or contact CUB National Headquarters listed under Iowa.)

Loveland 1-Net Connection, Susan Friel-Williams, Online researcher, P.O. Box 6006, Loveland, CO 80537, (970) 962-9463, fax (970) 593-9995, e-mail: LaznLady@aol.com

Carla Schuh, searcher, Colorado Confidential Intermediary Service, P.O. Box 260460, Lakewood, CO 80226-0460, (303) 237-6919

Betty Tyrell, researcher, P.O. Box 33937, Northglenn, CO 80233, (770) 974-5263 e-mail: Georgeit@aol.com

State Reunion Registry: Colorado has a Voluntary Adoption Registry. Refer to Chapter 8 for information on state and independent (group) reunion registries.

Age of Majority: 18/21 years or older

Laws Governing Opening Records: *Release of Confidential Information in Adoption.* "There are three ways that an adoptee or birth parent can access identifying information on the other party. They are as follows: 1. A Judge in a District or Juvenile Court can release the information for what the statutes state is "good cause" . . . 2. The Colorado Voluntary Adoption Registry . . . will release the information if both parties register . . . 3. The Adoption Intermediary Program . . . establishes a process for trained confidential intermediaries appointed by the court to arrange contact among consenting adult adoptees, adoptive parents, birth parents and siblings. You should contact the court where the adoption was final to initiate the procedure."

Laws Governing Inheritance: Article 4, 19-4-113. *Legal effects of formal decree.* (2) "The natural parents shall be divested of all legal rights and obligations with respect to the child and the adopted child shall be free from all legal obligations of obedience and maintenance with respect to the natural parents."

CONNECTICUT

State Agency: Department of Children and Youth Services, Office of Foster Care & Adoption Services, 505 Hudson St., Hartford, CT 06106.

Court of Jurisdiction: Probate Court

Birth and Death Records: Vital Records, Department of Health Services, 150 Washington St., Hartford, CT 06106. Check or money order should be made to Dept. of Health Services. Call (203) 566-2334. State office has records since July 1897.

Marriage Records: Vital Records (see address listed above) has records since July 1897; or contact Registrar of Vital Statistics, town where license issued.

Divorce Records: Clerk of Superior Court, town where divorce granted. Vital Records office does not have divorce decrees.

State Library/Record Holdings: Connecticut State Library, 231 Capitol Ave., Hartford, CT 06106, (860) 566-4971, fax 860-566-8866, Web site: <www.cslnet.ctstateu.edu>.

Department of Motor Vehicles: Motor Vehicles Dept., 60 State St., Wethersfield, CT 06109. In state call (860) 566-4710 or (800)-842-8222, out of state call (860) 566-4710, fax 860-566-1820, e-mail: Webmaster@dmv.state.ct.us, Web site: <www.state.ct.us>.

Search and Support Groups, Researchers/Searchers, Consultants, Intermediaries:

AASK, S&SG, 8 Homestead Dr., South Glastonbury, CT 06073, (860) 657-4005, fax (860) 657-4005

Adoption Crossroads Branch (Consult telephone operator or directory or contact the National Headquarters listed under New York.) For e-mail use cera@mail.idt.net or check their web site at <www.adoptioncrossroads.org/>.

Adoption Healing, SG, 2-F2 Hadik Pkwy, S., Norwalk, CT 06854, (203) 866-6475

State Reunion Registry: Connecticut has a State Reunion Registry. Refer to Chapter 8 for information on independent (group) reunion registries.

Age of Majority: 18 years or older

Laws Governing Opening Records: Probate Courts and Procedure, Chapter 803, Section 45a-750. *Termination of Parental Rights,* Adoption, Request for identifying information. "(a) Any adult adopted person or any adult adoptable person may request, in writing, in accordance with subsection (a) to (c) inclusive, of section 45a-751, release of information which would tend to identify the genetic parent or parents or blood or adoptive relative of such adult adopted person. In addition, a certificate of birth registration or a certified copy of the certificate of birth shall be issued in accordance with section 7-52 or 7-56 to any adoptable person by the department of health services whether or not such person knows the names of his or her birth parents . . . any agency, the department or any court having information which is needed to locate such certificate shall furnish it to the department of health services."

Laws Governing Inheritance: Substitute House Bill No. 5813. Sec. 18. (6). "The [genetic] BIOLOGICAL parent or parents and their relatives shall have no rights of inheritance from or through the adopted person, nor shall the adopted person have any rights of inheritance from or through his [genetic] BIOLOGICAL parent or parents and their relatives, except as provided in this section . . ."

Author's Observations: This state's laws are lengthy and contain many conditions. Searchers should read through each part carefully.

DELAWARE

State Agency: Department of Children, Youth & Their Families, 1825 Faulkland Rd., Wilmington, DE 19805, (302) 633-2500.

Court of Jurisdiction: Family Court

Birth and Death Records: Office of Vital Statistics, Division of Public Health, P.O. Box 637, Dover, DE 19903. Check or money order payable to Office of Vital Statistics. Call (302) 736-4721 for current fees. Death records since 1930 and birth records since 1920.

Marriage Records: Office of Vital Statistics (see address listed above) has records since 1930.

Divorce Records: Office of Vital Statistics (see address listed above) has records since 1935. Inquiries will be forwarded to appropriate office.

State Library/Record Holdings: Division of Libraries, State Library, 43 S. DuPont Hwy. Edgehill Shopping Center, Dover, DE 19901, (302) 739-4748, fax (302) 739-6787, e-mail: tsloan@lib.de.us, Web site: <www.lib.de.us>.

Department of Motor Vehicles: Division of Motor Vehicles, Public Safety Bldg., 303 Transportation Cr., P.O. Box 698, Dover, DE 19903, (302) 739-4421, fax 302-739-3152

Search and Support Groups, Researchers/Searchers, Consultants, Intermediaries:

Finders Keepers, Inc., S&SG, Ginger Farrow, searcher, P.O. Box 748, Bear, DE 19701-0748, (302) 834-8888, e-mail: SearchDE@aol.com

State Reunion Registry: Delaware does not currently have a state registry. Refer to Chapter 8 for information on independent (group) reunion registries.

Age of Majority: 18 years or older

Laws Governing Opening Records: Subchapter I, 925. *Inspection of court records.* "Anyone wishing to inspect any of the papers filed in connection with any adoption shall petition the Judge of the Superior Court concerning setting forth the reasons for the inspection."

Laws Governing Inheritance: Subchapter I, 920. *Effect of adoption on inheritance.* (a) "Upon the issuance of a decree of adoption, the adopted child shall lose all rights of inheritance from its natural parent or parents and from their collateral or lineal relative. The rights of the natural parent or parents or their collateral or lineal relatives to inherit from such child shall cease upon the adoption."

DISTRICT OF COLUMBIA

State Agency: District of Columbia Department of Human Services, 609 H St., NE, Washington, DC 20002, (202) 724-8602

Court of Jurisdiction: Superior Court

Birth and Death Records: Vital Records Branch, Room 3009, 425 I Street NW, Washington, DC 20001. Cashiers check or money order payable to DC Treasurer. Call (202) 727-9281 for current fees. Death records since 1855 and birth records since 1874, but no death records were filed during the Civil War.

Marriage Records: Marriage Bureau, 515 5th Street NW, Washington, DC 20001

Divorce Records: Clerk, Superior Court, District of Columbia, Family Division, 500 Indiana Avenue NW, Washington, DC 20001 (records since September 16, 1956). Clerk, U.S. District Court, District of Columbia, Washington, DC 20001 (records before September 16, 1956).

State Library/Record Holdings: Library of Congress Annex, Washington, DC 20540

Department of Motor Vehicles: Bureau of Motor Vehicle Services, 301 C Street NW, Washington, D.C. 20001, (202) 727-6680, fax (202) 727-5017

Search and Support Groups, Researchers/Searchers, Consultants, Intermediaries:

Adoptee Birthparent Support, Network, S&SG, (see Maryland)

American Adoption Congress, National Office, 1000 Connecticut NW #9, Washington, DC 20036, (202) 483-3399, Web site: <rdz.stjohns.edu/amer-adopt-congress>

CUB Branch: Washington, DC (Consult telephone directory or contact CUB National Headquarters listed under Iowa.)

National Adoption Information Clearinghouse, USA Referrals, P.O. Box 1182, Washington, DC 20013-1182, (703) 246-9095, fax 703-385-3205, e-mail: naic@calib.com

State Reunion Registry: The District does not currently have a registry. Refer to Chapter 8 for information and independent (group) reunion registries.

Age of Majority: 18 years or older

Laws Governing Opening Records: All adoption proceedings are confidential and shall be held in chambers or in a sealed court room. Records and papers in adoption proceedings are sealed. These papers may not be inspected except upon court order, if the court deems it in the child's best interest. Original birth certificates may be inspected only by court order.

Laws Governing Inheritance: The District gave me the following synopsis of their laws governing inheritance. "An adopted child may claim inheritance from the adoptive family but not the natural family."

Author's Observations: Searchers in Washington, DC, should contact a search and support group, visit their local library, or request more in-depth information from the Department of Human Services. The Laws Governing Open Records were obtained from the AdoptioNetwork, Summary of State Adoption Laws. Web site: www.adoption.org/legal/html/lawdc.htm

FLORIDA

State Agency: Department of HRS, Children, Youth & Families Adoption Program Office, 1317 Winewood Blvd., Tallahassee, FL 32399-0700.

Court of Jurisdiction: Circuit Court

Birth and Death Records: Department of Health and Rehabilitative Services, Office of Vital Statistics, 1217 Pearl St., Jacksonville, FL 32202. Check or money order payable to Office of Vital Statistics. Call (904) 359-6900 for current fees. Some birth records since April 1865. Some death records since August 1877. The majority of records date from January 1917.

Marriage and Divorce Records: Office of Vital Statistics (see address listed above) has records since June 6, 1927.

State Library/Record Holdings: State Library of Florida, R.A. Gray Bldg., 500 S. Bronough St., Tallahassee, FL 32399-0250, (904) 487-2651, fax (904) 487-6242, e-mail: locator@dlis.state.fl.us, Web site: <www.dos.state.fl.us/dlis/>.

Department of Motor Vehicles: Motor Vehicles Division, 2900 Apalachee Pkwy., B239, Tallahassee, FL 32399, (904) 487-4303, fax (904) 487-4080, Web site: <www.state.fl.us/hsmv>.

Search and Support Groups/Researchers/Searchers/Consultants/Intermediaries:

Active Voices in Adoption, S&SG, P.O. Box 24-9052, Coral Gables, FL 33124-9052, (305) 667-0387, fax (305) 667-2603, e-mail: avia@dcfreenet.seflin.lib.fl.us

Adoption Search & Support Group of Tallahassee, Judy Young, searcher, P.O. Box 3504, Tallahassee, FL 32315-3504, (850) 893-0004

Adoption Support & Knowledge of FL, S&SG, Susan Kuka, searcher, 11646 NW 19th Dr., Coral Springs, FL 33071, (954) 753-3878, e-mail: kukabeara@aol.com

Marilyn Carver, researcher, 2629 Gorda Bella Ave. , St. Augustine, FL 32086-5337, (904) 797-8830, e-mail: mcarver@aug.com

Circle of Hope—Florida, SG, 3603 Inlet Circle, Greenacres, FL 33463, (561) 967-7079, fax (561) 967-1279, e-mail: circle92@juno.com

CUB Representative, St. Augustine (Consult telephone directory or contact CUB National Headquarters listed under Iowa.)

Sue Eisman, ISC, searcher, Eisman Adoption Search Consulting, 16522 Offenhaur Rd., Odessa, FL 33556, (813) 926-9498, fax (813) 926-9636, e-mail: SueEisman@aol.com

Janice Fruland, searcher, TRIAD Adoption Search & Support, Inc., 3408 Neptune Dr., Orlando, FL 32804, (407) 644-7665

Bertie Hunt, searcher, TRIAD Adoption Search & Support, Inc., 3408 Neptune Dr., Orlando, FL 32804, (407) 843-2760, fax (407) 872-1433, e-mail: sherlock41@juno.com

Molly Johnson, searcher, Orphan Voyage, 1122 Marco Pl., Jacksonville, FL 32207, (904) 398-4269, fax (904) 396-8532

Mid-Florida Adoption Reunions, Inc. S&SG, Linda Knotts, searcher, P.O. Box 3475 Bellview, FL 34421, (352) 307-9600, fax (352) 307-9602

Organized Adoption Search, Information Services, Inc., S&SG, Rachel S. Rivers, searcher, P.O. Box 53-0761, Miami Shores, FL 33153

Alice Syman, searcher, formerly Orphan Voyage of Arizona, P.O. Box 5945, St. Augustine, FL 32085, (904) 810-5596, fax (904) 810-5596

State Reunion Registry: Florida has an Adoption Reunion Registry. Refer to Chapter 8 for information on state and independent (group) reunion registries.

Age of Majority: 18 years or older

Laws Governing Opening Records: Adoption, Chapter 63.162. *Hearings and records in adoption proceedings; confidential nature.* (1)(b) "All papers and records pertaining to the adoption, including the original birth certificate, whether part of the permanent record of the court or of a file in the Department of Health and Rehabilitate Services or in an agency, are subject to inspection only upon order of the court; . . ."

Laws Governing Inheritance: Adoption, Chapter 63.172. *Effect of judgment of adoption.* (b) "It terminates all legal relationships between the adopted person and his relatives, including his natural parents, except a natural parent who is a petitioner, so that the adopted person thereafter is a stranger to his former relatives for all purposes, including inheritance . . ."

GEORGIA

State Agency: State Adoption Unit, Division of Family & Children Services, Department of Human Resources, 2 Peachtree St. NW, Suite 13-400, Atlanta, GA 30303.

Court of Jurisdiction: Superior Court

Birth and Death Records: Georgia Department of Human Resources, Vital Records Unit, Room 217-H, 47 Trinity Ave. SW, Atlanta, GA 30334. Money order payable to Vital Records, GA. DHR. Call (404) 656-4900 for current fees. Records since January 1919.

Marriage and Divorce Records: Vital Records Unit (see address listed above) has records since June 9, 1952. Inquiries about marriages occurring before June 9, 1952, will be forwarded to appropriate probate judge in county where license was issued. Inquiries about divorce will be forwarded to appropriate Clerk of Superior Court in county where divorce was granted.

State Library/Record Holdings: Georgia State Historical Society, 501 Whitaker St., Savannah, GA 31499, fax (912) 651-2831.

Department of Motor Vehicles: Motor Vehicle Division, 1200 Tradeport Blvd., PO Box 740381, Hapeville, GA 30374-0381, (404) 362-6500.

Search and Support Groups/Researchers/Searchers/Consultants/Intermediaries:

Bill Jones, Researcher, Adoptees Search Network, 3317 Spring Creek Dr., Conyers, GA 30013-2366

State Reunion Registry: Georgia has an Adoption Reunion Registry. Refer to Chapter 8 for information on state and independent (group) reunion registries.

Age of Majority: 21 years of age or older

Laws Governing Opening Records: *Adoption Records:* 19-8-23 (a) "All records, including the docket book, of the court granting the adoption, of the department, and of the child placing agency that relate in any manner to the adoption shall be kept sealed and locked. The records may be examined by the parties at interest in the adoption and their attorneys when, after written petition having been presented to the court having jurisdiction with not less than 30 days after receipt of written notice to the department and the appropriate child-placing agency, the matter has come on before the court in chambers and good cause having been shown to the court and the court has entered an order permitting such examination."

Laws Governing Inheritance: Code Section 19-8-19(a). " . . . a decree of adoption terminates all legal relationships between the adopted individual and his relatives, including his parent, so that the adopted individual is thereafter a stranger to his former relatives for all purposes, including inheritance . . ."

Policies: In a letter from Georgia's Division of Family and Children, they state the following in regard to their policies: "Specific forms which must be requested and returned to the State Adoption Unit to request non-identifying information, birth parent registration and to initiate search. Forms may be requested by phone or mail. Requests are handled on a date received basis. Matches on the registry are notified at once. Medical emergencies, with Doctor's letter, are given priority."

HAWAII

State Agency: Department of Social Services and Housing, 810 Richards St., Honolulu, HI 96813, (808) 586-5705.

Court of Jurisdiction: Family Court

Birth and Death Records: Office of Health Status Monitoring, State Department of Health, P.O. Box 3378, Honolulu, HI 96801. Check or money order payable to State Department of Health. Call (808) 548-5819 for current fees. Records since 1853.

Marriage and Divorce Records: State Department of Health (see address listed above). Centralized state records since July 9, 1952.

State Library/Record Holdings: Hawaii State Library, 478 South King St., Honolulu, HI 96813, (808) 586-3500, fax (808) 586-3584, Web site: <www.hcc.hawaii.edu/hspls/hsplshp.html>.

Department of Motor Vehicles: Check local telephone book

Search and Support Groups/Researchers/Searchers/Consultants/Intermediaries:

Contact the American Adoption Congress, National Office (District of Columbia), Adoption Crossroads National Office (New York), or Concerned United Birthparents (Iowa) to learn of search help for Hawaii.

State Reunion Registry: Hawaii has a state registry. Those adopted/relinquished in the state of Hawaii may submit a "Request to Inspect Confidential Adoption Records of the Family Court." Refer to Chapter 8 for information on independent (group) reunion registries.

Age of Majority: 18 years or older

Laws Governing Opening Records: Hawaii Revised Statutes 578-1 to 578-17. The court records [adoption] shall be sealed by the court, but on written request of the adoptive parents the court may decide not to seal the records. The seal may be broken, and identifying information revealed by a family court order upon a showing of good cause. For adoption occurring prior to January 1, 1991, an adult adoptee or adoptive parents may petition the court for the records. The law provides for extensive procedures to notify the natural parents of this request. If the natural parents file an affidavit requesting continual confidentiality, the record will remain sealed. For adoption occurring after December 31, 1990, the adult adoptee or adoptive parents may have access to the records unless there is an effective affidavit of confidentiality on file.

Laws Governing Inheritance: Please write to the Department of Social Services and Housing with your direct question regarding inheritance in this state.

Policies: The "Laws Governing Open Records" information was taken from AdoptionNetwork, Summary of State Adoption Laws. Web site: www.adoption.org/legal/html/lawhi.htm

IDAHO

State Agency: Department of Health and Welfare, Center for Vital Statistics and Health Policy, P.O. Box 83720, Boise, ID 83720-0036.

Court of Jurisdiction: Magistrate Court

Birth and Death Records: Vital Statistics Unit, Idaho Department of Health and Welfare, 450 W. State St., Statehouse Mall, Boise, ID 83720-9990. Check or money order payable to Idaho Vital Statistics. Call (208) 334-5988 for current fees. Records since 1911. For records from 1907 to 1911, write to County Recorder in county where event occurred.

Marriage and Divorce Records: Vital Statistics Unit (see address listed above) has records since 1947. Earlier records are with County Recorder in county where license was issued or divorce was granted.

State Library/Record Holdings: Idaho State Library, 325 W. State St., Boise, ID 83702, (208) 334-2150, fax (208) 334-4016, e-mail: reference@isl.state.id.us, Web site: <www.state.idus/isl/hp.htm>.

Department of Motor Vehicles: Idaho Transportation Department, 3311 W. State St., P.O. Box 7129, Boise, ID 83707-1129, (208) 334-8000, fax 208-334-8739.

Search and Support Groups/Researchers/Searchers/Consultants/Intermediaries:

ICARE, S&SG, Maureen Pirc, searcher, 4348 Maverick Way, Boise, ID 83709, (208) 362-2281, fax (208) 362-1604, e-mail: MTYMO@aol.com

Search-Finders of ID, S&SG, Nancy Henderson, ISC, searcher, 1520 N. 17th St. Boise, ID 83702, (208) 336-5949, fax (208) 336-5949, e-mail: nancybm@rmci.net

Search-Finders of ID, S&SG, Lois Wight, ISC, searcher, P.O. Box 7941, Boise, ID 83707, (208) 375-9803, fax (208) 368-9885, e-mail: PHCF54A@prodigy.com

Triad Endeavors, S&SG, P.O. Box 249, Pinehurst, ID 83850, (208) 682-4280

State Reunion Registry: Idaho has a Voluntary Adoption Registry. Refer to Chapter 8 for information on state and independent (group) reunion registries.

Age of Majority: 18 years or older

Laws Governing Opening Records: Chapter 2, Vital Statistics. 39-258. Adoption of Persons Adopted In Idaho. (h) "All records and information specified in this section other than a new birth certificate issued hereunder, and all records, files and information of any court in this state relating to adoption proceedings, shall not be open to inspection except as provided in section 39-259A. . ."

Laws Governing Inheritance: Idaho Code, Title 16, Chapter 15.16-1509. Release of Child's Parents from Obligation-Termination of Rights of Parents and Children. "Unless the decree of adoption otherwise provides, the natural parents of an adopted child are, from the time of the adoption, relieved of all parental duties toward, and all responsibilities for, the child so adopted, and have no right over it, and all rights of such child from and through such natural parents including the right of inheritance, are hereby terminated unless specifically provided by will." Check this law for possible changes/updates.

ILLINOIS

State Agency: Dept. of Children & Family Services, 406 E. Monroe St., Springfield, IL 62701-1498.

Court of Jurisdiction: County Circuit Court

Birth and Death Records: Division of Vital Records, Illinois Department of Public Health, 605 W. Jefferson St., Springfield, IL 62702-5079. Check, money order, certified check payable to Illinois Dept. of Public Health. Call (217) 782-6553 for current fees. Records since January 1916. For earlier records and for copies of state records since January 1916, write to County Clerk in county where event occurred.

Marriage and Divorce Records: Division of Vital Records (see address listed above) has records since January 1962.

State Library/Record Holdings: Illinois State Library, 300 S. Second St., Springfield, IL 62701-1796, (217) 782-7596, fax (217) 524-0041, Web site: <www.library.sos.state.il.us/illinetw.html>.

Department of Motor Vehicles: Motor Vehicle Licensing, 213 State House, Springfield, IL 62706, (217) 782-2201, fax (217) 785-0358, e-mail: Secryan@ccgatesos.state.il.us, Web site: <www.sos.state.il.us>.

Search and Support Groups/Researchers/Searchers/Consultants/Intermediaries:

Adoption Triangle, Lydia Granda, researcher, 512 Oneida St., Joliet, IL 60435, (815) 722-4999, e-mail: Lydiaswrld@aol.com

CUB Branch & Representatives: (Consult telephone directory or contact CUB National Headquarters listed under Iowa.)

Healing Hearts, Inc., S&SG, P.O. Box 136, Stanford, IL 61774-0136, (309) 379-5401, fax (309) 379-5401, e-mail: dljfinger@aol.com

The Lost Connection, S&SG, Karen Saunders, searcher, 2661 N. Illinois St. #147, Belleville, IL 62226, (618) 235-9409, fax (618) 233-2715, e-mail: Gyspy22@aol.com

Missing Pieces, SG, P.O. Box 7541, Springfield, IL 62791-7541, (217) 787-8450, fax (217) 787-8450

Search Connection, S&SG, Mike Egan, ISC, searcher, P.O. Box 2425, Bridgeview, IL 60455, (708) 430-9133, e-mail: srchcon@ix.netcom.com

Truth Seekers in Adoption, SG, P.O. Box 366, Prospect Hts., IL 60070-0366, (847) 342-8742

State Reunion Registry: Illinois has a state registry. Refer to Chapter 8 for information on state and independent (group) reunion registries.

Age of Majority: 18 years or older

Laws Governing Opening Records: 750 ILCS 50/18 *Records Confidential.* (c) "All adoption records maintained by each circuit clerk shall be impounded in accordance with the procedures provided by the Illinois Supreme Court's General Administrative Order on Recordkeeping and shall be opened for examination only upon specific order of the court. . ."

Laws Governing Inheritance: 750 ILCS 50/17 *Effect of order terminating parental rights or order.* "After the entry either of an order terminating parental rights or the entry of an order of adoption, the natural parents of a child sought to be adopted shall be relieved of all parental responsibility for such child and shall be deprived of all legal rights as respects the child, and the child shall be free from all obligations of maintenance and obedience as respects such natural parents."

INDIANA

State Agency: Division of Family and Children, Bureau of Family Protection/Preservation, 402 W. Washington St., Room W364, Indianapolis, IN 46204-2739

Court of Jurisdiction: District Court

Birth and Death Records: Vital Records Section, State Board of Health, 1330 W. Michigan St., P.O. Box 1964, Indianapolis, IN 46206-1964. Check or money order payable to Indiana State Board of Health. Call (317) 633-0274 for current fees. Birth records since 1907 and death records since 1900. For earlier records, write to Health Officer in city or county where event occurred.

Marriage Records: Vital Records Section (see address listed above) has a marriage index since 1958; or contact Clerk of Circuit Court or Clerk of Superior Court, county where license issued.

Divorce Records: County Clerk, county where divorce granted.

State Library/Record Holdings: Indiana State Library, Genealogy Section, 140 N. Senate Ave., Indianapolis, IN 46204, (317) 232-3689, fax (317) 232-3728. Web site: www.statelib.lib.in.us

Department of Motor Vehicles: Bureau of Motor Vehicles, 100 N. Senate Ave., Room 440, Indianapolis, IN 46204, fax (317) 233-3135.

Search and Support Groups/Researchers/Searchers/Consultants/Intermediaries:

   Adoptees Identity Doorway, SG, Betty Heide, searcher, P.O. Box 361, South Bend, IN 46624, (219) 272-3520

   Adoption Triangle NW Indiana, S&SG, Kristin Lucas, CI, 7361 Wilson Place, Merrillville, IN 46410, (219) 736-5512, e-mail: adoption@mail.icongrp.com

   Common Bond, S&SG, Diana Hunter, researcher, P.O. Box 833, Kendallville, IN 46755, (219) 636-2404, e-mail: mdhunter@noblecan.org

   Connected by Adoption, S&SG, 1817 Woodland Dr., Elkhart, IN 46514, (219) 262-0210

Confidential Intermediary Program of Indiana, Cheri Freeman, Administrator, 61
Country Farm Rd., Peru, IN 46970, (765) 472-7425, fax (765) 472-2565, e-
mail: cfreeman@netusa1.net, Web site: <www.geocities.com/Heartland/
Prairie/9997/>

Double Heritage, S&SG, Lori Baxter, Confidential Intermediary of Indiana, 2345
W. 12th, Marion, IN 46953, (765) 677-7810, e-mail: smile@comteck.com

Double Heritage, SG, 2345 W. 12th, Marion, IN 46953, (765) 668-7675

Full Circle Adoption Support Group, S&SG, Pat Allen, Jody Moreen, Randi
Richardson, researchers, P.O. Box 2904, Indianapolis, IN 46206-2904, (317)
592-1998, e-mail: ADUE78A@prodigy.com

Lafayette Adoption Search & Support Organization, SG, 5936 Look Out Dr., W.
Lafayette, IN 47906, (765) 567-4139

Lafayette Adoption Search & Support Organization, SG, 3305 Longlois Dr.,
Lafayette, IN 47904, (765) 448-2949

Therese E. Maxwell, searcher, St. Elizabeth's Maternity Home, 2500 Churchman
Ave., Indianapolis, IN 46203-4699, (317) 787-3412, fax (317) 787-0482

Reflections, SG, P.O. Box 45, Wadeville, IN 47638-0045, (812) 464-9689, fax
(812) 464-9669, e-mail: rrin@ccsi.tds.net, Web site: <members.wbs.net/home
pages/a/d/o/adoptedbanker.html>.

Deb Schmidt, searcher, Catholic Charities, 315 E. Washington Bl., Ft. Wayne, IN
46802, (800) 686-7459 or (219) 439-0242, fax 219-439-0250, e-mail:
smileycake@aol.com

Search Committee of Madison County, Historical Society, S&SG, Phyllis Leedom,
Search Committee, P.O. Box 523, Anderson, IN 46015-0523, (317) 642-0187,
e-mail: phyllis@apl.acsc.net

SOS—Support of Search, S&SG, Candy Jones, searcher, CI, P.O. Box 1292,
Kokomo, IN 46965-0076, (765) 453-4427, fax (765) 453-7418, e-mail:
candylp@hotmail.com

State Reunion Registry: Indiana has an Adoption History State Registry. Refer to
Chapter 8 for information on state and independent (group) reunion registries.

Age of Majority: 18-21 years or older

Laws Governing Opening Records: Title 31, Article 31-3-1-5. "Such petition [peti-
tion to adopt], the report or reports of the investigation made, any and all other papers
filed in connection therewith, the record of evidence of such hearing, and the decree
made and entered by the court . . . are confidential. All files and records of the court
pertaining to such adoption proceedings shall be in the custody of the clerk of the court
and shall not be open to inspection except as provided in section 12(f)(2) of this
chapter."

Laws Governing Inheritance: Chapter I, Section 9. 31-3-1-9. *Effects of Adoption.* "The
natural parents of such adopted person, if living, shall after such adoption be relieved of
all legal duties and obligations due from them to such person and shall be divested of all
rights with respect to such person."

Policies: A pamphlet titled Medical Information for Adopted Persons states, "Any person may voluntarily transmit medical information to benefit an adopted person to the State Registrar for inclusion in the medical history files of the Registry regardless of the date of adoption."

IOWA

State Agency: Adoption Program Mgr., Department of Human Services, Division of Adult, Children and Family Services, Hoover Building, Des Moines, IA 50319; Fax (515) 281-4597.

Court of Jurisdiction: District Court

Birth and Death Records: Iowa Department of Public Health, Vital Records Section, Lucas Office Building, 321 E. 12th St., Des Moines, IA 50319. Check or money order payable to Iowa Dept. of Public Health. Call (515) 281-5871 for current fees. Records since July 1880.

Marriage Records: Iowa Department of Public Health (see address listed above) has records since July 1880.

Divorce Records: Iowa Department of Public Health (see address listed above); or contact Clerk of District Court, county where divorce granted. The Department of Public Health has a brief statistical record only since 1906. Inquiries will be forwarded to appropriate office.

State Library/Record Holdings: Iowa State Library, Old Historical Bldg., East 12th and Grand Ave., Des Moines, IA 50319, (515) 281-4102, fax 515-281-3384, Web site: <www.silo.lib.ia.us>.

Department of Motor Vehicles: Office of Vehicle Registration, 100 Euclid, Park Fair Mall, PO Box 9204, Des Moines, IA 50306-9204, (515) 237-3146, fax (515) 237-3152, e-mail: CPadget@idot.e-mail.com

Search and Support Groups/Researchers/Searchers/Consultants/Intermediaries:

  Concerned United Birthparents, CUB Headquarters, 2000 Walker St., Des Moines, IA 50317, (800) 822-2777, fax (515) 263-9541, e-mail: cub@webnations.com, Web site: <www.webnations.com/cub/>

  Origins, Inc., S&SG, Jim McDonald, searcher, P.O. Box 13134, Des Moines, IA 50310-0134, (515) 277-7700, fax (515) 277-9811

State Reunion Registry: Iowa does not currently have a state registry. Refer to Chapter 8 for information on independent (group) reunion registries.

Age of Majority: 18 years or older, except adult is 21 years or older for persons requesting medical and developmental histories (nonidentifying)

Laws Governing Opening Records: Chapter 600, Adoption, Section 600.16A. 2. "All papers and records pertaining to a termination of parental rights under chapter 600A and to an adoption shall not be open to inspection and the identity of the biological parents of an adopted person shall not be revealed except under any of the following circumstances: b. The court, for good cause, shall order the opening of the permanent adoption record. . .(1) A biological parent may file an affidavit requesting that the court reveal or not reveal the parent's identity. The court shall consider any such affidavit in determining whether there is good cause to order opening of the records. . ."

Laws Governing Inheritance: Section 633.223. *Effect of Adoption.* "A lawfully adopted person and his heirs shall inherit from and through the adoptive parents the same as a natural born child. The adoptive parents and their heirs shall inherit from and through the adopted person the same as though he were a natural born child."

A Section 600.13. Adoption decrees. 4. "A final adoption decree terminates any parental rights, except those of a spouse of the adoption petitioner, existing at the time of its issuance and establishes the parent-child relationship between the adoption petitioner and the person petitioned to be adopted. Unless otherwise specified by law, such parent-child relationship shall be deemed to have been created at the birth of the child."

KANSAS

State Agency: Department of Social and Rehabilitative Services, Division of Children and Family Services, 300 SW Oakley, West Bldg., Topeka, KS 66606.

Court of Jurisdiction: District Court

Birth and Death Records: Office of Vital Statistics, Kansas State Department of Health and Environment, 900 Jackson St., Topeka, KS 66612-1290. Check or money order payable to State Registrar of Vital Statistics. Call (913) 296-1400 for current fees. Records since July 1911. For earlier records, write to County Clerk in county where event occurred.

Marriage Records: Office of Vital Statistics (see address listed above) has records since May 1913; or contact District Judge, county where license issued.

Divorce Records: Office of Vital Statistics (see address listed above) has records since July 1951; or contact Clerk of District Court, county where divorce granted.

State Library/Record Holdings: Kansas State Historical Society, 6425 SW 6th Ave., Topeka, KS 66615.

Department of Motor Vehicles: Drivers Licensing & Control Bureau, 915 SW Harrison St., Topeka, KS 66612-1588, fax (913) 296-3852.

Search and Support Groups/Researchers/Searchers/Consultants/Intermediaries:

Adoption Concerns Triangle, S&SG, 411 SW Greenwood Ave., Topeka, KS 66606 (785) 235-6122, fax (785) 235-6122, e-mail: waugh5@aol.com

Shirley Lytle, searcher, Catholic Social Service, 2546 20th St., Great Bend, KS 67530, (316) 792-1393, fax (316) 792-1393

Wichita Adult Adoptees, S&SG, Rochelle Harris, searcher, 4551 S. Osage St., Wichita, KS 67217, (316) 522-8772, Web site: <www.southwind.net/~lpeters/waaindex.html>

State Reunion Registry: Kansas does not currently have a state registry. Refer to Chapter 8 for information on independent (group) reunion registries. Note "Policies" below.

Age of Majority: 18 years or older

Laws Governing Opening Records: K.S.A. 65-2423. *Adoption Cases.* "In cases of adoption the state registrar upon receipt of certified order of adoption shall prepare a supplementary certificate in the new name of the adopted person; and seal and file the original certificate of birth with said certified copy attached thereto. Such sealed documents may be opened by the state registrar only upon demand of the adopted person if of legal age or by an order of the court."

A K.S.A. 59-2122. Files and records of adoption. "The files and records of the court in adoption proceedings shall not be open to inspection or copy by persons other than the parties in interest and their attorneys, and representatives of the state department of social and rehabilitation services, except upon an order of the court expressly permitting the same."

Laws Governing Inheritance: K.S.A. 59-2118. *Name of adopted child, effect of adoption.* (b) ". . . Upon adoption all the rights of birth parents to the adopted person, including their right to inherit from or through the person, shall cease, except the rights of a birth parent who is the spouse of the adopting parent."

A K.S.A. 59-2124 (d). *Same: termination of rights.* ". . . all the rights of the parent or person in loco parentis shall thereupon be terminated, including the right to receive notice in a subsequent adoption proceeding involving said child."

Policies: Taken from *Adoption Picture*, prepared by the Kansas Department of Social Rehabilitation Service, October 1974. "We can and should inform the adult adoptee of the fact that they [sic] can, upon request to the Bureau of Vital Statistics, obtain their original birth certificate. (When Kansas adopted the Uniform Act on Vital Statistics in 1951 it became possible for an adopted adult to obtain their original birth certificate upon request). Those requesting a copy of their original birth certificate in person need to provide proof of identification such as a drivers license. Those requesting a copy of their original birth certificate by mail need to provide a notarized written request (all written requests need to be notarized)."

Author's Observations: In light of the many people who predict open records as a forerunner to ruined lives and adoptive-family breakups, Kansas has remained stable since 1951. This is a very progressive state.

KENTUCKY

State Agency: Department for Social Services, 275 E. Main St., 6W, Frankfort, KY 40621

Court of Jurisdiction: Circuit Court

Birth and Death Records: Office of Vital Statistics, Department for Health Services, 275 E. Main St., Frankfort, KY 40621. Check or money order payable to Kentucky State Treasurer. Call (502) 564-4212 for current fees. Records since January 1911 and some records for the cities of Louisville, Lexington, Covington, and Newport before then.

Marriage and Divorce Records: Office of Vital Statistics (see address listed above) has records since June 1958; or contact Clerk of County Court in county where marriage license issued, Clerk of Circuit Court in county where divorce decree issued.

State Library/Record Holdings: Department of Libraries & Archives, Public Records Division, 300 Coffee Tree Rd., P.O. Box 537, Frankfort, KY 40602-0537, (502) 564-8300, Web site: <www.kdla.state.ky.us>.

Department of Motor Vehicles: Transportation Cabinet, 501 High St., Frankfort, KY 40622

Search and Support Groups/Researchers/Searchers/Consultants/Intermediaries:

Adoptee Awareness, SG, P.O. Box 23019, Anchorage, KY 40223, (502) 245-2811

CUB Branch (Consult telephone directory or contact CUB National Headquarters listed under Iowa.)

Linda Cecil, searcher, Locators Unlimited, P.O. Box 1218, Nicholasville, KY 40340, (606) 885-1777, fax (606) 885-1778, e-mail: L CECIL@aol.com

State Reunion Registry: Kentucky has a state registry. Refer to Chapter 8 for information on state and independent (group) reunion registries.

Age of Majority: 21 years or older to do a search

Laws Governing Opening Records: Economic Security and Public Welfare, 199.570. *Adoption records confidential; exception; new birth certificate.* (1) "Upon the entry of the final order in the case, the clerk shall place all papers and records in the case in a suitable envelope which shall be sealed and shall not be open for inspection by any person except on written order of the court, except that upon the written consent of the biological parents and upon written order of the circuit court all papers and records including all files and records of the circuit court during proceedings for termination of parental rights provided in KRS 199.615 shall be open for inspection to any adult adopted person who applies in person or in writing to the circuit court as provided in KRS 199.572."

199.572. *Inspection of adoption records; limitations.* (1) "At the time the biological parents give up the child for adoption, they shall be asked by the cabinet whether they consent to the inspection of the adoption records, to personal contact by the child, or to both when he becomes an adult. If consent is then given, it can later be revoked. If consent is withheld at that time, the biological parents may give consent at any later time . . . . When a written consent is on file, the records shall be available to the adult adopted person, upon his request therefor in writing."

Laws Governing Inheritance: Protective Services for Children: Adoption, 199.611. *Order of Termination.* (1) "If the court determines that . . . it shall make an order terminating all parental rights and obligations in the parent in whom they have existed, and releasing the child from all legal obligations to his parents, and transferring such parental rights to some other person or authorized agency or department as may, in the opinion of the court, be best qualified to receive them, except that the child shall retain the right to inherit from its parents under the laws of descent and distribution until the child is adopted."

Policies: In order to receive information on a pre-adoptive brother or sister in Kentucky, both siblings must file a release of information and both must be 18 years or older.

Author's Observations: Adult adoptees may request a search be made for birthparents. The cost is $150 (non-refundable). The birthparent must give their written permission before any identifying information can be released. The Kentucky Department for Social Services states the following: "Hundreds of requests for adoption information are received each year. As a result, it can sometimes take a while to get the information you are requesting. Because each request and each adoption record is different, it is impossible to suggest an 'average' waiting period, but each request will be handled as quickly and fairly as possible."

LOUISIANA

State Agency: Division of Children, Youth, & Family Services, P.O. Box 3318, Baton Rouge, LA 70821; (504) 342-2297.

Court of Jurisdiction: Juvenile Courts of Caddo, East Baton Rouge, Orleans, Jefferson Parishes. All other parishes handled by the District Court.

Birth and Death Records: Vital Records Registry, Office of Public Health, 325 Loyola Ave., New Orleans, LA 70112. Check or money order payable to Vital Records. Call (504) 568-2561 for current fees. Records since July 1914. Birth records for City of New Orleans are available from 1790, and death records from 1803.

Marriage Records: Orleans Parish (see address listed above); if license issued in another parish, contact Clerk of Court for that parish.

Divorce Records: Clerk of Court, parish where divorce granted

State Library/Record Holdings: State Library, 760 N. Third St., P.O. Box 131, Baton Rouge, LA 70821-0131, (504) 342-4914, fax (504) 342-3547, e-mail: ladept@pelican.state.lib.la.us, Web site: <www.smt.state.lib.la.us/>.

Department of Motor Vehicles: Office of Motor Vehicles, P.O. Box 64886, Baton Rouge, LA 70896, fax (504) 925-3979, Web site: <www.dps.state.la.us/laomy.html>.

Search and Support Groups, Researchers/Searchers, Consultants, Intermediaries:

  Adoption Triad Network, S&SG, Johnnie Kocurek, searcher, 120 Thibodeaux Dr., Lafayette, LA 70503, (318) 984-3682

State Reunion Registry: Louisiana has a Voluntary State Registry. Refer to Chapter 8 for information on state and independent (group) reunion registries.

Age of Majority: 18 years or older

Laws Governing Opening Records: Louisiana Revised Statutes Annotated 9:400, Ch.C. Title XII, and 40:74 to 40:79. All adoption hearings are heard in the judge's chambers and records from the proceeding are kept confidential, except upon a court order.

Laws Governing Inheritance: Father and Child, Chapter 4, Of Adoption, Article 214. *Reciprocal rights and duties of adopter and adopted.* " . . . the blood parent or parents and all other blood relatives of the adopted person, except as provided by R.S. 9:572 (B), are relieved of all legal duties and divested of all of their legal rights with regard to the adopted person, including the right of inheritance from the adopted person and his lawful descendants; and the adopted person and his lawful descendants are relieved of all of their legal duties and divested of all of their legal rights with regard to the blood parent or parents and other blood relatives, except the right to inheritance from them."

Policies: Searchers in this state should check their local library or contact a search and support group to learn of any changes to the above laws. The "Laws Governing Opening Records" information was taken from the AdoptioNetwork, Summary of State Adoption Laws. Web site: www.adoption.org/legal/html/lawla.htm

MAINE

State Agency: Department of Human Services, State House, Station 11, Augusta, ME 04333-0011, (207) 624-5464, fax (207) 624-5470.

Court of Jurisdiction: County Probate Courts: Adoption

Birth and Death Records: Office of Vital Records, Human Services Bldg., Station 11, State House, Augusta, ME 04333. Check or money order payable to Treasurer, State of Maine. Call (207) 289-3184 for current fees. Records since 1892. For earlier records, write to the municipality where event occurred.

Marriage and Divorce Records: Office of Vital Records (see address listed above). Divorce record since January 1892; or contact Clerk of District Court, judicial division where divorce granted.

State Library/Record Holdings: Maine State Library, #64 State House Station, Augusta, ME 04333, (207) 287-5600, fax (207) 287-5615, e-mail: gary.nichols@ state.me.us, Web site: <www.state.me.us/msl/mslhome.htm>.

Department of Motor Vehicles: Bureau of Motor Vehicles, State House Station #29, Augusta, ME 07333-0029, (207) 287-9000, fax (207) 287-5219.

Search and Support Groups, Researchers/Searchers, Consultants, Intermediaries:

> *Barbara Hough, searcher,* SearchRight, Inc., P.O. Box 506, Yarmouth, ME 04096, (207) 846-9555, e-mail: bhough@worldnet.att.net

State Reunion Registry: Maine has an adoption reunion registry. See Chapter 8 for information on state and independent (group) reunion registries.

Laws Governing Opening Records: 19 MRSA, Section 1131. *Records of adoption.* "Nonwithstanding any other provision of law, all Probate Court records relating to any adoption decreed on or after August 8, 1953 are confidential. The Probate Court shall keep records of those adoptions segregated from all other court records. If a Probate

Court Judge determines that examination of records pertaining to a particular adoption is proper, the judge may authorize that examination by specified persons, authorize the register of probate to disclose to specified persons any information contained in the records by letter, certificate or copy of the record or authorize a combination of both examination and disclosure."

Laws Governing Inheritance: MRSA, 1105. Rights of adopted persons. ". . . An adoptee also retains the right to inherit from the adoptee's birth parents, if the adoption degree so provides as specified in Title 18-A, section 2-109, subsection (1)."

MARYLAND

State Agency: Department of Human Resources, Social Services Administration, 311 W. Saratoga St., Baltimore, MD 21201-3521, (410) 767-7423, Web site: <www.gl.umbc.edu/~hickman/adopt.htm>.

Court of Jurisdiction: 24 local court jurisdictions

Birth and Death Records: Division of Vital Records, Department of Health and Mental Hygiene, Metro Executive Bldg., 4201 Patterson Ave., P.O. Box 68760, Baltimore, MD 21215-0020. Check or money order payable to Division of Vital Records. Call (301) 225-5988 for current fees. Records since August 1898. Records for City of Baltimore are available from January 1875. Will not do genealogical studies. Must apply to State of Maryland Archives.

Marriage Records: Division of Vital Records (see address listed above) has records since June 1951; or contact Clerk of Circuit Court, county where license issued; Clerk of Court of Common Pleas, Baltimore City licenses.

Divorce Records: Division of Vital Records (see address listed above) has records since January 1961; or contact Clerk of Circuit Court, county where divorce granted.

State Library/Record Holdings: State of Maryland Archives, Hall of Records, 350 Roew Blvd., Annapolis, MD 21401, (410) 974-3915, fax (410) 974-3895, e-mail: archives@mdarchives.state.md.us, Web site: <www.mdarchives.state.md.us>.

Department of Motor Vehicles: Motor Vehicles Administration., 6601 Ritchie Hwy., NE, Glen Burnie, MD 21061, (800) 950-1MVA, fax 410-768-2654, e-mail: 103063.3627@compuserve.com, Web site: <www.inform.umd.edu;8080\ums+state\md_resources\mdot\mva\ad>.

Search and Support Groups, Researchers/Searchers, Consultants, Intermediaries:

Adoptee Birthparent Support Network, S&SG, P.O. Box 6485, Columbia, MD, 21045-6485, (202) 686-4611

Adoptees in Search, S&SG, Joanne Small, searcher, P.O. Box 41016, Bethesda, MD 20824, (301) 656-8555, fax (301) 652-2106

Adoption Search & Support Group, Western Md, S&SG, Ronda J. Barmoy-Wilt, searcher, 1427 Church St., Cumberland, MD 21502, (301) 724-4705, fax (301) 724-4705

Sue Cook, searcher, SEEK, P.O. Box 2, Hydes, MD 21082, (410) 592-7256, e-mail: XYNK67A@prodigy.com, <www.seek4you.com/seek.html>

CUB Branch: (Consult telephone directory or contact CUB National Headquarters listed under Iowa.)

State Reunion Registry: Maryland has a Mutual Consent Voluntary Adoption Registry. Refer to Chapter 8 for information on state and independent (group) reunion registries.

Age of Majority: 21 years or older

Laws Governing Opening Records: Family Law, Children. Section 5-329. *Access to adoption records.* (a) Court order to disclose medical information.- (ii) "On petition by an adopted individual or birth parent of an adopted adult, a court shall order that part of a court record or child placement agency record containing medical or nonidentifying information be opened to inspection by the individual". (b) "Limitation.- The court may not order opened for inspection any part of a record that contains any information that reveals the location or identity of the individual's birth parents."

Laws Governing Inheritance: Article 16, Section 78. *Legal effect of interlocutory decree of adoption.* (b) "The natural parents of the person adopted, if living, shall after the interlocutory decree is relieved of all legal duties and obligation due from them to the person adopted, and shall be divested of all rights with respect to such person. Upon the entry of a decree ofadoption, all rights of inheritance between the child and the natural relatives shall be governed by the Estates Article of the Code."

MASSACHUSETTS

State Agency: Department of Social Services, 24 Farnsworth St., Boston, MA 02110.

Court of Jurisdiction: Probate Court

Birth and Death Records: Registry of Vital Records, 150 Tremont St., Room B-3, Boston, MA 02111. Records since 1896. Check or money order payable to Commonwealth of MA. Call (617) 727-7388 for current fees.

Marriage Records: Registry of Vital Records (see address listed above) has records since 1896.

Divorce Records: Registry of Vital Records (see address listed above) has records since 1952; or contact Registrar of Probate Court, county where divorce granted.

State Library/Record Holdings: State Library of MA, State House, Room 341, Boston, MA 02133, (617) 727-2590, Web site: <www.magnet.state.ma.us>.

Department of Motor Vehicles: Registry of Motor Vehicles, 1135 Tremont St., Boston, MA 02120-2103

Search and Support Groups, Researchers/Searchers, Consultants, Intermediaries:

Adoption Healing, SG, Carolyn Canfield, searcher, 87 Chestnut St., E. Falmouth, MA 02536-6704, (508) 457-7181, fax (508) 457-4875

Adoption Healing, SG, P.O. Box 211, S. Orleans, MA 02662, (508) 255-8138

AdOption Resource Center (ARC), SG, P.O. Box 383246, Cambridge, MA 02238-3246, (617) 547-0909, fax (617) 497-5952, e-mail: kinnect@aol.com

Center for Family Connections, SG, 350 Cambridge St., East Cambridge, MA 02136, (617) 547-0909, fax (617) 497-5952

CUB Branch (Consult telephone directory or contact CUB National Headquarters listed under Iowa.)

TRY-Resource & Referral, S&SG, Ann Henry, searcher, P.O. Box 989, 214 State St., Northampton, MA 01061-0989, (413) 584-6599, fax (413) 568-3663, e-mail: try@javanet.com, Web site: <www.javanet.com/~try>

State Reunion Registry: Massachusetts does not have a registry but does allow for exchange of information if adoptee and birthparent have both submitted waivers: Adoption Search Coordinator, Department of Social Services, 24 Farnsworth St., Boston, MA 02210, (617) 727-3171, (800) 548-4802, fax (617) 261-7435. Refer to Chapter 8 for information on state and independent (group) reunion registries.

Age of Majority: 18 years or older

Laws Governing Opening Records: Adoption of Children and Change of Names, Chapter 210, Section 5D, *Release of information concerning adoption.* (b) "If a placement agency, as defined in section nine of chapter twenty-eight A, has received written permission from a biological parent of an adopted person to release the identity of the biological parent to the adopted person and the said agency has received written permission from the adopted person, or written permission from the adoptive parents if the adoptive person is under the age of twenty-one, to release the identity after adoption of the adopted person to the biological parent, then the agency shall release the identity of the adopted person to the biological parent and the identity of the biological parent to the adopted person; provided, however, that if the biological parent is surviving, that he or she has given written consent at least thirty days before the release of said identifying information." [those not having mutual permission to release information will not be given identifying information]

Laws Governing Inheritance: Adoption of Children and Change of Names, Chapter 210, Section 7. *Rights of Adopted Child as to Succession to Property.* "A person shall by adoption lose his right to inherit from his natural parents or kindred, except when one of the natural parents of a minor child has died and the surviving parent has remarried subsequent to such parent's death, subsequent adoption of such child by the person with whom such remarriage is contracted shall not affect the rights of such child to inherit from or through the deceased parent or kindred thereof." Check to see if this information is current.

MICHIGAN

State Agency: Family Independence Agency, 235 S. Grand Ave., P.O. Box 30037, Lansing, MI 48909.

Court of Jurisdiction: Probate Court

Birth and Death Records: Office of the State Registrar and Center for Health Statistics, Michigan Department of Public Health, 3423 N. Logan St., Lansing, MI 48909. Check or money order payable to State of Michigan. Call (517) 335-8655 for current fees. Records since 1867.

Marriage Records: Office of the State Registrar (see address listed above) has records since April 1867; or contact County Clerk, county where license issued.

Divorce Records: Office of the State Registrar (see address listed above) has records since 1897; or contact County Clerk, county where divorce granted.

State Library/Record Holdings: Michigan Library and Historical Center, 717 W. Allegan, P.O. Box 30007, Lansing, MI 48909, (517) 373-1300, Web site: <www.libofmich.lib.mi.us/>.

Department of Motor Vehicles: Records & Info. Services, Service Delivery Admn., Secondary Complex, 7064 Crowner Dr., Lansing, MI 48918, fax 517-322-6410.

Search and Support Groups, Researchers/Searchers, Consultants, Intermediaries:

Adoptees Search for Knowledge, Inc., S&SG, P.O. Box 762, East Lansing, MI 48826-0762, (517) 321-7291

Adoption Connection, S&SG, Julie Carter, searcher, P.O. Box 293, Cloverdale, MI 49035-0293, (616) 623-8060, fax (616) 623-4595, e-mail: Julesci@aol.com

Adoption Identity Movement, S&SG, Peg Richer, searcher, P.O. Box 9265, Grand Rapids, MI 49509, (616) 531-1380, fax (616) 532-5589

Adoption Identity Movement, S&SG, P.O. Box 812, Hazel Park, MI 48030, (248) 548-6291, e-mail: DGeorgeW@aol.com

Adoption Identity Movement, North MI, S&SG, P.O. Box 337, Kalkaska, MI 49646, (616) 922-1986

Adoption Insight, S&SG, Elaine Meints, searcher/researcher, confidential intermediary, P.O. Box 171, Portage, MI 49081, (616) 327-1999

Adoption Reform Movement, SG, 95 N. Whitesbridge Rd., Belding, MI 48809, (616) 897-5342

Bonding by Blood, Unlimited, S&SG, Mary Louise Foess, search assistant, 4710 Cottrell Rd., Rt. 5, Vassar, MI 48768-9256, (517) 823-8248 (weekends 2-5 p.m.)

Christine Buehrer, ISC, searcher, 1270 Grosvenor Hwy., Palmyra, MI 49268, (517) 486-3444

Catholic Services of Macomb, SG, Joanne Ales, searcher/researcher, Confidential Intermediary, 235 SB Gratiot, Mt. Clemens, MI 48043, (810) 468- 2616, fax (810) 468-6234

CUB Representative: (Consult telephone directory or contact CUB National Headquarters listed under Iowa.)

Kalamazoo Birthparent Support Group, P.O. Box 2183, Portage, MI 49081-2183, (616) 324-9987

Tri-County Genealogical Society, S&SG, Randy Ferrari, searcher, 21715 Brittany, Eastpointe, MI 48021, (810) 774-7953, fax (810) 268-0851, e-mail: REDTAG@Juno.com

Tri-County Genealogical Society, S&SG, 15492 MacArthur, Redford Township, MI 48239, (313) 255-7319, e-mail: REDTAG@juno.com

Truth in the Adoption Triad, S&SG, 1815 Sunrise Dr., Caro, MI 48723, (517) 672-2054

State Reunion Registry: Michigan has a state reunion registry. Refer to Chapter 8 for information on state and independent (group) reunion registries.

Age of Majority: 18 years or older

Laws Governing Opening Records: Michigan Adoption Code, Chapter 10, 710.67, Sec. 67. (1) "Except as otherwise provided in subsection (4) or in section 68 of this chapter, records of proceedings in adoption cases, including a notice filed under section 33(1) of this chapter, and a petition filed under section 34(1) of this chapter, and the papers and books relating to the proceedings shall be kept in separate locked files and shall not be open to inspection or copy except under order of a court of record for good cause shown expressly permitting inspection or copy. (5) Upon receipt of a written request for identifying information from an adult adoptee, a child placing agency, a court, or the department, if it maintains the adoption for that adoptee, shall submit a clearance request form to the central adoption registry. Within 28 days after receipt of a clearance reply form from the central adoption registry, the child placing agency, court, or department shall notify the adoptee in writing of the identifying information to which the adoptee is entitles under subsection (6) or (7), or, if the identifying information cannot be released pursuant to those subsection, the reason why the information cannot be released."

Laws Governing Inheritance: Michigan Adoption Code, Chapter X. 710.60 Sec. 60 Item 1. "After the entry of the order of adoption, the adoptee shall, in case of a change of name, be known and called by the new name. The person or persons adopting the adoptee than stand in the place of a parent or parents to the adoptee in law in all respects as though the adopted person had been born to the adopting parents and are liable for all the duties and entitled to all the rights of parents."

MINNESOTA

State Agency: Department of Human Services, 444 Lafayette Rd., St. Paul, MN 55155-3831.

Court of Jurisdiction: County Family Court or Juvenile Division of District Court

Birth and Death Records: Minnesota Department of Health, Section of Vital Statistics, 717 Delaware St. SE, P.O. Box 9441, Minneapolis, MN 55440. Check or money order payable to Treasurer, State of MN. Call (612) 623-5121 for current fees. Records since January 1908. Copies of earlier records may be obtained from Court Administrator in county where event occurred.

Marriage Records: Minnesota Department of Health (see address listed above). Index since January 1958. Inquiries will be forwarded to appropriate office. Contact Court Administrator, court where license issued.

Divorce Records: Minnesota Department of Health (see address listed above). Index since January 1970. Contact Court Administrator, county where divorce granted.

State Library/Record Holdings: Minnesota Historical Society, 345 Kellogg Blvd. West, St. Paul, MN 55102-1906, fax (612) 297-3343.

Department of Motor Vehicles: MN Dept. of Public Safety, 445 Minnesota St., Suite 100, Saint Paul, MN 55101, (612) 292-6911, fax (612) 296-3141, Web site: <www.dps.state.mn.us/dvshome.html>.

Search and Support Groups, Researchers/Searchers, Consultants, Intermediaries:

CUB Branch: (Consult telephone directory or contact CUB National Headquarters listed under Iowa.) Contact the American Adoption Congress (District of Columbia) or the Adoption Crossroads National Office (New York) to learn of additional search help in Minnesota.

State Reunion Registry: Minnesota does not have a state reunion registry. Refer to Chapter 8 for information on independent (group) reunion registries.

Age of Majority: 18/21. Age 19 to request post adoption or original birth certificate information.

Laws Governing Opening Records: Adoption, Section 259.61. *Hearings, Confidential.* " . . . the files and records of the court in adoption proceedings shall not be open to inspection by any person except the commissioner of Human Services or representatives, or upon an order of the court expressly so permitting pursuant to a petition setting forth the reasons thereof."

Laws Governing Inheritance: Adoption, Section 259.59. *Effect of Adoption.* "After a decree of adoption is entered the natural parents of an adopted child shall be relieved of all parental responsibilities for the child, and they shall not exercise or have any rights over the adopted child or his property. The child shall not owe his natural parents or their relatives any legal duty nor shall he inherit from his natural parents or kindred, except as provided in subdivision a."

Policies: In a pamphlet titled *Agency Services for Adopted Person, Adoptive Parents, and Birth Parents*, Minnesota states the following: "Requests for Original Birth Certificate Information 1. A birth parent, or an adopted adult over the age of 19 years, may request information on the original birth certificate from the Minnesota Department of Health. The Section of Vital Statistics may: A. Release to the birth parent a non-official copy of the original birth certificate B. Release to the adopted adult a non-official copy of the original birth certificate information on a birth parent a) who has consented, or b) the adult was adopted after August 1, 1977 unless birth parent had filed a non-disclosure."

MISSISSIPPI

State Agency: Department of Human Services, Adoption Unit, P.O. Box 352, Jackson, MS 39205.

Court of Jurisdiction: Chancery Court

Birth and Death Records: Vital Records, State Department of Health, 2423 N. State St., Jackson, MS 39216. For out-of-state requests, only bank or postal orders are accepted. For in-state requests, personal checks are accepted. Make check or money order payable to Mississippi State Dept. of Health. Call (601) 960-7981 for current fees. Records since 1912. Personal checks are accepted only for in-state requests.

Marriage Records: Vital Records (see address listed above) has statistical records only from January 1926 to July 1, 1938, and since January 1942; or contact Circuit Clerk, county where license issued.

Divorce Records: Vital Records (see address listed above) has records since 1926; or contact Chancery Clerk, county where divorce granted.

State Library/Record Holdings: Mississippi Library Commission, Serving the Information Generation. P.O. Box 10700, Jackson, MS 39289-0700, (601) 359-1036, fax (601) 354-4181, e-mail: mlcref@mlc.lib.ms.us, Web site: <www.mlc.lib.ms.us>.

Department of Motor Vehicles: Department of Public Safety, 1900 E. Woodrow Wilson Blvd., P.O. Box 958, Jackson, MS 39205-0958, (601) 987-1212

Search and Support Groups, Researchers/Searchers, Consultants, Intermediaries:

Contact the American Adoption Congress National Office (District of Columbia), Adoption Crossroads National Office (New York), or Concerned United Birthparents (Iowa) to learn of search resources for Mississippi.

State Reunion Registry: Mississippi does not have a state reunion registry. Refer to Chapter 8 for information on state and independent (group) reunion registries.

Age of Majority: 18/21 years or older

Laws Governing Opening Records: Chapter 17, Section 93-17-25. *Proceedings and records confidential-use in court or administrative proceedings.* "All proceedings under this chapter shall be confidential and shall be held in closed court without admittance of any person other than the interested parties, except upon order of the court. All pleadings, reports, files and records pertaining to adopting proceedings shall be confidential and shall not be public records and shall be withheld from inspection or examination by any person, except upon order of the court in which the proceeding was had on good cause shown; provided however, officers of the court, including attorneys, shall be given access to such records upon request."

Laws Governing Inheritance: Chapter 17, Section 93-17-13. *Final decree and effect thereof.* (d) " . . . that the natural parents and natural kindred of the child shall not inherit by or through the child except as to a natural parent who is the spouse of the adopting parent, and all parental rights of the natural parent, or parents, shall be terminated, except as to a natural parent who is the spouse of the adopting parent. Nothing in this chapter shall restrict the right of any person to dispose of property under a last will and testament."

MISSOURI

State Agency: Department of Social Services, Division of Family Services, P.O. Box 88, Jefferson City, MO 65103.

Court of Jurisdiction: Circuit Court

Birth and Death Records: Department of Health, Bureau of Vital Records, 1730 E. Elm, P.O. Box 570, Jefferson City, MO 65102. Check or money order payable to Missouri Dept. of Health. Call (314) 751-6387 (birth) or (314) 751-6376 (death) for current fees. Records since January 1910. If event occurred in St. Louis (City), St. Louis County, or Kansas City before 1910, write to the City or County Health Department.

Marriage Records: Department of Health (see address listed above). Indexes since July 1948. Correspondent will be referred to appropriate Recorder of Deeds in county where license was issued. Contact Recorder of Deeds, county where license issued.

Divorce Records: Department of Health (see address listed above). Indexes since July 1948. Inquiries will be forwarded to appropriate office. Contact Clerk of Circuit Court, county where divorce granted.

State Library/Record Holdings: Missouri State Library, 600 W. Main, P.O. Box 387, Jefferson City, MO 65102-0387, (573) 751-3615, fax 573-751-3612, Web site: <mosl.sos.state.mo.us>.

Department of Motor Vehicles: Division of Motor Vehicle & Driver Licensing, 301 W. High St., P.O. Box 200, Jefferson City, MO 65105-0200, (573) 751-4600, fax (573) 526-7367.

Search and Support Groups, Researchers/Searchers, Consultants, Intermediaries:

> *Donors' Offspring, S&SG,* Candace Turner, searcher, P.O. Box 37, Sarcoxie, MO 64862, (417) 673-1905, fax (417) 673-1906, e-mail: Candace@usa-net

> *Kansas City Adult Adoptees Organization, S&SG,* P.O. Box 11828, Kansas City, MO 64138, (816) 229-4075 (before 10 am), (816) 363-2810 (after 6 pm), e-mail: WHassler@Prodigy.net

State Reunion Registry: Missouri has an Adoption Information Registry. Refer to Chapter 8 for information on state and independent (group) reunion registries.

Age of Majority: 21 years or older.

Laws Governing Opening Records: Chapter 453, Adoption and Foster Care, Section 453.120. *Records of adoption proceedings not open to inspection except on order of court-penalty for violation.* 1. "The files and records of the court in adoption proceedings shall not be open to inspection or copy by any person or persons, except upon an order of the court expressly permitting the same in accordance with the provisions of section 453.121."

Laws Governing Inheritance: Chapter 453, Adoption and Foster Care, Section 453-090. *Consequences of Adoption.* 1. "When a child is adopted in accordance with the provisions of this chapter, all legal relationships and all rights and duties between such child and his natural parents (other than a natural parent who joins in the petition for adoption as provided in Section 453.010) shall cease and determine. Said child shall thereafter be deemed and held to be for every purpose the child of his parent or parent by adoption, as fully as though born to him or them in lawful wedlock."

MONTANA

State Agency: Department of Public Health & Human Services, Box 8005, Helena, MT 59604.

Court of Jurisdiction: District Court/Tribal Court

Birth and Death Records: Bureau of Records and Statistics, State Department of Health and Environmental Sciences, Helena, MT 59620. Check or money order payable to Montana Dept. of Health and Environmental Sciences. Call (406) 444-2614 for current fees. Records since late 1907.

Marriage and Divorce Records: Bureau of Records and Statistics (see address listed above) has records since July 1943. Inquiries will be forwarded to appropriate office. Contact Clerk of District Court, county where license issued or divorce granted.

State Library/Record Holdings: Historical Society, 225 N. Roberts, P.O. Box 201201, Helena, MT 59620-1201.

Department of Motor Vehicles: Motor Vehicle Division, 303 N. Roberts, P.O. Box 201430, Helena, MT 59620-1430, (406) 444-3292, fax (406) 444-1631.

Search and Support Groups, Researchers/Searchers, Consultants, Intermediaries:

Montana Adoption Resource Center, SG, Ella Gaffaney, researcher, 25 S. Ewing Rm. 509, P.O. Box 634, Helena, MT 59624-0634, (406) 449-3266, fax (406) 449-5648

State Reunion Registry: Montana has a Post Adoption Center registry. Refer to Chapter 8 for information on state and independent (group) reunion registries.

Age of Majority: 18 years or older

Laws Governing Opening Records: Family Law, Adoption, 40-8-126. *Confidentiality of record and proceedings.* (3) "All files and records, pertaining to said adoption proceedings in the county departments of public welfare, the department of social and rehabilitation services, or any authorized agencies shall be confidential and withheld from inspection except upon order of court for good cause shown."

Laws Governing Inheritance: Family Law, Adoption, 40-8-125. *Effect of final decree.* (2) "After a final decree of adoption is entered, the natural parents and the kindred of the natural parents of the adopted child, unless they are the adoptive parents or the spouse of an adoptive parent, shall be relieved of all parental responsibilities for said child and have no rights over such adopted child or to his property by descent and distribution."

NEBRASKA

State Agency: Nebraska Health & Human Services System, P.O. Box 95044, Lincoln, NE 68509-5044.

Court of Jurisdiction: County Court

Birth and Death Records: Bureau of Vital Statistics, State Department of Health, 301 Centennial Mall South, P.O. Box 95007, Lincoln, NE 68509-5007. Check or money order payable to Bureau of Vital Statistics. Call (402) 471-2871 for current fees. Records since late 1904. If birth occurred before then, write Bureau of Vital Statistics for information.

Marriage and Divorce Records: Bureau of Vital Statistics (see address listed above) has records since January 1909. Contact County Court, county where marriage license issued or Clerk of District Court, county where divorce granted.

State Library/Record Holdings: Nebraska State Historical Society, 1500 R St., P.O. Box 82554, Lincoln, NE 68501, (402) 471-4751, fax (402) 471-3100

Department of Motor Vehicles: Department of Motor Vehicles, 301 Centennial Mall S., P.O. Box 94789, Lincoln, NE 68509

Search and Support Groups, Researchers/Searchers, Consultants, Intermediaries:

Adoption Triad Midwest, SG, P.O. Box 45273, Omaha, NE 68145-0273, (402) 493-8047, e-mail: ralphsullivan@prodigy.com

Alice Beyke, ISC, searcher, 1850 S. Baltimore, Hastings NE 68901, (402) 462-6349, e-mail: ab35316@navix.net

Marge Brower, searcher, Box 489, Fullerton, NE 68638, (308) 536-2633

CUB Branch (Consult telephone directory or contact CUB National Headquarters listed under Iowa.)

State Reunion Registry: Nebraska does not currently have a state reunion registry. Refer to Chapter 8 for information on independent (group) reunion registries.

Age of Majority: 19 years or older

Laws Governing Opening Records: Infants, Section 42-130, subsection 12. "An adopted person twenty-five years of age or older born in this state who desires access to the name of relatives or access to his or her original certificate of birth shall file a written request for such information with the bureau. The bureau shall provide a form for making such a request."

Infants, Section 43-129, subsection 11. "If at any time an individual licensed to practice medicine and surgery pursuant to section 71-1, 102 to 107.14 or certified as qualified to practice clinical psychology pursuant to sections 71-1.222 to 71-3836, through his or her professional relationship with an adopted person, determines that information contained on the original birth certificate of the adopted person may be necessary for the treatment of the health of the adopted person, whether physical or mental in nature, he or she may petition a court of competent jurisdiction for the release of the information contained on the original birth certificate, and the court may release the information on good cause shown."

Laws Governing Inheritance: Infants, Section 43-106.01 *Adoption: relinquishment to Department of Public Welfare; relief from parental duties; no impairment of right to inherit.* "When a child shall have been relinquished by written instrument, as provided by sections 43-104 and 43-106, to the Department of Public Welfare or to a licensed child placement agency and the agency has, in writing, accepted full responsibility for the child, the person so relinquishing shall be relieved of all parental duties toward and all responsibilities for such child and have no rights over such child. Nothing contained in this section shall impair the right of such child to inherit."

NEVADA

State Agency: Division of Child and Family Services, 6171 W. Charleston Blvd., Bldg. No. 15, Las Vegas, NV 89158, (702) 486-7650.

Court of Jurisdiction: District Court

Birth and Death Records: Division of Health—Vital Statistics, Capitol Complex, 505 E. King St. #102, Carson City, NV 89710. Check or money order payable to Section of Vital Statistics. Call (702) 885-4480 for current fees. Records since July 1911. For earlier records, write to County Recorder in county where event occurred.

Marriage and Divorce Records: Division of Health—Vital Statistics (see address listed above) has indexes since January 1968. Inquiries will be forwarded to appropriate office. Contact County Recorder, county where marriage license issued or County Clerk, county where divorce granted.

State Library/Record Holdings: Nevada State Library and Archives, 100 N. Stewart St, Carson City, NV 89710, (702) 687-5160, fax (702) 687-8330, Web site: <www.clan.lib.nv.us./docs/nsla.htm>.

Department of Motor Vehicles: Public Safety Department, 555 Wright Way, Carson City, NV 89711-0900, fax (702) 687-1404.

Search and Support Groups, Researchers/Searchers, Consultants, Intermediaries:

Mary Buckley, researcher, Heritage Searching, 4308 San Mateo St., N. Las Vegas, NV 89030-2822

State Reunion Registry: Nevada has a state reunion registry. Refer to Chapter 8 for information on state and independent (group) reunion registries. no search

Age of Majority: 18 years or older

Laws Governing Opening Records: Chapter 127, Adoption of Children and Adults, Section 127.140. *Confidentiality of hearings, files and records.* 2. "The files and records of the court in adoption proceedings are not open to inspection by any person except upon an order of the court expressly so permitting pursuant to a petition setting forth the reasons therefor, or if a natural parent, and the child are eligible to receive information from the state register of adoptions."

Laws Governing Inheritance: Chapter 127, Adoption Children and Adults, Section 127.160. *Rights and duties of adopted child and adoptive parents.* ". . . After a decree of adoption is entered, the natural parents of an adopted child shall be relieved of all parental responsibilities for such child, and they shall not exercise or have any rights over such adopted child or his property. The child shall not owe his natural parents or their relatives any legal duty nor shall he inherit from his natural parent or kindred."

Policies: 127.007 State register for adoptions: Establishment; contents; release of information. 1. "The division shall maintain the state register for adoptions, which is hereby established, in its central office to provide information to identify adults who were adopted and persons related to them within the third degree of consanguinity."

NEW HAMPSHIRE

State Agency: Division for Children, Youth and Families, 6 Hazen Dr., Concord, NH 03301.

Court of Jurisdiction: Probate Court

Birth and Death Records: Bureau of Vital Records, Health and Human Services Building, 6 Hazen Dr., Concord, NH 03301. Check or money order payable to Treasurer, State of New Hampshire. Call (603) 271-4654 for current fees. Records since 1640.

Marriage Records: Bureau of Vital Records (see address listed above) has records since 1640; or contact Town Clerk, town where license issued.

Divorce Records: Bureau of Vital Records (see address listed above) has records since 1808; or contact Clerk of Superior Court where divorce granted.

State Library/Record Holdings: New Hampshire State Library, 20 Park St., Concord, NH 03301-6314, (603) 271-2144, fax (603) 271-2205, Web site: <www.state.nh.us/ nhsl/nhsl.htm/>. Information only, no responses.

Department of Motor Vehicles: Division of Motor Vehicles, 10 Hazen Dr., Concord, NH 03305, (603) 271-2484, fax (603) 271-3903.

Search and Support Groups, Researchers/Searchers, Consultants, Intermediaries:

Contact the American Adoption Congress National Office (District of Columbia), Adoption Crossroads National Office (New York), or Concerned United Birthparents (Iowa) to learn of search resources for New Hampshire.

State Reunion Registry: New Hampshire does not currently have a state reunion registry. Refer to Chapter 8 for information on independent (group) reunion registries.

Age of Majority: 18 years and older.

Laws Governing Opening Records: Chapter 170-B Adoption, Section 19, *Confidentiality of Records*. II. "All papers and records, including birth certificates, pertaining to the adoption, whether part of the permanent record of the court or of a file in the division, in an agency or office of the town clerk or the bureau of vital statistics are subject to inspection only upon written consent of the court for good cause shown."

Laws Governing Inheritance: Chapter 170-B, Section 20. *Effect of Petition and Decree of Adoption; Inheritance*. II. "Upon the issuance of the final decree of adoption, the adopted child shall no longer be considered the child of his natural parent or parents and shall no longer be entitled to any of the rights or privileges or subject to any of the duties or obligations of a child with respect to the natural parent or parents; but, when a child is adopted by a stepparent, his relationship to his natural parent who is married to the stepparent shall in no way be altered by reason of the adoption." III. "Upon the issuance of a final decree of adoption, the adopted child shall lose all rights of inheritance from his natural parents and from their collateral or lineal relatives. The rights of the natural parent or parents of their collateral or lineal relatives to inherit from such child shall cease upon the adoption."

NEW JERSEY

State Agency: Department of Human Services, Division of Youth & Family Services, CN 717, Trenton, NJ 08625-0717; e-mail: ggioglio@dhs.state.nj.us.

Court of Jurisdiction: Superior Court or County Court

Birth and Death Records: State Department of Health, Bureau of Vital Statistics, South Warren and Market Sts., CN 370, Trenton, NJ 08625. Check or money order payable to NJ State Dept. of Health. Call (609) 292-4087 for current fees. Records since June 1878. State Library Division, State Department of Education, Trenton, NJ 08625 has records from May 1848 to May 1878.

Marriage Records: State Department of Health (see address listed above); Archives and History Bureau (see address listed below). Records from May 1848 to May 1878.

Divorce Records: Superior Court, Chancery Division, State House Annex, Room 320, CN 971, Trenton, NJ 08625.

State Library/Record Holdings: State Library, CN 520, Trenton, NJ 08625-0520, fax (609) 292-7746.

Department of Motor Vehicles: Motor Vehicle Services, Certified Information Unit, 225 E. State St, CN-146, Trenton, NJ 08666-1046, (609) 292-6500.

Search and Support Groups, Researchers/Searchers, Consultants, Intermediaries:

Adoption Crossroads Branch, (Consult telephone operator or directory, write the National Headquarters listed under New York.)

Adoption Reunion Coalition of NJ, S&SG, Barbara Kelly, ISC, searcher, 15 Fir Pl. Hazlet, NJ 07730, (723) 739-9365

Angles & Extensions, SG, P.O. Box 7247, Sussex, NJ 07461, (973) 875-9869, fax (973) 875-9869

NJ Coalition for Openness in Adoption, S&SG, 206 Laurel Pl., Laurel Springs, NJ 08021, (609) 784-7532, fax (609) 784-7532, e-mail: mgpic@cyberenet.net

Origins, S&SG, Diane LeMasson, searcher, 289 E. Halsey Rd., Parsippany, NJ 07054, (973) 884-1695, e-mail: HUWV77A@prodigy.com

State Reunion Registry: New Jersey has a state adoption registry for State Agency Adoptions only. Refer to Chapter 8 for information on state and independent (group) reunion registries.

Age of Majority: 18 years or older

Laws Governing Opening Records: Chapter 367, Section 9:3-52. *Records of proceedings; filing under seal; inspection; change of birth record.* (a) "All records of proceedings, relating to adoption, including the complaint, judgment and all petitions, affidavits, testimony, reports, briefs, orders and other relevant documents, shall be filed under seal by the clerk of the court and shall at no time be open to inspection or copying unless the court, upon good cause shown, shall otherwise order . . . ."

Laws Governing Inheritance: Chapter 367, Section 9.3-50. *Effect of adoption; relationships of parent and child; rights of inheritance.* "The entry of a judgment of adoption shall terminate all relationships between the adopted child and his parents and all rights, duties and obligations of any person that are founded upon such relationships, including rights of inheritance under the interstate laws of this State, except such rights as may have vested prior to entry of the judgment of adoption; . . . For good cause, the court may in the judgment provide that the rights of inheritance from or through a deceased parent will not be affected or terminated by the adoption."

Policies: The following is taken from a letter from the New Jersey Division of Youth and Family Services. "In 1952, the current law (NJSA 9:3-52) was passed. It requires any person seeking access to SEALED adoption records to obtain a court order, for good cause, from the Superior Court. However, since records prior to 1940 WERE NOT SEALED, citizens should be able to review them."

NEW MEXICO

State Agency: Children, Youth & Families Department, Protective Services Division, Central Adoption Unit, P.O. Drawer 5160, Santa Fe, NM 87502.

Court of Jurisdiction: District Court

Birth and Death Records: Vital Statistics, New Mexico Health Services Division, 1190 St. Francis Dr., Santa Fe, NM 87503. Check or money order payable to Vital Statistics. Call (505) 827-2338 for current fees. Records since 1920 and delayed records since 1880.

Marriage and Divorce Records: County Clerk, county where marriage license issued. Contact Clerk of Superior Court where divorce granted.

State Library/Record Holdings: New Mexico State Library, 325 Don Gaspar, Santa Fe, NM 87501, (505) 827-3824, fax (505) 827-3888, Web site: <www.stlib.state.nm.us>.

Department of Motor Vehicles: Motor Vehicle Division, 1100 S. St. Francis Dr., P.O. Box 1028, Santa Fe, NM 87504-1028, (505) 827-0700, fax (505) 827-2397.

Search and Support Groups, Researchers/Searchers, Consultants, Intermediaries:

Leonie Boehmer, ISC, searcher, 805 Alvarado NE, Albuquerque, NM 87108, (505) 268-1310, fax (505) 268-1310, e-mail:BoehmerL@aol.com

CUB Representative (Consult telephone directory or contact CUB National Headquarters listed under Iowa.)

Operation Identity, S&SG, Sally File, searcher, 13101 Blackstone, NE, Albuquerque, NM 87111, (505) 293-3144

State Reunion Registry: New Mexico does not currently have a state reunion registry. Refer to Chapter 8 for information on independent (group) reunion registries.

Age of Majority: 18 years or older

Laws Governing Opening Records: Adoption, 40-7-16. *Inspection of adoption filed, limitations; new birth record.* A. "The files, records and entries in adoption proceedings in the custody of the court, or of the department or of the agency involved in the proceeding, shall be separately kept, locked and preserved after filing, except in the case of appeal. No person other than officials of the court, or the department of any agency who may be a party to the adoption proceedings, shall be permitted to inspect such files, records and entries except by order of the court."

Laws Governing Inheritance: Domestic Affairs, 40-7-15. *Effect of judgment of adoption; appeal.* A. "A judgment of adoption, whether issued by the court of this state or any other place, has the following effect as to matters within the jurisdiction of or before the court: (1) to divest the natural parent and the child of all legal rights, privileges, duties and obligations, including rights of inheritance, with respect to each other . . ."

NEW YORK

State Agency: State of New York, Department of Health, Corning Tower, The Governor Nelson A. Rockefeller, Empire State Plaza, Albany, NY 12237, (518) 474-9600, Web site: <www.state.ny.us>.

Court of Jurisdiction: The New York State court that finalized the adoption or the New York State Supreme Court

Birth and Death Records: (except New York City), Vital Records Section, State Department of Health, Empire State Plaza, Tower Building, Albany, NY 12237-0023. Check or money order payable to NY State Dept. of Health. Call (518) 474-3075 for current fees. Records since 1880. For records before 1914 in Albany, Buffalo, and Yonkers, or before 1880 in any other city, write to Registrar of Vital Statistics in city where event occurred. For the rest of the state, except New York City, write to the Vital Records Section (New York City), Bureau of Vital Records, Department of Health of New York City, 125 Worth St., New York, NY 10013. Money order payable to New York City Dept. of Health. Call (212) 619-4530 for current fees. Birth records since 1898 and death records since 1930. For Old City of New York (Manhattan and part of the Bronx) birth records for 1865-97 and death records for 1865-1929 write to Archives Division, Department of Records and Information Services, 31 Chambers St., New York, NY 10007.

Marriage Records: (except New York City) Vital Records Section (see address listed above). Records from 1880 to present. For records from 1880-1907 and licenses issued in the city of Albany, Buffalo, or Yonkers, apply to—Albany: City Clerk, City Hall, Albany, NY 12207; Buffalo: City Clerk, City Hall, Buffalo, NY 14202; Yonkers: Registrar of Vital Statistics, Health Center Building, Yonkers, NY 10701. Other addresses—Bronx Borough, (New York City); City Clerk's Office, 1780 Grand Concourse, Bronx, NY 10457. Brooklyn Borough, City Clerk's Office, Municipal Building, Brooklyn, NY 11201; Manhattan Borough, City Clerk's Office, Municipal Building, New York, NY 10007; Queens Borough, City Clerk's Office, 120-55 Queens Blvd. Kew Gardens, NY 11424; Staten Island Borough, City Clerk's Office, Staten Island Borough Hall, Staten Island, NY 10301. For records from 1847 to 1865, write Archives Division,

Department of Records and Information Services (see address above), except Brooklyn records for this period which are filed with County Clerk's Office, Kings County, Supreme Court Building, Brooklyn, NY 11201. For records from 1866 to 1907, write to City Clerk's Office in borough where marriage was performed. For records from 1908 to May 12, 1943, New York City residents write to City Clerk's Office in the borough of bride's residence; nonresidents write to City Clerk's Office in borough where license was obtained. For records since May 13, 1943, write to City Clerk's Office in borough where license was issued.

Divorce Records: Vital Records Section (see address listed above) has records since January 1963; or contact County Clerk, county where divorce granted.

State Library/Record Holdings: NY State Library, Cultural Education Center, Madison Avenue, Empire State Plaza, Albany, NY 12230, (518) 474-5355, fax (518) 474-5786, Web site: www.nysl.nysed.gov>.

Department of Motor Vehicles: Department of Motor Vehicles, Empire State Plaza, Swan St. Bldg., Albany, NY 12228.

Search and Support Groups, Researchers/Searchers, Consultants, Intermediaries:

Adoptee-Birthparent F.I.N.D., S&SG, Frank Piccarreto, searcher/researcher/CI, 104 Old Orchard Ln., Orchard Park, NY 14127-4637, (716) 648-6949, e-mail: Frankly 1@aol.com

Adoptees Liberty Movement Assn., (ALMA) Headquarters, P.O. Box 727, Radio City Station, New York, NY 10101, (212) 581-1568, e-mail: Almainfo@aol.com, Web site: <www.almanet.com>

Adoption Crossroads, HQ, S&SG, Joe Soll, searcher, 356 E. 74th St. #2, New York, NY 10021, (212) 988-0110, fax (212) 988-0291, e-mail: cera@mail.idt.net, Web site:

Adoption Crossroads Branch, (Consult telephone operator or directory, write the National Headquarters listed under New York.)

Adoption KinShip, S&SG, 817 Taylor Dr., Vestal, NY 13850-3933, (607) 772-6793, fax (607) 594-9015, e-mail: JeanVH@prodigy.net

ANGELS NETWORK, Inc. S&SG, P.O. Box 67789, Rochester, NY 14617, (716) 234-1864, fax (716) 594-9051, e-mail: ANGELSR5@aol.com

Birthparent Support Network, S&SG, Gail Davenport, ACSW, searcher, P.O. Box 120, N., White Plains, NY 10603, (914) 682-2250, e-mail: Gad52@aol.com

Birthparent Support Network of Long Island, Carole Whitehead, searcher, P.O. Box 34, Old Bethpage, NY 11804-0034, (516) 931-5929, fax 516-931-5537, e-mail: CAROLE401@aol.com

C.E.R.A., S&SG, Joe Soll, searcher, 356 E. 74th St., #2, New York, NY 10021, (212) 988-0110, fax (212) 988-0291, e-mail: cera@mail.idt.net, Web site:

Center for Reuniting Families, S&SG, Dominic & Sarah Telesco, searchers, 51 Burke Dr., Buffalo, NY 14215, (716) 835-6387, fax (716) 835-1609, e-mail: dstelesco@aol.com

CUB Representative, (Consult telephone directory or consult CUB National Headquarters listed under Iowa.)

KinQuest, Inc., S&SG, 89 Massachusetts Ave., Massapaqua, NY 11758, (516) 541-7383, fax (541) 7383, e-mail: AnmaCara@aol.com

The Missing Connection, S&SG, Sue Boyce, searcher/researcher, P.O. Box 712, Brownville, NY 13615, (315) 782-6245, e-mail: Jan905@aol.com

Missing Pieces, SG, P.O. Box 8041, Massena, NY 13662-8041, Missing Pieces of Massena, NY, SG

Anne Johnson, researcher, 30 Grant St., Potsdam, NY 13676, (315) 265-2619, e-mail: annehj@northnet.org

Triangle of Truth, S&SG, 4 Adler Ln., Liverpool, NY 13090, (315) 622-0620, e-mail: Rrichar763@aol.com

State Reunion Registry: New York has *The Adoption and Medical Information Registry.* Refer to Chapter 8 for information on state and independent (group) reunion registries.

Age of Majority: 18 years

Laws Governing Opening Records: Domestic relations, Section 114. *Order of Adoption.* "Notwithstanding the fact that adoption records shall be sealed and secret, they may be microfilmed and processed pursuant to an order of the court, provided that such order provides that the confidentiality of such records be maintained."

Laws Governing Inheritance: Article 117. *Effect of Adoption.* (b) "The rights of an adoptive child to inheritance and succession from and through his natural parents shall terminate upon the making of the order of adoption. . ."

Policies: This state has many laws regarding adoption. Persons adopted/relinquished in this state should spend much time reviewing their rights.

NORTH CAROLINA

State Agency: Children's Services Section, Division of Social Services, Department of Human Resources, 325 N. Salisbury St., Raleigh, NC 27603.

Court of Jurisdiction: Superior Court—address to Clerk of the Superior Court

Birth and Death Records: Department of Environment, Health and Natural Resources, Division on Epidemiology, Vital Records Section, 225 N. McDowell St., P.O. Box 27687, Raleigh, NC 27611-7687. Check or money order payable to Vital Records Section. Call (919) 733-3526 for current fees. Birth records since October 1913 and death records since January 1, 1930. Death records from 1913 through 1929 are available from Archives and Records Section (see address listed below).

Marriage Records: Department of Environment (see address listed above) has marriage records since January 1962; or contact Registrar of Deeds, county where marriage performed.

Divorce Records: Department of Environment (see address listed above) has records since January 1958; or contact Clerk of Superior Court where divorce granted.

State Library/Record Holdings: State Library of North Carolina, 109 E. Jones St., Raleigh, NC 27601-2807, (919) 733-3683, fax (919) 733-5679, Web site: <www.dcr.state.nc.us/ncs1home.htm>.

Department of Motor Vehicles: Department of Motor Vehicles, 1100 New Bern Ave., Raleigh, NC 27697, (919) 715-7000, e-mail: DMV-info.@mail.dot.state.nc.us.

Search and Support Groups, Researchers/Searchers, Consultants, Intermediaries:

> *Adoption Reunion Connection, S&SG*, P.O. Box 1447, Dunn, NC 28335, (910) 892-1072, fax 910-892-5514, e-mail: tammy@nceye.net, Web site: <www2.nceye.net/tammy>

> *Christine Lee-Pl, searcher*, Kinsolving Investigations, P.O. Box 471921, Charlotte, NC 28247-1921, (704) 537-5919, fax (704) 846-5123, e-mail: mzchrislee@aol.com, Web site: <kinsolving.com>

> *NC Adoption Connections, S&SG*, P.O. Box 4153, Chapel Hill, NC 27515-4153, (919) 967-5010, e-mail: NCCAAE@aol.com

State Reunion Registry: North Carolina does not currently have a state reunion registry. Refer to Chapter 8 for information on independent (group) reunion registries.

Age of Majority: 18 years or older

Laws Governing Opening Records: North Carolina General Statutes, ARTICLE 9, 48-9-104. *Release of identifying information.* "No person or entity shall release from any records, retained and sealed under this Article the name, address, or other information that reasonably could be expected to lead directly to the identity of an adoptee, an adoptive parent of an adoptee, an adoptee's parent at birth, or an individual who, but for the adoption, would be the adoptee's sibling or grandparent, except upon order of the court for cause pursuant to G.S. 48-9-105. 48-9-105. Action for release of identifying and other nonidentifying information. (a) Any information necessary for the protection of the adoptee or the public in or derived from the records, including medical information not otherwise obtainable, may be disclosed to an individual who files a written motion in the cause before the clerk of original jurisdiction. In hearing the petition, the court shall give primary consideration to the best interest of the adoptee, but shall also give due consideration to the interests of the members of the adoptee's original and adoptive family."

Laws Governing Inheritance: North Carolina General Statutes. ARTICLE 1. General Provisions. 48-1-106. *Legal effect of decree of adoption.* (c) "A decree of adoption severs the relationship of parent and child between the individual adopted and that individual's biological or previous adoptive parents. After the entry of a decree of adoption, the former parents are relieved of all legal duties and obligation due from them to the adoptee . . . and the former parents are divested of all rights with respect to the adoptee."

NORTH DAKOTA

State Agency: Department of Human Services, Children & Family Services, 600 E. Boulevard Ave., Bismarck, ND 58505, (701) 328-2316, fax (701) 328-2359.

Court of Jurisdiction: District Court

Birth and Death Records: Division of Vital Records, State Capitol, 600 E. Boulevard Ave., Bismarck, ND 58505. Money order payable to Division of Vital Records. Call (701) 224-2360. Some records since 1893. Years from 1894 to 1920 are incomplete.

Marriage and Divorce. Records: Division of Vital Records (see address listed above). Marriage records since July 1925. Requests for earlier records will be forwarded to appropriate office. Contact County Judge, county where license issued. Index of divorce records since 1949. Inquiries will be forwarded to appropriate office.

State Library/Record Holdings: State Historical Society, 604 E. Boulevard Ave., Bismarck, ND 58505-0800, (701) 328-4622, fax (701) 328-2040, e-mail: msmail.statelib@ranch.state.nd.us, Web site: <www.sendit.nodak.edu/ndsl/index.html>.

Department of Motor Vehicles: Department of Transportation, 608 E. Blvd. Bismarck, ND 58505, (701) 328-2725, fax (701) 328-3500, e-mail: ccmail.kkiser@ranch.state.nd.us, Web site: <www.state.nd.us/dot/>.

Search and Support Groups, Researchers/Searchers, Consultants, Intermediaries:

> Lutheran Social Services of North Dakota, S&SG, 1325 S. 11th St., Fargo, ND 58103, (701) 235-7341

State Reunion Registry: North Dakota does not currently have a state reunion registry. Refer to Chapter 8 for information on independent (group) reunion registries.

Age of Majority: 18/21 years or older.

Laws Governing Opening Records: Domestic Relations and Persons, 14-15-16. *Hearings and Records in Adoption Proceedings-Confidential Nature-Disclosure of Identifying and Nonidentifying Information.* Retroactive Operation. 4. "An adopted person who is eighteen years of age or over may request the Department of Human Services to secure and disclose information identifying the adopted child's genetic parents or to secure and disclose nonidentifying information not on file with the board or a child placing agency. The Department of Human Services shall, within five working days of receipt of the request, notify in writing the child placing agency having access to the information requested of the request by the adopted child." 5. "Within three months after receiving notice of the request of the adopted person, the child placing agency shall make complete and reasonable efforts to notify the genetic parents of the adopted child. The child placing agency may charge a reasonable fee to the adopted child for the cost of making a search pursuant to the subsection . . . ." 6. "If the child placing agency certifies to the Department of Human Services that it has been unable to notify the genetic parent within three months, the identifying information shall not be disclosed . . . ." 7. "If, within three months, the child placing agency certifies to the Department of Human Services that it has notified the genetic parents pursuant to subsection 5, the Department of Human Services shall receive the identifying information from the child placing agency and disclose the information sixty-one days after the date of the latest notice . . . ." 8. "If the genetic parent has died and has not filed an unrevoked affidavit with the Department of Human Services stating that identifying information shall not be disclosed, the information shall be forwarded to and released by the Department of Human Services to the adopted child . . . ."

Laws Governing Inheritance: Domestic Relations and Persons, 14-15-14. *Effect of Petition and decree of adoption.* 1a. "Except with respect to a spouse of the petitioner and relatives of the spouse, to relieve the natural parents of the adopted individual of all parental rights and responsibilities, and to terminate all legal relationships between the adopted individual and his relatives, including his natural parents, so that the adopted individual thereafter is a stranger to his former relatives for all purposes including inheritance and the interpretation or construction of documents, statutes, and instruments, whether executed before or after the adoption is decreed . . . ."

Policies: Domestic Relations and Persons, 14-15-01. *Definitions.* "Nonidentifying adoptive information means: a. Age of genetic parent in years at the birth of the adopted child. b. Heritage of genetic parent. c. Educational attainments, including the number of years of school completed by genetic parent at the time of birth of the adopted child. d. General physical appearance of genetic parent at the time of birth of the adopted child, including the weight, height, color of hair, eyes, skin and other information of a similar nature. e. Talents, hobbies, and special interests of genetic parents. f. Existence of any other children born to either genetic parent before the birth of the adopted child. g. Reasons for child being placed for adoption or for termination of parental right. h. Religion of genetic parent. i. Vocation of genetic parent in general terms. j. Health history of genetic parents and blood relatives in a manner prescribed by the Department of Human Services. k. Such further information which, in the judgment of the agency, will not be detrimental to the adoptive parent or the adopted person requesting the information, but the additional information must not identify genetic parents by name or location."

Author's Observations: A copy of these statutes would be valuable in discovering additional laws governing siblings and affidavits. *Note:* There is a charge to conduct the search. Find out the amount and what services are rendered.

OHIO

State Agency: Ohio Department of Human Services, 30 E. Broad St., 32nd Floor, Columbus, OH 43266-0423.

Court of Jurisdiction: Probate Court

Birth and Death Records: Division of Vital Statistics, Ohio Department of Health, G-20 Ohio Department Bldg., 65 S. Front St., Columbus, OH 43266-0333. Check or money order payable to State Treasury. Call (614) 466-2531 for current fees. Birth records since December 20, 1908. For earlier birth and death records, write to the Probate Court in the county where the event occurred. The Division of Vital Statistics has death records for the last 49 years. Death records from 50 or more years ago—through December 20, 1908—can be obtained from the Ohio Historical Society (see address listed below).

Marriage and Divorce Records: Division of Vital Statistics (see address listed above) has records since September 1949. Contact Probate Judge, county where marriage license issued or Clerk of Court of Common Pleas where divorce granted.

State Library/Record Holdings: Ohio Historical Society, Archives Library Division, 1982 Velma Ave., Columbus, OH 43211-2497 , (614) 297-2510, fax (614) 297-2546, e-mail: ohsref@winslo.ohio.gov, Web site: <winslo.ohio.gov/ohswww/ohshome.html>. Ohio State Library, 65 S. Front St., 11th Floor, Columbus, OH 43215-4163. (800) 686-1531, fax (614) 466-3584, e-mail: sloinfo@slonet.ohio.gov, Web site: <www.winslo.ohio.gov>.

Department of Motor Vehicles: Bureau of Motor Vehicles, P.O. Box 16520, Columbus, OH 43266-0020.

Search and Support Groups, Researchers/Searchers, Consultants, Intermediaries:

Adoption Network Cleveland, S&SG, 291 E. 222nd St., Room #229, Cleveland, OH 44123-1751, (216) 261-1511, fax (216) 261-1164, e-mail: bln2@po.cwru.edu, Web site: <pages.prodigy.com/adoptreform/anc.htm>

Birthmothers Sharing, S&SG, Denise Fossett, searcher, 3355 Scioto Rd., Cincinnati, OH 45244, (513) 271-5926, fax (513) 561-0074

Chosen Children, S&SG, Joanne Gall, researcher, 311 Springbrook Blvd., Dayton, OH 45405, (937) 274-8017, e-mail: ag802@daton.wright.edu

CUB Branch: (Consult telephone directory or contact CUB National Headquarters listed under Iowa.)

Full Circle, S&SG, Janet Anderson, researcher, 4110 North Ave., #4, Cincinnati, OH 45236, (513) 791-0441

Insight to the Adoption Triad, S&SG, Mary Lynn Fuller, searcher, 2599 3E Riverside Dr., Columbus, OH 43221, e-mail: mlfuller@aol.com

Pieces of Yesterday, SG, 856 Pine Needles Dr., Centerville, OH 45458-3329, (937) 436-0593

Sunshine Reunions, S&SG, Jean Batis, searcher, 1175 Virginia Ave., Akron, OH 44306, (330) 773-4691, e-mail: OdessaRose@aol.com

State Reunion Registry: Ohio has a reunion registry. Refer to Chapter 8 for information on state and independent (group) reunion registries.

Age of Majority: 18 years and older

Laws Governing Opening Records: Adoption. Records. 3107.17. *Confidentiality; records; access to histories of biological parents; rights of parties concerning proposed correction or expansion; procedures.* (A) "All hearings held under sections 3107.01 to 3107.19 of the Revised Code shall be held in closed court without the admittance of any person other than essential officers of the court, the parties, the witnesses of the parties, counsel, persons who have not previously consented to an adoption but who are required to consent, and representatives of the agencies present to perform their official duties." (B1) ". . . no person or governmental entity shall knowingly reveal any information contained in a paper, book, or record pertaining to a placement under section 5103.16 of the Revised Code . . . without the consent of a court."

Laws Governing Inheritance: Adoption. Section 3107.15. *Effects of final decree* (A2) "To create the relationship of parent and child between petitioner and the adopted persons, as if the adopted person were a legitimate blood descendant of the petitioner, for all purposes including inheritance and applicability of statutes, documents and instruments, whether executed before or after the adoption is decreed, which do not expressly exclude an adopted person from their operation or effect."

Policies: Adoption. Records. Section 3107.17. (D) "All forms that pertain to the social or medical histories of the biological parent of an adopted person and that were completed pursuant to division 6107.19 or 3107.91 of the Revised Code shall be filed only in the permanent record kept by the court. During the minority of the adopted person, only the adoptive parents of the person may inspect the forms. When an adopted person reaches majority, only he may inspect the forms. Under the circumstances described in this division, an adopted person or his adoptive parents are entitled to inspect the forms upon requesting the clerk of the court to produce them."

OKLAHOMA

State Agency: Child Welfare Services, Human Services Dept., Attention: Adoption Section, P.O. Box 25352, Oklahoma City, OK 73125, fax (405) 521-6458.

Court of Jurisdiction: District Court

Birth and Death Records: Vital Records Section, State Department of Health, 1000 Northeast 10th St., P.O. Box 53551, Oklahoma City, OK 73152. Check or money order payable OK State Dept. of Health. Call (405) 271-4040 for current fees. Records since October 1908.

Marriage and Divorce Records: Contact Clerk of Court, county where license issued or Clerk of Court, county where divorce granted

State Library/Record Holdings: Department of Libraries, 200 NE 18th St., Oklahoma City, OK 73105, (405) 521-2502, Web site: <www.state.ok.us/~odl/>.

Department of Motor Vehicles: Department of Public Safety, 3600 N. Martin Luther King, PO Box 11415, Oklahoma City, OK 73136, (405) 425-2424, fax (405) 425-2061, Web site: <www.dps.state.ok.us>.

Search and Support Groups, Researchers/Searchers, Consultants, Intermediaries:

Carol Davis, searcher, CI, Family Connection, Inc., P.O. Box 187, Perkins, OK 74059, (405) 547-1183, fax (405) 547-1184, e-mail: imssomeone@aol.com

Shepherd's Heart, S&SG, Karen Slagle, researcher, 158 Stevens Circle N, Newalla, OK 74857, e-mail: SQFK07B@prodigy.com

State Reunion Registry: Oklahoma has an adoption reunion registry. Refer to Chapter 8 for information on state and independent (group) reunion registries. Note "Policies" below.

Age of Majority: 18 years or older

Laws Governing Opening Records: Children, Section 60.17. *Confidential character of hearings and records.* (2) "All papers and records pertaining to the adoption shall be kept as a permanent record of the court and withheld from inspection. No person shall have access to such records except on order of the judge of the court in which the decree of adoption was entered, for good cause shown."

Laws Governing Inheritance: Children, Section 60.16. *Effect of Final Decree.* (2) "After a final decree of adoption is entered, the natural parents of the adopted child, unless they are the adoptive parents or the spouse of an adoptive parent, shall be relieved of all parental responsibilities for such child and have no rights over such adopted child or to his property by descent and distribution."

Policies: All non-DHS adoption inquiries will be sent to the International Soundex Reunion Registry.

Author's Observations: Children, Section 60.18. *Certificates.* (2) "The state registrar, upon receipt of a certified copy of an order of decree of adoption, shall prepare a supplementary certificate in the new name of the adopted person, the city and county of residence of adoptive parents, hospital of choice of adoptive parents, and the family physician of the adoptive parents if they are residents of the State of Oklahoma, provided, however, any change of name of the physician or the hospital shall first require that a written consent of such hospital and such physician is obtained. The state registrar shall then seal and file the original certificate of birth with said certified copy attached thereto. Such sealed documents may be opened by the state registrar only upon demand of the adopted person, if of legal age, or adoptive parents, by an order of the court."

[My understanding of this section of the law is that adopted persons must demand from the court or receive an order of the court to learn the true identity of his/her hospital and physician at birth. How can this law be in the best interest of the child? Adoptees from this state should be aware of the altered information on their birth certificates.]

OREGON

State Agency: Department of Human Resources, State Office for Services to Children & Families, 500 Summer St. NE, Salem, OR 97310-1017.

Court of Jurisdiction: Circuit Court

Birth and Death Records: Oregon Health Division, Vital Statistics Section, P.O. Box 116, Portland, OR 97207. Check or money order payable Oregon Health Division. Call (503) 229-5710 for current fees. Records since January 1903. Some earlier records for the City of Portland since approximately 1880 are available from the Oregon State Archives (see address listed below).

Marriage Records: Oregon Health Division (see address listed above) has records since January 1906; or contact County Clerk, county where license issued. Some County Clerks also have records before 1906.

Divorce Records: Oregon Health Division (see address listed above) has records since 1925; or contact County Clerk, county where divorce granted. Some County Clerks also have some records before 1925.

State Library/Record Holdings: Oregon State Archives, 1005 Broadway, NE, Salem, OR 97310. Oregon State Library, 250 Winter St. NE, Salem, OR 97310, (503) 378-4277, fax (503) 588-7119.

Department of Motor Vehicles: Motor Vehicles Division, Dept. of Transportation, 1905 Lana Ave. NE, Salem, OR 97314, (503) 945-5000.

Search and Support Groups, Researchers/Searchers, Consultants, Intermediaries:

Adoptee Birthfamily Connection, S&SG, P.O. Box 50122, Eugene, OR 97405, (541) 345-6710, fax (541) 345-6710 (call first), e-mail: BWDX83A@prodigy.com

Kathy Brown, researcher, 1076 Queens Branch Rd., Rogue River, OR 97537, (541) 582-2658

The Circle, SG, 1090 Ellendale Sp. C14, Medford, OR 97504, (503) 773-4554

The Circle, SG, 635 Elkader St., Ashland, OR 97520, (541) 482-5554, fax (541) 482-5554, e-mail: pjflorin@jeffnet.org

Helen Gallagher, ISC, searcher, Family Ties, 4537 Souza St., Eugene, OR 97402-6122, (541) 461-0752, e-mail: GRTJ72A@prodigy.com

Oregon Adoptive Rights Association (OARA), S&SG, P.O. Box 882, Portland, OR 97204, (503) 235-3669, e-mail: darlenew@worldaccessnet.com, Web site: <www.oara.org.>

Triad Connections, S&SG, Katherine M. Pedersen, Ed.M., researcher, 550 SE 123rd St., South Beach, OR 97366-6611, (541) 867-4649, e-mail: kpederse@orednet.org

Darlene Wilson, Confidential Intermediary, P.O. Box 882, Portland, OR 97204, (503) 235-3669, e-mail: darlenew@worldaccessnet.com

State Reunion Registry: Oregon has a Voluntary Adoption Registry. See Chapter 8 for information on state and independent (group) reunion registries.

Age of Majority: 18 years or older

Laws Governing Opening Records: Section 7.211. *Records in adoption, finalization, probate, domestic relations and juvenile proceedings.* Separate records in adoption cases; accessibility of records limited. "The clerk or court administrator of any court having jurisdiction over adoption cases shall keep a separate journal, index and fee register in all cases of adoption filed in such court. The journal, index and fee register shall not be subject to the inspection of any person, except upon order of the court . . . .Nothing contained in this section shall prevent the clerk or court administrator from certifying copies of a decree of adoption to the petitioners in such proceeding or their attorney."

Laws Governing Inheritance: Section 109.041. *Relationship between adopted child and his natural and adopted parents.* (1) "The effect of a decree of adoption heretofore or hereafter granted by a court of this state shall be that the relationship, rights and obligations between an adopted person and his descendants and (a) His adoptive parents, their descendants and kindred, and (b) His natural parents, their descendants and kindred shall be the same to all legal intents and purposes after the entry of such decree as if the adopted person had been born in lawful wedlock to his adoptive parents and had not been born to his natural parents."

PENNSYLVANIA

State Agency: Department of Public Welfare, Office of Children, Youth and Families, P.O. Box 2675, Harrisburg, PA 17105-2675, (800) 227-0225, fax (717) 772-6857.

Court of Jurisdiction: Court of Common Pleas

Birth and Death Records: Division of Vital Records, State Department of Health, Central Building, 101 S. Mercer St., P.O. Box 1528, New Castle, PA 16103. Check or money order payable to Division of Vital Records. Call (412) 656- 3147 for current fees. Records since January 1906. For earlier records, write to Register of Wills, Orphans Court, in county seat of county where event occurred. Persons born in Pittsburgh from 1870 to 1905 or in Allegheny City, now part of Pittsburgh, from 1882 to 1905 should write to Office of Biostatistics, Pittsburgh Health Department, City-County Building, Pittsburgh, PA 15219. For events occurring in City of Philadelphia from 1860 to 1915, write to Vital Statistics, Philadelphia Department of Public Health, City Hall Annex, Philadelphia, PA 19107.

Marriage Records: Division of Vital Records (see address listed above). Records since January 1906. Inquiries will be forwarded to appropriate office. Contact Marriage License Clerks, county Court House, county where license issued.

Divorce Records: Division of Vital Records (see address listed above). Records since January 1946. Inquiries will be forwarded to appropriate office. Contact prothonotary/ Court House, County seat, county where divorce granted.

State Library/Record Holdings: Commonwealth Libraries, Forum Building, Commonwealth & Walnut Sts, P.O. Box 1601, Harrisburg, PA 17105-1601, (717) 787-4440, fax (717) 783-2070, e-mail: ali@unixl.stlib.state.pa.us, Web site: <www.cas.psu.edu/docs/pde/lib1.html>.

Department of Motor Vehicles: Bureau of Motor Vehicles, 1101 S. Front St., Riverfront Office Center, Harrisburg, PA 17105.

Search and Support Groups, Researchers/Searchers, Consultants, Intermediaries:

Adoption Healing, SG, Judy Scott, searcher, 120 46th St., Pittsburgh, PA 15201, (412) 687-0100, fax (412) 687-0129

Lost Loved Ones, SG, Bob Mulvehill, searcher, 621 W. Crawford St., Ebensburg, PA 15931, (814) 472-7525, fax (814) 472-7525

Open Line Adoption Connection, S&SG, Holly Watson, searcher, 817 E. Third St., Oil City, PA 16301, (814) 677-7850

P.A.S.T., S&SG, Barbara Hakel & Rose Yeast, searchers, 8130 Hawthorne, Dr., Erie, PA 16509, (814) 899-1493, fax (814) 866-2535, e-mail: PACHAIN@aol.com

Pittsburgh Adoption Connection, S&SG, Glenda Shay, searcher, 37 Edgecliff Rd., Carnegie, PA 15106, (412) 279-2511, e-mail: G Shay@aol.com, Web site: <members.aol.com/GShay/index.html>

Pittsburgh Adoption Lifeline, S&SG, Jean Vincent, searcher, P.O. Box 52, Gibsonia, PA 15044, (412) 443-3370

SEARCHING, S&SG, Dee Hardy, 923 South Front St., Steelton, PA 17113, (717) 939-0138, e-mail: TRIAD2271@aol.com,

State Reunion Registry: Pennsylvania has an Adoption Medical History Registry. Refer to Chapter 8 for information on state and independent (group) reunion registries.

Age of Majority: 18 years or older

Laws Governing Opening Records: Title 23, Domestic Relations, Part III, Adoption, Section 2905 (a). "General Rule.-All petitions, exhibits, reports, notes of testimony, decrees, and other papers pertaining to any proceeding under this part or former statutes relating to adoption shall be kept in the files of the court as a permanent record thereof and withheld from inspection except on an order of court granted upon cause shown or except as otherwise provided in this section." (b) "Petition to court for limited information.—Upon petition by any adoptee at least 18 years of age or, if less than 18, his adoptive parent or legal guardian to the court in the judicial district in which the permanent records relating to the adoption have been impounded, the court shall furnish to the adoptee as much information concerning the adoptee's natural parents as will not endanger the anonymity of the natural parents. The information shall first be reviewed, in camera, by the court to insure that no information is revealed which would endanger the anonymity of the natural parents. The court shall, upon motion of the adoptee, examine the entire record to determine if any additional information can safely be revealed without endangering the anonymity of the natural parents."

Laws Governing Inheritance: Title 23, Domestic Relations, Part III, Adoption, Section 321. *Effect of decree of termination.* "A decree terminating all rights of a parent or a decree terminating all rights and duties of a parent entered by a court of competent jurisdiction shall extinguish the power or the right of such parent to receive notice of adoption proceedings."

Policies: A birthparent may file consent with the Department of Health's Division of Vital Records granting permission to release their name and address to an adoptee upon request. Adoptees searching should check this resource.

RHODE ISLAND

State Agency: Department for Children and Their Families, 610 Mount Pleasant Ave., Providence, RI 02908, (401) 457-4548.

Court of Jurisdiction: Adoptees over 18: Probate Court. Adoptees under 18: Family Court

Birth and Death Records: Division of Vital Records, Rhode Island Department of Health, Room 101, Cannon Bldg., 3 Capitol Hill, Providence, RI 02908-5097. Money order payable to General Treasurer, State of Rhode Island. Call (401) 277-2811 for current fees. Records since 1853. For earlier records, write to Town Clerk in town where event occurred.

Marriage Records: Division of Vital Records (see address listed above) has records since January 1835.

Divorce Records: Clerk of Family Court, One Dorrance Plaza, Providence, RI 02903.

State Library/Record Holdings: Rhode Island Historical Society Library, 121 Hope St., Providence, RI 02906, (401) 331-8575, fax (401) 751-7930.

Department of Motor Vehicles: Division of Motor Vehicles, 286 Main St., Pawtucket, RI 02860, (401) 277-2970.

Search and Support Groups, Researchers/Searchers, Consultants, Intermediaries: Contact the National Office (District of Columbia), Adoption Crossroads National Office (New York) or Concerned United Birthparents (Iowa) to learn of search resources for Rhode Island.

State Reunion Registry: Rhode Island has a state reunion registry. Refer to Chapter 8 for information on independent (group) reunion registries.

Age of Majority: 18 years or older

Laws Governing Opening Records: Courts and Civil Procedure—Courts. 8-10-21. *Records of Court.* "The records of the family court shall be public records, except that records of hearings in matters set forth in 14-1-5 (B. Concerning Adoption of Children), together with stenographic notes and transcripts of said hearings, shall not be available for public inspection unless the court shall otherwise order."

Laws Governing Inheritance: Adoption of Children. 15-7-17. *Rights of natural parents terminated—Inheritance by child from natural parents.* "The parents of such child shall be deprived, by the decree, of all legal rights respecting the child, and the child shall be freed from all obligations of maintenance and obedience respecting his natural parents except that the granting of the petition for adoption will not deprive an adopted child of the right to inherit from and through his natural parents in the same manner as all other natural children; provided, however, that the right to inherit from and through natural parents of an adopted child born out of wedlock shall be as provided in 33-1-8; and provided, further, however, that the decree of adoption shall in no way affect all legal rights of a natural parent respecting the right and all obligations of the child of maintenance and obedience respecting a natural parent if such natural parent is legally married to the adopting parent at the time of the decree of adoption."

SOUTH CAROLINA

State Agency: Department of Social Services P.O. Box 1520, Columbia, SC 29202-1520, fax (803) 734-6285, Post-Legal Administrator.

Court of Jurisdiction: Family Court

Birth and Death Records: Office of Vital Records and Public Health Statistics, South Carolina Department of Health and Environmental Control, 2600 Bull St., Columbia, SC 29201. Check or money order payable to Office of Vital Records. Call (803) 734-4830 for current fees. Records since January 1915, City of Charleston births from 1877 and deaths from 1821 are on file at Charleston County Health Department. Ledger entries of Florence City births and deaths from 1895 to 1914 are on file at Florence County Health Department. Ledger entries of Newberry City births and deaths from the late 1800s are on file at Newberry County Health Department. These are the only early records obtainable.

Marriage Records: Office of Vital Records (see address listed above) has records since July 1950; or contact Probate Judge, county where license issued, for records since July 1911.

Divorce Records: Office of Vital Records (see address listed above) for records since July 1962; or contact Clerk, county where petition filed, for records since April 1949.

State Library/Record Holdings: South Carolina State Library, 1500 Senate St., P.O. Box 11469, Columbia, SC 29211, (803) 734-8666, fax (803) 734-8676, e-mail: reference@leo.scsl.state.sc.us, Web site: <www.state.sc.us/scsl/>.

Department of Motor Vehicles: Motor Vehicles Division, 5410 Broad River Rd., Columbia, SC 29210, fax (803) 896-7881.

Search and Support Groups, Researchers/Searchers, Consultants, Intermediaries:

Adoptees and Birthparents in Search, S&SG, PO Box 5426B, Greenville, SC 29606 (803) 877-1458

Adoptees & Birthparents in Search, SG, P.O. Box 5551, West Columbia, SC 29171, (803) 791-1133, fax (803) 791-1133

Adoptees & Birthparents in Search, S&SG, Marci-Jo Mishoe, researcher, 4327 Helene Dr., Charleston, SC 29418-5710, (803) 552-0405, e-mail: marcijom@aol.com

Adoption Reunion Connection, S&SG, 263 Lemonade Rd., Pacolet, SC 29372, (864) 474-3479

Ever Check Where, S&SG, Brenda Craig, searcher, P.O. Box 849, Roebuck, SC 29376-0849, (864) 576-7593, fax (864) 587-7235, e-mail: ECWbrenda@aol.com

Liz White, researcher, Adoption Reunion Connection, P.O. Box 239, Moore, SC 29369, (864) 574-0681, fax (864) 574-6571, call first for fax, e-mail: LIZ_IN_SC@prodigy.com

State Reunion Registry: South Carolina has a state registry. See Chapter 8 for information on independent (group) reunion registries. Also note the "Author's Observations" section for this state.

Age of Majority: 18 years or older

Laws Governing Opening Records: Children's Code. Section 20-7-1780. *Hearings and records shall be confidential; access to records; furnishing nonidentifying information.* (B) "All papers and records, pertaining to the adoption and filed with the clerk of court are confidential from the time of filing and upon entry of the final adoption decree must be sealed and kept as a permanent record of the court and withheld from inspection. No person may have access to the records except for good cause shown by order of the judge of the court in which the decree of adoption was entered."

Laws Governing Inheritance: Domestic Relations. Section 20-7-1770. *Effect of Final decree.* (A) "After the final decree of adoption is entered, the relationship of parent and child and all the rights, duties, and other legal consequences of the natural relationship of parent and child exist between the adoptee, the adoptive parent, and the kindred of the adoptive parent." (B) "After a final decree of adoption is entered, the biological parents of the adoptee are relieved of all parental responsibilities and have no rights over the adoptee."

Author's Observations: Children's Code. Section 20-7-1780. *Hearings and records shall be confidential; access to records; furnishing nonidentifying information.* (E)(d) "The adoptee and his biological parents and siblings shall undergo counseling by the adoption agency concerning the effects of the disclosure. The adoption agency may charge a fee for the services, but services must not be denied because of inability to pay." Does this mean "you *shall*" even if such counseling is not needed?

SOUTH DAKOTA

State Agency: Department of Social Services, Child Protection Services, 700 Governors Dr., Pierre, SD 57501, (605) 773-3227, fax (605) 773-6834.

Court of Jurisdiction: Circuit Court

Birth and Death Records: State Department of Health, Center for Health Policy and Statistics, Vital Records, 523 E. Capitol, Pierre, SD 57501. Money order payable to South Dakota Dept. of Health. Call (605) 773-3355 for current fees. Records since July 1905 and access to other records for some events that occurred before that time.

Marriage and Divorce Records: State Department of Health (see address listed above) has records since July 1905. Contact County Treasury, county where marriage license issued or Clerk of Court, county where divorce granted.

State Library/Record Holdings: State Librarian, 900 Govenors Dr., Pierre, SD 57501-2217, fax (605) 773-6041.

Department of Motor Vehicles: Division of Motor Vehicles, 118 W. Capitol Ave., Pierre, SD 57501-2080, (605) 773-3541.

Search and Support Groups, Researchers/Searchers, Consultants, Intermediaries:

CUB Representative (Consult telephone directory or contact CUB National Headquarters listed under Iowa.)

The Lost Bird Society, S&SG, Marie Nohelpim, searcher/researcher, P.O. Box 952, Pine Ridge, SD 57770, (605) 867-5988, Web site: <www.montrose.net/users/fouche/zintka.htm>

State Reunion Registry: South Dakota has a Voluntary Registry. See Chapter 8 for information on state and independent (group) reunion registries.

Age of Majority: 18 years or older

Laws Governing Opening Records: Domestic Relations, 25-6-15. *Restrictions on access to court records in adoption proceedings—Court order required for disclosure of information.* "The files and records of the court in adoption proceedings shall not be open to inspection or copy by persons other than the parents by adoption and their attorneys, representatives of the office of community services, and the child when he reaches maturity, except upon order of the court expressly permitting inspection or copy. No person having charge of any birth or adoption records shall disclose the names of any parents, or parents by adoption, or any other matter, appearing in such records, or furnish certified copies of any such records, except upon order of the circuit court for the county in which the adoption took place or other court of competent jurisdiction."

Laws Governing Inheritance: Adoption of Children 25-6-17. *Rights and duties of natural parents terminated on adoption—Exception on adoption of stepchild.* "The natural parents of an adopted child are from the time of the adoption, relieved of all parental duties towards, and of all responsibility for the child so adopted, and have no right over it, except in cases where a natural parent consents to the adoption of his or her child by the child's stepfather or stepmother who is the present spouse of the natural parents."

TENNESSEE

State Agency: Department of Human Services, Post Adoption Unit, 8th Floor, Cordell Hull Bldg., 436 Sixth Ave. North, Nashville, TN 37243-1290.

Court of Jurisdiction: Adoptions prior to 1950: Probate or County Court; Afte: 1950: Chancery or Circuit Courts. Jurisdiction for the opening of sealed records includes Chancery or Circuit Court of First Degree.

Birth and Death Records: Tennessee Vital Records, Department of Health & Environment, Cordell Hull Bldg., Nashville, TN 37219-5402. Check or money order payable to Tennessee Vital Records. Call (615) 741-1763 to verify current fees. Call (800) 423-1901. Birth records for entire state since January 1914, for Nashville since June 1881, for Knoxville since July 1881, and for Chattanooga since January 1882. Death records for entire state since January 1914, for Nashville since July 1874, for Knoxville since July 1887, and for Chattanooga since March 6, 1872. For earlier Memphis records, write to Memphis-Shelby County Health Department, Division of Vital Records, Memphis, TN 38105.

Marriage and Divorce Records: Tennessee Vital Records (see address listed above) has records since July 1945. Contact County Clerk, county where marriage license issued or Clerk of Court, county where divorce granted.

State Library/Record Holdings: Tennessee State Library, 403 Seventh Ave., N, Nashville, TN 37243-0312, (615) 741-2764, fax (615) 532-2472, e-mail: referenc@mail.state.tn.us, Web site: <www.state.tn.us/sos/statelib/tslahome.htm>.

Department of Motor Vehicles: TN Department of Safety, 44 Vantage Way, Suite 160, Nashville, TN 37243, (615) 741-3101, fax 615-401-6782.

Search and Support Groups, Researchers/Searchers, Consultants, Intermediaries:

Adult Adoptees & Birthparents in Search, P.O. Box 901, Cleveland, TN 37364

Birthparents Search for Answers, S&SG, Kathy Albaum, searcher, 2750 Ward Rd. Millington, TN 38053, e-mail: Kathy_Albaum@prodigy.com

CUB Representative (Consult telephone directory or contact CUB National Headquarters listed under Iowa.)

F.A.I.T.H., S&SG, Nadeen Hart, ISC, searcher, 181 1/2 W. Sevier Ave., Kingsport, TN 37660, (423) 378-4679, e-mail: XKDL32A@prodigy.com

F.A.I.T.H., S&SG, Sharron Mauk, searcher, 1504 E. Sevier Ave., Kingsport, TN 37664, (423) 230-0061, e-mail: Pennygl@hotmail.com

Group for Openness in Adoption, SG, 518 Gen. George Patton Rd., Nashville, TN 37221, (615) 646-8116

R.O.O.T.S., SG, Sue Campbell, ISC, searcher, P.O. Box 9662, Knoxville, TN
37940, (423) 573-1344, e-mail: sis@icx.net

Linda Davilla, searcher, Tennessee Adoptees in Search, (see California listing)

Tennessee Right to Know, S&SG, Jalena Bowling, searcher, P.O. Box 34334,
Bartlett, TN 38134, (901) 373-7049, fax (901) 388-7722, e-mail:
FFMJ26B@prodigy.com

Tennessee Right to Know, S&SG, Denny Glad, searcher, 5182 Oak Meadow Ave.,
Memphis TN 38164, (901) 386-2197, fax (901) 385-5453

State Reunion Registry: Tennessee has a state registry. See Chapter 8 for information
on state and independent (group) reunion registries.

Age of Majority: 18/21 years or older

Laws Governing Opening Records: Domestic Relations, 36-1-127. *Availability of
records to adopted persons and certain other persons for adoption finalized or attempted prior
to March 16, 1951.* (3) (B) (1) (a). "All adoption records, sealed records, sealed
adoption records, post-adoption records, or any other records or papers for a person
relating to the adoption or ttempted adoption of a person, which adoption was finalized
by . . . March 16, 1951 . . . shall be made available to eligible persons [generally anyone
over the age of 21 with some exceptions]."

Contact Veto Registry Fact Sheet. *Release of Information.* "Records for persons placed
for the purpose of adoption which were finalized, . . . on or after March 16, 1951 will be
made available to the following individuals who are determined eligible: The adopted
person 21 years of age or older, the adopted person's birth/adoptive/step or legal parent
21 years of age or older, the adopted person's birth or adoptive siblings 21 years of age
or older . . . ."

Laws Governing Inheritance: Adoption, 36-126. *Effect of adoption on relationship.* "An
adopted child shall not inherit real or personal property from a natural parent or
relative thereof when the relationship between them has been terminated by adoption,
nor shall such natural parent or relative thereof inherit from the adopted child."

Policies: The policies of this state are being argued by the state supreme court. Write to
your state agency or reunion registry to insure the information is current.

TEXAS

State Agency: Texas Department of Protective and Regulatory Services, Voluntary
Adoption Registry [they will direct your inquiry], Mail Code Y-943, P.O. Box 149030,
Austin, TX 78714-9030, (512) 834-4485, fax (512) 834-4476.

Court of Jurisdiction: District Court

Birth and Death Records: Bureau of Vital Statistics, Texas Department of Health,
1100 W. 49th St., Austin, TX 78756-3191. Check or money order payable to Texas
Dept. of Health. Call (512) 458-7451 for current fees. Records since 1903.

Marriage Records: Bureau of Vital Statistics (see address listed above) has records
since 1966; or contact County Clerk, county where license issued.

Divorce Records: Bureau of Vital Statistics (see address listed above) has records since January 1968; or contact Clerk of District Court, county where divorce granted.

State Library/Record Holdings: Texas State Library, 1201 Brazos, P.O. Box 12927, Austin, TX 78711, (512) 463-5463, fax (512) 463-5436, e-mail: geninfo@tsl.state.tx.us, Web site: <www.tsl.state.tx.us/aris/genealogy.html>.

Department of Motor Vehicles: Texas Department of Motor Vehicles, P.O. Box 2293, Austin, TX 78768-2293, fax (512) 505-5180.

Search and Support Groups, Researchers/Searchers, Consultants, Intermediaries:

Adoption Knowledge Affiliates, Inc., S&SG, 2121 S. Lamar, Suite 112, Austin, TX 78704, (512) 442-8252

Adoption Search & Reunite, S&SG, Marilyn Morris-Rose, researcher/searcher, P.O. Box 371, Pasadena, TX 77501-0371, (713) 944-0599, e-mail: mrose@wt.net

Linda Crenwelge, researcher, Orphan Voyage, 1305 Augustine Ct., College Station, TX 77840, (409) 764-7157 (after 6:30), e-mail: lsc@ag-eco.tamu.edu

Marcia Morehead, searcher/researcher, 4601 N. 7th St., McAllen, TX 78504-2903, (956) 682-8748, e-mail: mamm@swbell.net

Pat Palmer, searcher, Searchline of Texas, 1516 Old Orchard, Irving, TX 75061, (214) 445-7005

Post Adoption Center Support, SG, 8600 Wurzbach Rd., #1110, San Antonio, TX 78240-4334, (210) 614-0299, fax (210) 614-0511

Bonnie P. Solecki, searcher, Texas Adoption Search Services, P.O. Box 14142, Ft. Worth, TX 76117, (817) 834-9713, fax (817) 834-0001

Linda Strength, searcher, P.O. Box 8445, Bacliff, TX 77518, (281) 339-1129, e-mail: srchgrl@wtnet

TxCARE & Adoption Triad Forum, SG, P.O. Box 832161, Richardson, TX 75083-2161, (972) 699-8386, fax (972) 699-1269, e-mail: TxCARE@aol.com, Web site: <www.visualimage.com/txcare>

State Reunion Registry: Texas has a Voluntary Adoption Registry. Refer to Chapter 8 for information on state and independent (group) reunion registries.

Age of Majority: 18 years or older

Laws Governing Opening Records: The Texas Family Code, Title 5, Section 162.022, *Confidentiality Maintained by Clerk*. "The records concerning a child maintained by the district clerk after entry of an order of adoption are confidential. No person is entitled to access to the records or may obtain information from the records except for good cause under an order of the court that issued the order."

Laws Governing Inheritance: The Family Code, Title 5, Section 161.206, *Effect of Adoption*. (b) "An order terminating the parent-child relationship divests the parent and child of all legal rights and duties with respect to each other, except that the child retains the right to inherit from and through the parent unless the court otherwise provides."

UTAH

State Agency: Division of Family Services, Department of Human Services, 120 North 200 West, Salt Lake City, UT 84103.

Court of Jurisdiction: District Court

Birth and Death Records: Bureau of Vital Records, Utah Department of Health, 288 North 1460 West, P.O. Box 16700, Salt Lake City, UT 84116-0700. Check or money order payable to Utah Dept. of Health. Call (801) 538-6105 for current fees. Records since 1905. If event occurred from 1890 to 1904 in Salt Lake City or Ogden, write to City Board of Health. For records elsewhere in the state from 1898 to 1904, write to County Clerk in county where event occurred.

Marriage and Divorce Records: Bureau of Vital Records (see address listed above) has records since 1978. Contact County Clerk, county where marriage license issued or County Clerk, county where divorce granted.

State Library/Record Holdings: Utah State Library, 2150 S. 300 W. #16, Salt Lake City, UT 84115, (801) 468-6777, fax (801) 468-6767, e-mail: Sub@inter.state.lib.ut.us, Web site: <www.state.lib.ut.us>.

Department of Motor Vehicles: Tax Commission Customer Service, 210 N. 1950 W., Salt Lake City, UT 84134, (800) DMV-UTAH, fax (801) 297-7697, Web site: <www.tax.ex.state.ut.us>.

Search and Support Groups, Researchers/Searchers, Consultants, Intermediaries:

Adoption Connection of Utah, S&SG, Sharlene Lightfoot, searcher, 1349 E. Mariposa Ave., Salt Lake City, Utah 84106, (801) 278-4858

State Reunion Registry: Utah has a Voluntary Adoption Registry. See Chapter 8 for information on state and independent (group) reunion registries.

Age of Majority: 18 years or older

Laws Governing Opening Records: Judicial Code, 78-30-15. *Petition and Report to be sealed and filed.* "The court shall order that the petition, the written report provided for in section 78-30-14, above, or any other documents filed in connection with the hearing, shall be sealed and shall not be open to inspection or copy except upon order of the court expressly permitting such inspection or copy after good cause therefor has been shown."

Laws Governing Inheritance: Judicial Code, 78-30-11. *Rights and liabilities of natural parents.* "The natural parents of an adopted child are, from the time of the adoption, relieved of all parental duties toward and all responsibility for the child so adopted, and shall have no further rights over it."

Judicial Code, 78-30-11. *Decisions under former law. Inheritance by adopted child.* "This section neither by express terms nor by necessary implication prevented an adopted child from inheriting from or through its natural parents; nor did the mere fact that the adopting parent was a blood relative prevent him from inheriting both from the adoptive parent and also from his natural parent by right of representation. In other words, the child could inherit in a dual capacity."

VERMONT

State Agency: Agency of Human Services, Department of Social and Rehabilitation Services, 103 S. Main St., State Complex, Waterbury, VT 05671-0201.

Court of Jurisdiction: District Probate Court

Birth and Death Records: Vermont Department of Health, Vital Records Section Box 70, 60 Main St., Burlington, VT 05402. Check or money order payable to Vermont Dept. of Health. Call (802) 863-7275 for current fees. State has records since 1955. Division of Public Records, 6 Baldwin St., Montpelier, VT 05602 has records prior to 1955.

Marriage Records: Vermont Department of Health (see Division of Public Records address listed above) has records since 1955; or contact Town Clerk, town where license issued.

Divorce Records: Vermont Department of Health (see address listed above) has records since 1968.

State Library/Record Holdings: Vermont State Library, 109 State St., Montpelier, VT 05609, (802) 828-3268, Web site: <dol.state.vt.us>.

Department of Motor Vehicles: Department of Motor Vehicles, 120 State St, Montpelier, VT 05603, (802) 828-2000, fax (802) 828-2170, Web site: <www.AOT.STATE.VT.US/DMV/DMVHP.1>.

Search and Support Groups, Researchers/Searchers, Consultants, Intermediaries:

Adoption Alliance of VT, S&SG, Enoch Thompkins, searcher, 104 Falls Rd., Shelburne, VT 05482, (802) 985-2464

Adoption Alliance of VT, S&SG, Mary Lighthall, searcher, RR 2, Box 2280, Charlotte, VT 05445, (802) 425-2478

Adoption Alliance of VT, S&SG, Maureen S. Vincent, searcher, 17 Hopkins St., Rutland, VT 05701, (802) 773-7078

Adoption Crossroads Branch (Consult telephone operator or directory, write the National Headquarters listed under New York.)

Adoption Search & Support Network, S&SG, RR1, Box 83, E. Calais, VT 05650, (802) 456-8850, fax (802) 456-8850, call first for fax, e-mail: BeLeaf4u@aol.com

B & C Search Assistance of Vermont, S&SG, Carolyn Flood, ISC, searcher, Beth Thomas, searcher, P.O. Box 1451, St. Albans, VT 05478, (802) 524-9825 or (802) 527-7507, e-mail: cbflood@sover.net or bcfind4u@together.net

Central VT Support Group, S&SG, RR 1, P.O. Box 83, East Calais, VT 05650, (802) 456-8850, e-mail: BeLeaf4U@aol.com

CUB Representative (Consult telephone directory or contact CUB National Headquarters listed under Iowa.)

Wendi Whitaker, ISC, searcher, 30 Martindale, Rd., Shelburne, VT 05482, (802) 985-8775, e-mail: wjw8775@sover.net

State Reunion Registry: Vermont has a State Adoption Registry. See Chapter 8 for information on state and independent (group) reunion registries.

Age of Majority: 18/21 years or older

Laws Governing Opening Records: Domestic Relations, Title 15, Article 6-105. *Disclosure of Identifying Information.* (a) "Identifying information about an adoptee's former parent shall be disclosed by the registry to any of the following persons upon request: (1) An adoptee who is 18 or more years old. (2) An adoptee who is emancipated. (3) A deceased adoptee's direct descendant who is 18 or more years old . . . (b) For adoptions that were finalized prior to July 1, 1986, the registry shall disclose identifying information if the former parent has filed in any probate court or agency any kind of document that clearly indicates that he or she consents to such disclosure. (2) For adoptions that were finalized on or after July 1, 1986, the registry shall disclose identifying information without requiring the consent of the former parent except . . . if the parent has filed a request for nondisclosure."

Laws Governing Inheritance: Domestic Relations, Chapter 9, Section 448. *Rights, duties, obligations.* "The natural parents of a minor shall be deprived, by the adoption, of all legal right to control of such minor, and such minor shall be freed from all obligations of obedience and maintenance to them. A person adopted shall have the same right of inheritance from and through his natural parents as though the adoption had not occurred, but the natural parents, predecessors in line of descent, and collateral kin of a person adopted shall be deprived of all right on inheritance from or through such person."

VIRGINIA

State Agency: Department of Social Services, 730 E. Broad St., Richmond, VA 23219-1849, (804) 692-1290.

Court of Jurisdiction: Circuit Court (see "Policies" listed below)

Birth and Death Records: Division of Vital Records, State Health Department, P.O. Box 1000, Richmond, VA 23208-1000. Check or money order payable to State Health Department. Call (804) 786-6228 for current fees. For records from January 1853 to December 1896 and since June 14, 1912, write to the Health Department in the city where event occurred.

Marriage Records: Division of Vital Records (see address listed above) has records since January 1853; or contact Clerk of court, county/city where license issued.

Divorce Records: Division of Vital Records (see address listed above) has records since January 1918; or contact Clerk of Court, county/city where divorce granted.

State Library/Record Holdings: Virginia State Library, 800 E. Broad St., Richmond, VA 23219-1905, fax (804) 892-3594.

Department of Motor Vehicles: Department of Motor Vehicles, 2300 W. Broad St., Richmond, VA 23269-0001, (804) 367-0538, fax (804) 367-0390.

Search and Support Groups, Researchers/Searchers, Consultants, Intermediaries:

Adoptees and Natural Parents Organization, S&SG, Sandra Shaw, researcher, 949 Lancon Drive, Newport, VA 23608, (757) 874-9091, e-mail: ros77@aol.com

Anita L. Steagall, searcher, P.O. Box 192, Abingdon, VA 24212-0192, (540) 623-1661, e-mail: asteagall@nl@naxs.com

State Reunion Registry: Virginia does not currently have a state reunion registry. Refer to Chapter 8 for information on independent (group) reunion registries.

Age of Majority: 18 years or older

Laws Governing Opening Records: Chapter 11, Adoptions, Section 63.1-236. *Disposition of reports.* "No information with respect to the identity of the biological family of the adopted child shall be disclosed, opened to inspection or made available to be copied except (i) upon application of the adopted child, which child is eighteen or more years of age, (ii) upon the order of a circuit court entered upon good cause shown, and (iii) after notice to and opportunity for hearing by the applicant for such order, and the person or agency which made the investigation required by Section 63.1-223 or Section 63.1-228."

Laws Governing Inheritance: Wills and Decedents' Estates, Section 54-1-5.1 *Meaning of child and related terms.* 1. "An adopted person is the child of an adopting parent and not of the biological parents, except that adoption of a child by the spouse of a biological parent has no effect on the relationship between the child and either biological parent."

Policies: Adoptees and Birthparents should request the *Access to Information from a Finalized Adoption Record in Virginia.* The right to exchange medical information, photographs, and letters are allowed with certain restrictions.

WASHINGTON

State Agency: Division of Children and Family Services, Adoption Program Mgr., P.O. Box 45713, Olympia, WA 98504, (800) 562-5682.

Court of Jurisdiction: Superior Court

Birth and Death Records: Vital Records, 1112 S. Quince, P.O. Box 9709, ET-11, Olympia, WA 98504-9709. Money order payable to Vital Records. In state call (800) 331-0680, out of state call (800) 551-0562 for current fees. County Auditor of county of birth has registered births prior to July 1907.

Marriage and Divorce Records: Vital Records (see address listed above) has records since January 1968. Contact County Auditor, county where marriage license issued or County Clerk, county where divorce granted.

State Library/Record Holdings: Washington State Library, 415 15th Ave. SW, P.O. Box 42460, Olympia, WA 98504-2460, (360) 753-5590, fax (360) 586-7575, e-mail: nzussy@statelib.wa.gov, Web site: <www.wa.gov>.

Department of Motor Vehicles: Department of Licensing, Technical Reporting Unit, P.O. Box 9030, Olympia, WA 98507-9030, (360) 902-3900, Web site: <www.wa.GOV/DOL>.

Search and Support Groups, Researchers/Searchers, Consultants, Intermediaries:

Adoptee/Birthparent Reunion Searches, S&SG, Mary Lively, searcher, 1509 Queen Anne Ave., N. #331, Seattle, WA 98109, (206) 233-8888

Adoption Resource Center of Childrens Home Society of Washington, Provide: Search services & referrals, PO Box 15190, Seattle, WA 98133, (206) 524-6062

Adoption Triad Support Group, MaryLou Netzer, searcher, CI, P.O. Box 742, Sumner, WA 98390, (253) 891-8122

Janet Nixon Baccus, searcher, CI, Baccus Genealogical Research, 5817 144th St. E., Puyallup, WA 98375-5221, (253) 537-8288, e-mail: JanetGB@worldnet.att.net

Joanie Brink, genealogist, P.O. Box 1760, Eatonville, WA 98328, e-mail: NENT78B@prodigy.com

Bellingham Birth Mothers Support Group, P.O. Box 841, Femdale, WA 98248-0841, (360) 647-5184, e-mail: gretchen@admsec.wwu.edu

Marilyn Dean, ISC, searcher, 9901 SE Shoreland Dr., Bellevue, WA 98004, (206) 454-3793, e-mail: MJDean@juno.com

William Eigenberger, searcher, CI, Safe Passage, 4022 39th Ave. S., Seattle, WA 98118, (206) 725-2472, e-mail: spassage@accessone.com

Michele Heiderer, searcher/researcher, 16315 Jim Creek Rd., Arlington, WA 98223-8531, (360) 435-2629, fax (360) 435-2720

Lost & Found, S&SG, Zoe Waggoner, searcher, 3232 Laurel Dr., Everett, WA 98201, (206) 339-1194, e-mail: zoe@halcyon.com

Janet Mackey, ISC, searcher, 1114 N. Locust Rd., Spokane, WA 99206-4078, (509) 891-1876, fax (509) 926-1493, e-mail: BNBG86A@prodigy.com

Mike O'Shaughnessey Adoption Support Group, SG, 63 Bear Gulch Rd., Aberdeen, WA 98520, (360) 533-6953, fax (360) 533-8444, e-mail: zastrow@techline.com

Marlene Smith, searcher, CI, Madrona Research, P.O. Box 29001, Bellingham, WA 98228-1001, (360) 647-8126, fax (360) 647-8126, e-mail: marlenesmi@aol.com

Carole A. VandenBos, ISC, searcher, 14435 22nd Ave., SW, Seattle, WA 98166 (206) 244-5134, fax (206) 244-5134 (call first), e-mail: GWGS04A@prodigy.com

Washington Adoptees Rights Movement (WARM), 5950 Sixth Ave. S., Suite 107, Seattle, WA 98108, (206) 767-9510, fax (206) 763-4803, e-mail: warm@wolfenet.com

WARM, SG, Joan M. Degroot, researcher, 2409 Baker Ave., Everett, Wa 98201, (425) 258-3080

Warm, SG, 7835 Forest Ridge Ln. NE, Bremerton, WA 98311, (360) 377-3041, fax (360) 373-9053, For additional WARM, SG's contact the WARM Seattle office for current information.

Darlene Wilson, CI, (360) 256-8795, fax (360) 260-1750, e-mail: darlenew@worldaccessnet.com

Rita Zastrow, searcher, CI, 63 Bear Gulch Rd., Aberdeen, WA 98520, (360) 533-6953, fax (360) 533-8444, e-mail: zastrow@techline.com

State Reunion Registry: Washington does not currently have a state reunion registry. Refer to Chapter 8 for information on independent (group) reunion registries.

Age of Majority: 18 years or older

Laws Governing Opening Records: RCW 26.33.330. *Records sealed—Inspection only upon court order.* (1) "An adopted person over the age of twenty-one years, or under twenty-one with the permission of the adoptive parent, or a birth parent or member of the birth parent's family after the adoptee has reached the age of twenty-one may petition the court to appoint a confidential intermediary. The intermediary shall search for and discreetly contact the birth parent or adopted person, or if they are not alive or cannot be located within one year, the intermediary may attempt to locate members of the birth parent or adopted person's family." (5) "If the confidential intermediary locates the person being sought, a discreet and confidential inquiry shall be made as to whether or not that person will consent to having his or her present identity disclosed . . . If the party being sought consents to the disclosure of his or her identity, the confidential intermediary shall obtain the consent in writing and shall include the original of the consent in the report filed with the court. If the party being sought refuses disclosure of his or her identity, the confidential intermediary shall report the refusal to the court and shall refrain from further and subsequent inquiry without judicial approval."

RCW 26.33 Sec. 2. (2) "The department of vital records shall make available a noncertified copy of the original birth certificate of a child to the child's birth parents upon request."

Laws Governing Inheritance: RCW 26.33.270 *Decree of adoption—Effect.* "The entry of a decree of adoption divests any parent or alleged father who is not married to the adoptive parent or who has not joined in the petition   for adoption of all legal rights and obligations in respect to the adoptee, except past-due child support obligations. The adoptee shall be, to all intents and purposes, and for all legal incidents, the child, legal heir, and lawful issue of the adoptive parent, entitled to all rights and privileges, including the right of inheritance and the right to take under testamentary disposition, and subject to all the obligations of a natural child of the adoptive parent."

WEST VIRGINIA

State Agency: Department of Health & Human Resources, Bureau for Children & Families, State Capitol Complex, Bldg. 6, Room 850, Charleston, WV 25305, (304) 558-9048, fax (304) 558-3240.

Court of Jurisdiction: Circuit Court

Birth and Death Records: Vital Registration Office, Division of Health, State Capitol Complex Bldg. 3, Charleston, WV 25305. Check or money order payable to Vital Registration. Call (304) 348-2931 for current fees. For records earlier than January 1917, write to Clerk of County Court in county where event occurred.

Marriage Records: Vital Registration Office (see address listed above) has records since 1921; or contact County Clerk, county where license issued.

Divorce Records: Vital Registration Office (see address listed above) has records since 1968; or contact Clerk of Circuit Court, Chancery Side, county where license issued.

State Library/Record Holdings: Cultural Center, 1900 Kanawha Blvd. East, Capital Complex, Charleston, WV 25305, (304) 558-2041, fax (304) 558-2044, Web site: <www.wvlc.wvnet.edu>.

Department of Motor Vehicles: Department of Motor Vehicles, 1800 Kanawra Blvd., E. Capitol Complex, Bldg. 3, Charleston, WV 25317, (304) 558-3900 or (800) 642-9066, fax (304) 558-0037.

Search and Support Groups, Researchers/Searchers, Consultants, Intermediaries:

Legacies, S&SG, Loretta Hopson, researcher, 826 Honaker Ln., Charleston WV 25312, (304) 984-0305

Legacies, S&SG, Karl Slater, researcher, 3728 Sissonville Dr., Charleston, WV 25312, (304) 343-3641

State Reunion Registry: West Virginia has a mutual consent voluntary adoption registry. Refer to Chapter 8 for information on state and independent (group) reunion registries.

Age of Majority: 18 years or older

Laws Governing Opening Records: Adoption, Section 48-4-10. *Recordation of order; fees; disposition of records; names of adopting parents not to be disclosed; certificate for state registrar of vital statistics; birth certificate.* "All records of proceedings in adoption cases and all papers and records relating to such proceedings shall be kept in the office of the clerk of the circuit court in a sealed file, which file shall be kept in a locked or sealed cabinet, vault or other container and shall not be open to inspection or copy by anyone, except as otherwise provided in this article, or upon court order for good cause shown . . . Nonidentifying information, the collection of which is provided for in article four-a of this chapter, shall be provided to the adoptive parents as guardians of the adopted child, or to the adult adoptee, by their submitting a duly acknowledged request to the clerk of the court." (b) "If an adoptee, or parent of a minor adoptee, is unsuccessful in obtaining identifying information by use of the mutual consent voluntary adoption registry provided for in article four-a of this chapter, identifying information may be sought through the following process: (1) Upon verified petition of an adoptee at least eighteen years of age . . . (2) Upon the filing of a verified petition as provided in subdivision (1) of this subsection . . . (c) Identifying information may only be obtained with the duly acknowledged consent of the mother or the legal or determined father . . ."

Laws Governing Inheritance: Domestic Relations, Section 48-4-11. *Effect of order as to relations of parents and child and as to rights of inheritance; intestacy of adopted child.* (a) "Upon the entry of such order of adoption, any person previously entitled to parental rights, any parent or parents by any previous legal adoption, and the lineal or collateral kindred of any such person, parent or parents, except any such person or parent who is the husband or wife of the petitioner for adoption, shall be divested of all legal rights, including the right of inheritance from or through the adopted child under the statutes of descent and distribution of this State . . . ."

WISCONSIN

State Agency: Division of Health & Social Services, P.O. Box 7851, 1 West Wilson St., Madison, WI 53701-7851. Searchers in this state can call a toll-free telephone number, (800) 522-6882, to obtain information.

Court of Jurisdiction: Circuit Court

Birth and Death Records: Vital Records, 1 West Wilson St., P.O. Box 309, Madison, WI 53701. Check or money order payable to Center for Health Statistics. Call (608) 266-1371 for current fees. Scattered records earlier than 1857. Records before October 1, 1907 are very incomplete.

Marriage Records: Vital Records (see address listed above). Records since April 1836. Records before October l, 1907 are incomplete.

Divorce Records: Vital Records (see address listed above). Records since October 1907.

State Library/Record Holdings: State Historical Society of Wisconsin, University of Wisconsin, 816 State St., Madison, WI 53706, fax (608) 264-6404.

Department of Motor Vehicles: Division of Motor Vehicles, Department of Transportation, P.O. Box 7910, Madison, WI 53707-7910

Search and Support Groups, Researchers/Searchers, Consultants, Intermediaries:

Adoption Resource Network, S&SG, Shelley Borreson, searcher, P.O. Box 8221, Eau Claire, WI 54702-8221, (715) 835-6695, e-mail: borreson@eau.net

Adoption Roots Traced, S&SG, Mary Sue Wedl, searcher, N 6795 Hwy. A #44, Lake Mills, WI 53551, (920) 648-2917, fax (920) 648-2744, e-mail: mswedl@intaccess.com

Carolyn F. Seierstad, ISC, searcher, Milestone Search & Support, Inc., 3214 Beckshire Rd., Janesville, WI 53546, (608) 754-4005, fax (608) 754-4644, email: bluejay@jvlnet.com

Mary Weidling, searcher, ICARE, N. 5080 17th Ave., Mauston, WI 53948, (608) 847-5563, fax (608) 524-2836, e-mail: ICARE@jvinet.com, Web site: <www.jvlnet.com/~icare>

State Reunion Registry: Wisconsin does not currently have a reunion registry that allows adoptees and birthparents to agree to a match. A centralized file of genetic and medical information, provided by the birthparent, is kept at the Department of Health and Social Services. A search must be requested from the agency. See Chapter 8 for information on independent (group) reunion registries.

Age of Majority: 18 years or older

Laws Governing Opening Records: Children's Code, 49.93. *Records closed.* (1d) "All records and papers pertaining to an adoption proceeding shall be kept in a separate locked file and may not be disclosed except under sub. (1g) or (1r), . . . or by order of the court for good cause shown."

Laws Governing Inheritance: 26.32.140. *Effect of Decree of Adoption.* "By a decree of adoption the natural parents shall be divested of all legal rights and obligations in respect to the child, and the child shall be free from all legal obligations of obedience and maintenance in respect to them, and shall be, to all intents and purposes, and for all legal incidents, the child, legal heir, and lawful issue of his or her adopter or adopters."

WYOMING

State Agency: Department of Family Services, Hathaway Bldg., Cheyenne, WY 82002

Court of Jurisdiction: District Court

Birth and Death Records: Vital Records Services, Hathaway Bldg., Cheyenne, WY 82002. Money order payable to Vital Records Services. Call (307) 777-7591 for current fees. Records since July 1909.

Marriage and Divorce Records: Vital Records Service (see address listed above) has records since May 1941. Contact County Clerk, county where marriage license issued or Clerk of District Court, county where divorce granted.

State Library/Record Holdings: Wyoming State Library, Supreme Court & State Library Bldg., 2301 Capitol Ave., Cheyenne, WY 82002-0060, (307) 777-5914, fax (307) 777-6289, e-mail: jyeo@windy.state.wy.us, Web site: <www-ws1.state.wy.us>.

Department of Motor Vehicles: Department of Revenue & Taxation, 5300 Bishop Blvd., Cheyenne, WY 82009, P.O. Box 1708, Cheyenne, WY 82003-1708, (307) 777-4810, fax (307) 777-4773.

Search and Support Groups, Researchers/Searchers, Consultants, Intermediaries:

Contact the American Adoption Congress National Office (District of Columbia), Adoption Crossroads National Office (New York) or Concerned United Birthparents (Iowa) to learn of search help in Wyoming.

State Reunion Registry: Wyoming does not currently have a state reunion registry. Refer to Chapter 8 for information on independent (group) reunion registries.

Age of Majority: 18 years or older

Laws Governing Opening Records: State House Bill No. 144, 1-726:4. *Petition for adoption of minor; by whom filed; requisites: confidential nature; inspection: separate journal to be kept.* (d) "The petition and documents filed pursuant to this section, and the interlocutory decree, if entered, and the final decree of adoption shall constitute a confidential file and shall be available for inspection only to the judge, or, by order of court, to the parties of the proceedings or their attorneys . . . The court may order inspection of all or part of the confidential file in adoption proceedings only if it appears to the court that the welfare and best interests of the child will be served by the inspection."

Laws Governing Inheritance: House Bill No. 144, 1-726.14. *Effect of Adoption.* "Upon the entry of a final decree of adoption the former parent, guardian or putative father of the child shall have no right to the control or custody of the child."

Policies: Section 1. W.S. 1-22-201 through 1-22-203 created Confidential Intermediaries in this state.

NOTE

1. The definition of nonidentifying information comes from Mary Sullivan, *Task Force on Confidentiality in the Adoption Program—A Report to the California State Department of Health*, Sacramento, CA, 1977, p. 24.

APPENDIX 2

Searcher's Checklist

W hat follows is a checklist of information sources that have been referred to, although some have been treated at more length than others. Use it as an aid to developing leads in areas you've not yet covered. Use it as a record of sources you've referred to. While the listing here is extensive, it is not definitive—other sources may prove open to you. You yourself will decide how efficient your search turns out to be. Review carefully all information you receive, follow any new sources of information you discover, and always proceed in a positive manner.

Adoption Papers

___ Change of Name
___ Finalized Court Papers
___ Home Study Report
___ Petition to Adopt
___ Relinquishment Papers

Agency Records

___ Application to Adopt
___ Baptismal Certificate
___ Financial Agreements
___ Foster Homes
___ Home Study Reports
___ Medical Information
___ Petition to Adopt
___ Relinquishment Papers

Birth Records

___ Altered Certificate
___ Baptismal Certificate
___ Christening Certificate
___ Original Certificate
___ Published Birth Notice

Cemetery Records

___ Obituaries
___ Interment Orders
___ Perpetual Care

Census Records
___ City or County
___ State
___ Federal
___ School District
___ Soundex

Church Records
___ Birth Records
___ Baptism and Christening Records
___ Confirmation Records
___ Contributors List
___ Death Records
___ Marriage Records
___ Membership Rolls
___ Published Events
___ Subscribers List
___ Sunday School Records
___ Tithe Records

City Directories
___ Cole Directory
___ Polk Directory
___ Telephone Directory
___ Other (List: _____)

Computer Records
___ Computer Reunion Registries
___ Computer Search Sites
___ Genealogical Records

Court Records
___ Adoption Records
___ Change of Name
___ Citizenship
___ Relinquishment

Death Records
___ Burial Permit
___ Death Certificate
___ Obituaries
___ Plot Records

___ Probate Records
___ Published Accounts
___ Tombstones or Monuments
___ Will

Divorce Records
___ Grant of Annulment
___ Divorce Index
___ Published Accounts

Employment Records
___ Payroll Records
___ Profession or Trade
___ Union Membership
___ Work History

Engagement Records
___ Church Records
___ Newspaper Accounts

Estate Docket
___ Administrator(s)
___ Executor(s)
___ Index to Probate Records
___ Will

Family Records
___ Correspondence
___ Insurance Records
___ Personal Recollections
___ Photographs

Genealogy
___ Genealogy Societies
___ Historical Societies
___ LDS Genealogy Records
___ Library of Congress
___ National Archives
___ Published Genealogies

Hospital Records
___ Admittance
___ Delivery Room
___ Medical Records
___ Nursery Records
___ Release Records

Immigration Records
___ Applications for Entry
___ Customs Records
___ Naturalization Papers

Land Records
___ Abstracts
___ Change of Title
___ Index to Records
___ Property Tax Lists

Licenses
___ Building
___ Business
___ Gun Registration
___ Hunting
___ Marriage
___ Professional
___ Trade
___ Vehicular

Marriage Records
___ Announcements
___ License Application
___ Certificates
___ Church Records
___ Marriage Index
___ Justice of the Peace
___ Licenses
___ Published Accounts
___ Wedding Announcements

Military Records
___ Death Rolls
___ Discharge Papers
___ Enlistment Records
___ Pension Records
___ Published Events
___ VA Records

Mortuary Records
___ Burial Permits
___ Burial Registers
___ Funeral Cards
___ Memorial Cards
___ Obituaries

Newspapers
___ Accomplishments
___ Church Events
___ Club and Organization
     Events
___ Engagements
___ Graduations
___ Local History
___ Military Service
___ Obituaries
___ Passenger Lists
___ Passport Records
___ Published Births
___ Published Deaths
___ Published Divorces
___ Published Marriages

Search Resources
___ Adoption-related literature
___ Reunion Registry
___ Search and Support Group
___ Search Newsletters,
     Magazines, Newspapers
___ Search Workshops

APPENDIX 3

Reference Sources

The following list contains reference sources discussed in this book; see especially Chapter 4, "Reference Resources," and Chapter 9, "Search Resources and Services." Also included are other sources of information that you might find useful in your search.

Access: The Supplementary Guide to Periodicals. New York: Gaylord Bros., 1975 to present.

Adoption Law and Practice, John H. Hollinger, editor-in-chief. Albany, NY: Matthew Bender, 1990 supplement.

African American Genealogical Sourcebook, edited by Paula K. Byers. Detroit: Gale Research, Inc., 1995.

Aigner, Hal, *Faint Trails: Western States Edition.* Greenbrae, CA: Paradigm Press, 1980.

American Library Directory, 49th ed. New York: R.R. Bowker Company, annual.

Ayer Directory of Publications. Philadelphia: Ayer Press, annual.

Baran, Annette and Pannor, Reuben, *Lethal Secrets.* New York: Warner Books, 1989.

Beard, Timothy F., and Demong, Denise, *How to Find Your Family Roots!* New York: McGraw-Hill, 1977.

Bentley, Elizabeth Petty, *County Courthouse Book*, 2nd ed. Baltimore, MD: Genealogical Publishing Co., 1995.

——*Genealogist's Address Book.* Baltimore: Genealogical Publishing Co., 1991.

Blockson, Charles L., *Black Genealogy.* Englewood Cliffs, NJ: Prentice-Hall, 1977.

Books in Print. New York: R.R. Bowker Company, annual.

Carroll's State Directory, Harris, Lela E., editor. Washington, DC: Carroll Publishing, 1996-1997.

Code of Federal Regulations. Washington, DC: Government Printing Office, annual.

County and City Data Books. Pittsburgh: U.S. Bureau of the Census, U.S. Department of Commerce, 1949 to present.

Cumulative Book Index. New York: H.W. Wilson Company, 1928 to present.

Directories in Print, 2 parts, 13th ed. Julie E. Towell and Charles B. Montney, eds. Detroit: Gale Research, Inc., 1995.

Directory of Historical Organizations in the US and Canada, 14th Edition, edited by Mary Bray Wheeler, Nashville: ASSL Press, 1990.

Doane, Gilbert H. and Bell, James B., *Searching for Your Ancestors: The How and Why of Genealogy*, 5th ed. Minneapolis, MN: University of Minnesota Press, 1992.

Editor and Publisher International Year Book. New York: Editor and Publisher, annual.

Ehrlick, Henry, *A Time to Search.* New York and London: Paddington, 1977.

Encyclopedia of Associations, 31st ed. Detroit: Gale Research Company, 1996.

Everton, George B., Sr., *The Handy Book for Genealogists*, 8th ed. Logan, UT: Everton Publishers Inc., 1991.

FaxUSA. Detroit, MI: Omnigraphics, 1994 annual edition.

Federal Registry. Washington, DC: Government Printing Office, daily.

Freedom of Information Guide, Know your Government Series, Washington, DC: WANT Publishing Company, 1982.

Gormley, Myra Vanderpool, *Family Diseases: Are You At Risk?* Baltimore, MD: Genealogical Publishing Co., 1989.

Greenfield, Stanley R., ed., *National Directory of Addresses and Telephone Numbers*, rev. ed., New York: Bantam Books, 1995.

Greenwood, Val D., *The Researcher's Guide to American Genealogy*, 2nd ed. Baltimore, MD: Genealogical Publishing Co., 1990.

Guide to American Directories, 12th ed., edited by Bernard Klein, Coral Springs, FL: B. Klein Publications, 1989.

Haley, Alex, *Roots.* New York: Doubleday, 1976.

Handbook for Genealogical Correspondence, prepared by Cache Genealogical Library, Logan, UT, 1963.

Harley, Hahn and Stout, Rick. *The Internet Yellow Pages*, 2nd ed. Berkeley, CA: Osborne McGray-Hill, 1995.

Index to U.S. Government Periodicals. Chicago: Infordata International, quarterly, 1974 to present.

Kempt, Thomas J., *International Vital Records Handbook*, 3rd ed., Baltimore, MD: Genealogical Publishing Co., 1994.

Johnson, Lt. Col. Richard S., *How to Locate Anyone Who is or has been in the Military.* Ft. Sam Houston, TX: Military Information Enterprises, 1990.

Jones, Mary Ann, *The Sealed Adoption Record Controversy: Report of a Survey of Agency Policy, Practice and Opinions.* New York: Child Welfare League of America, Inc., 1976.

Kirkham, E. Kay, *A Survey of American Church Records*, IV Edition. Logan, UT: Everton Publishers Inc., 1978.

Landau, Elaine, *Black Market Adoption.* New York: Franklin Watts, 1990.

Mann, Thomas, *A Guide To Library Research Methods.* NY: Oxford University Press, 1987.

Marindale-Hubbell Law Directory. Summit, NJ: Martindale Hubbel, annual.

Maxtone-Graham, Katrina, *An Adopted Woman.* New York: Remi Books, 1983.

McCormick, Mona, *The New York Times Guide To Reference Materials*, revised edition. New York: Dorset Press, a division of Marboro Books Corp. by arrangement with Times Books, 1988.

Musser, Sandy, *To Prison with Love.* Cape Coral, FL: The Awareness Press, 1995.

National Directory of State Agencies. Washington, DC: Information Resources Press, 1976.

The New York Times Index. New York: The New York Times, 1851 to present.

Niles, Reg, *Adoption Agencies, Orphanages and Maternity Homes*, 2 vols. NY: Phileas Deigh Corp., 1981.

The Official Congressional Directory. Washington, DC: Government Printing Office, 1809 to present.

Oryx Family Tree Series, different authors for each book in series. Phoenix, AZ: Oryx Press, 1996. Web site: <www.oryxpress.com/>.

Patterson's American Education. Chicago: Educational Directories, 1904 to present.

Peskett, H., *Discover Your Ancestors: A Quest for your Roots.* New York: Arco Publishing Company, 1978.

Popcorn, Faith and Marigold, Lys, *Clicking.* New York: HarperCollins, 1996.

Rabkin, Jacob, and Johnson, Mark, *Current Legal Forms with Tax Analysis.* New York: Matthew Bender and Company, 1980.

Reader's Guide to Periodical Literature. New York: H.W. Wilson Company, 1905 to present.

Rottenberg, Dan, *Finding Our Fathers: A Guidebook to Jewish Genealogy.* New York: Random House, 1986.

Sheehy, Eugene P., *Guide to Reference Books.* Chicago: American Library Association, 1968 to present.

Smith, Robert Sellers, *Handbook of Law Office Forms 1974.* Englewood Cliffs, NJ: Prentice-Hall, Inc., 1974.

Social Science Index. New York: H.W. Wilson Company, annual.

Standard Periodical Directory, 19th ed. New York: Oxbridge Communications, 1996.

State Censuses, Library of Congress, Census Library Project, prepared by Henry J. Dubester. Washington, DC: Government Printing Office.

Survey of American Census Schedules, 1790–1950. Salt Lake City: Deseret Book Company, 1959.

Ulrich's International Periodicals Directory. New York: R.R. Bowker Company, annual.

United States Government Manual. Washington, DC: Government Printing Office, 1935 to present.

Where to Write for Vital Records. Washington, DC: Government Printing Office, #PHS 90-1142, 1990.($2.25).

The WPA Historical Records Survey. Edited by William B. Hassletine and Donald R. McNeil. Madison: University of Wisconsin Press, 1958.

Yearbook of American and Canadian Churches, 1990, edited by Constant H. Jacquet, Jr. Nashville TN: Abingdon Press, 1990.

Young, M.L., *Directory of Special Libraries and Information Centers*, Detroit: Gale Research Company, 1987.

INDEX

Compiled by Janet Perlman